GOD, LIFE, AND THE COSMOS

God, Life, and the Cosmos: Christian and Islamic Perspectives is the first book in which Christian and Muslim scholars explore the frontiers of science-religion discourse. Leading international scholars present new work on key issues in science and religion from Christian and Islamic perspectives.

Following an introduction by the editors, the book is divided into three sections: the first explores the philosophical issues in science-religion discourse; the second examines cosmology; the third analyses the issues surrounding bioethics. One of the first books to explore aspects of science-religion discourse from the perspective of two religious traditions, *God, Life, and the Cosmos* opens up new vistas to all interested in science and religion, and those exploring contemporary issues in Christianity and Islam.

God, Life, and the Cosmos

Christian and Islamic Perspectives

Edited by
TED PETERS
MUZAFFAR IQBAL
SYED NOMANUL HAQ

ASHGATE

Published by
Ashgate Publishing Limited
Wey Court East
Union Road
Farnham, Surrey
GU9 7PT England

Ashgate Publishing Company
Suite 420
101 Cherry Street
Burlington, VT 05401-4405
USA

Ashgate website: http://www.ashgate.com

British Library Cataloguing in Publication Data
God, life, and the cosmos.
    1. Islam and science. 2. Religion and science. 3. Life - Origin
    - Religious aspects - Islam. 4. Life - Origin - Religious
    aspects - Christianity.
    I. Peters, Ted, 1941- . II. Iqbal, Muzaffar. III. Haq, Syed
Nomanul.
    291.1'75

Library of Congress Cataloging-in-Publication Data
God, life, and the cosmos: Christian and Islamic perspectives / [edited by] Ted Peters,
Muzaffar Iqbal, Syed Nomanul Haq.
        p. cm.
    Includes index.
    ISBN 978-0-7546-0883-7
        1. Religion and science. 2. Islam and science. I. Peters, Ted, 1941- .
    II. Iqbal, Muzaffar. III. Haq, Syed Nomanul.

BL240.3.G63 2002
291.1'75–dc21   2002022547

ISBN 978 0 7546 0883 7

Reprinted 2010

Mixed Sources
Product group from well-managed
forests and other controlled sources
www.fsc.org Cert no. SA-COC-1565
© 1996 Forest Stewardship Council
FSC

Printed and bound in Great Britain by
MPG Books Ltd, Bodmin, Cornwall

Contents

List of Contributors

S. Nomanul Haq is currently on the faculty of the University of Pennsylvania with appointments in two departments – the History of Art, and History and Sociology of Science. He studied physics as an undergraduate at England's Hull University, and then, at University College London, the history of Philosophy and Science, and Islamic Studies. He did his PhD work at Harvard in the history of Arabic Science and Near Eastern Languages and Civilizations. He has held positions at Tufts, Brown, and Rutgers and has published widely. Among these publications are: *Names, Natures, and Things* (Kluwer Academic Publishers 1994), and he is general editor of the *Studies in Islamic Philosophy* series of Oxford University Press.

Muzaffar Iqbal is the founder-president of the Center for Islam and Science (CIS), and former Regional Director for the Muslim World for the Science and Religion Course Program (SRCP) of The Center for Theology and the Natural Sciences (CTNS) Berkeley. He is the author/editor *Science in Islamic Polity in the Twenty-first Century* (ed., 1995), *Health and Medical Profile of the Muslim World* (ed., 1993), *Possible Strategy for Energy Mixes in the Muslim World (Co-ed.,* 1994), and *Islam and Science* (Ashgate, 2002). He was the Guest Editor for the special issue of *Islamic Studies,* on Islam and Science (Winter 2000).

Ibrahim Kalin is currently with the Human Sciences Program at George Washington University, Washington DC, working and teaching in the field of humanities and Islamic studies. His field of concentration is post-Avicennan Islamic philosophy and Mulla Sadra with interests in the school of Ibn Arabi, Ottoman intellectual history, Islamic scientific tradition and contemporary philosophy of science.

Since 1996, Kalin has been working with and under the direction of Seyyed Hossein Nasr on a number of projects at George Washington University. His publications include: "Scientific and Religious Instrumentalism: Some Considerations on Science-Religion Controversy", *Iqbal Review*, Volume 38, Number 1 (April 1997), pp. 83-104; and "Knowledge as Light: Critical Remarks on M. Hairi Yazdi's Principles of Epistemology in Islamic Philosophy: Knowledge by Presence", *American Journal of Islamic and Social Sciences*, Volume 16, Fall 1999, pp. 85-97.

Ted Peters is a professor of systematic theology at Pacific Lutheran Theological Seminary and the Graduate Theological Union in Berkeley, California. He served as Program Director for the Science and Religion Course Program of the Center for Theology and the Natural Sciences, Berkeley. He is editor of *Dialog: A Journal of Theology*, and co-editor of *Theology and Science*. His publications include: *Playing God? Genetic Determinism and Human Freedom* (Routledge 1997; revised edition, 2002); *For the Love of Children: Genetic Technology and the Future of the Family* (Westminster John Knox 1996), *Sin* (Eerdmans 1994), *God as Trinity* (Westminster John Knox 1993), *God The World's Future* (Fortress Press 1992; 2000), and *The Cosmic Self* (HarperCollins 1990).

Mustansir Mir, originally from Pakistan, teaches Islamic Studies at Youngstown State University in Ohio, USA. He has previously taught at colleges in Lahore, at the University of Michigan, Ann Arbor, and at the International Islamic University, Malaysia. Dr. Mir's main academic interest is Qur'anic studies. He also has an interest in Iqbal studies. His publications include: *Coherence in the Qur'an: A Study of Islahi's Concept of Nazm in Tadabbur-i Qur'an* (American Trust Publications 1986); *Dictionary of Qur'anic Terms and Concepts* (Garland 1987); and *Tulip in the Desert: A Selection of the Poetry of Muhammad Iqbal* (Hurst & Co. 2000). He is co-editor of a biannual journal, *Studies in Contemporary Islam*.

William C. Chittick is Professor of Comparative Studies at the State University of New York, Stony Brook. He is the author, editor and/or translator of some 20 books and monograms and 100 articles on Islamic Philosophical Theology, Shi'ism, and Sufism. These publications include: *The Heart of Islamic Philosophy: The Quest for Self-Knowledge in the Teachings of Afdal al-Din Kâshânî* (Oxford University Press 2001); *Sufism: A Short Introduction* (Oneworld 2000); *The Self-Disclosure of God: Principles of Ibn al-'Arabî's Cosmology* (SUNY Press 1998); and, *Varolmann Boyutlari* ("The Dimensions of Existence"), seventeen articles with new introduction, translated into Turkish by Turan Koç (Istanbul: Insan Yayinlari 1997).

Roshdi Rashed received his doctorate in History and Philosophy of Sciences at the University of Paris. He serves as the Director of Research at CNRS (Centre National de la Recherche Scientifique), Honorary Professor at the University of Tokyo, and Professor Emeritus at the University of Mansourah in Egypt. His publications include: *The Development of Arabic Mathematics: Between Arithmetic and Algebra* (Kluwer Academic Publishers 1994); editor and co-author of *Encyclopedia of the History of Arabic Science* (Routledge 1996); and, in collaboration with B. Vahabzadeh, *Al-Khayyam, Mathematician* (Bibliotheca Persica Press 2000).

Ahmad Dallal is Associate Professor of Middle Eastern History at Stanford University in California. He receive his PhD in Middle East Languages in Cultures from Columbia University. His publications include: *An Islamic Response to Greek Astronomy* (Brill 1995); *Traditions of Reform: Trends in Eighteenth Century Islamic Thought* (Forthcoming); and *Islam and the Modern World* (Forthcoming).

Mehdi Golshani joined the faculty of Sharif University of Technology in Tehran in 1970, where, in 1995, he founded the Faculty of the Philosophy of Science and has been its chairman since then. Golshani has been the director of the Institute for Humanities and Cultural Studies in Tehran since 1993. His books include: *The Holy Qur'an and the Sciences of Nature* (Global Publications 1998); *English Translation of the Holy Qur'an*, Vol. 1 (Islamic Propagation Organization 1991); *From Physics to Metaphysics* (Institute for Humanities and Cultural Studies 1998); and *Can Science Dispense with Religion?* (ed.) (Institute for Humanities and Cultural Studies 1998).

Philip Clayton is former Professor and Chair of Philosophy at the California State University, Sonoma. He has been guest professor at Harvard Divinity School, Humboldt Professor at the University of Munich, and Fulbright Professor at the University of Munich. He is currently Principal Investigator of the Science and the Spiritual Quest program at the Center for Theology and the Natural Sciences, Berkeley. His publications include: *The Problem of God in Modern Thought* (Eerdmans 2000); *God and Contemporary Science* (Edinburgh University Press 1997); and *Explanation from Physics to Theology: An Essay in Rationality and Religion* (Yale University Press 1989).

Mark Worthing is Dean of Studies at Tabor College in Adelaide, Australia. He is an ordained pastor of the Lutheran Church of Australia and former head of the Department of Systematic Theology and Church History at Luther Seminary, Adelaide, Australia. He also served as the regional director of the CTNS Science and Religion Course Program in Australia and New Zealand. His publications in the area of the natural sciences and theology include: *God, Creation, and Contemporary Physics* (Fortress Press 1996), for which he was awarded the 1997 Templeton Book Prize for Outstanding monograph on science and religion; and *Foundations and Functions of Theology as Universal Science: Theological Method and Apologetic Praxis in Wolfhart Pannenberg and Karl Rahner* (Peter Lang 1996).

Audrey R. Chapman is Director of both the Dialogue on Science, Ethics, and Religion, and the Science and Human Rights Program, of the American Association for the Advancement of Science. She has taught courses institutions such as: Georgetown University, Andover Newton Theological Seminary, and Wesley Theological Seminary. Her books include: *Consumption, Population and the Environment: Perspectives from Science and Religion*, co-editor with Rodney Petersen and Barbara Smith-Moran (Island Press 2000); *Unprecedented Choices: Religious Ethics at the Frontiers of Genetic Science* (Augsburg Fortress Press 1999); *Perspectives on Genetic Patenting: Science, Religion, Industry and Government in Dialogue*, editor and co-author (American Association for the Advancement of Science 1999); and *Human Rights and Health: The Legacy of Apartheid*, co-author and co-editor with Leonard Rubenstein (American Association for the Advancement of Science 1998).

Ebrahim Moosa is Associate Professor in the Department of Religious Studies at the University of Cape Town and Visiting Associate Professor in the Department of Religious Studies at Stanford University (1998-2002). He is editor of the *Journal for Islamic Studies*. He is the founder of and former Director of the Center for Contemporary Islam at the University of Cape Town. He is the author/editor of many publications including: *Ghazali of Tus: A Poetics of Imagination* (Oneworld 2001); and editor of the posthumous publication of Fazlur Rahman's *Revival and Reform: A Study of Islamic Fundamentalism* (Oneworld 1999).

Nancey Murphy is Professor of Christian Philosophy at Fuller Theological Seminary in California. Her first book, *Theology in the Age of Scientific Reasoning* (Cornell University Press 1996), won prizes from both the American Academy of Religion and the Templeton Foundation. She is also co-author with George F.R. Ellis of *On the Moral Nature of the Universe: Theology, Cosmology, and Ethics* (Fortress 1996), as well as co-author with Warren Brown, and Newton Maloney of *Whatever Happened to the Soul* (Fortress 1998). Murphy is a member of the Board of Directors of the Center for Theology and the Natural Sciences and an ordained minister in the Church of the Brethren.

Preface

God, Life, and the Cosmos: Christian and Islamic Perspectives is the first book of its kind in which scholars and representatives of two major religious traditions reflect on the tensions, support, and overlap between science and religion with regard to the fundamental questions of the origin and purpose of life and cosmos.

All but three chapters in this volume are revised versions of the papers presented at the International Conference, "God, Life and the Cosmos: Theistic Perspectives", held on November 6-9, 2000 at Islamabad, Pakistan. The conference brought together 23 scientists and scholars from various parts of the world for three days of presentations and discussions. It was jointly organized by the Center for Theology and the Natural Sciences, Berkeley, California, USA, the Islamic Research Institute of the International Islamic University, Islamabad, Pakistan, and the International Institute of Islamic Thought, Islamabad.

The 14 chapters that make up this volume deal with the philosophical issues in the science-religion discourse, cosmology, and bioethics. Providing the context for the whole volume, the first section of the book explores the philosophical, historical, and methodological foundations of the relationship between science and the two religious traditions. It also presents various aspects of the Islamic scientific tradition and its relationship with the religious faith that is considered to have shaped and defined it. The second section focuses on cosmology, and the third on life, consciousness, and bioethics.

This book does not address all facets of the rich and intricate discourse on the relationship between science and religion – no single volume can. Neither does it attempt to establish an interfaith dialogue in the context of the science-religion discourse; it is still too early to make such an attempt. The book, however, does attempt to present a broad overview of Christian and Islamic perspectives on the relationship between faith and science in general, and between the two religious traditions and some aspects of modern cosmology and bioethics.

This is a small beginning toward addressing some urgent concerns in the field of science and religion. They are urgent because, after all, science and religion are the two most important forces that make up the warp and weft of contemporary life as it is lived in various parts of the globe. Both have global impact, both are powerful, and both claim to provide answers to some of the most enigmatic questions that humanity has ever faced.

When these papers were written and presented, the world had not yet witnessed the shocking events which closed the year 2001. Then we had a different kind of war and peace in our minds: the alleged war between science and religion. We hoped to ferret out consonance and dissonance between faith and science and explore various facets of science in the Christian and Islamic traditions. But since then, war and peace have attained completely new meanings. In this changed global situation, there is an urgent need to pursue dialogue between various peoples of our larger world community. In this volume, our method of inquiry is indeed dialogue; and dialogue too is the mode of our interaction with the pluralism of our ideas. This way we have sought to enhance understanding – understanding of the subject matter and of one another. Our hope has been that this will lead to a peaceful sharing of our enormously rich intellectual, cultural, and religious legacies and resources, and to a deepened sense of our human unity.

In addition to the hosts of the Islamabad Conference mentioned earlier, the three editors would like to thank Whitney Bauman, Publications Assistant at the Center for Theology and the Natural Sciences for attending to all the details necessary to bring this book from chaos into order. Gratitude goes as well to Kevin Lucid for the complex yet invaluable job of preparing the index.

Introduction

S. Nomanul Haq

As a fully differentiated arena of thought and scholarship with its own independent set of methodological principles, the field of Religion and Science is just beginning to claim its own territory. And so the leading authorities in the field, authorities who provide the point of departure for practically everyone else, are all living contemporary pioneers. Pioneers speak not as expounders, but as discoverers; they do not observe rules that are already established, they seek to promulgate rules; to them questions are not given as such, questions are formulated by them. "The science-religion divide is particularly difficult to traverse", and "the science-religion dialogue is a very complex and time-consuming enterprise", writes Audrey Chapman in her thorough and critical survey of Christian responses to the whole array of ethical, religious, and philosophical questions arising out of the genetic revolution. These words, taken from her chapter included in this volume, announce a pioneering spirit; and they also show that the field of religion and science is still in the making.

When we planned the Islamabad conference, whose revised and select proceedings make up this volume, we had no models to follow. The idea was to ponder the science-religion question in a pluralistic religious perspective, in particular to include the Islamic perspective whose minimal presence – in fact, practical absence – in this discourse is ruefully noted by Audrey Chapman. As I see it, and I say this emphatically, this effective absence is not simply a matter of neglect or apathy or "politics of hegemony"; it is a profoundly significant phenomenon and deserves very serious attention. At the planning stage, then, it was not at all clear how we ought to apply to Islam the emerging methodological framework of the science-religion dialogue whose builders happen to be largely on the Christian theological side, people such as Ian Barbour, Arthur Peacocke, or Ted Peters who is a co-editor of, and contributor to, this book. We decided that while issues arising from and within cosmology and biology would be our specific focus, the very question of methodology and the fundamental task of defining the very terms of discourse, these would themselves be a central concern for reflection, investigation, and articulation – and this burden, let us note, is the burden of the pioneer.

Mustansir Mir takes up this question directly in his chapter. His position is that there exists, indeed, a community of concerns between the Christian and Islamic perspectives on religion and science. But more, Mustansir Mir feels that even contemporary Christian theological methods can appropriately serve today's Muslim thought; he singles out with approval Ted Peter's notion of "hypothetical consonance" between theology and science, a consonance considered to hold the promise of benefitting both. "In its essential form", he says, "this method seems to be correct, though it remains for Muslim scholars to work out its details ...". Evidently, Mustansir Mir is seeking to set the very terms of the Islamic discourse on religion and science, and this is precisely what Ted Peters undertook for a theistic discourse in his chapter, "Science and Faith: From Warfare to Consonance", cited by the former. Both of these chapters prepare new ground for a new synthesis, and both appear in the first and the largest part of this volume dealing with philosophical, historical, and methodological issues.

Muzaffar Iqbal's chapter, with which the first section appropriately begins, also speaks in the tone of a discoverer. On a wide canvass, the chapter carries out an extensive historical excursus into the whole question of the relationship between the Islamic scientific tradition and the post-Renaissance science of Latin Christendom. In the opinion of this co-editor of this volume, though these are not his words, there was a metaphysical rupture between science as it was created and pursued in the medieval Islamic world, and as it developed in a secularized mode in the modern West. This thesis brings to bear a large body of historical data, and yields far-reaching consequences for the contemporary science-religion dialogue in the perspective of Islam. It also functions as a cautionary backdrop to Mustansir Mir's position, since it seeks a reformulation of basic questions. In this context, Ibrahim Kalin's very useful survey of what he considers three different views of science in the contemporary Islamic world serves to highlight the gaps between historical narratives and contemporary perceptions.

The learned chapter of Roshdi Rashed, an outstanding historian of Arabic science, and my own chapter, fall roughly into the same genre. We both undertake historical case studies, focusing on the same grand figure Ibn Sīnā (Lat. Avicenna), discovering a cross-fertilization between science and what were extra-scientific disciplines and concerns in medieval Islam. Rashed also speaks of a highly creative interplay *within* various branches of science pursued in the Islamic world, in particular between different branches of mathematics. But in this specific instance, he rigorously demonstrates a "double movement" between metaphysics and mathematics, a phenomenon embodied in the exchange between combinatorial analysis and ontological doctrines. The latter involved the question of the One and many, of God and his creation, of intellects and angels – and so, we may legitimately say, here we have a case of science-religion linkage. And this is precisely what I explicitly say in my own chapter in which I speak about the fateful Islamic recasting of the Greek intellectual legacy: "Historical evidence teaches once again that the very doctrinal framework of science ... is conceived not in isolation from the religious context, but within it ...".

Sitting quite literally in the middle of the first part of this book is William Chittick's "The Anthropocosmic Vision in Islamic Thought". Chittick, who was the keynote speaker at the Islamabad conference, operates here exclusively in a philosophical-speculative framework. Borrowing the expression "anthropocosmic vision" from the historian of Chinese philosophy Tu Weiming of Harvard, Chittick says that with minor adjustments Tu Weiming's depiction of the Confucian anthropocosmism "could easily be employed to describe the overarching worldview of Islamic civilization in general and Islamic thought in particular". What is anthropocosmism? Chittick explains that in contrast to Western dichotomies "between reason and revelation, or between Athens and Jerusalem", anthropocosmism is a mode of thought that understands human beings and the cosmos as a single, organismic whole. Evidently, Chittick's thesis implies a fundamental incompatibility between the foundations of Islamic scientific tradition and those of modern western science; and this reinforces Muzaffar Iqbal's position, but – as does that position – it also opens up a host of messy questions.

The second and third parts of the book contain expert writings on specific questions in the science-religion discourse. The former opens with Ahmad Dallal's "Islamic Paradigms for the Relationship between Science and Religion", a work with impressive historical richness, carrying the pioneer's onus of recasting the basic framework of the science-religion question in the Islamic tradition. We need a different approach to the study of this question, "one that examines both the cultural environment, and the interaction among different cultural dynamics at work", he writes. Dallal points out the nuances *within* the Islamic religious milieu and argues cogently that we cannot, without glossing over historical complexities, identify a unified, traditional Islamic attitude toward science. This is a profoundly significant message that redefines the whole field of Islam and science.

Mehdi Golshani's "Creation in the Islamic Outlook and in Modern Cosmology" is a Muslim physicist's impassioned response to contemporary science. He juxtaposes modes of thought that are often considered incommensurable: juxtaposing in a comparative analysis the "hard science" of modern cosmology with mysticism, theology, and philosophy. The position is clear – "I do not believe that science alone can ever settle the problem of the absolute beginning of the universe", he writes, "we should explore our universe by science as much as we can, but we must avoid making claims about the absolute origination of the universe on physical grounds". In a complex manner, Golshani reinforces both Ted Peters' position of science-religion consonance, as well as that of Stephen Jay Gould's idea of science having no concern with ultimate questions.

The problem of causality happens to be a central concern of *kalam*, a discipline usually referred to as Islamic theology; and it was also the grand question for David Hume, trickling down from him through the Vienna Circle to Karl Popper in the 20th century. Philip Clayton, a philosopher, takes up this question again and presents a new doctrine of causation in his "The Impossible Possibility: Divine Causes in the World of Nature". Clayton explicates the physicist's presupposition of *causal closure*, embodied in the principle of conservation of energy, and the grand principle of causal or physical determinism, pointing out that theism and physical determinism are incompatible. "The problem of divine agency therefore stands on the center court for theists today", he says. He takes up this challenging problem by proposing in detail and meticulously a metaphysical revision of our existing theory of causation.

Mark Worthing deals with the theistic responses, in particular Christian and Islamic, to the models of an oscillating universe that arise out of contemporary Big Bang cosmologies. His chapter, in addition to its cosmological interest, is striking in that it speaks of possible contribution of the Islamic tradition to the Christian worldview in overcoming the difficulties encountered in incorporating the oscillating universe model into this worldview. This makes Mustansir Mir's flow move in the other direction – from the Islamic to the Christian.

The final part of this collection entitled "Life, Consciousness, and Genetics" takes up issues arising at the science-religion junction in the large domain of biology. I have already spoken of Audrey Chapman's chapter at the outset, a chapter that lies at the beginning of this third section. Ebrahim Moosa, whose chapter follows, gives a very crisp and erudite account of the contemporary relationship between scientific developments in biology and Islamic law. He demonstrates, and – by means of actual case studies – places before us in full view the absence of what he calls a "common epistemic vocabulary" between modern science and the inherited perceptions of the Muslim legal practice today. Ebrahim Moosa feels that the very viability of the Islamic legal system lies in the dynamic process of updating and reconstruction in view of the ever-shifting boundaries of scientific theories and ever-growing body of scientific discoveries.

The volume closes with Nancey Murphy's "Neuroscience and Human Nature: A Christian Perspective". Murphy addresses the perennial questions of the human person, soul, resurrection, and immortality, and gives a synoptic view of how these matters have been handled throughout Christian history. She also examines contemporary arguments against dualism, and finally speaks strongly in favor of what she calls "nonreductive physicalism – that is, to show that neurobiological determinism does not threaten our self-image as free and rational creatures". It is most interesting to note that Murphy's concerns coincide with those of Clayton, but they look at the issue from two different angles – the former speaks as a Christian philosopher about neuroscience, the latter as a logician and metaphysician; together, they function as mutual reinforcement.

Again, note that in a newly emerging independent discipline concerned with science, whose contours by definition shift constantly, scholars and thinkers carry the particularly heavy onus of pioneers, innovators, and trend setters. Evidently, all contributors to this volume have undertaken this onus with uncompromising integrity.

S. Nomanul Haq
University of Pennsylvania

Part I

Philosophical, Historical, and Methodological Issues

Chapter 1
Islam and Modern Science: Questions at the Interface
Muzaffar Iqbal

Taken as a whole, modern science is a unique enterprise. Though ultimately a product of Western civilization, today modern science and its more utilitarian offspring, technology, is eagerly sought by all cultures and societies throughout the world. In its triumphal march, modern science has been able to obliterate all other ways of exploring nature, at least in a practical sense. One does not need years of research to verify this aspect of modern science: from Islamabad to Jeddah and from Beijing to Niamey, contemporary scientific research is based on the same foundations and methods as those found in any Western university or research laboratory. Obviously, the mere presence of an NMR spectrometer in Makkah does not make it Islamic, just like the presence of thousands of Muslim scientists in European and North American laboratories does not make their scientific research Islamic.

This extraordinary universality of modern science makes it a unique and unprecedented phenomenon. The sheer magnitude of its reach, its ability to penetrate cultures as different as Islamic and Hindu, Chinese, and those of the North American aboriginal people, has no parallel in human history. The manner in which science has been able to obliterate all other ways of studying nature and its irresistible appeal are unique to this modern enterprise which arose in a small part of Europe in the 17th century and which has since been able to penetrate our whole living habitat.

But perhaps more wondrous is the fact that on a small part of this tiny planet that orbits around a star in the suburbs of a galaxy of a billion stars, which, in turn, is *a* galaxy among millions of galaxies, there arose a science which was able to penetrate into diverse cultures within the short span of three centuries and change the way human beings live, die, communicate, marry, give birth to children, produce their food, clothing and housing, and conduct the other thousand and one daily routines of their lives. The fact that electrons, atoms, and molecules on the one hand, and gears, levers, and beams on the other, have become universally accepted words in which contemporary scientists and engineers as well as ordinary citizens of various nation-states communicate and conduct their daily business is indicative of the vast reach of the scientific enterprise. This aspect of the universality of modern science is a *fait accompli*, whether one likes it or not.

If history can be our guide, it does not seem possible to return to a concept of matter – and ultimately of the whole universe – which is built upon the pre-17th century notions of matter, space, and time. Whatever judgment we may choose to pass on modern science, there is no escape from it. Even in the domain of non-western medicine, where results of alternative philosophies of the human body and its maladies and treatments have been effectively demonstrated, modern Western medicine is rapidly replacing traditional practices, resulting in an irreplaceable loss for the whole human race.

The West and Modern Science

In its onward march, the structure of scientific knowledge has passed through many revolutions in its various branches as well in its foundational philosophies. For example, in a century-long, successful struggle, the Copernican Revolution was able to establish that the earth is not the stationary center of the solar system and this was enough to shake the very foundation of the worldview that was based on a geocentric system.

But this was just the beginning. With Galileo, modern science not only discovered the use of a wonderful little tool, the telescope, it also entered a structural revolution of its epistemology: henceforth, the study of nature had to be based on experiments in a manner that was fundamentally different from the methods of natural philosophy. We are not concerned here about the debates about how this was achieved. It is, ultimately, immaterial that Galileo did not in fact go on the Leaning Tower of Pisa to perform his experiments in the 1580s; what was established was a principle which was as sound as any principle can be. And Galileo did have a tool – his little telescope – from which he could see what no other human being had seen before: the satellites of Jupiter. Galileo also established that acceleration creates force and that the mass of an object measured by its weight on Earth must be identical with the mass inferred from what happens when it collides with other objects anywhere in the universe or when it is accelerated by some force. This principle – known as the *equivalence principle* – which was later to become one of the foundations for the theory of relativity, is one of the fundamental formulations of modern science which changed the way human beings perceived "objects".

Likewise, William Harvey's (1578-1657) experiments and René Descartes' (1596-1650) philosophical account of nature were foundational to the understanding of nature that developed in the 17th century and that was to affect subsequent centuries. Similarly, Newtonian physics, which set the agenda for modern science for the next two centuries, was not merely an isolated and internal development in physics; it was and still is a profound meditation on the nature of nature, God, life and their mutual relationships.

The transforming ability of modern science was in full force in the 18th century – a century in which science seems to have been preoccupied with electricity and magnetism, on the one hand, and invention of tools, on the other. It was a century during which technological innovations would start to change the way human beings lived at a scale never observed before: steam engines, new and powerful telescopes, improved frictional machines for the mechanical generation of electrical charges, the condenser for its accumulation and storage, and electroscope and electrometer for its detection and measurement.

The 18th century also saw an increasing preoccupation with quantification,[1] standardization of instruments (for example, improvements in barometers and thermometers) and inventions such as hygrometer and wind-gauges.

The language of science also changed drastically. This was the single most important factor in attaining universality for the new science. Henceforth, science could formulate its discoveries in highly mathematized constructs which relied upon notations and numbers rather than linguistic constructs specific to a particular language. This, in fact, gave birth to its own language of expression that could be understood all over the world. Of course, this new language of science was ultimately rooted in its European home, yet the nomenclature of various branches of science soon achieved a universality unknown to any other language. Like ideas, equations started to change the world.

The process of refinement and standardization of symbols and notations along with the development of new apparatuses for various experiments occupied a central position in the 18th century. But most of all, the 18th century brought to Europe an immense amount of observational and experimental data from other parts of the world – a development made possible, to a large extent, by improved navigational techniques. Individual and organized expeditions explored Africa, Asia, North America, and the Pacific Ocean and its coasts. The use of new techniques in the textile industry,[2] application of scientific principles and technological tools in the construction of public and private buildings, roads, bridges, canals, lighthouses, extensive use of improved steam-engines in mines and water-works and, above all, the use of locomotives, steam-carriages, and steam boats transformed the way human beings lived and moved from one place to another.

The combined impact of all these new scientific developments and the corresponding changes in the philosophical foundations of science produced a century which would later be variously known as the century of Enlightenment, the Age of Reason, the Age of Criticism, and the Philosophical Century. It was a century which produced a definite break with the past by focusing on this worldliness with a concentration that had never been observed in human history at such a large scale. The 18th century also produced an unprecedented confidence in human reason. It produced the notion that human reason can understand all that *can* be understood in a world which operates in an orderly manner without the need of any magical or supernatural interference.

The next century produced even more dramatic changes. Within the first two decades of the 19th century, John Dalton (1766-1844) had established that all matter was made up of atoms and that each kind of atom has a unique specific weight.[3] By 1851, James Prescott Joule (1818-1889) had established his law of conservation of energy.[4] With the introduction of Rudolf Clausius' (1822-1888) idea of *entropy* in 1865, a new beginning was made which would eventually produce a vastly powerful concept, eventually known as the Second Law of Thermodynamics.[5] This led to the introduction of the idea of "arrow of time" into the mainstream of western science which was to have far reaching influence through its interpretive power, which established that most physical systems evolve only in one direction.

Perhaps the most important event in the history of the 19th century science was the formulation and articulation of the theory of the evolution of species by natural selection by Charles Darwin (1809-1882). In his paper entitled "On the Tendency of Species to Form Varieties; and on the Perpetuation of Varieties and Species by Natural Means of Selection", first presented on the afternoon of July 1, 1858, by his friends Charles Lyell (1797-1875) and Joseph Dalton Hooker (1817-1911), at a meeting of the Linnaean Society,[6] Darwin formally announced the results of his long research using a key term that was to become a household word: Natural Selection.[7]

The publication of Darwin's books, *The Origin of Species by Means of Natural Selection*[8] in 1859 and his second major work, *The Descent of Man* in 1871, were to transform the terms of debate about the place of human beings in the cosmos. In his second book, Darwin presented his "evidence" for the descent of Man from some lower form (chapter I) along with a complete "mechanism" of the "manner of development of man from some lower form" (chapter III). By emphasizing that human beings are part of nature in a manner akin to other animals, Darwin opened a chasm in the scientific and religious understanding of human nature which continues to draw attention.

The 19th century, often called the Age of Certainty, was also deeply interested in the formulation of vast systems, universal theories and explanations.[9] Before the end of the century, Louis Pasteur (1822-1895) had established the existence of bacteria and had shown some of their behavior, he had also formulated his germ theory of infectious disease; Heinrich Hertz[10] (1857-1894) had generated invisible Maxwell waves in the radio-frequency range (1880) and Guglielmo Marconi (1874-1937) had founded a global communication industry by spanning the Atlantic Ocean with these waves. In 1895, W.K. Röntgen[11] (1845-1923) discovered a new kind of radiation which could penetrate human flesh but not bones, X rays. A year later, Antoine Becquerel (1852-1908) in Paris identified the same radiation being emitted by atoms of uranium, the first of several elements to be known as radioactive.

Three years before the close of the century, J.J. Thompson (1856-1940), the winner of the 1906 Nobel Prize for Physics, would make another fundamental discovery: atoms have parts. This discovery produced a major transformation of all the ideas that human beings had held about the nature of material that makes up the physical universe.

Deeply interested in the "Why?" of natural phenomenon, the 19th century formulated its answers in mathematical terms. Fundamental problems of physics were thus investigated in mathematical terms – a process that further mathematized our notions about nature. This gave rise to certain physical constants. For example, in his efforts to explain why the amount of energy radiated at a particular frequency increased with temperature, Max Planck (1858-1947) proposed in 1900 that radiation of a particular frequency exists only as *quanta*; the greater the frequency, the greater the energy of the quanta concerned. In 1905, Einstein (1879-1955) was able to explain why a certain minimum frequency of light was required to extract electrons from metals or to make semiconductors carry an electrical current.

By the end of the first decade of the 20th century, Ernest Rutherford (1871-1937) had shown that all atoms were constructed from electrons and a nucleus, which contained most of the mass of the atom as well as its positively charged particles. In 1913, Niels Bohr (1885-1962) would reconcile the properties of the simplest atom, hydrogen, with Planck's discovery that energy is transferred between atoms only in quanta. This would explain much more: the so-called spectral lines always have a very precise and well-defined frequency. Bohr proposed that electrons travel around the nucleus just as if they were planets revolving around a star, except that only a restricted number of orbits is available, each with a well-defined energy; each spectral line corresponds to the change of the position of electrons from one orbit to another; the frequency of the spectral line being the difference between two energies. It seemed, then, that radiation (a ray of light or heat coming from a radiator) can be understood as a series of indivisible quanta, each with its specific frequency, or as a wavelike phenomena, first advocated by Huyghens in the 18th century and substantiated by Maxwell in the 1860s.

But by 1913, when Einstein published his second important paper on quantum mechanics, it became clear that radiation had to be both a wavelike function as well as a corpuscular phenomena; corpuscles were called photons. This led the French scientist Louis de Broglie (1875-1960) to propose that perhaps electrons (which had been thought of as corpuscles) might also have wavelike properties; by 1926, this had become an experimentally-proven and generally accepted idea.

The crowning achievement of the first quarter of the 20th century was the independent work of Werner Heisenberg (1901-1976) and Erwin Schrödinger (1887-1961). Heisenberg, a German scientist working with Max Born (1882-1970) and Pasqual Jordan (1902-) at

Göttingen, proposed a system to calculate the properties of quantized systems; this was called "matrix mechanics". Heisenberg had already proved that it was impossible to simultaneously measure the position and the speed of a particle, such as an electron. This principle, which became known as Heisenberg's uncertainty principle, had an enormous philosophical impact on the certainty of scientific enterprise which had become entrenched during the 19th century.

Quantum indeterminacy was to play a large role in the emergence of a new theology in the western world – a theology that acknowledges contingency. But Einstein supported the old theology.

Einstein's famous aphorism, "God does not play dice", is indicative of his contempt for quantum uncertainty. His strongest counter-argument was to call attention to a paradoxical implication of quantum mechanics now known as the Einstein-Podolsky-Rosen (EPR) Paradox. This can be explained by taking a pair of protons whose quantum spins cancel out. Separation and measurement of the spin of one proton "collapses" the wave equation and determines the spin of the other. Thus, it appears that a measurement in one place can have an instantaneous effect on something that may be light years away. Einstein took this as a proof for the incompleteness of quantum mechanics. He argued that this result only made sense if the spins were determinate, but unknown to us, *before* the protons were separated. In this case, measurement would merely tell us what was always the case. But, according to the orthodox interpretation of quantum mechanics, it is not merely a matter of ignorance; the spin is *not determined* until it has been measured. In other words, the pair of protons cannot be regarded as separate entities until the measurement has been made.

Quantum mechanics is one of the most important branches of modern science for it has not only broken the hold of 19th century determinism and scientism but has also led the way to an understanding of processes which seem to violate natural laws. Einstein and his colleagues had assumed two laws in formulating the EPR Paradox: "The principle of reality" which states that individual particles possess definite properties even when they are not being observed and "The locality principle" which states that a measurement in one of the two isolated systems can produce no real change in the other. Taken together, these principles imply an upper limit to the degree of cooperation that is possible between isolated systems.

In 1982 a team of physicists at the University of Paris led by Alain Aspect demonstrated experimentally that this limit is exceeded in nature. In other words, our physical descriptions of the world in which we live cannot be both real and local in the above sense. Most physicists interpret this result by abandoning the reality principle – the property (spin in this case) has no definite value until the measurement is made.

David Bohm (1906-) disagreed. He distinguished between the quantum particle (an electron, for example) and a hidden 'guiding wave' that governs its motion. In his opinion, electrons are treated as particles. In a two-slit experiment, they go through one slit rather than the other but their choice of slit is not random; it is governed by the guiding wave, resulting in the wave pattern that is observed.[12]

Islam and Modern Science

The foregoing cursory survey of the emergence of modern science and several developments within its various disciplines makes it abundantly clear that modern science is not even remotely similar to what was known as science prior to the Scientific Revolution of the 17th century. It also briefly mentions the role played by some of the main producers of this science, none of whom is a Muslim. Modern science has also formulated theories concerning the origins of the cosmos and life that are not always in harmony with the Islamic worldview, just as they are not always in agreement with the biblical tradition when taken in its traditional sense. Moreover, in its abstraction and mathematization of nature, modern science not only attempts to describe and explain nature, it also formulates its own theology of nature.

This new scientific theology finds the notion of God alien and formulates its theories on the basic assumption that the cosmos is merely an aggregate of matter that functions on the basis of certain laws that can be understood by the scientific method. Once understood, these laws can then be used to explain everything without recourse to anything other than science. True, many contemporary scientists hold theistic beliefs but these beliefs are held by them as articles of their faith and not because their science carries these beliefs within its working mechanism. In other words, modern science operates without any internal need of a deity. If it produces ideas, perceptions and theories that come into conflict with religious worldviews or which raise fundamental questions about God's omnipotence and freedom, it does not shun from doing so out of any commitment to any faith.

In fact, sometimes such theories emerge as a result of discoveries within specific branches of science. For example, it was recognized in the 1830s that cells are essential units of living things but it was not until the 1880s that differentiation was made between body cells (*somatic cells*) and those that are responsible for reproduction (*germ cells*). This was the work of German physiologist August Weissman (1834-1914) who also discovered the structures within the cell nuclei that appeared to be responsible for the transference of inheritable characteristics from one generation of cells to their successors; these were called *chromosomes*. He also discovered that in sexually reproducing organisms, germ cells only had half the number of chromosomes as compared to the somatic cells.

This led to the discovery that inheritable characteristics are determined by genes; genes are arranged in a linear fashion along the chromosomes, like beads on a string. But what were genes made of? The development of the ultra centrifuge in the 1940s made it possible to separate the components of chromosomes and it was discovered that chromosomes were made of two components: protein and a nucleic acid. But it was not until after the Second World War that science could establish the identity of the nucleic acid: it was deoxyribonucleic acid (DNA). Its structural model was built by J.D. Watson (1928-) and

Francis C. Crick (1916-) at the Cavendish Laboratory at Cambridge in April 1953; it illustrated how these molecules could function as repositories of genetic information. DNA also contained the recipe needed by the cells to carry out specific functions; in other words, the secret of life was thought to be contained within the genetic code. This not only firmly established the field of genetics, it also brought ontogeny[13] within the bounds of scientific inquiry – an event which has been ranked with Copernicus' successful advocacy of the heliocentric hypothesis.[14]

These developments in various branches of science have raised fundamental questions about the origin of the cosmos and life, and modern science seems to have answers for these questions. But these answers need to be interpreted through religious reflections. This process has not been ignored in the West and serious theological reflection by a whole range of theologians from all denominations has produced an impressive amount of literature which deals with various issues at the interface of Christianity and science, a subject that has always been part of the Western tradition in one or the other form – from Augustine to Newton, every major philosopher and scientist has reflected on the implications of scientific discoveries for their faith.

How do these issues relate to Islam and Muslims? Is it a legitimate subject of inquiry? Or is it one of those fields like "Islam and women", "Islam and democracy" and "Islamic socialism", which have come to the Muslim world through its encounter with the West as foreign entities and which lose all legitimacy when placed within the matrix of Islamic thought?[15] Seen in its proper historical perspective, the Islam and science discourse has certainly changed from what it was during the time when Islamic scientific tradition was fully alive. In order to understand these changes, let us attempt to articulate the main questions.

Briefly stated, the defining questions of the contemporary science and religion discourse in the West revolve around a central core: The questions related to *the origin of the cosmos and life* formulated in such disciplines as cosmology, quantum physics, and evolutionary biology; the questions springing from the various *concepts of nature*: Is nature merely a huge coagulate of purposeless matter that has somehow emerged on the cosmic plane? Or is there any teleology observable in natural phenomena? Does God act in the physical world? Or are natural causes sufficient to explain everything – from the thunderstorm to the formation of galaxies?

During the last 40 years, a surging interest in the field of science and religion has produced a large body of scholarly responses and interactions which seek to build bridges between science and Christian theology.[16] Of course, there are others, such as Stephen J. Gould, who advocate the principle of Non-Overlapping Magisteria (NOMA), implying that science and religion belong to two separate realms and never shall the twain meet.[17]

But despite the fact that modern science has produced an overwhelming impact on the Muslim world, the study of the relationship between Islam and modern science remains under-developed. There is an overwhelming interest in modern science (or perhaps one should say hunger for science), yet there exists very little interest in the study of its impact on the Muslim world or in its relationship with Islam. This is not surprising.

The Muslim world received modern western science at a time when most of the traditional Muslim lands were under direct colonial rule. Seen from the perspective of the colonized, it was the sheer force of Western science and technology that made it possible for England and France to colonize a large part of the world. Of course in retrospect, it seems more like a partial truth; but, for the early 20th century Muslim reformers, it was *the reason* for their subjugation. They saw Western science and technology as the most desirable aspect of Western civilization and implored their people to acquire it at all costs. This attitude continues to be the reigning paradigm in various development-related debates in the Muslim world.

Of course, there are notable exceptions to this general trend. There is, indeed, a small group of Muslim scholars who has devoted their intellectual energies to the study of the relationship between

Islam and science.[18] But the average Muslim scientist is not typically interested in this discipline. As a result of this general apathy toward the discipline, the Islam and science discourse remains a marginal issue in contemporary Muslim intellectual life.

But this marginality is only in reference to serious scholarship. At the popular level, there exists a large body of literature that attempts to show evidence for particular modern scientific discoveries in the Qur'ān. This apologetic literature, which ranges from the enormously popular book of the French Muslim physician Maurice Bucaille, *The Bible, the Qur'an and Science* – first published as *La Bible, le Coran et la science* in 1976[19] and since then translated into every language spoken in the Muslim world – to dozens of websites which attempt to prove that the Qur'ān *is,* in fact, the word of God because it contains scientific theories and facts that modern science has only recently discovered.[20]

As a result, any attempt to articulate Islamic perspectives on various aspects of contemporary science has to first formulate valid questions and develop a language of discourse. This is a daunting task. But it is also an essential task that needs to be undertaken by a large number of Muslim scientists who are deeply rooted in various Islamic sciences. Unfortunately, such a species does not exist in the Muslim world. Muslim scientists are, by and large, a product of western-style secular institutions where they do not receive any formal training in Islamic thought. And Islamic scholars in the Muslim world generally remain oblivious to science.

One must also note that whereas it is Christian *theology*[21] that has been posited as a counterweight to science in the science-religion discourse, one cannot consider Islamic theology to play a similar role. For any meaningful discourse between Islam and science, Islamic theology cannot be expected to play a similar role because in the Islamic tradition theology deals with a totally different subject matter. The main foci of Islamic theology have ranged from reflections on God's attributes to that of heaven and hell and the nature of reward and punishment. Islamic theology is, therefore, a poor counterbalance for science in any discourse on Islam and science.

For a creative exploration of the relationship between Islam and modern science, one needs to view it from the perspective of the Islamic concept of nature taken as a whole and within its own matrix, which is defined by the revealed text, the Qur'ān. This is not an easy task because as soon as one brings the revealed text into the contemporary discourse, there appears to be a hardening of attitudes and closing of doors; the science-religion discourse in the West is construed in the framework of theology and science and not in terms of the Bible and science, at least not in the mainstream. But perhaps the worst impediment is the parallel that is more likely to be drawn between such a stance and the presence of a fundamentalist strand in the West which posits the Bible as a counterweight in the science-religion discourse – a strand that is despised in the academic world. However, notwithstanding this difficulty, one cannot think of a genuine Islam and science discourse which is not rooted in the Qur'ān.

Likewise, the Islam and science discourse cannot attain any degree of authenticity without its roots going back to the Islamic scientific tradition. What was Islamic in Islamic Science? How was the Islamic scientific tradition rooted in the Qur'ānic worldview and whatever happened to that tradition? Equally important are the epistemological considerations concerning the status of the Qur'ān in relation to modern science and the nature and meaning of the so-called "scientific verses" of the Qur'ān. Likewise, the concepts of the cosmos, the nature of divine action, and God's relationship to created beings as defined by the Qur'ān cannot be ignored in any discourse on Islam and science. One also needs to examine the process of appropriation and transformation of the Islamic scientific tradition in Europe during the centuries prior to the emergence of modern science. This will provide insights into the making of the foundational structure of modern science and the relationship of its underlying philosophical structure to the Islamic worldview. Only then, and on the basis of these explorations, can one build models and methodologies for the Islam and science discourse.

Thus, for any meaningful discourse on Islam and science, the following points are essential:

1. Islamic concepts of God and the nature of the divine role in the created universe.
2. The concept of the cosmos in Islam, including the plurality of the worlds and the unseen.
3. The relationship between the Islamic concept of nature – as a sign and as a trust given to humans – and various concepts of the physical cosmos in modern science.
4. The vast corpus of Qur'ānic exegesis in relationship to modern science, particularly the interpretation of the so-called "scientific verses" of the Qur'ān.
5. An epistemological framework for the exploration of the relationship between Islam and modern science.

Each of these points demands in-depth studies. In addition to these fundamental questions, there are many other questions that need to be explored. These include a whole range of issues dealing with ethics and Islamic Law (*Sharīʿa*) in relation to certain branches of modern science such as biotechnology and genetics. Considering the limitations of space, this essay is limited to only a few observations on these issues. The following sections examine the historic process of transmission of the Islamic scientific tradition to Europe and the emergence of modern science. This inquiry is essential for understanding the points of consonance and dissonance that exist between the Islamic scientific tradition and modern science.

Transmission of the Islamic Scientific Tradition

Fortunately, we can reconstruct the process of transmission of the Islamic scientific tradition to Europe, at least in part. We do not know the whole picture but we do know, with reasonable accuracy, what was translated as well as when and by whom:[22] Ibn Sī nā's works were among the first to be translated into Latin. The physical and philosophical portions of his *Kitāb al-Shifā'* were translated by Dominicus Gundissalinus and John of Seville in Toledo in the 12th century; Alfred of Sareshel translated the chemical and the geographical parts in Spain at the beginning of the 13th century and *al-Qānūn fī'l-Ṭibb* was translated by Gerard of Cremono in Toledo in the 12th century. Among others who were translated between the 11th and the 13th centuries are Ibn Rushd, known to the Latin Christendom as Averroes, who was translated by Micheal Scot in the early 13th century; Ibn al-Haytham (354/965-430/1039), called Alhazen by his Latin translators, was translated by more than one translators toward the end of the 12th century; al-Fārābī (d. 339/950) was translated by Gerard of Cremona in Toledo during the 12th century; Abū Bakr al-Rāzī (ca. 250/854-313/925), known to his translators as Rhazes, was translated by Gerard of Cremona and Moses Farachi, in Toledo and Sicily, in the 12th and 13th centuries; al-Kindī (ca. 185/801-252/866) was translated by Gerard of Cremona in Toledo, in the 12th century; al-Khwārazmī (ca. 184/800-ca. 233/847) was translated by Adelard of Bath and Robert of Chester in the 12th century and Jābir ibn Hayyān (d. 200/815) was translated by various translators in the 12th and 13th centuries.

Notice the omission of Abū Rayḥān al-Bīrūnī (362/973-442/1050), Ibn Sīnā's able contemporary whose vast corpus of scientific writings includes 180 works of varying length embracing vast fields of knowledge, in this feverish translation activity. This omission is more than accidental. Al-Bīrūnī was not translated because he was *not needed* at that stage by the European scientific tradition. In fact, real appreciation for his work had to wait until the 20th century. And this is not an isolated example. Medieval Europe was equally uninterested in a host of other Muslim scientists whose contributions did not fit the requirements of the nascent scientific enterprise in Europe.[23] Those who were translated, were translated *because* of their importance for Aristotelian studies and *not* for their contributions to the Islamic scientific tradition. Had the Islamic scientific tradition been the need and focus of the European science, the list of translated material would not have been restricted to the above group of scholars and scientists, all of whom were profoundly interested in Aristotle.

This somewhat incomplete, but representative, list clearly shows that the European intellectual tradition was looking for a particular type of material, that it was not interested in the Islamic scientific tradition *per se;* rather, in the dynamics of its own development, it had come to a point where it needed to recover its own antiquity and it found it in Aristotle's Arab home and recovered it. In this process, it came across Ibn Sīnā, Al-Kindī, and Ibn Rushd and accepted them as well – not as the true representatives of the Islamic scientific tradition but as commentators on the Aristotelian corpus. Dante called Ibn Rushd *che'l gran comento*, the Grand Commentator. In his *Inferno* (IV), he placed him among the greatest non-Christian thinkers (Euclid, Ptolemy, Hippocrates, Avicenna, and Galen) who were, nevertheless confined to the first circle of Hell.

Appropriation of the Received Tradition

We also know that the large-scale translation activity of the 13th century that opened the floodgates of knowledge from a civilization which was considered to be hostile, pagan, and dangerous, posed a serious threat to intellectual life in Europe. The new material was simply irresistible in its utility, power, and quality. And some of it was considered harmless, as far as the religious and philosophical beliefs were concerned. Thus treatises on mathematics, optics, meteorology, and medicine were welcomed. Euclid's *Elements*, al-Khāwarazmī's *Algebra*, Ibn al-Haytham's *Optics*, and Ibn Sīnā's *Canon of Medicine* posed no serious threat, but when it came to those works which had profound metaphysical implications, there could be no easy solution. Once translated and circulated, these works could not be un-translated and removed from the intellectual horizon of Western Europe; their presence posed a serious threat to religious beliefs, which demanded an immediate response.

Aristotle and his Muslim commentators were the first to meet resistance. In 1210, a council of Christian bishops issued a decree forbidding instruction on Aristotle's natural philosophy within the faculty of arts; this decree was renewed in 1215 by the papal legate Robert de Courçon.[24] Though this decree was only applicable to Paris, it marks the beginning of a long process that would eventually cast shadows over the later history of the science and religion discourse in the West. Bans on Aristotle (1210, 1215, and 1231) had a short life and by 1240 Aristotle's works on natural philosophy were again being taught in Paris just like they were being taught in Oxford and Bologna. By 1255, Aristotle had won a respectable place in the academia; in that year the faculty of arts at Paris passed new statutes which made it mandatory to include all known works of Aristotle in the curriculum.

This change was accompanied by another change which is significant to our topic. Aristotle did not barge upon the intellectual tradition of the West unaided; he was received in the company of Ibn Sīnā whose Platonized versions of the Aristotelian corpus had posed serious threats of pantheism. However, around 1230, the commentaries of Ibn Sīnā began to be replaced by those of Ibn Rushd, in whom Europe discovered a more authentic and less Platonized commentator. It was for this reason that Ibn Rushd, the Commentator, was to enjoy immense respect and popularity in the West. The University of Padua became the main center of Averroism, though the Universities of Paris and Bologna were not far behind in their appreciation.

But in spite of his new companion, Aristotle was still as unacceptable to Christendom as he had been to the Muslims when he first arrived in his Arab home. Both the Islamic and Christian traditions had to struggle with an Aristotelian cosmos that was made up of eternal elements and destined to last forever because the elements had not come into being at any moment and hence would not cease to be. This was obviously in direct contradiction to the opening chapters of Genesis and to the Qur'ānic worldview. Likewise, both traditions were threatened by the Aristotelian notion of the Prime Mover as the deity that was eternally unchanging and hence incapable of intervening in the operation of the cosmos that ran on its own, merely on the basis of cause and effect relationships. Obviously there was no room for miracles – a major element in both the Islamic and Christian traditions. But this was not all. There were other troubling elements in the Aristotelian system which had sparked intense debates in the Muslim world a few centuries ago and which now arrived in Europe through the translation movement: the astrological theories which accompanied Aristotle's philosophy taught that human acts and will were influenced by celestial objects and hence they impinged upon Christian notions of sin and salvation. Likewise, the nature of soul in Aristotle's philosophy was patently unchristian: Aristotelian philosophy conceived of the soul as form and organizing principle of the body, which had no independent existence and which needed a body to exist and hence at death both the individual's form (i.e. body) and soul ceased to exist. This notion was obviously incompatible with earlier platonized Christian teachings on the immortality of the soul.

These specific concepts which were incompatible with Christian teachings were merely the tip of the iceberg; at a more fundamental level, Aristotle posed the same threat to Latin Christendom as he had posed to Muslims: his system was taken to be a rational alternative to the revealed knowledge. This opened floodgates of another kind; now, Aristotelian philosophy was standing on a par with theology and as a rival to biblical studies. A chasm had opened; one could follow theological methods and arrive at one conclusion or follow philosophical methods to arrive at a totally opposite conclusion, with both claiming to be true. This was another battle in the classical fight for authority; the rivalry between Athens and Jerusalem, a fight which was won by Jerusalem for a short while and then lost.

As the century ran its course, Aristotle bloomed in the new universities. The most attractive feature of Aristotelian philosophy was its completeness. Aristotle had constructed a cosmos in which everything was in place; everything followed a simple basic set of logical assumptions. He offered a cosmology in which the universe and its constituents were convincingly mapped – from the outer heavens to the earth in the center, everything had a function and all functions were explained. He provided details which the West had never known before. From his account of motion to the rich and detailed descriptions of his biological corpus, everything fit so well in an orderly cosmos which ran its course and which was explained in terms such as form, matter, substance, actualities and potentialities, the four causes, the four elements, contraries, nature, change, purpose, quantity, quality, time, and space.

By the second half of the 13th century, new commentaries had started to appear and the Latin West had begun to come to terms with Aristotle. Robert Grosseteste (ca. 1168-1253) was one of the first to produce a commentary on Aristotle's *Posterior Analytics*, which tried to harmonize Aristotelian notions with Christian beliefs through Platonic and Neoplatonic influences. Grosseteste's cosmology made use of Neoplatonic emanationism to reintroduce the biblical account of creation *ex nihilio* into Aristotle's cosmology.[25]

Roger Bacon (ca. 1220-1292) was to continue Grosseteste's work well into the 13th century. Bacon was a tireless champion of the new learning and he saw no conflict between Aristotelian philosophy and his own theology. But others were more cautious. In particular, the attitude of the Franciscan order around the middle of the 13th century was one of extreme caution. Bonaventure (ca. 1217-74), who studied liberal arts and theology at the University of Paris and then stayed on to teach theology from 1254 to 1257 before resigning to become a minister general of the Franciscan order, respected Aristotelian philosophy but he was much more cautious than Bacon about the utility of philosophy in matters of faith.

Grosseteste, Bacon, and Bonaventure made important contributions to finding a way out of the impasse that the Aristotelian corpus had produced; but it was left to two Dominicans, Albert the Great and Thomas Aquinas, who were active in the middle and later years of the 13th century, to forge a powerful synthesis between Aristotelian philosophy and Christian faith. Albert the Great (ca. 1200-1280) was born and raised in Germany, and educated at Padua and the Dominican school in Cologne. He arrived in Paris in the early 1240s to study theology and became the master of theology in 1245. Between 1245-1248 he was the Dominican professor at Paris; Thomas Aquinas studied under him and when Albert was called back to Cologne in 1248, Thomas accompanied him.

Albert wrote his voluminous commentaries on Aristotle after his departure from Paris. Until then, no one in Western Christendom had paid such serious and sustained attention to Aristotle. In many ways, he resembled Ibn Sīnā: Both men were profoundly impressed by Aristotle, both wanted to remain independent of Aristotle's influence, and both tried to harmonize their faiths with Aristotelian philosophy. No wonder Albert was heavily influenced by Ibn Sīnā's works. The twelve volume 19th century edition of Albert's works, consisting of more than 8,000 pages, stands as a monumental testimony to Albert's contribution in forging a synthesis between Aristotelian philosophy and Christian faith. Albert was able to produce this synthesis because he not only knew his Aristotle, he was also at home with the works of masters of Islamic philosophy, who had produced their own synthesis of Islam and Aristotelian philosophy before him. Thus, one finds in Albert's works a heavy dependence and borrowing from a range of Muslim and Greek authors such as al-Kindī, Ibn Rushd, Plato, Euclid, Constantine the African, and many others.

Albert's able student, Thomas Aquinas (ca. 1224-1274), was to add to the contributions made by his teacher. Both respected philosophy but not at the expense of theology, both understood the power of philosophy and both tried to use that power in service of faith. But Thomas went further than his teacher in addressing thorny issues. In his book, *On the Unicity of the Intellect Against the Averroists*, he dealt with the issue of monopsychism and the nature of the soul. He agreed with the Aristotelian doctrine that the soul is the substantial form of the body, but he argued that this is a special kind of form, one that is capable of existing independent of the body so that when the body perishes, the soul does not.

Along with the efforts to harmonize Aristotelian philosophy with Christian faith, there was a parallel current in the later half of 13th century Europe that disregarded the dictates of theology and opted for pure philosophy. Siger of Brabant (ca. 1240-84), in his earlier years, and Boethius of Dacia (fl. 1270) were two representatives of this current. Both felt that a compromise between philosophy and theology was not possible. As a philosopher, one has to remain true to its principles and, though in the end he remained attached to his faith as a Christian, Boethius felt that as a philosopher he could not defend his belief in a created universe. Natural philosophy cannot admit the possibility of creation, he felt, because such an admission will introduce a supernatural element to the natural causes. Although Boethius professed his faith openly, he and other members of his group were considered radicals and in 1270 and 1277, two condemnations were issued by Etienne Tempier, the bishop of Paris. The first condemned 13 philosophical propositions allegedly taught by Siger and his fellow radicals in the faculty of arts and the second condemned 219 propositions. This was a strong official response to the radical Aristotelianism that had spread in academic circles in Paris.

Rather than serve a severe blow to Aristotelian philosophy, these condemnations merely added fuel to the fire; Aristotle had arrived in Europe from his Arab home to stay. And men such as Thomas Aquinas had made a place for him in the main discourse. The force of condemnation wore off with time. In 1323, Pope John XXII elevated Thomas to the rank of saint and in 1325, the bishop of Paris revoked all articles of the condemnation of 1277 applicable to Thomas' teachings.

The problems were not resolved, however. With time, they became more sophisticated. It was realized that at the heart of the problem were two epistemological claims: one by philosophy and the other by theology. Toward the end of the 13th century and early in the 14th, men such as John Duns Scotus (ca. 1266-1308) and William of Ockham (ca. 1285-1347) tried to diminish the area of overlap between theology and philosophy by questioning the ability of philosophy to address articles of faith with demonstrative certainty. In this attempt to separate theology and philosophy, there was also an effort to achieve peace and cohabitation. The central doctrine of this peace plan was that the Articles of Faith could not be challenged by philosophy, and natural philosophy could not encroach on religious grounds.

The influence of the Islamic scientific tradition and the debates which it sparked in the theological circles ran their course, often echoing an earlier era when these issues were bitterly contested within the Islamic world. A good example is the emphasis on Divine omnipotence in the theological debates of the 14th century – a theme which was central to Christianity. If God is absolutely free and omnipotent, then the physical world is contingent rather than necessary. This means that there is no necessity that it should be what it is; it is entirely dependent on God's Will in all respects: in its form, function, operation, in fact, in its very existence. The observed physical laws are not necessary, they are imposed by the divine will. The cause and effect relationships, too, are not necessary; they are contingent. Fire burns but not because fire and the act of burning are necessarily connected; rather it is so because God chose to connect them, empowering fire for the function of burning. God is free and can choose to "disconnect" the relationship between fire and its power to burn, as He did in the case of Shadrach, Meshach, and Abednego when they were cast into the burning furnace but were not harmed, as the Book of Daniel recounts (3:19-29); this miracle demonstrated a perfect example of God's omnipotence and His right to suspend natural causation when He chose. It is no accident that this line of argument reads as if one is reading al-Ghazālī (450/1058-505/1111): "In our opinion, the connection between what is habitually believed to be a cause and what is habitually believed to be an effect is not necessary", al-Ghazālī had written in his seminal work, *Tahāfut al-Falāsifah (The Incoherence of the Philosophers)*:

> But [with] any two things, where 'this' is not 'that' and 'that' is not 'this' and where neither the affirmation of the one entails the affirmation of the other nor the negation of the one entails negation of the other, it is not a necessity of the existence of the one that the other should exist, and it is not a necessity of the nonexistence of the one that the other should not exist – for example, the quenching of the thirst and drinking, satiety and eating, burning and contact with fire, light and the appearance of the sun, death and decapitation, healing and the drinking of medicine ... so on, to include all observable among connected things in medicine, astronomy, arts and crafts. Their connection is due to prior decree of God, who creates them side by side, not to its being necessary in itself, incapable of separation. On the contrary, it is within [divine] power to create satiety without eating, to create death without decapitation, to continue life after decapitation, and so on to all connected things. The philosophers denied the possibility of [this] and claimed it to be impossible.[26]

And this is not an isolated coincidence; the medieval European debates on natural laws and their relationship with religion bear a striking resemblance to similar debates in the Muslim world. This resemblance is the result of a similar process in two different contexts in the two civilizations. In the Muslim world, al-Ghazālī's reflections on causality were the mature product of discourse on Aristotelian philosophy which had gone through a full cycle – from initial encounter through translations to acceptance and then appropriation and critical reflection. The debates in 14th century Europe were likewise a product of refinement and critical reflection on fundamental questions which arose from the encounter between Christianity and the Aristotelian corpus which had arrived in Europe from Aristotle's Arab homeland by way of a feverish translation activity.

In both cases, this produced two divergent views. According to the first view, nature did not have its own permanently assigned laws; rather, it depended, wholly and without exception, on divine will for the continuous validity of its laws. According to this view, any other explanation of natural laws would amount to compromise on God's omnipotence. According to the second view, it was held that God could have chosen to create any world He wished, but He chose to create *this* world with its laws; hence natural philosophy can only discover those laws which this world exhibits and these laws are universal and unchanging.

The former view provided an easy explanation of miracles. It also created room for God's absolute and ordained powers by arguing that God's omnipotence gave Him the power to create any kind of world out of an infinite number of possibilities but having created *this* world, God chose to manifest His power in a particular mode; since He is a consistent God, He does not tinker with His creation and having created *this* world, God's activity manifests within the existing order (i.e. His ordained power). Of course there are exceptions to this general rule, but they are extremely rare.

According to the latter view, unless the natural world was taken on its own absolute value, with its own well-established laws, there was no serious way of studying the order and laws which were inherent in the world. This view provided impetus for "going out" and discovering these laws; but this did not begin to happen until three centuries later and by the time it began, the medieval world had been shattered and pushed into the pale of history.

Transformation of the Islamic Scientific Tradition

Chaucer (ca. 1340-1400) tells us in *The Canterbury Tales,* that his Doctor of Physic:

Well knew he the olde Esculpius
And Deyscorides, and eek Rufus,
Olde Ypocras, Haly and Galyen,
Serpion, Razis and Avicen,
Averrois, Damascien and Constantyn,
Bernard and Gatesden and Gilbertyn.[27]

Out of the 15 authorities quoted above, there are five Greeks (including one mythical), seven Muslims, one Frenchman and two Englishmen. Written in the 1390s by a man who was a public servant, a courtier, and a diplomat trusted by three successive English kings – Edward III (1312-1377), Richard II (1367-1400) and Henry IV (1366-1413) – these tales, told by a group of pilgrims, reflect the general status of these men and an appraisal of their contributions to the Medieval Ages.

But within a century, that appraisal was going to change. Islam and Muslims were going to be cast out of the European memory as major players in the advancement of science and their role was to be delegated to second class citizenship – a position that was to remain firmly entrenched in Western scholarship for almost 500 years and only yielded to a revised appraisal toward the end of the 20th century.[28]

In retrospect, the normative Western tradition was to pass a judgment not only on Islam and the Islamic scientific tradition but also on the Middle Ages. The Middle Ages were to be looked upon as a period of darkness, stagnation, and decay. This was already the verdict of the major voices in the 17th century. Francis Bacon (1561-1626), Voltaire (1694-1778), his younger contemporary Condorcet (1743-94), and the Swiss historian Jacob Burchhardt (1818-97), who is generally credited with the coinage of the ubiquitous term "Renaissance", all conceived of the Middle Ages as the dark period. This judgment was to remain unchallenged until the early years of the 20th century when theoretical physics opened a chasm in the certainty of scientific knowledge. But by then, the popular notion about the Middle Ages as the dark ages had attained a universal currency and anyone voicing an opposite view had to fight a difficult battle.

But slowly, a respectable body of literature did emerge which challenged the prevalent view.[29] Shortly after World War II, the revisionist history witnessed a dramatic expansion, both in quality as well as in quantity. There were many reasons for this. The worldview, which had produced the condescending attitude toward the Middle Ages – and, in fact, toward the whole history – was badly shaken through the experience of the World War. The revised view owes its existence to a thorough re-examination of a significant number of new scientific and mathematical texts and to the works of historians such as Marshall Clagett (1916-), Anneliese Maier (1905-1971), and Alexandre Koyré (1892-1964). Koyré, a respected French historian of science, powerfully articulated an alternate view which was supported by impressive scholarship.[30] According to Koyré, what the founders of modern science did was neither refinement, nor improvement of what they had inherited; they had to actually "destroy one world and to replace it with another. They had to reshape the framework of our intellect itself, to restate and to reform its concepts, to evolve a new approach to Being, a new concept of knowledge, a new concept of science".[31]

However, in spite of these efforts of reappraisal, there remains the task of establishing a proper link between the Islamic scientific tradition and the emergence of modern science. To be sure, the Islamic scientific tradition contributed to the process that led to the emergence of the Medieval European scientific tradition, which viewed nature from a perspective that was not wholly alien to Islamic perspectives. But, the overlap was never complete, as is natural for any two distinct civilizations. Nevertheless, there was a broad sphere of commonality in the way the two traditions viewed nature. But this shared perspective was short-lived and as the Middle Ages gave way to Renaissance and Medieval science to the 17th century Scientific Revolution, the common area between the Islamic scientific tradition and the new science emerging in Europe rapidly shrank and finally there remained nothing of that old commonality.

The breach produced was only to widen with time. The inner dynamics of post-Renaissance European civilization led the way to the final rupture. First the notion of essential nature of qualities – which was an integral part of matter in the Islamic as well as the Greek scientific traditions – was abandoned. Then emphasis shifted to the geometric properties of corpuscles (shape, size, motion), and finally the mathematization of nature at an unprecedented scale produced the total cleavage with whatever was received from the Islamic scientific tradition.

Thus, it is safe to say that prior to the Scientific Revolution of the 17th century, there was a common universe and a common language of discourse between the sciences that were emerging in Europe and those that had developed in the Islamic civilization. But "this common universe of discourse", notes Professor Nasr in his *Religion and the Order of Nature*, "was rent asunder by the rise of modern science as a result of which the religious view of the order of nature, which is always based on symbolism, was reduced either to irrelevance or to a matter of mere subjective concern, which made the cosmic teachings of religion to appear as unreal and irrelevant".[32]

In the same work, Professor Nasr clearly traces the point of cleavage between the received material and the new science:

> From the idea of cosmic order and laws created by God through His Will and applicable to both men and nature to the idea of 'laws of nature' discoverable completely by human reason and usually identified with mathematical laws, divorced from ethical and spiritual laws, there is a major transformation that played a central role in the rise of modern science. This new idea of laws of nature also eclipsed the earlier Christian understanding of the subject, although later theologians tried to 'Christianize' the seventeenth-century scientific concept of laws of nature. Interestingly enough, such an event did not take place in other civilizations with a long scientific tradition such as the Chinese, Indian, and Islamic, and this is of great significance in the parting

of ways between the modern West and other civilizations as far as the understanding of the order of nature and its religious significance are concerned.[33]

In the final analysis, it seems that Europe attempted to rebuild a civilization based on its antiquity. It needed to establish direct relationship with its own antiquity and this led the Renaissance philosophers and scientists to discover their Greek heritage. But once this was over, the task of the reconstruction of science in the post-17th century took place in an atmosphere which was hostile to Islam and Muslims and thus ripe for bypassing the contributions made by the European translation movement which had been responsible for bringing a large body of sophisticated works of Islamic scientific tradition into European science.[34] This reappraisal of the Muslims and their contributions to science was also the result of major shifts in the European outlook on life and nature. This shift in the philosophical foundations of the new science was already apparent in the 15th century. Plato had replaced Aristotle as the most important influence and mathematics had acquired the status of being the queen of sciences. And for almost a century, mathematics and astronomy would reign. Thus it is no accident that posterity was to honor a scholarly Polish priest, Nicholas Copernicus (1473-1543) – who, out of sheer demands of mathematical elegance, placed the sun in the center of the universe – as the harbinger of a new science. Copernicus had no reason for placing the sun at the center of his cosmos except for the elegance that could be derived from such a construction because this imaginative leap eliminates circles within circles, or epicycles, that Ptolemy had to assign to the moving planets to explain their heavenly positions in relation to the earth.

It was this imaginative leap that many Muslim astronomers, including Ibn al-Haytham, Abū 'Ubayd al-Jūzjānī (d. ca. 462/1070), al-Bīrūnī, Mu'ayyid al-Dīn al-'Urḍī (d. 664/1266), Naṣīr al-Dīn Ṭūsī (d. 597/1201-672/1274), and Ibn al-Shāṭir (d. 777/1375) had failed to take that distinguishes Copernicus from Muslim astronomers.[35] In fact, since the publication of Swerdlow's and Neugebauer's *Mathematical Astronomy in Copernicus's De Revolutionibus*,[36] it has become impossible for anyone to deny the relationship between Copernicus and the Islamic astronomical tradition, especially the period associated with the Marāgha school – a fact which has been eloquently pointed out by Swerdlow and Neugebauer who referred to Copernicus as "the last of the Marāgha astronomers". Both Copernicus and his predecessors were dealing with the same problem. Copernicus used the same theorem that was first stated by al-ʿUrḍī to reform the Ptolemaic model for the upper planets. He also made use of another theorem now called the "Ṭūsī Couple" after the name of its inventor, Naṣīr al-Dīn al-Ṭūsī.[37] In their criticism of Ptolemaic astronomy, both Copernicus and his Muslim predecessors were concerned with a central issue in the philosophy of science. Both objected to the Ptolemaic model on the grounds that any system of "science must be inherently consistent, and its premises must always have the same meaning throughout its development".[38] Thus, if a sphere is a physical body with certain properties, as was accepted by Ptolemy and all medieval astronomers after him, then that sphere cannot, through the mechanism of an equant or the like, be made to move in a mathematical system in a manner that is not consistent with its properties as a sphere. The original accepted notion of a sphere is that the sphere is capable of uniform motion in place around an axis that passes through its center. That notion would no longer make sense if the axis was later assumed to pass through a point other than the center.[39]

This is the same objection that was raised by Ibn al-Haytham in his monumental work, *al-Shukūk ʿalā-Baṭlamūs*.[40] The weight of centuries which prevented Copernicus from publishing his theory for several years,[41] had also prevented al-ʿUrḍī from publishing his theory. We have documented evidence which shows this reluctance on the part of al-ʿUrḍī who states that he was afraid of publishing his astronomical theory because it was so different from what was commonly accepted.[42]

When Copernicus finally decided to publish his book, *De revolutionibus orbium coelestium*,(On the Revolution of the Heavenly Spheres) in 1543, he had only a few days to live. In fact, a copy of the published work is supposed to have been brought to him at Frauenburg on the very last day of his life, May 24, 1543.[43] It was left to Galileo Galilei (1564-1642) and Johannes Kepler (1571-1630) to take Copernican thought to its logical conclusion in a manner that would have even astonished Copernicus. Copernicus had proposed a revolutionary idea but he had done so through a reform *within* the generally accepted model of Ptolemaic and Aristotelian astronomy; by the time Kepler and Galileo finished their careers, the limited reformation of planetary theory within the broad outlines of the accepted framework of an Aristotelian cosmos had become a radical revolution and the beginning of a true scientific revolution that would take two centuries to complete; but once completed, this new science would change forever the way human beings looked at matter, sky, planets, and their own beings.

It was this radical revolution in science that produced an unbridgeable chasm between the concepts of nature in Islam and in modern science. It happened gradually, within the intellectual climate of Europe and through the interaction of a vast number of direct and indirect influences. These included invention of various powerful instruments and tools, construction of machines, an unprecedented rise in Europe's military and naval power, vast improvements in hydraulics, metallurgy, mining, agriculture, and the use of the printing press to rapidly reproduce results of new science for quick dissemination to an increasingly receptive and enlarging readership. A mélange of fundamentally new assumptions had to be accepted before the new science could take root. Along with this shift came a revolution in epistemology; it was the new science, with all its powerful tools of discovering nature that held the supreme authority. If scriptural texts were in conflict with what the new science discovered, then they had to be reinterpreted and Galileo himself earnestly initiated this process. In his letter of 1615 to Madam Christina of Lorraine, the Grand Duchess of Tuscany, "Concerning the Use of Biblical Quotations in Matters of Science", he reinterprets Joshua 10:12-13 in the light of his own discoveries by emphasizing that the verse 10:13 tells us that the sun stood still *in the midst of the heavens*. He then argues in a passionate manner that the command *Sun, stand thou still, stand thou still*, must have been issued toward the end of the day because had it been in the early part of the day, Joshua would have no need to request the miracle to pursue victory in battle: "for if it had been near the meridian, either it would have been needless to request a miracle, or it would have been sufficient merely to have prayed for some retardation".[44] And finally, he proves that the verse can be best understood if "in agreement with the Copernican system, we place the sun in the 'midst' – that is, in the center – of the celestial orbs and planetary rotations, as it is most necessary to do".[45] He then goes on to make the epistemological leap:

> As regard to other scriptural passages which seem to be contradictory to this opinion, I have no doubt that if the opinion itself were known to be true and proven, those very theologians who, so long as they deem it false, hold these passages to be incapable of harmonious exposition with it, would find interpretations for them which would agree very well, and especially if they would add some knowledge of astronomical science to their knowledge of divinity.[46]

In spite of these preemptive measures, Galileo could not save himself from the condemnation of the *Congregatio Sanctae Inquistitionis* which condemned the proposition "Sol est centrum mundi ..." (The sun is the center of the universe) in 1616. But by then Galileo, humanist, artist, experimenter, inventor, scientist and courtier, had international fame and his defense was not for one of his theories but for experimental science itself and for the right of the scientists to study nature as it was – a congregate of bodies made up of matter, shape, size, and motion. Galileo's self-defense was bold, confident, even aggressive. "First they have endeavored to spread the opinion that such propositions in general are contrary to the Bible and are consequently damnable and heretical", he wrote to the Grand Duchess Christina, "... they had no trouble in finding men who would preach damnability and heresy of the new doctrine from their pulpits with unwonted confidence, thus doing impious and inconsiderate injury not only to that doctrine and its followers but to all mathematics and mathematicians in general".[47] But Galileo's public condemnation could not stop new science; all it did was to drive it out of Italy into the Protestant world which had a particular favorable attitude toward the ideology of opposition to the power of the Roman Church and its clergy and support for Copernicanism as well as a mechanism for rapid dissemination of new scientific knowledge without the fear of Inquisition.

The work of the scientific revolution was brought to culmination by Darwin, not only in the biological sciences but also by completing the philosophical revolution that had accompanied it. The new science was to dispense the ancient doctrine of teleology and replace it with continuous variations through natural selection. But Darwin did not spring out of a vacuum; ground had been prepared for his arrival by a steady flow of discoveries and theories throughout the preceding centuries. The publication of *Zoonomia or the Laws of Organic Life* (1794) by Erasmus Darwin (1731-1802), Charles Darwin's grandfather, suggested that organisms must adapt to the physical conditions in which they find themselves. Erasmus argued that sensations, hunger, sex, the need for security – all of these and many other factors played a role in the acquisition of new parts and modification of species. But it was left to his grandson, Charles, to demolish the now cracking structure of the old worldview.

These developments were accompanied by philosophical reflections of a similar nature. For example, the social utility of the new science was articulated by the Lord Chancellor of England, Francis Bacon (1561-1626), who conceived a grand plan to put the new science in the service of the empire. In time, the new science entered into a new orbit in which its pursuit was interlinked with politics and economics in a manner that was totally unimaginable during the era of Islamic scientific tradition. The journey from the discovery of nature's secrets to gaining command over nature was somehow also accompanied by the loss of that built-in quality of medieval science which had linked it with the glory of God. The new science would launch into new domains, it would discover millions of new facts and construct thousands of new theories and it would serve humans as no other enterprise had ever done before, but it would achieve all of this on a philosophical foundation which treated matter as autonomous units that somehow came into existence to live forever in a universe that needed neither God nor miracles to function.

Conclusion

For a proper understanding of the relationship between Islam and modern science, fundamental assumptions of modern science should be studied from an Islamic point of view, not the specific scientific facts and theories. Thus, instead of finding the Big Bang in the Qur'ān, a deeper reflection would focus on the relationship between the fundamental assumptions of modern cosmology and the Qur'ānic cosmos, its metaphysical roots, and its ontological structure. Likewise, instead of debating the consonance or dissonance between Islam and the theory of evolution, a better route is to explore the Qur'ānic data on creation, life, death, and resurrection in its totality and examine the underlying principles of the theory of evolution in all its complexity in light of the revealed knowledge. Such reflection will also examine the epistemological questions because ultimately, the discourse on Islam and science will have to be framed within an epistemology of knowledge that is characteristically Islamic.

Notes

[1] For example, Coulomb's experimental proof that the forces between electrical charges are subject to the law of the inverse square; the law of variation of the force of a magnetic pole with distance, variation of the compass and its distribution was

mapped in increasing detail, diurnal and annual fluctuations were established, the magnetic dip was charted and attempts were made to compare the intensities of the Earth's magnetic field at various places on its surface.

[2] The invention of Wyatt's and Paul's spinning rollers, Arkwright's water-frame, and various new looms.

[3] Hydrogen atoms are the lightest, carbon atoms are roughly 12 times the weight of hydrogen atoms, etc. Dalton's papers have been collected by Hyde Wollaston and Thomas Thomson in *Foundations of the Atomic Theory* (Edinburgh: Alembic Club, 1969).

[4] That is: if disturbing influences are avoided, no energy is lost in the conversion from one form to another. This principle of conservation of energy was termed as the first law of thermodynamics.

[5] Entropy is a measure of the degree to which the internal energy of an object is not accessible for practical purposes, degree of internal disorder on an atomic scale. The Second Law of Thermodynamics states that other things being equal, there will be a tendency for the entropy or the disorder of an isolated system to increase.

[6] Linnean Society of London, named after the Swedish naturalist Carl Linnaeus (1707–1778), had leading botanists, zoologists, and geologists in England as its members.

[7] In fact, Lyell and Hooker presented two papers, one by Darwin and the other by Alfred Russell Wallace (1823-1913). They appended a letter to the papers by "two indefatigable naturalists" who had "independently and unknown to one another, conceived the same very ingenious theory to account for the appearance and perpetuation of varieties and of specific forms on our planet". See, Howard Mumford Jonesan and Bernarad I. Cohen, *Science Before Darwin* (London: Andre Deutsch, 1963), 338.

[8] First published on November 24,1859, by John Murray, London. All references to this work are from Charles Darwin, *The Origin of Species* (New York: Mentor Books, 1958).

[9] For example, James Clerk Maxwell's one set of mathematical equations which described electricity and magnetism, systems of classification of plants and animals, etc.

[10] Then at Karlsruhe in Germany.

[11] Then working at Würtzburg in Bavaria.

[12] Bohm's aim was to demonstrate that hidden-variables theories are indeed possible. Hidden-variables theories, with their underlying determinism, must be non-local, maintaining the existence of instantaneous causal relations between physically separated entities. Such a view contradicts the simple location of events in both classical atomism and relativity theory. It points to a more holistic view of the quantum world. Indeed Bohm himself stressed the holistic aspect of quantum theory in his later years, after his conversion from Marxism to theosophy.

[13] The development or developmental history of an individual organism.

[14] John Maddox, *What Remains to be Discovered* (New York: The Free Press, 1998), 20.

[15] These are not passing remarks; they are the product of serious reflection on these areas of modern scholarship which have been imposed upon the Muslim world either in imitation of corresponding debates in the West (for example, feminism and many shades of scholarly studies related to this movement) or they are totally irrelevant subjects within Islamic polity (for example, the subject of Islam and democracy) because they deal with nature of rights and obligations of individuals in a system of governance which have evolved on the basis of fundamentally different notions about the goal and purpose of life of the individuals as well as that of the cosmos.

[16] This recent tide owes its existence to the pioneering work of Ian Barbour who is recognized as the "father of contemporary science-religion discourse" in the West. His 1966 book, *Issues in Science and Religion* (Englewood Cliffs, NJ: Prentice-Hall, 1966), mapped out a topology of issues which has been further refined and elaborated by many scientists-theologians. It is outside the scope of this paper to cover this vast scholarship or even mention the key participants in the contemporary discourse. Fortunately, there are a number of excellent works which provide the history of this discourse as well as helpful bibliographies. There are many web-based resources, including the website of the Center for Theology and the Natural Sciences (CTNS), *www.ctns.org*, which contains useful definitions, a bibliography, and other online resources.

[17] See Stephen Jay Gould, *Rocks of Ages* (New York: The Ballantine Publishing Group, 1999), for his formulation of NOMA.

[18] See Ibrahim Kalin's chapter in this book.

[19] Maurice Bucaille, *La Bible, le Coran et la science: les Écritures saintes examinées à la lumière des connaissances modernes* (Paris: Seghers, 1976), trans., Alastair D. Pannell and the author as *The Bible, the Qur'an and Science*. The English translation was first published in 1978 by the North American Trust Publications, Indianapolis.

[20] A recent search on "Islam and science", using the altavista search engine, listed 1,873,545 occurrences, a random sampling of these listings showed that of all the relevant entries, a large majority were related to the efforts to prove the divine nature of the Qur'ān through modern science. See, E. Harder and Basit Kareem Iqbal, "Islam and Science Online", *Islamic Studies*, vol 39: 4 (Winter 2000), pp. 685-692.

[21] "The field of study and analysis that treats of God and of God's attributes and relations to the universe; study of divine things or religious truth; divinity". *Random House Compact Unabridged Dictionary* (New York: Random House Inc., 1987).

[22] A. C. Crombie, *The History of Science: From Augustine to Galileo* (New York: Dover Publications, 1995), pp. 56-58. This seminal, though now dated, work by Crombie has an interesting publication history. This Dover edition, first published in 1995,

is an unabridged republication of the second revised and enlarged edition (1959), reprinted with corrections in 1970 and reprinted in one volume in 1979 by Heinemann Educational Books, London, under the title *Augustine to Galileo*; Volume I. *Science in the Middle Ages: 5th to 13th Centuries;* Volume II. *Science in the Later Middle Ages and Early Modern Times: 13th to the 17th Centuries.* (Original publication: Falcon Press Limited, London, 1952, under the title, *Augustine to Galileo: The History of Science A.D. 400–1650.*)

[23] While the responsibility for the views expressed here is mine, I would like to acknowledge the input of many discussions held with Syed Nomanul Haq on these matters over the years; these discussions have contributed to the process of crystallization of these views.

[24] On reception of Aristotle in Paris, see, Fernand Van Steenberghen, *Aristotle in the West*, trans. Leonard Johnston (Louvian: Nauwelaerts, 1955).

[25] For details of Grosseteste's cosmology, see James McEvoy, *The Philosophy of Robert Grosseteste* (Oxford: Clarendon Press, 1982), 149-88 and 369-441.

[26] Al-Ghazālī, *Tahāfut al-Falāsifah*, trans. Michael E. Marmura as *The Incoherence of the Philosophers* (Provo: Brigham Young University Press, 2000), 166.

[27] Geoffrey Chaucer, *The Canterbury Tales* (Norman: University of Oklahoma Press, 1979), II: 429.

[28] Even now, the true appreciation of Muslim contributions to science remains sketchy and writers like Toby Huff continue to present accounts of science in which Muslim contributions appear marginal and cosmetic. See, his *The Rise of Early Modern Science: Islam, China and the West* (Cambridge: Cambridge University Press, 1993).

[29] One of the earliest to cast a stone was the French physicist and philosopher Pierre Duhem (1861-1916). While inquiring into the intellectual predecessors of Leonardo da Vinci, Duhem discovered a series of remarkable medieval texts and authors to whom he attributed many later discoveries. These included the works of Jean Buridan (d. ca. 1358), Nicole Oresme (d. 1382). This led Duhem to formulate his influential, but flawed, theories about the anticipation of Copernicus' theory of the diurnal rotation of the earth, Descartes' analytic geometry and Galileo's law relating time and distance traveled in free fall by Oresme. See Pierre Duhem, *Le Système du Monde*, 10 vols. (Paris: Hermann, 1913-1959), 7: 534. A little later, historians like Charles Homer Haskins (1870-1937) and Lynn Thorndike (1882-1965) were to add considerable weight to the counter arguments which tried to rehabilitate the Middle Ages. See, Charles Homer Haskins, *Studies in the History of Mediaeval Science* (Cambridge: Harvard University Press, 1924), and Lynn Thorndike, *A History of Magic and Experimental Science*, 8 vols. (New York: Columbia University Press, 1923-1958), also his *Science and Thought in the Fifteenth Century* (New York: Columbia University Press, 1944).

[30] See, for examples, Clagett Marshall, *Greek Science in Antiquity* (London: Abelard-Schuman, 1957); *The Science of Mechanics in the Middle Ages* (Madison: University of Wisconsin Press, 1959); *Studies in Medieval Physics and Mathematics* (London: Variorum, 1979); and Anneliese Maier, *On the Threshold of Exact Science: Selected Writings of Anneliese Maier on Late Medieval Natural Philosophy*, Selected and translated with an introduction by Steven D. Sargent (Philadelphia: University of Pennsylvania Press, 1982). Anneliese Maier is one of the most insightful historians of science who paid special attention to the philosophical underpinnings of Medieval science. Most of her work remains unavailable in English. Her other works on the subject include the nine volume series *Storia e Letteratura* (Rome: Edizioni di Storia e Letteratura, 1966); five volumes of her *Studien zur Naturphilosophie der Spätscholstik* [*Studies on late scholastic natural philosophy*] all published by Edizioni di Storia e Letteratura, between 1949 and 1958; three volumes of *Ausgehendes Mittelalter*, collective essays on 14th century intellectual history published in 1964, 1967, and 1977 by Edinioni di Storia e letteratura. A memorial volume in her honor was published in 1981 as *Studi sul XIV secolo in Memoria di Anneliese Maier*, ed. A. Maierù and A. Paravicini Bagliani (Rome: Edizioni di Storia e Letteratura, 1981), which includes an updated bibliography of her works.

[31] Alexandre Koyré, *Metaphysics and Measurement: Essays in the Scientific Revolution* (London: Chapman and Hall, 1968), p. 21.

[32] Seyyed Hossein Nasr, *Religion and the Order of Nature* (New York: Oxford University Press, 1996), p. 129.

[33] Ibid., 133.

[34] Already in the 14th century, Dante Alighieri (1265–1321) had placed Ibn Sīnā and Ibn Rushd in Limbo, in the First Circle of Hell, with the greatest non-Christian thinkers (Electra, Aeneas, Caesar, Aristotle, Plato, Orpheus, Cicero), where they must live without hope of seeing God, and in perpetual desire though not in torment. But he had placed Prophet Muḥammad (and his son-in-law, ʿAlī) among a group of "sowers of scandal and schism", whose mutilated and bloody shades, many of whom are ripped open, with entrails spilling out, bemoan their painful lot. See, Alighieri Dante, *The Divine Comedy, Inferno*, trans. Mark Musa (New York: Penguine, 1971), Cantos IV: 142–144 and Canto XXVIII: 31-33, p.101 and 326. Canto XXVIII: 31–33 reads: "See how Mohomet is deformed and torn!/In front of me, and weeping, Ali walks, /his face cleft from his chin up to the crown".

[35] See, for example, George Saliba, *A History of Arabic Astronomy: Planetary Theories During the Golden Age of Islam* (New York: New York University Press, 1994), especially the articles in section V, "Arabic Astronomy and Copernicus". Also see, Seyyed Hossein Nasr, *An Introduction to Islamic Cosmological Doctrines* (New York: State University of New York Press, 1993), 135–136, where Nasr quotes a passage from al-Bīrūnī in which al-Bīrūnī states, "I have seen the astrolabe called Zuraqī invented by Abu Saʿīd Sijzī. I liked it very much and praised him a great deal, as it is based on

the idea entertained by some to the effect that the motion we see is due to the Earth's movement and not to that of the sky. By my life, it is a problem difficult of solution and refutation ...".

[36] Noel M. Swerdlow and Otto Neugebauer, *Mathematical Astronomy in Copernicus's De Revolutionibus* (New York: Springer, 1984).

[37] See Saliba, *A History of Arabic Astronomy: Planetary Theories During the Golden Age of Islam*, op. cit., p.29, where he mentions the work of Neugebauer which established the fact that diagrams representing Ṭūsī Couple were found in the manuscripts which were accessible to Copernicus.

[38] Ibid., p. 27.

[39] Ibid.

[40] See, 'Abd al-Ḥamīd Ṣābrā and Nabīl Shehābī, *Al-Shukūk 'alā Baṭlamyūs* (Cairo: National Library Press, 1971), quoted in George Saliba, *A History of Arab Astronomy*, op. cit. 251.

[41] He had conceived of his heliocentric system as early as the 1520s but did not publish it until 1543.

[42] See, Mu'ayyid al-Dīn al-'Urḍī, *Kitāb al-Hay'a, The Astronomical Works of Mu'ayyid al-Dīn al-'Urḍī*, ed. George Saliba, (Beirut, no publisher mentioned, 1990), 340, quoted by George Saliba, *History of Arab Astronomy*, op. cit., 27.

[43] Note that later theories about fear of persecution by the Church as being a reason for hesitation of publishing his work hold no weight in the light of abundant evidence which shows that Copernicus had in fact circulated his work in manuscript form as early as 1514; the manuscript was then called *De hypothesibus motuum coelestium a se constitutes commentariolus* ("A Commentary on the Theories of the Motions of Heavenly Objects from Their Arrangements"); he gave lectures on his theory in Rome in 1533 before Pope Clement VII, who approved, and a formal request was made to Copernicus to publish his theory in 1536. See, "Copernicus" in *The Encyclopaedia Britannica*, 15th ed. (Chicago: Encyclopaedia Britannica, 1985), 16: pp. 814-15.

[44] *Discoveries and Opinions of Galileo*, trans. Stillman Drake (New York: Anchor Books, 1957), 214.

[45] Ibid., 214.

[46] Ibid., 215.

[47] Ibid., 177.

Chapter 2
Three Views of Science in the Islamic World
Ibrahim Kalin

There is hardly any subject as vexed and vital for the contemporary Islamic world as the question of modern science. Since its earliest encounter with modern Western science in the 18th and 19th centuries, the Islamic world has had to deal with science for practical and intellectual reasons. At the level of practical needs, modern science was seen as the *sine qua non* of the advancement and defense of Muslim countries in the field of military technology. The Ottoman political body, which unlike the other parts of the Islamic world was in direct contact with European powers, was convinced that its political and military decline was due to the lack of proper defense mechanisms against the European armies. To fill this gap, a number of massive reforms were introduced by Maḥmūd II with the hope of stopping the rapid decline of the Empire, and a new class of military officers and bureaucrats, who became the first point of contact between the traditional world of Islam and the modern secular West, was created.[1] A similar project, in fact a more successful one, was introduced in Egypt by Muḥammad Ali whose aspirations were later given a new voice by Ṭāhā Ḥūssain and his generation. The leitmotif of this period was that of extreme practicality: the Muslim world needed power, especially military power, to stand back on its feet and new technologies powered by modern science were the only way to have it.[2] The modern conception of science as a medium of power was to have a profound impact on the relations between the Muslim world and modern science, which was then already equated with technology, progress, power, and prosperity – a mode of perception still prevalent among the masses in the Islamic world.

The second level of encounter between traditional beliefs and modern science was of an intellectual nature with lasting consequences, the most important of which was the re-shaping of the self-perception of the Islamic world. Using Husserl's analysis of *Selbstverständnis*, a key term in Husserl's anthropology of "Western man", von Grunebaum takes the reception of modern science to be a turning point in the self-view of traditional Islamic civilization and its approach to history.[3] One of the recurring themes of this epochal event, viz. the incompatibility of traditional beliefs with the dicta of modern science, is forcefully stated in a speech by Atatürk (the founder of modern Turkey), who was as much aware of the practical urgencies of the post-independence war Turkey as he was passionately engaged in creating a new identity for Turkish people:

> We shall take science and knowledge from wherever they may be, and put them in the mind of every member of the nation. For science and for knowledge, there are no restrictions and no conditions. For a nation that insists on preserving a host of traditions and beliefs that rest on no logical proof, progress is very difficult, perhaps even impossible.[4]

On a relatively smaller scale, the clash between the secular premises of modern science and the traditional Islamic worldview was brought home to many Muslim intellectuals with the publication of Rènan's famous lecture "L'Islamisme et la science" given in Sorbonne in 1883. In this lecture, he strongly argued for the irrationality and inability of Muslim peoples to produce science. Today, Rènan's quasi-racist attack on the Islamic faith and crude promulgation of positivism as the new religion of the modern world makes little sense. Nevertheless, it was an eye opener for the Muslim intelligentsia about the way in which the achievements of modern Western science were presented. Spearheaded by Jamāl al-Dīn Afghānī in Persia and Nāmik Kemāl in the Ottoman empire, the Muslim men of letters took upon themselves the task of responding to what they considered to be the distortion of modern science at the hands of some anti-religious philosophers, and produced a sizable discourse on modern science with all the fervor and confusion of their tumultuous times.[5] As we shall see below, Afghānī, *inter alia*, came to epitomize the mind-set of his time when he based his historical apology against Rènan on the assumption that there could be no clash between religion and science, be it traditional or modern, and that modern Western science was nothing other than the original true Islamic science shipped back, via the Renaissance and Enlightenment, to the Islamic world. By the same token, there is nothing essentially wrong with modern science, and it is the materialistic representation of science that lies at the heart of the so-called religion-science controversy.[6] Nāmik Kemāl joined Afghānī with a rebuttal of his own in his *Rènan Mudāfānāmesi* (*The Defense against Rènan*), focusing on the scientific achievements of the Arabs, namely the Muslim countries of the past.[7] In contrast to these Muslim intellectuals who sought to place modern science within the context of an Islamic worldview, a number of prominent Christian writers in the Arab world, including Jurjī Zaydān (d. 1914), Shiblī al-Shumayyil (d. 1916), Faraḥ ʿĀntūn (d. 1922), and Yaʿqūb Ṣarrūf (d. 1927), began advocating the secular outlook of modern science as a way of joining the European path of modernization – hence taking a primarily philosophical and secular stance on the ongoing debate between religion and science.[8]

These two positions are still with us today and continue to represent the ambitions as well as failures of the Islamic world in its elusive relationship with modern science. Islamic countries spend billions of dollars every year for transfer of technology, science education, and research programs. The goal set by the Ottomans in the 19th century has remained more or less the same: gaining power through technological advancement. Furthermore, the financial wedding between science and technology, begun with the industrial revolution, makes it ever harder to search for "pure science", and the bottom line for the Muslim as well as the Western world becomes technology rather than science. The willingness of Islamic countries to participate in the modernization process through transfer of technology obscures the philosophical dimension of the problem, leading to the kind of simplistic and reductionist thinking upon which we will touch shortly.

As for the intellectual challenge posed by modern science, it can hardly be said to have dwindled or disappeared in spite of the diminishing sway of positivism and its allies among the learned. There is a peculiar situation in the wake of the rise of new philosophies of science with new developments in scientific research, extending from the ousting of positivism and physical materialism to quantum mechanics and anti-realism. The postmodernist wave has shaken our confidence in science and ripple effects can be felt far beyond the scientific field. As a result, many young Muslim students and intellectuals see no problem with adopting the relativist and anti-realist stances of a Kuhn or Feyerabend. With the dike of modern science broken, it is assumed that religion and science can now begin talking to each other; the truth is that neither has a firm standing because both of them have been deprived of their truth-value by the anti-realist and relativist philosophies of our time. The popularity of the current discussions of philosophy of science in Muslim countries is indicative of the volatile nature of the subject as well as its long history among the Muslim intelligentsia.[9]

It would not be a stretch to say that the contemporary Islamic world is gripped by the challenges of these two divergent yet related points of view, which shape its perception of science in a number of fundamental ways. On the one hand, the governments and ruling elite of Islamic countries consider one of their highest priorities keeping up with the global race of technological innovation, from communications and medical engineering to weapon industry and satellite technology.[10] Arguments to the contrary are seen as a call for resisting the irreversible process of modernization, or for backwardness, to say the least. On the other hand, it has become common wisdom that the consequences of the application of modern, natural sciences to fields that have never been encroached upon before pose serious threats to the environment and human life. This is coupled with the threat of modern science becoming the pseudo-religion of the age, thereby forcing religion to the margins of modern society or at least making it a matter of personal choice and social ethics. This creates a bitter conflict of consciousness in the Muslim mind, a conflict between sacred and worldly power, between belief and scientific precision, and between seeing nature as the cosmic book of God and seeing nature as a source of exploitation and domination.

When we look at the current discourse on science in the Islamic world, we see a number of competing trends and positions, each with its own claims and solutions. Without pretending to be exhaustive, they can be classified under three headings: ethical, epistemological, and ontological/metaphysical views of science. The ethical/puritanical view of science, which is the most common attitude in the Islamic world, considers modern science to be essentially neutral and objective, dealing with the book of nature as it is, with no philosophical or ideological components attached to it. Such problems as the environmental crisis, positivism, materialism, etc., all of which are related to modern science in one way or another, can be solved by adding an ethical dimension to the practice and teaching of science. The second position, which I call the epistemological view, is concerned primarily with the epistemic status of modern physical sciences, their truth claims, methods of achieving sound knowledge, and function for the society at large. Taking science as a social construction, the epistemic school puts special emphasis on the history and sociology of science. Finally, the ontological/metaphysical view of science marks an interesting shift from the philosophy to the metaphysics of science. Its most important claim lies in its insistence on the analysis of the metaphysical and ontological foundations of modern physical sciences. As we shall see below, it is this school, represented *inter alia* by such Muslim thinkers as Seyyid Hossein Nasr and Naquib al-Attas, that the concept of Islamic science goes back to, a concept which has caused a great deal of discussion as well as confusion in Islamic intellectual circles.

Science as the Servant of God: The Dimension of Social Ethics

The most common attitude towards science in the Islamic world is to see it as an objective study of the world of nature, namely as a way of deciphering the signs of God in the cosmic book of the universe. Natural sciences discover the Divine codes built into the cosmos by its Creator, and in doing so, help the believer marvel at the wonders of God's creation. Seen under this light, science functions within a religious, albeit overtly simplistic, framework. The image of science as the decoder of the sacred language of the cosmos is certainly an old one, going back to the traditional Islamic sciences whose purpose was not just to find the direction of the *qiblah* or the times of the prayers but also to understand the reality of things as they are. Construed as such, science is seen as a noble enterprise. It was within this framework that the Muslim intellectuals, when they encountered the edifice of modern science in the 18th and 19th centuries, did not hesitate to translate the word *'ilm* (and its plural *'ulūm*) as "science" in the sense of modern physical sciences.[11]

   This attitude can best be seen among the forerunners of Islamic modernism, especially among those who addressed the question of science as the most urgent problem of the Islamic world. Jamāl al-Dīn Afghānī in his celebrated attack on the "materialists", i.e. *Haqiqat-i mazhab-i naichīrī wa bayān-i ḥāl-i nachīrīyān*, translated into Arabic by Muḥammad 'Abduh as *al-Radd 'ala'l-dahriyyin*, was engaged in a self-proclaimed battle of saving science from the positivists, a battle for which he derived support from the history of both Islamic and modern sciences. He had the following to say in his celebrated response to Renan:

If it is true that the Muslim religion is an obstacle to the development of sciences, can one affirm that this obstacle will not disappear someday? How does the Muslim religion differ on this point from other religions? All religions are intolerant, each one in its way. The Christian religion, I mean the society that follows its inspirations and its teachings and is formed in its image, has emerged from the first period to which I have just alluded; thenceforth free and independent, it seems to advance rapidly on the road of progress and science, whereas Muslim society has not yet freed itself from the tutelage of religion. Realizing, however, that the Christian religion preceded the Muslim religion in the world by many centuries, I cannot keep from hoping that Muhammadan society will succeed someday in breaking its bonds and marching resolutely in the path of civilization after the manner of Western society? No I cannot admit that this hope be denied to Islam.[12]

Afghānī's voice, which was carried on by such figures as Muḥammad ʿAbduh, Sayyid Aḥmad Khān, Rashid Riḍā, Muhammad Iqbal, Mehmet Akif Ersoy, Namik Kemal, Said Nursi, and Farid Wajdi, was the epitome of the sentiments of the time: modern science is nothing but Islamic science shipped back to the Islamic world via the ports of the European Renaissance and Enlightenment. In other words, science is not a culture-specific enterprise, and as such it is not the exclusive property of any civilization. Afghānī puts it in the following way:

> The strangest thing of all is that our ulama these days have divided science into two parts. One they call Muslim science, and one European science. Because of this they forbid others to teach some of the useful sciences. They have not understood that science is that noble thing that has no connection with any nation, and is not distinguished by anything but itself. Rather, everything that is known is known by science, and every nation that becomes renowned becomes renowned through science. Men must be related to science, not science to men ...
>
> The father and mother of science is proof, and proof is neither Aristotle nor Galileo. The truth is where there is proof, and those who forbid

science and knowledge in the belief that they are safeguarding the Islamic religion are really the enemies of that religion. The Islamic religion is the closest of religions to science and knowledge, and there is no incompatibility between science and knowledge and the foundation of Islamic faith.[13]

For this generation of Muslim thinkers, Western science was clearly and categorically distinguishable from Western values, the underlying assumption being that the secular worldview of the modern West had no inroads into the structure and operation of the natural sciences. The task is therefore not to unearth the philosophical underpinnings of modern science but to import it without the ethical component that comes from Western culture, which is alien to the Islamic ethos. The best example of this attitude was given by Mehmet Akif Ersoy, the famous intellectual of the Ottoman empire and the poet of the national anthem of Turkey. Akif, who lived at a time when the Ottoman empire and parts of the Islamic world were being divided and fiercely attacked by European powers, made a clear-cut distinction between Western science and European life-style, calling for the full-fledged adoption of Western science while totally rejecting the manners and mores of European civilization.

The idea of locating modern science within the framework of Islamic ethics is an attitude that is still with us today. Most of the practitioners of science in the Islamic world, namely engineers, doctors, chemists, and physicists, believe in the inherent neutrality of the physical sciences; therefore, the questions of justification, domination, control, etc., simply do not arise for them. Since science is a value-free enterprise, the differences between various scientific traditions, if such a thing is allowed at all, come about at the level of justification, not experimentation and operation. Thus when a scientist, be he or she a Muslim, Hindu, or simply non-believer, looks at the chemical components of the minerals he or she sees the same thing, operates on the same set of elements under the same set of conditions, and arrives presumably at the same or commensurable conclusions. It is the practical application of these findings to various fields and technologies that makes the difference, if any, between a Ptolemy, an Ibn al-Haytham, and a F. Bacon.

It is not difficult to see the imagery of the torch of science inherent in this view. Being the most prevalent attitude towards the history of science both in the Islamic and Western world, this view considers the history of science as progressing along a linear trajectory of discoveries and heuristic advancements. The torch of science transmitted from one nation to another, from one historical period to another, signifies the constant progress of scientific research, relegating such facts as religious convictions, philosophical assumptions and/or social infrastructure to a set of preparatory conditions necessary for the advancement of science. Thus the only difference between the science of the 13th century Islamic world and that of 19th century Europe turns out to be quantitative, that is, in terms of the accumulation and further specialization of scientific knowledge about the physical world. By the same token, the scientific revolution of the 17th and 18th centuries was a revolution not in the outlook of the modern man concerning nature and the meaning of scientific investigation but in the methodological tools and formulations of the natural sciences. This is how the majority of the 19th century intellectuals would have interpreted the history of science and the rise of modern natural sciences, and this is how the subject is still taught today in schools in the Islamic world.[14]

A logical result of this view of science is the incorporation of scientific findings as confirmations of the Islamic faith. In the pre-modern era when the religious worldview was strong, no scientist deemed it necessary to subject the Qur'ānic verses to a "scientific" reading, thereby hoping (perhaps) to improve one's faith in religion or showing the religious basis of scientific investigation. However, a trait of the modern period is that many believers of different religions and denominations look for possible confirmation from the sciences for their religious belief, confirmations that will, it is hoped, both increase the truth-value of the sacred book and ward off the hegemonic onslaught of the positivists. A good example of this approach in the

Islamic world is without doubt Said Nursi (1877-1960), the famous scholar, activist, and founder of the Nurcu movement in Turkey.

Said Nursi's views on the relation between faith and science were formulated at a time when the rude positivism of the late 1900s was made the official ideology of the newly established Turkish republic. Unlike many of his contemporaries, Nursi had considerable knowledge of the scientific findings of his time. His method in confronting Western science was a simple yet highly influential one: instead of taking a position against it, he incorporated its findings within a theistic perspective, thus preempting any serious confrontation between science and religion. Nursi – like many of his contemporaries – was acutely aware of the power of modern natural sciences and, as we see in his great work *Risāle-i Nūr*, he certainly believed in the universal objectivity of their discoveries.[15] For him, reading the verses of the Qur'ān through the lens of modern physical sciences had not only an instrumental value for protecting the faith of the youth who were coming under the sway of 19th century positivism and empiricism; it was also the beginning of a new method of substantiating the Islamic faith on the basis of the certainties of modern physical sciences, and reading the cosmic verses of the Qur'ān within the matrix of scientific discoveries.

As a religious scholar well grounded in traditional Islamic sciences, Nursi was aware of the apparent discrepancy between traditional cosmology articulated by Muslim philosophers and Sufis, and the Newtonian world-picture which contained no religious terms. Instead of rejecting the mechanistic view of the universe presented by modern science, Nursi saw an interesting parallel between it and the *kalam* arguments from design (*niẓām*). In his view the classical arguments from design – used profusely by Muslim and Christian thinkers alike – were meant to prove the eternal order and harmony built into the texture of the cosmos by the Divine creator and as such do not contradict Newtonian determinism. If the mechanistic view of the universe presents a world-picture in which nothing can remain scientifically unaccounted for, then this proves not the fortuitous generation of the cosmos but its creation by an intelligent agent, which is nothing other than the Divine artisan.[16] Therefore, the depictions of the universe as a machine or clock, the two favorite symbols of the deists of the 19th century, do not nullify the theistic claims of creation. On the contrary, rationality as regularity, harmony, and predictability, Nursi would wholeheartedly argue, lies at the heart of the religious view of the cosmos. Thus the mechanistic view of the universe, which was hailed by the secularists and positivists of the 19th century as the indisputable triumph of reason over and against religion, poses no threat to the theistic conception of the universe. As Mardin points out, this attitude was so influential among Nursi's followers that vocabulary taken from 19th century thermodynamics and electricity became household terms of the Nurcu movement. Thus the physical world is described as 'a *fabrika-i kāinat* (factory of the universe) (*Lem'alar*, 287); life is a machine of the future from the exalted bench work of the universe (*hayat kainatin tezgah-i azaminda ... bir istikbal makinesidir*) (*Lem'alar*, 371). Sabri, one of the first disciples of Bediuzzaman, speaks of "machines which produce the electricity of the Nur factory" when speaking of the work of disciples.[17]

Nursi's approach to modern science has been interpreted in a number of variant and, sometimes, conflicting, ways. There are those who take his coping with science as a powerful way of deconstructing its metaphysical claims by using the language of Newtonian physics, chemistry, and astronomy.[18] The opposite side of the controversy is represented by those who tend to emphasize the influence of modern science and positivism on Nursi – an influence visible in the entire generation of 19th century Muslim scholars, intellectuals, and activists. Even though one can easily detect an apparent incongruity between what Nursi had intended by his so-called "scientific commentary" (*al-tafsīr al-ilmī*) and what his followers made out of it,[19] the roots of his theistic scientism, one may claim, are ultimately traceable to his *Risāle-i Nūr*.[20] A few examples will suffice to illustrate this point. When discussing the miracles of the prophets mentioned in the Qur'ān, Nursi identifies two main reasons for their dispensation by the Divine authority. The first reason pertains to the veracity of the prophets of God, viz. they have been sent with an undeniable truth (*burhān*) to summon people to God's eternal word. The second reason, and this is what concerns us here, is that the prophetic miracles contain in them the seed of the future developments of human civilization. The story of the Prophet Sulayman (Solomon) mentioned in the Qur'ān (Saba' 34:12) for instance, predicts the invention of modern aviation systems. As Nursi interprets it, the fact that God has given the wind under Sulayman's command to travel long distances in a short period of time points to the future possibility of traveling in the air in general, and to the invention of aircraft (*teyyāre*) in particular.[21] Another example is the Prophet Moses' miracle to bring out water from the earth, as mentioned in the Qur'ān (Baqarah 2:60), when he and his followers were searching for water in the middle of the desert. According to Nursi, this event predicts the development of modern drilling techniques to dig out such indispensable substances of modern industry as oil, mineral water, and natural gas. Following the same line of thinking so typical of his generation of Qur'ānic commentators, Nursi explains the mention of iron and "its being softened to David" (Saba' 34:10) as a sign of the future significance of iron and, perhaps, steel for modern industry.[22] Another striking example of how Nursi was deeply engaged in scientific exegesis is his interpretation of the verse of the light (Nur 24:35), upon which such colossal figures of Islamic history as Ibn Sina and Ghazzali have written commentaries. Among many of the other profound and esoteric meanings of the light verse, which depicts God as the "light of the heavens and the earth", is the allusion to the future invention of electricity whose continuous diffusion of light is compared to the Qur'ānic expression "light upon light" (*nūrun 'alā nūr*) mentioned in the verse.[23]

These examples, the number of which can easily be multiplied, and the way they are justified were in tandem with a presiding idea, which Nursi adopted and elaborated with full force. This he called the "miracle of the teaching of Divine names to Adam" (*talim-i esmā mucizesi*). The Qur'ān tells us in Baqarah 2:31 that God, after creating

Adam as his viceregent on earth – to which the angels had objected for fear of corruption on earth – taught him "all the names" (or according to another reading "the names of all things", *asmā'a kullahā*). Throughout Islamic intellectual history, this verse has been interpreted in a myriad of different ways ranging from the most literalist to the most esoteric readings. In a daring statement, Nursi takes this miracle of Adam, the father of humanity, as greater and more perfect than those of all the other prophets after him because (according to Nursi) it embodies and comprises the entire spectrum of "all the progress and perfection human beings will ever achieve in the course of their history".[24] It is essentially on the basis of this principle that Nursi justifies his scientific and "progressive" exegesis of various verses of the Qur'ān. True, interpretations of this kind can be found in traditional commentaries on the Qur'ān or among the Sufis. What is peculiar about Nursi's new hermeneutics, if we may use such an appellation here, is the scientific and modern context in which it is articulated and carried out.

In its vulgarized version, Said Nursi's encounter with modern science has led to a torrent of one-to-one correspondences between new scientific findings and Qur'ānic verses, generating unprecedented interest in the natural sciences among his followers. Moreover, his position on science as the decoder of the sacred language of nature influenced a whole generation of Turkish students, professionals, and lay people with repercussions outside the Turkish-speaking world. Today, his followers are extremely successful in matters related to the sciences and engineering, and they continue Nursi's method of integrating the findings of modern physical sciences into the theistic perspective of Abrahamic religions. They are, however, extremely poor and unprepared when it comes to the philosophical aspects of the subject. The pages of the journal *Sizinti*, published by Nursi's followers in Turkish, and its English version *Fountain*, are filled with essays trying to show the miracle of creation through comparisons between the cosmological verses of the Qur'ān and new scientific discoveries. Not surprisingly, every new discovery from this point of view is yet another proof for the miracle and credibility of the Qur'ān. In this sense, Nursi's progeny is the father of what we might call "Bucaillism" in the Islamic world. The idea of verifying the cosmological verses of the Qur'ān via the scrutiny of the science of the day is a highly modern attitude by which it is hoped to confront and overcome the challenges of modern secular science. The fact that the same set of scientific data can be used within different contexts of justification and thus yield completely different and incommensurable results does not arise as a problem, neither is the overtly secular nature of the worldview of modern science considered to be a threat to the religious view of nature and the universe. The deliberate ignorance of the problem is seen as the solution, and the most poignant result of this approach is the rise of a class of Muslim scientists and engineers who pray five times a day but whose concepts of science are largely determined by the postulates of the modern scientific worldview.

This, however, does not prevent the proponents of this view from seeing the problems inflicted upon the world of nature and human life by modern science. The environmental crisis, hazards of genetic engineering, air pollution, rapid destruction of countless species, and the nuclear and chemical weapons industries are all admitted as problems we have to deal with. Yet the proposed remedy is an expected one: inserting a dimension of social and environmental ethics will put under control, if not completely solve, the problems mentioned. In other words, science should be subjected to ethics at the level of policy decisions. Accordingly, the aforementioned problems of modern science can be overcome by better management and advanced techniques in environmental engineering. Reminiscent of Habermas' defense of the project of modernity, which he considers incomplete as of yet, this view looks for the solution in the problem itself: further advancement in scientific research and technologies will create new methods of controlling the environmental crisis and all the problems associated with modern science. In short, we need more science to overcome its misdeeds.

The great majority of people in the Islamic as well as Western world share the sentiments of the above view of science that we have just summarized. Many people from all walks of life believe in the necessity of upholding an ethical framework within which scientific investigation should be carried out and controlled. This certainly has important policy implications for scientific research funded by federal governments and business corporations in many parts of the world. The point that is inevitably obscured, however, is much more crucial than having an influence at the policy decision-making level. To limit ethics to policy implementations is to make it a matter of personal preference for the scientific community, whose political and financial freedom against that of the governments and giant corporations is highly questionable. The fact that the scientists who approve of human cloning and genetic alteration believe in theistic evolution does not change the course of modern science. The conflict of consciousness to which we referred above resurfaces here in the form of people whose hearts and emotions are attached to the mandates of their respective religions but whose minds are empty of the religious view of the universe.

The Epistemic View of Science: For and Against the Method

An important channel through which the contemporary Islamic world, especially in the last three decades of the 20th century, has come to terms with modern science is the philosophy of science as developed in the West. The impact of the deconstruction of the epistemological hegemony of 19th century positivism, together with the critique of Newtonian physics and scientific objectivism and realism, on the Islamic world has been stupendous and caused a torrential release of intellectual energy among students and intellectuals. Needless to say, the influx of ideas associated with such names as Kuhn, Feyerabend, Popper, and their current students continues almost unabated in spite of the fact that the post-antirealist thinking on science seems to have come to a serious stalemate. Being on the receiving end of this debate, many Muslim students and intellectuals are still experimenting with these ideas but with little success – as we shall see shortly – in extrapolating their full implications. Before analyzing the current research being done by Muslim students and intellectuals, a few words of clarification about the scope of the contemporary field of the philosophy of science are in order.

The primary concern of contemporary philosophy of science is to establish the validity, or lack thereof, of the truth claims of modern, natural sciences. Theory-observation dichotomy, fact-value distinction, experimentation, objectivity, scientific community, history and sociology of science, and a host of other problems stand out, *inter alia*, as the most important issues of the field, a field which leaves no aspect of the scientific enterprise untouched. What concerns us here, however, is the emphasis in the philosophy of science on epistemology to the point of excluding any ontological or metaphysical arguments. The majority of contemporary philosophers of science, including such celebrated vanguards as Kuhn, Popper, and Feyerabend, construe science primarily as an epistemic structure that claims to explain the order of physical reality within the exclusive framework of the scientific method. Scientific realism, anti-realism, instrumentalism, and empiricism are all, needless to say, anchored in different notions of knowledge with profound implications for both the natural and human sciences. Given its exclusive concern with the epistemic claims involved, contemporary philosophy of science can be equated with the epistemology of science. In this regard, the epistemic view of science is surely a respected member of modern philosophy, for which any concept other than the knowing subject and its paraphernalia is no foundation for a proper understanding of the world.

Thinking about the question of being in terms of how it is known, to use Heideggerian language, is the leitmotif of modern philosophy, including its prima facie foes: rationalism and empiricism.[25] Whether we consider the knowing subject as a rationalist, empiricist, structuralist, or deconstructionist, an anthropocentric ethos runs through the veins of how we perceive the world around us, how we interact with it, and how we position ourselves vis-à-vis the other human beings with whom we share the intentional as well as physical space of our life-world. Here the eternal paradox of all subjectivist epistemologies is brought into clarity: to put the subject before the world, of which he or she is a part, is to claim the square inside the circle to be larger than the circle. Said differently, to ground the intelligibility of the world in the discursive constructions of the knowing subject is to see the world, or rather anything outside the subject, as essentially devoid of intrinsic meaning and intelligibility.[26] The Muslim critique of modern science – based on the premises of modern epistemology – has usually lost sight of this crucial fact as we see in the otherwise commendable literature produced by Ismail Faruqi and his protégée, the International Institute of Islamic Thought (mentioned hereafter as IIIT).

There is no denying the fact that Kuhn's radical anti-realism or Popper's concept of verisimilitude cannot be interpreted as lending support to the epistemic hegemony of modern science. On the contrary, they are meant to destroy it once and for all. The anti-realist component of their positions, however, reinforces the anthropocentric imagery: it is the knowing subject who is willing to deny science its self-proclaimed objectivity and appeal to credibility.[27] It is this aspect of contemporary philosophy of science, I believe, that has been totally mistaken and ignored by its adherents in the Islamic world. Today we can hardly come across a book or article written in English, Arabic, Turkish, or Bahasa Malaysia that does not have recourse to Foucault, Kuhn, Feyerabend, or Lyotard in order to denounce the philosophical underpinnings of modern science. From the academic papers of Muslim graduate students to the writings of the so-called "ijmalis" led by Ziauddin Sardar, the names of numerous philosophers of science sweep through the literature, including additions indigenous to the Islamic point of view. To put it mildly, this has led to the overemphasis of epistemology and methodology among many Muslim thinkers and young scholars while questions of ontology and metaphysics have been either left out or taken for granted. The concept of Islamic science, in this point of view, is centered around a loosely defined epistemology, or rather a set of discrete ideas grouped under Islamic epistemology whose content is yet to be determined. In many ways, the idea of Islamizing natural and social sciences has been equated with producing a different structure of knowledge and methodology within what we might call the epistemological fallacy of modern philosophy. The crucial issue has thus remained untouched: to reduce the notion of Islamic science to considerations of epistemology and methodology – which are without doubt indispensable in their own right – is to seek out a space for the Islamic point of view within, and not outside, the framework of modern philosophy.

Ismail Faruqi's work known under the rubric of "Islamization of knowledge" is a good example of how the idea of method or methodology ("manhaj" and "manhajiyyah", the Arabic equivalents of method and methodology, which are the most popular words of the proponents of this view) can obscure deeper philosophical issues involved in the current discussions of science. Even though Faruqi's project was proposed to Islamize the existing forms of knowledge imported from the West, his focus was exclusively on the humanities, leaving scientific knowledge virtually untouched. This was probably due to his conviction that the body of knowledge generated by modern natural sciences is neutral and as such requires no special attention. Thus, Faruqi's work and that of IIIT after his death concentrated on the social sciences and education.[28] This had two important consequences. First, Faruqi's important work on Islamization provided his followers with a framework in which knowledge (al-'ilm) came to be equated with social disciplines, thus ending up in a kind of socio-logism. The prototype of Faruqi's project is, we may say, the modern social scientist entrusted as arbiter of the traditional 'ālim. Second, the exclusion of modern scientific knowledge from the scope of Islamization has led to negligent attitudes, to say the least, toward the secularizing effect of the modern scientific worldview.[29] This leaves the Muslim social scientists, the ideal-types of the Islamization program, with no clue as to how to deal with the questions that modern scientific knowledge poses. Furthermore, to take the philosophical foundations of modern, natural sciences for granted is tantamount to reinforcing the dichotomy between the natural and human sciences, a dichotomy whose consequences continue to pose serious challenges to the validity of the forms of knowledge outside the domain of modern physical sciences.[30]

A similar position, with some important variations, is to be found in the works of Ziauddin Sardar and a number of closely associated scholars known as the "ijmalis". Although the ijmalis do not accept the appellation of being "merely Kuhnian", one can hardly fail to see the subtext of their discourse – based on Kuhn, Feyerabend, and others – in their critique of modern Western science.[31] Sardar's definition of science shares much of the instrumentalist and anti-realist spirit of the Kuhnian definition of science. For him, science is "a basic problem-solving tool of any civilization. Without it, a civilization cannot maintain its political and social structure or meet the basic needs of its people and culture".[32] The ijmalis' socio-cultural point of view certainly points to an important component of scientific activity, viz. the social setting in which the sciences are cultivated and flourish. It should be noted, however, that the relegation of physical sciences, or any scholarly activity for that matter, to social utility is bound to have serious consequences insofar as the philosophical legitimacy of the sciences is concerned. As we see in the case of Van Fraassen and Kuhn, the instrumentalist definition of science entails a strong leaning towards anti-realism, a position whose compatibility with the concept of Islamic science is yet to be accounted for.

Yet, there is another paradox involved here. The most common critique of modern science has been to present it as a culturally conditioned and historical endeavor with claims to universality and objectivity. Kuhn's philosophy of paradigm, which has become the single most fashionable buzz word in the Islamic world, Feyerabend's defense of society against science, and Van Fraassen's scientific instrumentalism are all used profusely to show the utter historicity and relativity of modern science. Since every scientific and, by extension, human activity is embedded in a historical and cultural setting, we can no longer speak of the sciences in isolation from their socio-historical conditions. This implies that no account of science, be it Western or Islamic, is possible without the history and – more importantly – sociology of science, the task of which is to deconstruct the historical formation and genealogy of the sciences. Furthermore, this approach has been applied to the humanities with almost total disregard to the implications for what is proposed in its place, i.e. Islamic science and methodology.

At this point, philosophy of science becomes identical with sociology of science and any appeal to universal validity and objectivity for the physical sciences is rejected on the basis of their utter historicity, ideology, cultural bias, and so on. Even though these terms are used as household terms by many Muslims writing and thinking about modern science, they rarely appear in their defense of Islamic science, which is proposed as an alternative to the Western conceptions of science. If science is culture-specific with no right to universal applicability, as the advocates of this view seem to imply, then this has to be true for all scientific activity whether it takes place in 11th century Samarqand or 20th century Sweden. This is what is so clearly stated and intended by all the major expositors of the philosophy of science. If modern secular science is culturally and historically constructed, then Islamic science – as understood by this group of scholars – has to explain how and why it is entitled to universal validity and applicability. It would be short of logical consistency to say that Kuhn's language of paradigms is an adequate tool to explain the history of Western but not Islamic science.

What I have called the epistemic view of science, which has taken the form of an extremely common tendency rather than a single school of thought, has certainly raised the consciousness of the Islamic world about modern science and contributed to the ongoing discussion of the possibility of having a scientific study of nature based on an Islamic ethos. However, we can hardly fail to see the contradictions in this point of view, especially when it is most vulnerable to the temptations of modern epistemology. The emphasis put on epistemology to the point of excluding ontology and metaphysics has grave consequences for any notion of science, and it is for this reason that we do not see any serious study of philosophy, metaphysics, or cosmology among the followers of this point of view. Furthermore, there is a deliberate resistance to these disciplines in spite of the fact that traditional Islamic philosophy and metaphysics had functioned as a gateway between scientific knowledge and religious faith. At any rate, it remains to be seen whether or not the adherents of the epistemic view of science will be able to overcome the subjectivist fallacy of modern philosophy, i.e. building an epistemology without articulating an adequate metaphysics and ontology.

The Sacred versus the Secular: The Metaphysics of Science

The last major position on science, of which we can give here only a brief summary, is marked off from the other two positions by its emphasis on metaphysics and the philosophical critique of modern science. Represented chiefly, *inter alia*, by such thinkers as Rene Guenon, Seyyed Hossein Nasr, Naquib al-Attas, Osman Bakar, Mahdi Golshani and Alparslan Acikgenc, the metaphysical view of science considers every scientific activity operating within a framework of metaphysics whose principles are derived from the immutable teachings of Divine revelation. In contrast to philosophy and sociology of science, metaphysics of science provides the sciences with a sacred concept of nature and cosmology within which to function.[33] At this point, the sacred view of nature taught by religions and ancient traditions takes on a prime importance in the formation and operation of physical sciences and all of the traditional sciences. Regardless of the historical and geographic settings the sciences were cultivated in, they were based on principles that enabled them to produce highly advanced scientific disciplines and techniques while maintaining the sacredness of nature and the cosmos. The traditional natural sciences, Nasr and others argue, derived not only their work-ethics and methodology but also metaphysical and ontological *raison d'etre* from the principles of Divine revelation because they were rooted in a conception of knowledge according to which the knowledge of the world acquired by man and the sacred knowledge revealed by God were seen as a single unity. As a result, the epistemological crisis of the natural and human sciences – that we try to overcome today – did not arise for the traditional scientist who did not have to sacrifice his religious beliefs in order to carry out a scientific experiment, and vise versa.

Traditional, western metaphysics claims that reality is a multi-layered structure with different levels and degrees of meaning. The polarity between the Principle and Its manifestation, which is translated into the language of theology as God and His creation, gives rise to a hierarchic view of the universe because manifestation already implies a domain of reality lower than its sustaining origin. Moreover, since reality is what it is due to the Divine nature it cannot be seen as a play-thing or the product of a series of fortuitous events. On the contrary, the cosmos, as the traditional scientists firmly believed, is teleological throughout, displaying a remarkable order and purposiveness. Nature, depicted by modern science as a ceaseless flow of change and contingency, never fails to restore itself into an abode of permanence and continuity with the preservation of species and self-generation.[34] Seen under this light, nature, which is the subject matter of the physical sciences, cannot be reduced to any one of these levels. With reductionism out, the traditional metaphysics of science uses a language built upon such key terms as hierarchy, *telos*, interconnectedness, isomorphism, unity, and complexity. These qualities are built into the very structure and methodology of traditional sciences of nature, which can be taken to be one of the demarcation lines between the sacred and modern secular views of science.[35] It is therefore impossible, the proponents of this view would insist, to create or resuscitate the traditional Islamic sciences of nature without first articulating its metaphysical framework. Any attempt to graft Islamic ethics and epistemology to the metaphysically blind outlook of modern science is bound to be a failure.

The philosophical underpinnings of Islamic science, as defined by Nasr, Attas, and others are derived from the metaphysical principles of Islam. Just as the Islamic revelation determines the social and artistic life of Muslim civilization, it also gives direction to its understanding of the natural environment and its scientific study.[36] The doctrine of *tawḥīd*, the most essential tenet of Islamic religion, affirms the unity of the Divine Principle and it is projected into the domain of the natural sciences as the essential unity and interrelatedness of the natural order. A science can thus be defined as Islamic, Acikgenc states, to the extent that it conforms to and reflects the cardinal principles of the Islamic worldview.[37] In a similar way, Nasr insists that "the aim of all the Islamic sciences – and more generally speaking, of all the medieval and ancient cosmological sciences – is to show the unity and interrelatedness of all that exists, so that, in contemplating the unity of the cosmos, man may be led to the unity of the Divine Principle, of which the unity of Nature is the image".[38] Thus the Islamic sciences of nature function in a two-fold way. First, they look at nature as a single unity with all of its parts interconnected to each other. Second, they are meant to lead both the scientist and the layman to the contemplation of Nature as the sacred artifact of the Divine. For Nasr, the sacred cosmology of the Sufis, which is grounded in metaphysics and inspiration rather than physical sciences per se, is related to the second function of the sciences of nature, and maintains its validity even today because it is based on the symbolic significance of the cosmos. This brings us to the other important feature of the Islamic sciences of nature, i.e. their intellectual function.

Nasr uses the word "intellect" in its traditional sense, viz. as related to contemplation. The modern connotation of the words "intellect" and "intellectual" as logical analysis or discursive thinking is the result of the emptying of their metaphysical and mystical content. Having rejected the usage of the word "intellect" as abstract analysis or sentimentality, Nasr seeks to regain its medieval and traditional usage.

> 'Intellect' and 'intellectual' are so closely identified today with the analytical function of the mind that they hardly bear any longer any relation to the contemplative. The attitude these words imply toward Nature is the one that Goethe was to deplore as late as the early nineteenth century – that attitude that resolves, conquers, and dominates by force of concepts. It is, in short, essentially abstract, while contemplative knowledge is at bottom concrete. We shall thus have to say, by way of establishing the old distinction, that the gnostic's relation to Nature is 'intellective', which is neither abstract, nor analytical, nor merely sentimental.[39]

Defined as such, the Islamic sciences of nature do not lend themselves to being a means of gaining power and domination over nature. Their contemplative aspect, rooted in the Qur'ānic teachings of nature as well as in traditional cosmologies, ties them to metaphysics on the one hand, and to art on the other.

By the same token, the function of philosophy cannot be confined to being a mere interpreter of the data produced by natural sciences. In sharp contrast to the Kantian notion of philosophy, which has turned philosophy into a handmaid of Newtonian physics, Nasr gives to philosophy an important role in establishing a harmonious relation between the givens of religion and the demands of scientific investigation. In the post-Kantian period, philosophy was gradually reduced to a second-order analysis of the first-order facts of physical sciences, and this assigned the philosophical pursuit to a completely different task. In contrast to this new mission, Nasr insists on the traditional meaning and function of philosophy. On the one hand philosophy is related to the life-world in which we live, including the physical environment, and as such it cannot remain indifferent to a veritable understanding of the universe and the cosmos. On the other hand it is closely related to metaphysics and wisdom and as such cannot be reduced to a branch of physical sciences. In fact, this is how the relationship between philosophy and science was established in classical classifications of knowledge both in the West and the Islamic world. The scientist and the philosopher were united in one and the same person, as we see in the case of an Aristotle or Ibn Sīnā, and this suggests that the scope of philosophical thinking could not be relegated to quantitative analyses of natural sciences. Thus, in Nasr's concept of science, philosophy – in addition to metaphysics and aesthetics – plays a crucial role that cannot be substituted by any other science.[40] Moreover, the sciences of nature always function within a definite framework of ontology and cosmology, which is articulated primarily and essentially by philosophy in the traditional sense of the term. This is why philosophy is an integral part of Nasr's metaphysical concept of science.

The metaphysical view of traditional civilizations concerning nature and its scientific study has been lost in modern science, whose philosophical foundations go back to the historical rupture of Western thought with its traditional teachings. The rise of modern science, Nasr and others would insist, was not simply due to some ground-breaking advancements in scientific methods of measurement and calculation.[41] On the contrary, it was the result of a fundamental change in human outlook concerning the universe.[42] This outlook is predicated by a number of premises, among which the following five are of particular significance. The first is the *secular view of the universe*, which allows no space for the Divine in the order of nature. The second is the *mechanistic world-picture* presented by modern science, which construes the cosmos as a self-subsisting machine and/or a pre-ordained clock. The third is the *epistemological hegemony of rationalism and empiricism* over the current conceptions of nature. The fourth is the *Cartesian bifurcation*, based on Descartes' categorical distinction between *res cogitans* and *res extensa*, which can also be read as the ontological alienation of the knowing subject from his or her object of knowledge. The fifth and the final premise of the modern scientific worldview, which can be seen as the end-result of the preceding points, is the *exploitation of the natural environment as a source of global power and domination.*[43] This is coupled with the hubris of modern science, which does not accept any notion of truth and knowledge other than that which is verifiable within the context of its highly specialized, technical, and hence restricted means of verification.

The metaphysical view of science, which points to an interesting shift from the philosophy to the metaphysics of science, takes aim at the intellectual foundations of modern science and, unlike the other two views of science, proposes a well-defined philosophy of nature and cosmology based on the principles of traditional Islamic sciences. Its critique of modern science is not confined to ethical considerations or methodological amendments as it claims to restore the religious view of the universe. In this regard, the metaphysical view of science, as formulated by Nasr and others, is part of the larger project of deconstructing the modernist worldview of which science is considered to be only an offshoot.

Conclusion

The three views of science presented here testify to the vibrancy of the ongoing debate over science in the present world of Islam. Needless to say, there are many aspects to this debate, and many borderline cases and crisscrossings have to be admitted as part of the continuous struggle of the Muslim world to come to terms with the problem of science both in its traditional-Islamic and modern Western senses. It is nevertheless certain that the growing awareness of the Islamic world concerning its scientific tradition, on the one hand, and the ways in which it tries to cope with the challenges of modern Western science, on the other, are among the momentous events of the history of contemporary Islam. The kind of interaction that will play out between the three positions analyzed above remains to be seen. Be that as it may, the future course of the debate on science in the Islamic world is more than likely to be shaped by these positions with all of their ambitions and promises.

Notes

[1] Among those who were sent to Europe as the reconnoiterer of the Islamic world was Yirmisekiz Mehmet Çelebi (Chalabi). He arrived at Paris as the Ottoman ambassador in 1720 and became one of the first Ottomans to give a first-hand report of "modern" Europe, especially France. When compared with the accounts of earlier Muslim travelers to Europe, such as that of Evliya Çelebi, his reports and letters show in an unequivocal way the psychology of the 18th century: a proud Muslim soul torn between the glory of his history and the mind-boggling advancement of the "afranj", the infidels of Europe. Mehmet Çelebi's reports published under the title of *Sefâretnâme* became a small genre of its own to be followed by later Ottoman envoys to Europe. His *Sefâretnâme* has also been translated into French by Julien Galland as *Relation de l'embassade de Mehmet Effendi a la cour de France en 1721 ecrite par lui meme et traduit par Julien Galland* (Constantinople and Paris, 1757). For a brief account on Mehmet Çelebi in English, see Bernard Lewis, *The Muslim Discovery of Europe* (New York: W.W. Norton & Company, 1982), 114-116.

[2] See, among others: Lewis, *The Muslim Discovery of Europe*, 221-238; and H.A.R. Gibb and Harold Bowen (eds), vol 1, parts 1 and 2 of *Islamic Society and the West: A Study of the Impact of Western Civilization on Moslem Culture in the Near East* (Oxford: Oxford University Press, 1957).

[3] G. E. Von Grunebaum, *Modern Islam: The Search for Cultural Identity* (Connecticut: Greenwood Press, 1962), 103-111.

[4] *Atatürk'ün Söylev ve Demeçleri* (Ankara, 1952), II, 44, from a speech given in October 27, 1922; quoted in Von Grunebaum, *Modern Islam*, 104.

[5] Although the most celebrated responses to Rénan belong to J. Afghānī and N. Kemāl, a number of other refutations have been written. The Turkish scholar Dücane Cündioglu lists 12 major refutations, 10 of which are by Muslims, and the list comprises such names as Sayyid Amir Ali, Rashīd Riḍā, Celal Nuri, Louis Massignon, and Muhammad Hamidullah. For an excellent survey of the subject, see Ducane Cundioglu, "Ernest Renan ve 'Reddiyeler' Baglaminda Islam-Bilim Tartişmalarina Bibliyografik Bir Katki", in vol. 2, *Dīvān* (Istanbul, 1996), 1-94.

[6] The full text of Afghānī's rebuttal "Refutation of the Materialists" is translated by Nikki R. Keddie in *An Islamic Response to Imperialism, Political and Religious Writings of Sayyid Jamal al-Din al-Afghani* (Berkeley: University of California Press, 1983), 130-174.

[7] Namik Kemāl's *Defense* has been published in Turkish many times. For a brief account of his political thought in general and apology in particular, see Şerif Mardin, *The Genesis of Young Ottoman Thought: A Study in the Modernization of Turkish Political Ideas* (Syracuse: Syracuse University Press, 2000; originally published in 1962), 283-336.

[8] For the radical positivism of Shumayyil and 'Antūn, see Albert Hourani, *Arabic Thought in the Liberal Age: 1798-1939* (Cambridge: Cambridge University Press, 1993), 245-259; Hisham Sharabi, *Arab Intellectuals and the West: The Formative Years 1875-1941* (Washington DC: The Johns Hopkins Press, 1970). See also Osman Bakar's "Muslim Intellectual Responses to Modern Science" in his *Tawhid and Science: Essays on the History and Philosophy of Islamic Science* (Kuala Lumpur: Secretariat for Islamic Philosophy and Science, 1991), 205-207.

[9] Turkey is a case in point. The growing literature on the philosophy of science in Turkish, with translations from European languages and indigenous contributions of Turkish scholars, is far beyond the other Islamic languages both in quality and quantity. Interestingly enough, the Muslim intellectuals have been more vocal in this debate, carrying the heritage of the Islamic sciences of nature into the very center of the current discourse on science. In addition to philosophical discussions, there is now serious work done on the history of Islamic and especially Ottoman science, which was begun some years back under the direction of Ekmeleddin İhsanoglu, head of the department of the history of Ottoman science at the University of Istanbul.

[10] See the remarks of the Nobel laureate Abdus Salam in C.H. Lai, ed., *Ideals and Realities: Selected Essays of Abdus Salam* (Singapore: World Scientific, 1987).

[11] Osman Amin, one of the prominent figures of the Egyptian intellectual scene of the last century and perhaps the most outspoken vanguard of the 19th century Islamic modernism represented by Afghānī, 'Abduh, and 'Abd al-Rāziq, interprets 'Abduh's vision of modern science as a veritable attempt to revive the traditional concept of knowledge (*'ilm*). He has the following to say: "Islam has been accused of being hostile to the development of science and culture. For 'Abduh there is nothing more false than such hasty or partial judgements. In the search for truth, Islam prescribes reasons [sic.], condemns blind imitation and blames those who attach themselves without discernment to the habits and opinions of their forefathers. How then can Islam, based on the requirements of human nature and reason, and itself urging its faithful to seek, and reason to develop their knowledge and to perfect their understanding–how can such a faith be incapable of satisfying the demands of science and culture? ... Did not the Prophet of Islam say: 'Seek to learn science even though you have to find it in China'. ... undoubtedly the religion which declared that 'the ink of a scholar is as precious as the blood of martyrs' cannot be accused of obscurantism in its essential nature". Osman Amin, *Lights on Contemporary Moslem Philosophy* (The Renaissance Bookshop: Cairo, 1958), 140-141; cf. 105-106.

[12] Afghānī's "Letter to Rénan", first published in *Journal de Débats* (May 18, 1883), translated in Kiddie, *An Islamic Response to Imperialism*, 183.

[13] Afghānī, "Lecture on Teaching and Learning" in Keddie, *An Islamic Response to Imperialism*, 107.

[14] Perhaps the most notable exception, albeit in a rather negative sense, was Sayyid Aḥmad Khān who had called for the complete rejection of the traditional notions of nature under the name of "new theology" (*'ilm-i kalām-i jadīd*). Afghānī was well aware of the perils of this point of view and thus did not hesitate to include Ahmad Khān among the "materialists", whom he called "neicheri", namely the naturalists. For Afghānī's response see his "The Materialists in India" in *al-'Urwa al-Wuthqā'* (August 28, 1884), translated in Keddie, *An Islamic Response to Imperialism*, 175-180.

[15] In one of his famous aphorisms, Nursi stresses the importance of the unity of the heart and reason for the future of humanity. But he qualifies reason (*akil*, *'aql* in Arabic) as "the sciences of modern civilization" (*fünūn-u medeniye*): "The light of the heart (*vicdan*, *wijdān* in Arabic) are the religious sciences whereas the light of reason are the modern sciences. The truth emerges out of the blend of the two. When they are separated, the former causes dogmatism and the latter deception and suspicion", in Said Nursi, *Münāzarāt* (Istanbul: Tenvir Nesriyat, 1978), 81.

[16] Nursi's works, especially the *Sözler* (Istanbul: Sinan Matbaasi, 1958), are replete with references to God as the Great or Absolute Artisan (*sāni-i mutlak*) of the universe. It goes without saying that Nursi was not alone in approaching the deterministic and orderly universe of modern science from this peculiar point of view. In fact, this was a common attitude among the forerunners of what is called the "scientific method of commenting upon the Qur'ān" (*al-tafsīr al-'ilmī* and/or *al-tafsīr al-fannī*) such as Muḥammad 'Abduh, Muḥammad ibn Aḥmad al-Iskandarānī, Sayyid Abd al-Raḥman al-Kawākibī, and Muḥammad 'Abdullah Draz. Like Nursi, these figures were passionately engaged in reconciling the scientific findings of 19th century physical sciences with the cosmological verses of the Qur'ān and, in some cases, the sayings (*hadith*) of the Prophet of Islam. For these figures and the concept of scientific commentary, see Ahmad Umar Abu Hijr, *al-Tafsīr al-'Ilmī li'l-Qur'ān fī'l-Mīzān* (Beirut, 1991), and Muḥammad Ḥusayn al-Dhahabi, *al-Tafsīr wa'l-Mufassirūn*, 2 vols (Beirut, 1976).

[17] Şerif Mardin, *Religion and Social Change in Turkey: The Case of Bediuzzaman Said Nursi* (New York: SUNY Press, 1989), 214. Mardin also makes interesting remarks concerning Nursi's ambivalent relation to Sufi cosmology represented especially by Ibn Arabi in Mardin, *Religion and Social Change*, 203-212.

[18] Without exception, all of Nursi's followers appeal to the first view, rejecting any association with positivism. For a defense of this position, see, among others, Yamine B. Mermer, "The Hermeneutical Dimension of Science: A Critical Analysis Based on Said Nursi's *Risale-i Nur*", in *The Muslim World* vol. LXXXIX, Nos. 3-4

(July-October, 1999): 270-296. Mermer's essay is also interesting for making a case for occasionalism on the basis of Nursi's views.

[19] I am grateful to Drs. Ali Mermer and Yamine B. Mermer for drawing my attention to this incongruity, which should perhaps be more emphasized than I can do here. I will be dealing with Nursi's position on science in full detail in a separate study.

[20] The ambiguity, for want of a better term, of Nursi's position on modern science is illustrated by an interesting incident which Nursi narrates in his *Kastamonu Lāhikasi* (Ankara: Dogus Matbaasi, 1958), p. 179. According to the story, a Naqshibandi darwish, a member of the Naqshibandiyyah order, had read a section of the Risāle-i Nūr on the meaning of 'ism-i Hakem (the Divine name of the Arbiter) dealing with the sun and the solar system, and concluded that "these works [i.e. the *Risaleler*] deal with scientific matters just like the scientists and cosmographers". In response to this "delusion" (*vehim*), Nursi had the same treatise read to him in his presence, upon which the darwish admitted his misunderstanding. This incident is narrated by Nursi, we may presume, as a preemptive act to separate Nursi's "scientific exegesis" from the method of modern physical sciences.

[21] Nursi, *Sözler* (Istanbul: Sinan Matbaasi, 1958), p. 265; and *Ishārāt al-i'jāz fi mazānni'l-ijāz* (Istanbul: Sinan Matbaasi 1994), p. 311.

[22] Nursi, *Sözler*, 266.

[23] Ibid., 263; cf. *Sikke-i Tasdik-i Gaybī* (Istanbul: Sinan Matbaasi 1958), p. 76.

[24] Nursi, *Sözler*, 272-273; Nursi, *Isharat*, 310.

[25] Heidegger makes his case in two of his famous essays "The Question Concerning Technology", and "The Age of the World Picture". These essays have been published in *The Question Concerning Technology and Other Essays*, trans. William Lowitt (New York: Harper Colophon Books, 1977). See also, in the same collection of essays, his "Science and Reflection", 155-182.

[26] Charles Taylor puts it in the following way: "Is the expression which makes us human essentially a self-expression, in that we are mainly responding to our way of feeling/experiencing the world, and bringing this to expression? Or are we responding to the reality in which we are set, in which we are included of course, but which is not reducible to our experience of it?". See Charles Taylor, *Human Agency and Language: Philosophical Papers*, vol. 1 (Cambridge: Cambridge University Press, 1985), 238.

[27] Heidegger calls this "projection", through which the world of nature is made the subject-matter of mathematico-physical sciences: "What is decisive for its development [viz. the development of mathematical physics] does not lie in its rather high esteem for the observation of 'facts', nor in its 'application' of mathematics in determining the character of normal processes; it lies rather in the way in which Nature herself is mathematically projected. In this projection, something constantly present-at-hand (matter) is uncovered beforehand, and the horizon is opened so that one may be guided by looking at those constitutive items

in it, which are quantitatively determinable (motion, force, location, and time). Only 'in the light' of a Nature which has been projected in this fashion can anything like a 'fact' be found and set up for an experiment regulated and delimited in terms of this projection. The 'grounding' of 'factual science' was possible only because the researchers understood that in principle there are no 'bare facts'. ... When the basic concepts of that understanding of Being by which we are guided have been worked out, the clues of its method, the structure of its way of conceiving things, the possibility of truth and certainty which belongs to it, the ways in which things get grounded or proved, the mode in which it is binding for us, and the way it is communicated – all these will be Determined. The totality of these items constitutes the full existential conception of science". *Being and Time*, trans. J. Macquarrie and E. Robinson (Oxford: Basil Blackwell, 1978), 413-4.

[28] See Ismail R. al-Faruqi, *Islamization of Knowledge: General Principles and Work Plan* (Washington DC: International Institute of Islamic Thought, 1982). This book has been largely revised and expanded in its 1989 edition by a group of scholars associated with the International Institute of Islamic Thought.

[29] Jamal Berzinji, one of the family members of IIIT, mentions the natural sciences only once (p. 28) in his informative article on Islamization of knowledge and IIIT's role in its development. See his "History of Islamization of Knowledge and Contributions of the International Institute of Islamic Thought" in *Muslims and Islamization in North America: Problems & Prospects*, ed. Amber Haque (Maryland: Amana Publications, 1999), 13-31.

[30] For an informative analysis of Faruqi's work on Islamization, see Leif Stenberg, *The Islamization of Science: Four Muslim Positions Developing an Islamic Modernity* (Lund: Lund Studies in History of Religions, 1996), 153-219.

[31] Ziauddin Sardar, *Explorations in Islamic Science* (London: Mansell Publishing Ltd., 1989), 155. This emphatic denial itself is quite telling for our discussion here.

[32] Z. Sardar, *Islamic Futures* (London: Mansell Publishing Ltd., 1985), 157.

[33] Nasr uses the word metaphysics as the all-inclusive science of the Divine Principle, which comprises both ontology and theology: "If Being is envisaged as the principle of existence or of all that exists, then It cannot be identified with the Principle as such because the Principle is not exhausted by its creating aspect. Being is the first determination of the Supreme Principle in the direction of manifestation, and ontology remains only a part of metaphysics and is incomplete as long as it envisages the Principle only as Being in the sense defined". *Knowledge and the Sacred* (New York: SUNY Press, 1989), 136.

[34] Perhaps the most systematic and comprehensive exposition of this idea is to be found in Mulla Sadra's concept of nature (*ṭabī'ah*) and substantial movement (*al-ḥarakat al-jawhariyyah*). See the section on natural philosophy (*'ilm al-ṭabī'ah*) in his *al-Ḥikmat al-muta'āliyah fī'l-asfār al-arba'at al-'aqliyyah*, ed. M. Riḍa al-Muẓaffar (Beirut: Dar Ihya al-Turath al-'Arabi, 1981), vol. 3, part. 1. Sadra's work is also

important for its highly articulated cosmology which is comparable in Islamic history only to that of Ibn al-'Arabi.

[35] For an analysis of such concepts as quality, quantity, unity, simplicity, regularity, etc., from the traditional point of view, see Rene Guenon, *The Reign of Quantity and the Signs of the Times* (London, 1953), especially, pp. 19-100.

[36] S.H. Nasr, *Islamic Science: An Illustrated Study* (Kent: World of Islam Festival Publishing Company Ltd, 1976), 3-9; and S.M. Naquib al-Attas, "Islam and the Philosophy of Science" in his *Prolegomena to the Metaphysics of Islam: An Exposition of the Fundamental Elements of the Worldview of Islam* (Kuala Lumpur: ISTAC, 1995), and *Islam and Secularism* (Kuala Lumpur: Muslim Youth Movement of Malaysia, 1978).

[37] "Islamic science is that scientific activity which takes place *ultimately* within the Islamic worldview (which can now be identified also as the Islamic conceptual environment); but as an extension of it *directly* within the *Islamic scientific conceptual scheme* (which can be identified also as the Islamic context of sciences)". Alparslan Acikgenc, *Islamic Science: Towards a Definition* (Kuala Lumpur: ISTAC, 1996), 38.

[38] S. H. Nasr, *Science and Civilization in Islam* (New York: Barnes and Noble Books, 1992), 22.

[39] *Ibid.*, 24.

[40] For Nasr's concept of philosophy, see his "The Meaning and Concept of Philosophy in Islam" and "The Qur'an and the Hadith as Source and Inspiration of Islamic Philosophy" in *History of Islamic Philosophy*, 2 vols, eds. S.H. Nasr and O. Leaman (London: Routledge, 1996), 21-39.

[41] This has been noted by many Western historians of science. See, for instance, Edwin Arthur Burtt, *The Metaphysical Foundations of Modern Physical Science* (New York: Doubleday Anchor Books, 1932), and Wolfgang Smith, *Cosmos and Transcendence: Breaking Through the Barrier of Scientistic Belief* (Illinois: Sherwood Sugden and Company, 1984). For the transformation of the concept of nature in the Western tradition, see R.G. Collingwood, *The Idea of Nature* (Oxford: Oxford University Press, 1972), especially 133-177. For a thorough study of the ongoing debate on the meaning of the Scientific Revolution, see H. Floris Cohen, *The Scientific Revolution: A Historiographical Inquiry* (Chicago: The University of Chicago Press, 1994). Cohen's book has also a useful section (384-417) on Islamic science in relation to the Scientific Revolution.

[42] Russell has provided one of the most elegant expressions of the secular outlook of modern physical sciences in his celebrated essay "A Free Man's Worship", in his *Mysticism and Logic* (New York: Doubleday Anchor Books, 1957), 44-54. It would not be out of place to quote him here to underline the sharp contrast between the secular and traditional conceptions of science: "Such in outline, but even more purposeless, more void of meaning, is the world which Science presents for our belief. Amid such a world, if anywhere, our ideals henceforward must find a home. That Man is the product of causes which had no prevision of the end they were

achieving; that his origin, his growth, his hopes and fears, his loves and his beliefs, are but the outcome of accidental collocations of atoms; that no fire, no heroism, no intensity of thought and feeling, can preserve an individual life beyond the grave; that all the labors of the ages, all the devotion, all the inspiration, all the noonday brightness of human genius, are destined to extinction in the vast death of the solar system, and that the whole temple Man's achievement must inevitably be buried beneath the debris of a universe in ruins – all these things, if not quite beyond dispute, are yet so nearly certain, that no philosophy which rejects them can hope to stand" (45).

[43] Nasr has given a full account of this process in his *Religion and the Order of Nature* (Oxford: Oxford University Press, 1997), which is a comprehensive and detailed sequel to his earlier work *Man and Nature: The Spiritual Crisis in Modern Man* (Chicago: ABC International, 1999). I have dealt with Nasr's conception of science in greater detail in my essay, "The Sacred versus the Secular: Nasr on Science" in *The Philosophy of Seyyed Hossein Nasr*, ed. Lewis Hahn, R.E. Auxier, and L.W. Stone (Chicago: Open Court, 2001), 445-462.

Chapter 3

Science and Faith:
From Warfare to Consonance

Ted Peters

If there exists a war between science and faith, it appears that science is winning. Along with its ally, technology, science like Charlemagne or Tamerlane is continually conquering new domains of human living and expanding its hegemony so as to create a worldwide cultural empire. No people or religious tradition has remained unaffected.

Like a swaggering soldier, science takes nothing to be sacred. No noble tradition, no way of life, no tender religious affections, no tightly held dogma, no reverence for the sublime, no high moral resolve are protected from attacks by upsetting empirical evidence and by cold calculating reason. Science takes no prisoners. As it marches on it leaves a trail of religious debris, broken beliefs, and crumbling worldviews.

We in the citadels of religious faith, when spying advancing science on the horizon, are tempted to put up the defenses and wall out the invasion. Faith fears a repeat of the Trojan horse: if we allow scientific authority to enter our city of belief, we risk letting loose an internal enemy who will defeat us from within.

Yet, I ask that we pause in the midst of battle to consider this question: is science actually our enemy? Is it actually the case that the warfare image is the most accurate way to describe the interaction between science and faith, whether Christian faith or Islamic faith? Are there any qualities shared by both faith and science that suggest a partnership, a peaceful coexistence if not cooperation? Even if science remains partly the enemy, might there be some ways in which it could be our friend?[1]

Peace Through Truth

I submit that the honest pursuit of truth may be the key to peace, the door to cooperation. Both Christian theology and Islamic thought at their best revere truth, especially ultimate truth. Oh yes, our respective histories have been replete with dogmas and fragmentation, hierarchies and despots, crusades and aggressive invasions, schisms and wars. Yet, beneath all of this, we share a deep reverence for God and a heartfelt gratitude to God for the beauty of creation.

It is God's creation that is studied by science, viewed through microscopes and telescopes, dissected and disconnected, analyzed and theorized. This creation, dubbed "nature" in science, the Book of Genesis describes as "very good". This cosmos, which we understand to be a creation, was brought into existence by God out of love, and for a purpose, a divinely appointed purpose. Christians would add that, because God so loves this cosmos, God became incarnate in Jesus Christ and actually experienced finite physical life on our side of the Creator-creature line (John 3:16).

The import of this understanding of the natural world as God's creation is this: our growing knowledge of the natural world through scientific investigation has the potential for enhancing our appreciation of God's creative handiwork. Or, to put it more forcefully, any truth we might learn about the natural world – if it turns out really to be the truth and not falsehood – should not be a threat to our knowledge of God or gratitude to God; it may even enhance our appreciation of God. Science at its best, and theology at its best, pursues truth and rests at ease only when confident that it relies upon truth.

Hypothetical Consonance

This leads me to propose a model for understanding the interaction between science and faith that differs from the warfare model. I call my proposed alternative *hypothetical consonance*.[2] If there be one God and one creation, then what natural scientists study is the same cosmos that God has created. We should expect in the long run, then, that knowledge gained from empirical research and knowledge gained from special revelation will be consonant.

The term 'consonance' prompts us to look for areas of correspondence or connection or compatibility between what theologians say about God's creation and what scientists say about nature. Such consonance comes in two varieties, strong and weak. 'Consonance' in the strong sense would require full accord or complete harmony between scientific knowledge and special revelation. This would be too much to ask of the current inter-disciplinary dialogue, I think. To be realistic, 'consonance' in a milder or weaker sense would be sufficient to promote fruitful discussion. In this second sense, consonance would serve as an initial hypothesis to direct our attention toward looking for possible connections, overlaps, and reinforcements. Hypothetical consonance is not something we already have; rather, it is an agenda to pursue that circumvents warfare.

In what follows, I would like to review briefly a number of models for understanding the relationship between science and theology. I will divide these models into two categories, warfare models and non-warfare models. Within the second category, I will advocate that both Muslim and Christian thinkers give serious consideration to adopting the approach of hypothetical consonance. This approach might have an additional side benefit. If each religious tradition, Islam and Christianity, could benefit from cultivating a more healthy relationship to the natural sciences, the two traditions might find openings for a healthier relationship with each other. The principle of hypothetical consonance might show value for Muslim-Christian dialogue as well.

In the meantime, let us turn to delineating nine alternative ways of relating science to faith's theological reflection. Among the five warfare models I include scientism, scientific imperialism, ecclesiastical authoritarianism, creationism, and intelligent design arguments.

Among the four non-warfare models I include the two-language theory, hypothetical consonance, ethical overlap, and New Age spirituality. Most but not all of my examples are drawn from existing patterns involving Christian theology and western spirituality. I proffer this list as suggestive, recognizing that additional models might be drawn from Islamic history.

The Warfare Model

To the extent that a war between science and religion is ongoing, we can identify two ranks of soldiers in the scientific army. What both have in common is that they carry the flags of reductionism and materialism, meaning that all that we can know about reality is reducible to a material substrate and that science is the only gatekeeper to this knowledge. Critics point out that what is going on here is that scientific knowledge is expanded into a materialist philosophy, a philosophical worldview that goes well beyond what is warranted from genuine knowledge of the physical world.

Scientism

The first rank is *scientism*. The military goal of scientism – sometimes called 'naturalism' or 'scientific materialism' or 'secular humanism' or even 'atheism' – is to pursue war against religion, declaring total victory over the forces of superstition, dogma, and pseudo-knowledge. Scientism, like other '… isms', is an ideology. This ideology is built upon the assumption that science provides all the knowledge that we can know. There is only one reality, the natural, and science has a monopoly on the knowledge we have about nature. What theologians have to say about things supernatural is only pseudo-knowledge – that is, false impressions about non-existent fictions.[3] Accordingly, "*scientism* is a secular religion, in the sense of generating loyal commitments (a type of faith) to a method, a body of knowledge, and a hope for a better future".[4]

Scientific Imperialism

The second rank in the advancing army is *scientific imperialism*. The military goals of scientific imperialism differ slightly from those of scientism. Rather than obliterating its religious enemy, scientific imperialism seeks to conquer the territory formally possessed by theology and claim it as its own. The assumption is that science can explain religion better than religion can explain itself. Ordinarily, theology is religion in its self-reflective mode and theology explains religion's foundations. In the case of scientific imperialism, science takes over theology's role.[5]

The sociobiologists provide a good example, because they presume they can reduce the transcendental claims of religious intuition to material processes active in human evolution. "Blind faith, no matter how passionately expressed will not suffice", writes E.O. Wilson. "Science for its part will test relentlessly every assumption about the human condition and in time uncover the bedrock of the moral and religious sentiments. The eventual result of the competition between the two world views, I believe, will be the secularization of the human epic and of religion itself."[6]

Whereas scientism is atheistic, scientific imperialism may actually affirm the existence of something divine. Key is the scientific imperialist's claim that knowledge of the divine comes from scientific research rather than religious revelation. Physicist Paul Davies leads the vanguard: "Science has actually advanced to the point where what were formerly religious questions can be seriously tackled ... [by] the new physics".[7] What Davies does is demonstrate how the field of physics transcends itself, opening us in the direction of the divine reality. "I belong to a group of scientists", he writes, "who do not subscribe to a conventional religion but nevertheless deny that the universe is a purposeless accident. ... There must, it seems to me, be a deeper level of explanation. Whether one wishes to call that deeper level 'God' is a matter of taste and definition".[8]

Ecclesiastical Authoritarianism

Now, still within the warfare model, we will turn to the other side for the third form of army. When Roman Catholics enter into battle, their primary weapon is *ecclesiastical authoritarianism*. This was a defense tactic in the 19th century, not characteristic of the present period. The Vatican perceived science and scientism as a threat. Presuming a two-step route to truth in which natural reason is followed by divine revelation, theological dogma was ceded authority over science on the grounds that it is founded on God's revelation. In 1864, Pope Pius IX promulgated *The Syllabus of Errors*, wherein item 57 stated it to be an error to think that science and philosophy could withdraw from ecclesiastical authority. A century later the Second Vatican Council dropped the defenses by declaring the natural sciences to be free from ecclesiastical authority and called them "autonomous" disciplines (*Gaudium et Spes*: 59). Pope John Paul II, who has a serious interest in fostering dialogue between theology and the natural sciences, is negotiating a new peace between faith and reason.[9]

Scientific Creationism and Intelligent Design

In American Evangelical and Fundamentalist Protestant circles, a warfare is taking place. Is it a warfare between science and faith? No, although it may look like it. Two religious armies are marching: *scientific creationism* and *intelligent design* argumentation. The first is more well known than the second. Both attack Darwinian evolutionary theory; but their attack is with scientific weapons, not religious ones.

    Sometimes called "creation science", creationism is not a Protestant version of church authoritarianism, even though it is frequently so mistaken. The grandparents of today's scientific creationists were the fundamentalists of the 1920s, to be sure. Yet, there is a marked difference between fundamentalist authoritarianism and contemporary creation science. Today's creation scientists are willing to argue their case in the arena of science, not biblical authority. They assume that biblical truth and scientific truth belong to the same domain. When there is a conflict between a scientific assertion and a religious assertion, then we could see this as a conflict in scientific theories. Yet, this does not apply here, according to creationists. Creationists argue that the book of Genesis is itself a theory which tells us how the world was physically created: God fixed the distinct kinds (species) of organisms at the point of original creation. They did not evolve. Geological and biological facts attest to biblical truth, they argue.

With regard to theological commitments, scientific creationists typically affirm: (1) the creation of the world out of nothing; (2) the insufficiency of mutation and natural selection to explain the process of evolution; (3) the stability of existing species and the impossibility of one species evolving out of another; (4) separate ancestry for apes and humans; (5) catastrophism to explain certain geological formations, e.g. the flood explains why sea fossils appear on mountains; and (6) at least the young earth creationists argue that the earth was formed only six to ten thousand years ago.[10]

A new force in the warfare is *Intelligent Design*, what we will nickname ID. Between two already fighting armies, scientific creationism on the right and Neo-Darwinian evolutionism on the left, Intelligent Design enters the war from the middle. It is important here to avoid the mistake made repeatedly by the media and by the scientific establishment of thinking that ID is just another variant of creationism. It is not. Creationists reject macroevolution – that is, they reject evolutionary development from one species to another. They accept microevolution – that is, they accept the kind of mutations and natural selection we can witness in laboratory experiments with fruit flies. The theological commitment of the creationists is this: God created each species independent of the others at the moment of creation. The theological commitment of the ID school, in contrast, is that evolutionary development is designed by a transcendent designer. This permits, though it does not require, support of macroevolution. On the other side of the battlefield we find defenders of neo-Darwinian evolutionary theory. Proponents of Darwinism affirm both microevolution and macroevolution; and they argue further that the long process of species change and development is due strictly to randomness and chance. No guiding purpose or supernatural intervention is engineering the evolutionary process. Rejected by Darwinians is any kind of *telos* or direction or progress. Natural selection and its corollaries provide an inclusive and exhaustive explanation for evolutionary wanderings.

Between the creationists and evolutionists enter the ID forces. Key figures here are biologist Michael Behe, lawyer Philip Johnson, philosopher Alvin Plantinga, and mathematician William Dembski. Affirming both micro- and macro- evolution, what ID adds is intelligent design to evolutionary direction. The first of two key terms is "irreducible complexity", meaning that emergent life forms are not reducible to random natural events. They must have been designed. To be designed, they must have had a designer. The second key term is "information". Information is a third reality in addition to matter and energy; and information in the universe could come only from a mind, a divine mind. Materialistic explanations for evolution are not enough.[11]

Both creationists and IDers see themselves as warriors in the battle for the modern cultural psyche. This is by no means an ivory tower or laboratory discussion about the finer points of evolutionary theory. This is a struggle to see if social values and human self-understanding will be brought down to the level of animals who know only the survival of the fittest, for whom survival depends upon defeating and destroying and devouring. More is at stake than merely a theoretical discussion within the science-religion dialogue. There is no dialogue here – only war.[12]

Non-warfare Models: The Two-Language Detente

Turning from warfare to non-warfare models, the first of the four attempts to bring peace is a form of detente: *the two-language theory*. This is a form of truce because it respects the sovereign territory of both science and theology, and because it is advocated by highly respected persons in both domains. Albert Einstein – remembered for his remark that "science without religion is lame and religion without science is blind" – distinguished between the language of fact and the language of value. "Science can only ascertain what *is*, but not what *should be*", he once told an audience at Princeton; "religion, on the other hand, deals only with evaluations of human thought and action". Note the use of "only" here. Each language is *restricted* to its respective domain.

More recently, the U.S. National Academy of Sciences released an official statement: "Religion and science are separate and mutually exclusive realms of human thought whose presentations in the same context lead to misunderstanding of both scientific theory and religious belief".[13] Note the emphasis: "separate and mutually exclusive".

As of this writing, the current president of the American Association for the Advancement of Science, anthropologist Stephen Jay Gould, advocates the two-language view. Responding to Pope John Paul II's elocution on evolution, Gould argues that science and religion need not be in conflict because their teachings occupy different domains. Their respective *magisteria* (teaching authorities) are "nonoverlapping".[14]

What is said among scientists is repeated among theologians. Neoorthodox theologian Langdon Gilkey has long argued for the two-language approach. Science, he says, deals only with objective or public knowing of *proximate* origins, whereas religion and its theological articulation deals with existential or personal knowing of *ultimate* origins. Science asks *"how?"*, while religion asks "why?".[15] What Gilkey wants, of course, is for one person to be a citizen in two lands – that is, to be able to embrace both Christian faith and scientific method without conflict.[16] To speak both languages is to be bilingual, and bilingual intellectuals can work with one another in peace.

The modern two-language theory of the relation between science and theology ought not to be confused with the premodern concept of the two books. In medieval times, revelation regarding God could be read from two books, the *book of nature* and the *book of scripture*. Both science and theology could speak of things divine. Both natural revelation and special revelation pointed us in one direction: toward God.[17] The two-language theory, in contrast, points us in two different directions: either toward God or toward the world.

A problem appears with the two-language theory. What it gains is peace through separation, by establishing a demilitarized zone that prevents communication. In the event that a scientist might desire to speak about divine matters or that a theologian might desire to speak about the actual world created by God, the two would have to speak past one another on the assumption that shared understanding is impossible. Why begin with such an assumption? The method of hypothetical consonance makes just the opposite assumption, namely, there is but one reality and sooner or later scientists and theologians should be able to find some areas of shared understanding.

Hypothetical Consonance

As I mentioned earlier, *hypothetical consonance* is the name I give to the negotiations that carry the two-language theory beyond truce to a fuller cooperation. The term 'consonance', coming from the work of Ernan McMullin, indicates that we are looking for those areas where there is a correspondence between what can be said scientifically about the natural world and what the theologian understands to be God's creation.[18] 'Consonance' in the strong sense means accord, harmony. Accord or harmony might be a treasure we hope to find, but we have not found it yet. Where we find ourselves now is working with consonance in a weak sense – that is, by identifying common domains of question asking. The advances in physics, especially thermo-dynamics and quantum theory in relation to Big Bang cosmology, have in their own way raised questions about transcendent reality. As Paul Davies has shown, the God question can be honestly asked from within scientific reasoning. Theologians and scientists may now be sharing a common subject matter, and the idea of hypothetical consonance encourages further cooperation.

Theologian Mark William Worthing challenges us to be theologically responsible by investigating what science is saying about the world, the world we believe God to be the creator and redeemer of. "Theology ... has the responsibility to demonstrate to what extent and in what ways Christian faith is compatible with cosmologies that may in fact prove to be an accurate description of the universe."[19] Princeton theologian Wentzel van Huyssteen puts it this way: "As Christians we should therefore take very seriously the theories of physics and cosmology; not to exploit or to try to change them, but to try to find interpretations that would suggest some form of complementary consonance with the Christian viewpoint".[20]

Hypothetical consonance asks theologians to view their dogmas non-dogmatically. Rather than beginning from a rigid position of inviolable truth, the term 'hypothetical' asks theologians to subject their own assertions to further investigation and possible confirmation or disconfirmation. An openness to learning something new on the part of theologians and scientists alike is essential for hypothetical consonance to move us forward.

It is my judgment that, at least for the near future, the model of hypothetical consonance should lead the conversation between natural science and Christian theology. Scientists are already recognizing the limits to reductionist methods and peering into the deeper questions about the nature of nature and the significance of all that is real. Theologians are mandated to speak responsibly about the natural world we claim to be the creation of a divine creator; and natural science has demonstrated its ability to increase our knowledge and understanding of this wondrous world. If God is the creator, then we should expect growth in our understanding of God as we grow in understanding of the creation. Conversely, we should expect that, if the world is a creation, then it cannot be fully understood without reference to its creator.

Ethical Overlap

The above seven models have placed science and theology into direct relationship or direct opposition. In addition, at least two indirect venues are connecting them as well. One is *ethical overlap* – that is, theologians need scientists in order to speak credibly to the questions of human survival created by our industrial and technological society. And, even more urgently, they need to speak up on the ethical challenges posed by the environmental crisis and the need to plan for the long range future of the planet. The ecological challenge arises from the crisis-crossing forces of population overgrowth, increased industrial and agricultural production that depletes nonrenewable natural resources while polluting air and soil and water, the widening split between the haves and the have-nots around the world, and the loss of a sense of responsibility for the welfare of future generations. Modern technology is largely responsible for this ecological crisis, and theologians along with secular moralists are struggling to gain ethical control over technological and economic forces that, if left to themselves, will drive us toward destruction.[21]

One can embrace both hypothetical consonance and ethical overlap, to be sure. At root, the ecological crisis poses a spiritual issue, namely, the crying need of world civilization for an ethical vision. An ethical vision – a vision of a just and sustainable society that lives in harmony with its environment and at peace with itself – is essential for future planning and motivating the people's of the world to fruitful action. Ecological thinking is future thinking. Its logic takes the following form: *understanding-decision-control*. Prescinding from the scientific model, we implicitly assume that to solve the eco-crisis we need to understand the forces of destruction; then, we need to make the decisions and take the actions that will put us in control of our future and establish a human economy that is in harmony with earth's natural ecology.

New Age Spirituality

Islam and Christianity have their respective investments in retrieving a sense of cooperation between science and theology. Yet, the world of religion on our planet includes many other traditions and these traditions are undergoing rapid change. Many spiritual concepts and practices have cut loose from the traditions that gave birth to them and now they meander on their own throughout the world of high tech pluralism.

This is where we find *New Age Spirituality*. It owes allegiance to no tradition and to no ethnic group and to no nation. Like science, it owes no allegiance to any theological orthodoxy. It has no priesthood, no church. Yet it is a powerful religious force. The key to New Age thinking is holism – that is, the attempt to overcome modern dualisms such as the split between science and spirit, ideas and feelings, male and female, rich and poor, humanity and nature. New Age artillery is loaded with three explosive sets of ideas: (1) discoveries in 20th century physics, especially quantum theory; (2) acknowledgment of the important role played by imagination in human knowing; and (3) a recognition of the ethical exigency of preserving our planet from ecological destruction.

On the roster of New Age physicists we find Fritjof Capra and David Bohm, who combine Hindu mysticism with physical theory. Bohm, for example, argues that the explicate order of things that we accept as the natural world and that is studied in laboratories is not the fundamental reality; there is under and behind it an implicate order, a realm of undivided wholeness. This wholeness, like a hologram, is fully present in each of the explicate parts. Reality, according to Bohm, is ultimately "undivided wholeness in flowing movement".[22] When we focus on either objective knowing or subjective feeling we temporarily forget the unity that binds them. New Age spirituality seeks to cultivate awareness of this underlying and continually changing unity.

In a recent *Christian Century* article on science and religion we can see holism – and pantheism as well – at work. "When I am dreaming quantum dreams", writes Barbara Brown Taylor, "the picture I see is more like a web of relationships – an infinite web, flung across the vastness of space like a luminous net. ... God is the web ... I want to proclaim that God is the unity – the very energy, the very intelligence, the very elegance and passion that make it all go".[23]

Narrative construction comes into play here. Some New Age theorists add evolutionary theory to physics and especially to Big Bang cosmology, then they create a grand story – a myth – regarding the history and future of the cosmos of which we human beings are an integral and conscious part. On the basis of this grand myth, New Age ethics tries to proffer a vision of the future that will guide and motivate action appropriate to solving the ecological problem. Science here provides the background not only for ethical overlap but also for a fundamental religious revelation. Brian Swimme and Thomas Berry put it this way:

> Our new sense of the universe is itself a type of revelatory experience. Presently we are moving beyond any religious expression so far known to the human into a meta-religious age, that seems to be a new comprehensive context for all religions. ... The natural world itself is the primary economic reality, the primary educator, the primary governance, the primary technologist, the primary healer, the primary presence of the sacred, the primary moral value.[24]

From Models to Theological Construction

The above nine models, whether they feed on warfare or pursue peace, are merely formal plans for connecting or disconnecting science and religious thought. Among the many agendas we could adopt, one important one is constructive theology. Both Muslims and Christians center their faith on God, a faith that is founded on the combination of divine revelation and awareness of God's unfathomable mystery. In recent years Christian theologians have begun adopting agendas of inquiry that are driven by their own distinctive concerns. Many Christian thinkers feel they can be true to their own vocations as theologians only if they pursue science questions in earnest and with honesty.

What I would like to do here is report briefly on the field of Christian systematic theology, showing some of the apparent points of contact with recent developments in natural science. Such points of contact are apparent in that they appear to provide paths for inquiry to follow; yet in most cases following them has not led to any final destinations. Some may lead to dead ends, others to orchards of new theological fruit.

Christian Systematic Theology

Systematic Theology in the Christian context refers to that branch of reflection responsible for articulating the doctrines of belief, especially as belief engages the surrounding contemporary culture. It is systematic for two reasons. First, theology here reviews systematically the full round of belief commitments offered by the Apostles' Creed and Nicene Creed. Second, theology here seeks coherence; it tries to wed doctrinal conviction with philosophical reasonableness. In the words of St. Anselm, theology is "faith seeking understanding". Today, theology seeks to understand Christian belief in light of scientific knowledge about the natural world.

Working out of the model of hypothetical consonance, some Christian theologians are ready to engage in exploration, in inquiry. Sufficient respect for the mystery of God pervading authentic revelation will guide the gaze of the theologian, praying for an expanding horizon and increased vision regarding new and more complex ways for understanding the relation of the world to its divine creator and redeemer.

Specifically, the theologian will formulate questions arising from centuries of scriptural interpretations and doctrinal commitments. Following the two ecumenical creeds, the Apostles' and Nicene, the topics or *loci* that the systematic theologian uses to orient such inquiries usually appear in a list such as the following.

1. Methodology
2. God and Creation
3. Anthropology
4. Imago Dei
5. Sin and Evil
6. Christology
7. The Person of Christ: Christology
8. The Work of Christ: Soteriology
9. Pneumatology
10. Ecclesiology
11. Eschatology
12. Ethics

By 'methodology', the Christian theologian includes epistemological questions regarding our knowledge of God through revelation and our relation to God through faith. Over the last four decades, theological methodology has been enlivened by the philosophy of science wherein the relativity of scientific knowledge has come to the fore, as well as the admission that science too works with faith. Science has faith that the world it studies is rational, that it is mathematically organized; and, it also has faith that the human mind is correspondingly rational and can thereby understand the world around. Both science and theology, then, may turn out to share a structure, namely, they both begin from faith, move to reflection upon faith, and then arrive at further understanding.[25]

The relation of God to creation is what Christian theologians refer to as "first article" matters. One of the most exciting areas of conversation over the last two decades has involved the question of divine action in nature, a question posed by theologians engaging physicists about quantum mechanics, relativity, chaos and complexity, and Big Bang cosmology. Is the existence of the natural world self-explanatory, or does it require reference to a transcendent origin? Should we think of divine action within the natural world in interventionist or non-interventionist terms? If at the quantum level physical processes are indeterminate, might we think of God acting in a non-interventionist manner to further the divine will?[26]

Still within the first article, the locus dealing with anthropology has drawn attention. Discussions surrounding the Anthropic Principle have raised within science a matter dear to the heart of the theologian: does the history of the universe seem to be oriented toward making a home for human beings? The question of purpose rises with force in dialogue with evolutionary biology: given the apparent blindness in natural selection to purposeful direction, do we have any grounds for postulating a divine guidance to the evolution of the human race? Can we, by connecting the creative advance in evolution with observable human creativity, apply the *imago dei* (divine image) in such a way as to define the human race as the "created co-creator"?[27]

Central to discussions of anthropology are questions arising from apparent biological determinism. In the neurosciences, brain biology appears increasingly to challenge traditional notions of the self and the soul.[28] The field of genetics may be even more forceful. Two forms of determinism pose challenges: *puppet determinism*, according to which the DNA pulls the strings to make the entire human organism dance, and *Promethean determinism*, wherein we ask our molecular biologists to alter the DNA so that the human race can take control of its own evolutionary future. The latter, Prometheanism, has elicited a cultural outcry: "thou shalt not play God!".[29] Such challenges of biological determinism force theologians to ask once again what they mean by concepts such as sin and freedom.

Christology belongs to the second article. The term "christology" can refer two things. First, as an encompassing term, it refers to everything a Christian theologian wants to say about Jesus Christ. Second, more specifically, it refers to the *person* of Christ – that is, the divine and human natures combined into a single person. Its sister term "soteriology" refers to the *work* of Christ on behalf of our salvation. To date, very little in the science-religion dialogue has been applied here. A few scholars have attempted to draw in sociobiology with its "selfish gene" theory of natural selection, asking where Jesus with his emphasis on unselfish love (*agape*) fits with kin altruism. Does Jesus mark an evolutionary advance?[30]

With pneumatology we move to third article theology, the Holy Spirit. Again, relatively little drawn from science has to date seemed relevant. Some theologians have proffered the notion that the work of God's spirit in the world can be compared to a force field.[31] Nonlocality and action-at-a-distance in quantum field theory attract theologians. Should we think of the Holy Spirit as a force field, even literally as a field of force active in the natural causal nexus?

Ecclesiology and eschatology also belong to the third article, with ecclesiology nearly completely ignored by theologians interested in science. Eschatology has just recently drawn interest for two reasons. First, physical cosmologists forecast a future for the universe that is not consonant with Christian symbols for a new creation. Considering the law of entropy and projections of a cosmic heat death some 65 billion years ahead, it appears to the eyes of the scientist that our cosmos has a finite future that will end in its demise. Is this dissonant with Christian promises of redemption, transformation, and renewal?[32] Second, debate has begun over the scientific contribution, if any, to understanding what resurrection from the dead could mean. Does it make conceptual sense to imagine what finite life without death would look like?[33]

Conclusion

Two impulses guide Christian theology, impulses that may be at work among Islamic thinkers as well. The first is the impulse inherent in faith to seek further understanding. Faith is based upon revelation, to be sure; yet, by appreciating the mystery surrounding our creator God, faith presses for further understanding about the complex relation between creator and creation. In the modern world, science has dramatically demonstrated its ability to prosecute progressive research, yielding incalculable excitement over new knowledge. The sheer appreciation of the wonders of nature that science makes possible is itself an event of God's spirit within the human soul.

The second impulse is the drive toward truth. God is the ultimate reality. What is true about anything is finally true about God. Nothing about faith could elicit our confidence if we could not trust in its truth. Because of this tacit yet vitally important theological commitment to truth, scientific inquiry has an innate appeal to the theological mind. Science, at its best, pursues truth. Theology, at its best, should find sisterhood and brotherhood in the laboratory.

Even if something looking like warfare is taking place on some battlefields, a faith that seeks understanding should also be a faith that seeks peace between science and theology. Beyond the struggle for intellectual dominance, the quest for truth causes us to strain our eyes, looking to the horizon to spot the dove of peace.

Notes

[1] Muzaffar Iqbal suggests that scientific inquiry belongs inherently to Islamic faith. "The Qur'ān emphasizes learning. It repeatedly asks the believers to contemplate upon and try to understand the mysteries of the universe. It provides a vast array of natural and historical phenomena and asks people to reflect in order to derive conclusions for themselves." "Five Eminent Early Muslim Scientists and their Contributions to Islamic Scientific Thought", *Islamic Thought and Scientific Creativity*, 3:3 (1992): 8.

2 See the discussion of "hypothetical consonance" in the Introduction and Chapter 1 of *Science and Theology: The New Consonance*, ed. Ted Peters (Boulder CO: Westview Press, 1998).

3 "Scientism", writes Pope John Paul II, "is the philosophical notion which refuses to admit the validity of forms of knowledge other than those of the positive sciences; and it relegates religious, theological, ethical and aesthetic knowledge to the realm of mere fantasy". *Fides et Ratio*, 1999.

4 Michael Shermer, *How We Believe: The Search for God in an Age of Science* (New York: W. H. Freeman and Co., 2000), 61.

5 Physicist Fred Alan Wolf illustrates the scientific takeover by explaining the existence of the soul in terms of quantum physics. "We march forward to modern science's view of the universe. Balancing new with old, we find a scientific view of heaven, hell, immortality, reincarnation, and Karma." *The Spiritual Universe: How Quantum Physics Proves the Existence of the Soul* (New York: Simon and Schuster, 1996), 34.

6 Edward O. Wilson, *Consilience* (New York: Alfred A. Knopf, 1998), 265.

7 Paul Davies, *God and the New Physics* (New York: Simon and Schuster, Touchstone, 1983), ix.

8 Paul Davies, *The Mind of God* (New York: Simon and Schuster, 1992), 16. In reviewing Davies' new book, *The Fifth Miracle: The Search for the Origin and Meaning of Life* (New York: Simon and Schuster, 1999), Philip Hefner alerts us to the manner in which Davies challenges science to go beyond its current limits. "*The Fifth Miracle* has an important subtext, which presses the claim: the current understanding of nature's laws is insufficient to understand the origin of life. Religious people have perennially perceived such insufficiencies as occasions to invoke the action of God" (622). "Mysterious Beginnings", *Christian Century*, 116:17 (June 2-9, 1999): 522-623. Davies does not invoke a religious God-of-the-gaps to fill the insufficiency, of course, but rather presses science to expand to fill this gap with a fuller understanding of nature.

9 *John Paul II On Science and Religion: Reflections on the New View from Rome*, eds. Robert John Russell, William R. Stoeger, and George V. Coyne (Notre Dame: University of Notre Dame Press, and Vatican City State: Vatican Observatory Publications, 1990). In October 1992 the pope completed a 13 year study of the Galileo affair, proclaiming that the church erred on condemning the astronomer for disobeying orders regarding the teaching of Copernicus' heliocentric theory of the universe. John Paul II described Galileo as "a sincere believer" who was "more perceptive [in the interpretation of Scripture] than the theologians who opposed him". Because in the myths of scientism Galileo is touted as a martyr for truth over against the narrow-mindedness of theology, Owen Gingerich took the occasion to write to clear up the facts. One noteworthy fact is that Galileo was never condemned for heresy,

only disobedience. "How Galileo Changed the Rules of Science", *Sky and Telescope*, 85:3 (March 1993): 32-26.

[10] See Duane T. Gish, *Evolution: The Fossils Say No!* (San Diego: Creation-Life Publishers, 1973) and Roger E. Timm, "Scientific Creationism and Biblical Theology", in *Cosmos as Creation*, ed. Ted Peters (Nashville: Abingdon, 1989), 247-264.

[11] See William A. Dembski, *Intelligent Design* (Downer's Grove IL: InterVarsity Press, 1999).

[12] Informative here is a brief compilation of documents: *Voices for Evolution*, ed. Molleen Matsumura (Berkeley, CA: The National Center for Science Education, 1995).

[13] National Academy of Sciences, *Science and Creationism* (Washington, DC: National Academy Press, 1984), 6.

[14] Stephen Jay Gould, "Nonoverlapping Magisteria", *Natural History* 106 (March 1997): 16-22.

[15] Langdon Gilkey, *Creationism on Trial* (San Francisco: Harper, 1985), 49-52, 108-113.

[16] In his more recent works, Gilkey has pressed for a closer relationship – a mutual interdependence – between science and religion. Gilkey attacks scientism (what he calls naturalism or scientific positivism) when it depicts nature as valueless, determined, and void of the sacred, on the grounds that these are supra-scientific or philosophical judgments that go beyond science itself. Science, therefore, must be supplemented by philosophy and religion if we are to understand reality fully. *Nature, Reality, and the Sacred* (Minneapolis: Fortress Press, 1993), 3, 11, 75, 111, 129.

[17] The "two books" approach is embraced today by the organization, Reasons to Believe, a publishing house that "examines how the facts of nature and the truths of the Bible give each of us a reason to believe". Reasons to Believe, P.O. Box 5978, Pasadena, CA 91117.

[18] Ernan McMullin, "How Should Cosmology Relate to Theology", in *The Sciences and Theology in the Twentieth Century*, ed. Arthur Peacocke (Notre Dame: University of Notre Dame Press, 1981), 39. See Peters, *Cosmos as Creation*, 13-17.

[19] Mark William Worthing, *God, Creation, and Contemporary Physics* (Minneapolis: Fortress Press, 1996), 193.

[20] Wentzel van Huyssteen, *Duet or Duel? Theology and Science in a Postmodern World* (Harrisburg, Pennsylvania: Trinity Press International, 1998), 78.

[21] See Ted Peters, *Fear, Faith, and the Future* (Minneapolis: Augsburg Press, 1980).

[22] David Bohm, *Wholeness and the Implicate Order* (London: Routledge and Kegan Paul, 1980), 11. See Fritjof Capra, *The Tao of Physics* (New York: Bantam, 1977). See Ted Peters, "The New Physics and Wholistic Cosmology", in his *The Cosmic Self: A Penetrating Look at Today's New Age Movements* (San Francisco: Harper, 1991), 133-168.

[23] Barbara Brown Taylor, "Physics and Faith: The Luminous Web", *Christian Century*, 116:17 (June 2-9, 1999): 619.

[24] Brian Swimme and Thomas Berry, *The Universe Story* (San Francisco: Harper, 1992), 255. A variant would be the team work of physicist Joel R. Primack and musician Nancy Ellen Abrams who are trying to construct a myth out of big bang inflationary cosmology and medieval Jewish Kabbalah, not because the myth would be true but because our culture needs a value orienting cosmology. "In the Beginning ... Quantum Cosmology and Kabbalah", *Tikkun*, 10:1 (January-February 1995): 66-73.

[25] In the area of methodology, key contributors are Nancey Murphy, *Theology in an Age of Reasoning* (Ithaca: Cornell University Press, 1990); Philip Clayton, *Explanation from Physics to Theology* (New Haven and London: Yale University Press, 1989); and Wentzel van Huyssteen, *Theology and the Justification of Faith* (Grand Rapids: Wm. B. Eerdmans, 1989).

[26] Leading the divine action discussion has been the joint effort by the Vatican Observatory and the Center for Theology and the Natural Sciences. See the series of books that includes, *Physics, Philosophy, and Theology*, eds. Robert John Russell, William R. Stoeger, and George V. Coyne (Vatican City State: Vatican Observatory and Notre Dame University Press, 1988); and *Quantum Cosmology and the Laws of Nature*, eds. Robert John Russell, Nancey Murphy, and C.J. Isham (Vatican City State: Vatican Observatory and Notre Dame University Press, 1993).

[27] See Philip Hefner, *The Human Factor* (Minneapolis: Fortress Press, 1993).

[28] See Niels Henrik Gregersen, William B. Drees, and Ulf Görman, eds., *The Human Person in Science and Theology* (Edinburgh: T&T Clark, 2000); James B. Ashbrook and Carol Rausch Albright, *The Humanizing Brain* (Cleveland: Pilgrim Press, 1997); and Robert John Russell, Nancey Murphy, Theo Meyering, and Michael Arbib, eds., *Neuroscience and the Human Person* (Vatican City State: Vatican Observatory; and Berkeley: CTNS, 2000).

[29] See Ted Peters, *Playing God? Genetic Determinism and Human Freedom* (New York and London: Routledge, 1997); and Ted Peters, ed., *Genetics: Issues of Social Justice* (Cleveland: Pilgrim Press, 1998).

[30] See Hefner, *The Human Factor*.

[31] See Wolfhart Pannenberg, *Toward a Theology of Nature: Essays on Science and Faith*, Ted Peters, ed. (Louisville: Westminster/John Knox, 1993), 37-40; and Michael Welker, *God the Spirit* (Minneapolis: Fortress Press, 1994), 235-248.

[32] See John Polkinghorne and Michael Welker (eds) *The End of the World and the Ends of God* (Harrisburg PA: Trinity Press International, 2000).

[33] This debate was kicked off by Frank Tipler, *The Physics of Immortality* (New York: Doubleday, 1994). See Ted Peters, "The Physical Body of Immortality", *CTNS Bulletin*, 15:2 (Spring 1995): 1-20.

Chapter 4

Christian Perspectives on Religion and Science and their Significance for Modern Muslim Thought

Mustansir Mir[1]

I will explore five questions in this chapter:

1. Why do Muslims need to know what Christians have to say about religion and science?
2. Assuming that Muslims need to know about them, what are the Christian perspectives on religion and science?
3. Are there any guidelines that Muslims should follow in studying those perspectives?
4. What are some examples of Christian perspectives that Muslims might find helpful?
5. Is there a task ahead for Muslims?

Importance of the Subject

Many Muslims believe that the historical conflict between religion and science was a conflict between a particular religion – Christianity – and science, and that while it is too bad that Christianity emerged from the engagement badly bruised, Islam need have no fears of any such clash.[2] The conclusion drawn about Islam requires comment. The modern scientific outlook, which is born of a secular and materialistic worldview and in turn reinforces that worldview, constitutes a challenge to all those philosophies of life that take a supreme being, like the God of theistic religions, as their basic reference point in life, thought, and

conduct. Islam is one such religion.[3] As such, it is a target of the so-
called scientific – or rather, scientistic – critique, the fundamental
assumption of which is that the physical world, which is in principle
amenable to observation and quantification, is the *ne plus ultra* of
human inquiry and concern. Islam differs with a crucial aspect of this
assumption. Islam does grant that the physical world as we know it has
order, stability, and integrity, implying that it is, consequently,
observable and quantifiable. Thus, the Qur'ān refers to the world's
order, stability, and integrity when it says, *wa-huwa'l-ladhī fī's-samā'i
ilāhun wa-fī'l-arḍi ilāhun* (43:84), "And He is the One who is deity in the
heavens and deity in the earth".[4] However, the Qur'ān also calls the
world an *āya*, "sign" – or rather, *āyāt*, a series or multiplicity of "signs".
By definition, a "sign" points beyond itself to something else to which
it bears the same relationship as that of a means to an end. The sign
itself, therefore, cannot be an end in itself; there is, about it, a certain
inconclusiveness that calls for conclusion, a certain incompleteness that
calls for completion. This conclusion or completion must be sought
outside the sign itself. Qur'ānic verses – such as 2:164 – which refer to
the world as containing so many signs, maintain that God, known as
One and as possessing certain attributes, is the supreme reality to
which the signs of the universe point. Thus God, rather than the
physical world, is the *ne plus ultra* – not only of human inquiry and
concern, but also of human devotion and worship; according to the
Qur'ān, recognition of God as the supreme reality not only alters our
theoretical understanding of the physical world, but it also draws from
us a certain kind of practical response or commitment. The Qur'ānic
invitation to human beings to reflect on the universe and the signs it
contains demands, as its logical end, *sajda* and *'ibāda – fa's-judū li'l-lāhi
wa-'budū* (53:62), "Prostrate yourself before God and worship Him".

On this matter, Christianity holds a position essentially similar
to that of Islam's. The two religions share the beliefs: in a personal
God; in a world that is not only dependent for its existence and
continuance on that God, but also gives evidence of His existence and
providence; in the involvement of God in the shaping of human history

and human destiny; and in the imperative need for human beings to submit to God's will. It is in light of these similarities that the study of Christian perspectives on religion and science becomes relevant for Muslims.

Of all the religions of the world, it is Christianity that has had to face head-on the attack by scientism. It was in Christendom that modern science was born and nourished, and it was the medieval Christian paradigm of life and thought that modern science sought to repudiate and dislodge. In the now longstanding encounter between religion and science, Christian writers have produced an extensive – and impressive – body of literature.[5] Modern Islam cannot boast of a significant body of literature dealing with issues arising from that encounter. If the above-stated two assumptions – namely, that the scientistic challenge is addressed not only to Christianity but also to Islam, and that there are essential similarities between the Christian and Islamic worldviews – are correct, it will follow that Christian literature on religion and science can be of value to Muslim thinkers. Muslim thinkers should realize that just because science and the scientific worldview have not yet engaged and challenged the Muslim world with the same amount of time and energy they have spent engaging and challenging Christianity, it does not mean that they pose no challenge to Islam. A full-scale encounter between Islam and modern science is yet to come, and Muslims would do well to prepare for it; and, in preparing for it, they can derive some fruitful lessons from Christianity's encounter with science. There may actually exist Qur'ānic warrant for studying this encounter.

Chapter 31 of the Qur'ān, after predicting that the Byzantine Christians, though defeated by the Sasanians in a then recent battle, will eventually defeat their foes, adds: *wa yawma'idhin yafraḥu'l-mu'minūn* ("And on that day will the Muslims rejoice"). The Qur'ānic comment was made not in the context of the Christian-Muslim doctrinal divide but in the context of a perceived conjunction or coalescence of Christian-Muslim views and interests. The Muslims of 7th century Arabia felt that they had stakes in the Byzantine-Sasanian conflict and the Muslims of modern times would not be mistaken to think that they have stakes in the conflict between science and the Christian faith.[6] A number of modern, and especially Christian, writers have stressed the need for the three great monotheistic religions to mount a joint initiative to stem and counter the forces of atheistic materialism and moral rootlessness. This call is not without merit and, if it were to be heeded, would require that a serious critical examination be undertaken – by Muslims no less than by Jews and Christians – of the so-called scientism which now informs the outlook of the dominant secular Western civilization.

Christian Perspectives: Background and Nature

Christian perspectives on religion and science developed against a rich intellectual background. Christian thinkers naturally draw on the Bible and on medieval Christian authorities and sources for ideas and insights, but the substantive issues they deal with took shape in the post-Renaissance West. The intellectual background against which these thinkers write, and to which they respond, is made up of a rich tapestry of philosophical, theological, and scientific ideas. Among those whose ideas, thought-systems, and discoveries these writers draw on are: the Polish astronomer Nicolaus Copernicus (1473-1543), the German astronomer and physicist Johannes Kepler (1571-1630), the Italian scientist and philosopher Galilei Galileo (1564-1642), the French mathematician and philosopher René Descartes (1596-1650), the English thinker John Locke (1632-1704), the English mathematician, scientist, and philosopher Isaac Newton (1642-1747), the Scottish philosopher David Hume (1711-1776), the English naturalist Charles Darwin (1809-1882), the German philosopher Immanual Kant (1724-1804), the German theologian and philosopher Friedrich Schleiermacher (1768-1834), the British mathematician and philosopher Alfred North Whitehead (1861-1947), the Swiss theologian Karl Barth (1886-1968), and the German theologian Rudolf Bultmann

(1884-1976). Among the ideas, theories, and concepts that come under discussion are: agency, causality, autonomy, chance, indeterminacy, chaos, empiricism, rationalism, transcendence, special and continuous creation, general and special providence, kenosis, reductionism, thermodynamics, quantum theory, and relativity. Even these partial lists of names and issues indicate that the Christian literature on the religion-science encounter reckons with a centuries-long history of intellectual development, and, as one would suspect – or rather, expect – is quite sophisticated and nuanced in its own right. What gives this literature further depth is the fact that a significant number of modern Christian writers have a thorough training not only in theology, but also in the natural sciences; this enables them to view and examine the interaction of religion and science from a unique vantage point.

In view of both the breadth and the depth of this literature it would be difficult, even for one who knew it intimately, to summarize its contents or character in a few propositions. Since I have no pretensions to such knowledge, I will not make such an attempt and will make only one or two points.

Christian thought on religion and science has gone through several phases and has seen the rise and eclipse of several methodologies. It hardly needs stating that there is no single Christian position and no single set of Christian perspectives on the relationship between religion and science; there are, for instance, the conservative and liberal approaches. Understandably, the principal endeavor of the Christian writers is to deny the existence of an irreconcilable gulf between science and Christianity, whether in respect of the general Christian view of nature or in respect of specific Christian doctrines like creation and providence. But several Christian writers (especially in modern times) have, instead of passively defending Christianity against the attacks of a secular science, argued both on scientific and religious grounds that the "establishment" scientist's view of nature and life is hopelessly inadequate. Furthermore, they argue that this inadequacy can only be made good by means of a religious worldview. These writers, some of them acknowledged authorities in fields of science, place constructions on scientific data that are generically different from those of secular scientists; many of them are led by their professional research to conclude that consonance rather than conflict marks the relationship between religion and science.

But, these writers do not take a facile view of such consonance. They recognize that both religion and science make conflicting truth claims and that such claims cannot be wished away. In 1930, 12 distinguished British thinkers, including scientists like Julian Huxley, John S. Haldane, Bronislaw Malinowski, Arthur Eddington, and churchmen like Ernest W. Barnes, Burnett H. Streeter, and William R. Inge, participated in a symposium. The proceedings from this symposium were published the following year under the title *Science and Religion*. Most of the speakers expressed the opinion that religion and science could coexist harmoniously if each confined itself to its proper domain – science dealing with fact and religion with value. Dean Inge, however, registered a note of dissent. Rejecting the view that no real conflict between science and religion exists, he said:

> If by religion we mean theology, and if by science we mean naturalism, this [view of the absence of a conflict] is not true. Theology and naturalism are both theories about ultimate reality. They are both poachers; theology cannot be content with religion, nor naturalism with science; and when they meet on each other's ground, or on no-man's land, they are likely to fight.[7]

Modern Christian writers would agree with Dean Inge that rival claims about reality by science and religion exist but they would argue – and it is a measure of the sophistication that Christian thought has acquired since his time – that these claims can be plausibly resolved on grounds whose acceptance would impugn the integrity neither of science nor of religion. In the fourth section of this paper, we will note an example or two illustrating this approach.

Guidelines for Muslim Study of Christian Works on Religion and Science

An open and receptive Muslim attitude should characterize such study. Christian works on religion and science proceed from theistic principles, which, as we have already noted, are broadly shared between Christianity and Islam. The main objective of a Muslim study of these works should be to use them as guide and fillip in the attempt, first, to cultivate an authentic Islamic understanding of the religion-science relationship and, second, to envision how scientific method and scientific activity can be integrated into the larger cultural processes of an Islamic society. It should be obvious that the Muslim attitude toward the Christian literature in question cannot be that of a shopper at the supermarket. For, it would not do to ask which of the particular Christian responses to the scientific challenge Muslims may adopt or take over. Not only has the course of the religion-science relationship been different in historical Islam – and that is because of Islam's distinctive structures of belief and conduct – but there is every likelihood that, in the future as well, a genuine Muslim response to science and the scientific worldview will emerge from within Islam and, following its own impulse, will chart its own course. It is, therefore, necessary that Muslim engagement with Christian writings on religion and science be both sympathetic and creative.

The imperative to ground Muslim study of these writings in a proper Islamic framework of reflection and inquiry requires that such study seek to follow, clarify, and build on leads and emphases culled from Islamic sources; these sources include not only the great Islamic texts with the Qur'ān at their center, but also the historical practice of science by Muslim individuals and societies. This, admittedly, is a gigantic and daunting project that, for an ideal execution, requires dedicated work by teams of qualified Muslim scholars and thinkers over an extended period of time. But regardless of the level at which and manner in which the project is undertaken, a commitment to

Islamic principles of interpretations of life and nature would appear to be a *sine qua non*.

Several Christian writers not only attempt to make room for religion in a world that, allegedly on strict scientific grounds, disallows the existence of a divine being, but also go on to establish the validity of such specific and distinctive Christian doctrines as Trinitarianism.[8] Needless to say, Muslims will have little interest in pursuing such lines of argument; not only because such doctrines are un-Islamic, but also because the attempt to validate such doctrines on a scientific basis takes one outside the proper limits of the subject. By the same token, however, Muslims may not seek scientific validation of a particular belief in its specific Islamic formulation – the belief in angels, for example. This brings up the question of the relative extent to which revelation and reason can serve as sources of knowledge and this question falls outside the scope of our inquiry.

Much of the early Christian thought on religion and science developed – beginning about the middle of the 19th century – when the Church of Rome, to use Ted Peters' words, "felt it was under siege".[9] Christian thought has come a long way since the middle of the 19th century, but Muslims have to guard against falling prey to a similar siege mentality. In a sense this mentality is the product of a need for closure, for definitive answers reached in a hurry. Significant solutions, definitive or tentative, are reached after deliberation that can be – one might say, ought to be – time-consuming. The urge to come up with quick, fully-baked solutions and the tendency to enshrine such solutions as indubitable verities, must be resisted. A period of gestation must be allowed for, and this period should be used to canvass the Muslim and Christian – and other – sources, in the search for answers. "They also serve who only stand and wait", wrote John Milton. Muslims need not merely stand with folded arms. They must apply themselves to the task at hand, but they must be prepared to wait for mature answers to emerge.

Examples of Christian Perspectives

Critique of Scientism

It is generally agreed that in the present age science supplies the reigning paradigm in the fields of human knowledge and action. For a variety of reasons, paradigms, once entrenched, tend to become tyrannical, preventing the rise and growth of alternative or rival paradigms; so, there is always a need for a view from the edge – that is, for a critical view that would help curb the excesses committed in the name of the ruling paradigms. Christian writers have been among the forefront of those who have drawn attention to the tyranny perpetrated in the name of scientific paradigms. They have done so by distinguishing between scientific fact and scientific speculation, calling the latter scientism. Ted Peters offers a succinct explanation of scientism:

> Scientism, like other '-isms', is an ideology, this one built upon the assumption that science provides all the knowledge that we can know. There is only one reality, the natural, and science has a monopoly on the knowledge we have about nature. Religion, which claims to purvey knowledge about things supernatural, provides only pseudo-knowledge – that is, false impressions about non-existent fictions.[10]

In other words, scientism is scientific absolutism. This absolutism results from a failure to recognize that science is a social activity that, like any other social activity, is subject to analysis and critique. Wolfgang Smith writes:

> We must remember that science does not operate in a vacuum, and that only the smallest portion of what is normally presupposed in technical discourse is itself subject to scientific analysis. Recognized or not, there is always a dark field around the white spot, a grey region that shades off into obscurity. [In this] rationally obscure and protean realm [is to be found] 'the other side' of

the intellectual coin: hidden imprecisions, for instance, that mitigate the formidable exactitudes of science, and the groundless fantasies that temper its austere sobriety. And here, too, most assuredly, are to be found those sweeping tenets that filter down into the non-scientific strata of the technological society to become its officially recognized worldview.[11]

Thus, science runs the risk of becoming an ideology – of becoming an oppressive system of thought and practice that seeks to impose its dominant will alike on stubborn data and on reluctant minds. It is true that secular writers too have expressed apprehensions about science donning the mantle of a ruthless monarch.[12] But they propose an in-house solution – that of injecting bigger doses of the "pure" scientific method into the conduct of scientific activity. Christian writers, on the other hand, subject the overall scientistic model to critique, pointing out that the model is in principle incapable of overcoming certain inherent limitations and blind spots. In so doing, they do not wish to debunk science, though it is their aim to puncture the *hubris* of scientism. From an Islamic standpoint, the Christian critique of scientism is not only relevant, but judicious.

Setting the Historical Record Straight

Another important contribution of Christian writers on the critical side consists in their attempt to set straight the historical record of the relationship between religion and science. Science and religion are often perceived to be irreconcilable foes.[13] Albert Einstein's remark that "the churches have always fought science and persecuted its devotees" not only reflects but also reinforces such a view.[14] It is true that the relations between science and Christianity have not always been smooth and cordial, but on the other hand the case for the warfare between Christianity and science appears to have been overstated. Two *causes célèbres* often cited to prove the Church's hostility toward science are those involving Giordano Bruno (1548-1600), who was burnt at the stake, and Galileo Galilei, who was forced to recant his heretical views and put under house arrest. But one wonders if the general indictment handed down against Christianity on account of the Church's treatment of Bruno and Galileo is not a little too severe and the conclusion drawn about Christianity's ingrained antipathy toward science not a little too rash. As Charles Raven says, "the evidence [against Christianity] is slight, and has been exaggerated in the interest of later controversy".[15] The cases of Bruno and Galileo themselves are indicative of the exaggeration. Bruno was punished mainly for political reasons; in Frederick Copleston's words, "his unhappy end was due not to his championship of the Copernican hypothesis, nor to his attacks on Aristotelian Scholasticism, but to his apparent denial of some central theological dogmas".[16] The story of Galileo's condemnation leads one to a similar conclusion. In an interesting paper, "Galileo and the Church", William R. Shea demonstrates that the treatment meted out to Galileo by the Church has to be seen in the context of the Counter-Reformation and "related to a period [after the Council of Trent (1545-1564)] in which modern liberal values were far from commanding the assent that we have come to take for granted".[17] Drawing on Galileo's correspondence and a number of other contemporary sources, Shea maintains that "Galileo's condemnation was the result of the complex interplay of untoward political circumstances, personal ambitions, and wounded prides".[18] And we should not forget that the same Galileo had previously enjoyed the favor of several ecclesiastical authorities and received medals and other honors from Pope Urban VIII,[19] and that his work *Two New Sciences*, when it appeared in Protestant Holland in 1638, was left unchallenged by the Church.[20] At any rate, it can hardly be claimed that the Church was always relentlessly hostile to science. The truth is that many early scientists professed belief in Christianity and saw no conflict between their faith and their scientific pursuits. Edward Grant's statement that "Science and theology were never more closely interrelated than during the Latin Middle Ages in Western Europe" may appear surprising,[21] but it becomes plausible when one learns about the deeply religious orientation of many scientists[22] – people who were motivated

in their professional work by a religious vision of life and nature.[23] A
list of such scientists would include many names from later – and from
our own – times as well.[24] To take only one or two examples from the
latter category: Gregor Johann Mendel, who founded the discipline of
genetics in the 19th century, was an Austrian monk, and the famous
French paleontologist Teilhard de Chardin, who died in 1955, was a
Jesuit priest. A number of professional scientists today are qualified
theologians, and there is, in Britain, a Society of Ordained Scientists.

Christian scholars' interpretations of the historical relationship
between science and religion are of crucial academic significance, but
the psychological significance is no less great: it is a tremendous
confidence-booster for those in the theistic camp – a fact that Muslims
would appreciate. The scientistic charge-sheet against Christianity
becomes, in the final analysis, a charge-sheet against all theistic
religions – Islam included. To demonstrate that the charges brought
against Christianity are an overstatement is to demonstrate, by clear
and valid analogy, that the charges brought against all theistic religions
– again, Islam included – are an overstatement.

Science and Theology: Methodological Affinities

Many Christian writers have pointed out that science and religion, far
from bearing each other a natural grudge, have several meeting-points
– and even overlap. Thus, theology – which is systematic reflection on
such religious matters as the existence of God – and science have
certain methodological affinities. In the popular mind, the words
"science" and "religion" evoke contrary images. As Ian Barbour puts
it, "Many people view science as objective, universal, rational, and
based on solid observational evidence. Religion, by contrast, seems to
be subjective, parochial, emotional, and based on traditions or
authorities that disagree with each other".[25] But this neatly
dichotomous view does not accurately represent the ground realities.
Furthermore, recent developments in science and theology have
tended to erase, or at least significantly blur, the subjective/objective

and personal/impersonal distinctions that were formerly made between theology and science.[26] Arthur Peacocke notes five similarities between what he calls the scientific and theological enterprises:

1. Both involve a process of abstraction from human experience, and in both, personal imagination and intuition play a significant role;[27]
2. Both carry on, each within its own domain, a constant dialogue between the old and the new, and it is a mistake to think that theology always holds on to the old whereas science always goes for the new;
3. Both appeal to experience as validating criterion;
4. Both deal with – which is to say, religion no less than science is capable of dealing with – process, change, and development, so that both are describable in terms of dynamic images; and
5. Both place reliance on communal authority, requiring intellectual integrity on the part of their practitioners.[28]

It is not difficult to see that methodological similarities between science and theology have implications both for a philosophy of physical nature and for a philosophy of human nature: it establishes the presumption of unity between the physical world and the spiritual realm – something that is affirmed by the Qur'ān, which, as was noted at the beginning this paper, speaks of the world as a repository of spiritual insights; and it integrates the human self by grounding it in a unified matrix of loyalties – again something that would find strong support in the Qur'ān, which demands from human beings total commitment to the truth – *dukhūl fi's-silmi kaffatan* (see 2:208).

Typologies of Approaches and Issues

Arthur Peacocke outlines eight ways in which science and theology can interact:

1. Science and theology are concerned with two distinct realms.
2. Science and theology are interacting approaches to the same reality.
3. Science and theology constitute two distinct non-interacting approaches to the same reality.
4. Science and theology constitute two different language systems.
5. Science and theology are generated by quite different attitudes in their practitioners.
6. Science and theology are both subservient to their objects and can only be defined in relation to them.
7. Science and theology may be integrated.
8. Science generates a metaphysic in terms of which theology is then formulated.[29]

Peacocke himself inclines to the second position. The eighth approach would be preferred by Ted Peters, whose own typology, though it differs somewhat from Peacocke's, includes – under the name "hypothetical consonance"[30] – an approach similar to Peacocke's eighth.[31]

At this stage in Islamic scholarship it would be premature to speak of a definitive Islamic view – or of one or more authoritative Islamic understandings – of the relationship between science and theology; such a view will emerge only after a careful discussion of the matter among Muslim thinkers has taken place. A word about Peacocke's typology is in order, however. It seems that any view in which a radical disjunction between science and theology is effected (such as the first, third, fourth,[32] fifth, and sixth) is unlikely to gain acceptance as Islamic; the same can be said about a view (such as the eighth) in which religion is given a subservient position. The second and the seventh approaches seem to be the most viable from an Islamic standpoint.

Several Christian authors list and discuss issues that arise from a religion-science encounter. The following chapter titles from John Haught's *Science and Religion* give an idea of the range of issues:

> Is Religion Opposed to Science?
> Does Science Rule Out a Personal God?
> Does Evolution Rule Out God's Existence?
> Is Life Reducible to Chemistry?
> Was the Universe Created?
> Do We Belong Here?
> Why is There Complexity in Nature?
> Does the Universe have a Purpose?
> Is Religion Responsible for the Ecological Crisis?

Most of these issues now have a fairly longstanding history, and their persistence to this day shows their continued relevance. But note that the last issue – that of ecology – is of relatively recent provenance, which indicates that Christian writers are alive to modern developments that call for a religious response. Also, these issues, as set forth by Haught, are actually summations that include and implicate other issues, such as transcendence, providence, value, chance, cause, matter, soul or spirit, mind, and autonomy. Besides these substantive issues, methodological and procedural issues are also involved – for example, those of *a priori* assumption, abstraction, subjectivity, and verification.[33]

These typologies of approaches and issues are helpful for a theistic study of the relationship between science and theistic religion. Muslim scholars can use them as guides, first in their study of their own tradition – in their attempt to determine whether, and to what extent, they can draw on that tradition in coming to grips with modern issues – and, second in developing new approaches and prioritizing issues.

The God Question

Central to the religion-science encounter is the question of whether God exists and, if so, what God's relationship to the world is. A host of issues arise here. We will review briefly some of the insights Christian literature offers on two of them – providence and prayer.

As theistic religions, both Christianity and Islam maintain that God acts in the world and in history. From a scientific – or rather, from a scientistic – viewpoint, this doctrine is open to the charge of needless divine interventionism: the world as we know it follows certain unbreakable laws and, as such, does not allow for interference by a supernatural agency.

In an article bearing the title "Does the God 'Who Acts' Really Act in Nature?", Robert Russell argues that, historically, there have been only two ways of conceptualizing special providence: as objective divine acts or as subjective responses to otherwise uniform divine acts. But, according to Russell, modern developments in science and philosophy give us a third option. Today, nature is no longer regarded as a closed causal system. The replacement of Newtonian physics and philosophical reductionism by, respectively, quantum physics and holistic thought now enables us to think of the world as "an open, temporal process with the ontology of 'Swiss cheese' – one in which the genuine, material effects of human and even divine agency are at least conceivable".[34] These developments open up the possibility of "non-interventionist objective special providence".[35] Russell distinguishes between epistemological indeterminacy and ontological indeterminacy, maintaining that "some natural processes are, in fact, ontologically indeterministic", so that "[t]he future is ontologically open, influenced, of course, but *under*determined [Russell's emphasis] by the factors of nature acting in the present. ... there is no exhaustive set of underlying natural causes. In, through and beyond the causal conditions we can describe scientifically, things just happen".[36] In Russell's view, "quantum mechanics allows us to think of special divine action without God overriding or intervening in the structure of nature. God's action will remain hidden within that structure, and it will take the form of realizing one of several potentials in the quantum system ...".[37]

Russell's argument that modern developments in science and philosophy make the theistic view of special providence not only plausible but entirely rational and credible should be of great interest to Muslim thinkers. As can be seen, Russell does not reject the so-called scientific view, but builds on it, taking into account the relatively recent findings in science. Of course, he cannot be said to have *proved* – and he himself would not claim that he has proved – special providence on scientific basis. What he has done, however, is effectively blunted the edge of the scientistic attack that science excludes special providence.

We will now look at the question of prayer. Does the idea of petitionary prayer make sense? On scientific construal, it would seem that to petition God for something would be either pointless or presumptuous. For, in presenting your prayer, you either want God to grant you something that God would grant you whether you ask for it or not, or you want God to violate the principles of order and stability that underlie and uphold this world. In the former case prayer is pointless and in the latter, presumptuous. But according to Donald MacKay, this judgment is based on a false dichotomy between ourselves and our environment:

> The temptation is always to think of our environment as a created thing, but ourselves as essentially independent settlers in it. ... We ourselves and our fellow human beings are just as much continually dependent on the divine fiat as our environment is. God's drama is one and indivisible, both in its conception and in its moment-by-moment dependence on the agency of the Creator. It follows that if a man finds himself in a situation that calls for petitionary prayer, the circumstances that move him to pray are just as much an integral part of the Creator's conception as the circumstances that lead up to whatever God brings about in response.[38]

The issue, for MacKay, is perspectival: two different understandings of a phenomenon gained from two different standpoints may equally be correct if "[t]here is, on the one hand, the divine standpoint of extra-temporality or eternity and, on the other hand, the human standpoint of created space-time. When we say 'this would have happened even if that had not', there is always an unspoken qualification '... other things being equal'". In other words, if I petition God for something, then we cannot ask whether God would have granted my petition even if I had not made it. For the drama in which I make the petition is different from the drama in which I do not make it, and each drama comes as a complete package in itself, "for there could be no guarantee that if God had created a drama in which you had not prayed [say, for help or rescue], he would still have made it one in which help was sent off in time to rescue you".[39] MacKay goes on to say, quoting Romans 8:28, 29:

> What we do have is a firm promise that God is 'the hearer of the prayer of the needy' and that 'in everything ... he cooperates for good with those who love God. ... God knew his own before ever they were'. Thus the rational thing for those who love God to do when in trouble is to express their trust in this and related promises by praying for help, confident that if their Creator sees that good would be served by a positive response, he will have ordered accordingly events that may otherwise have no 'causal connection' (in the scientific sense) with their action in prayer.[40]

> A Christian can justly argue that to *refuse* to ask God's help in trouble would make it *irrational* for him to expect to receive it.[41]

MacKay's argument is set in a dynamic understanding of the relationship of the petition-maker (human being) and the petition-granter (God), and it should be comprehensible against the backdrop of modern developments in science. In advancing theological positions, Christian writers like Robert Russell and Donald MacKay make competent use of scientific data, and their works furnish a solid basis for building a case for theistic religion.

But, notably, modern Christian writers on religion and science, while they put up a stout defense of theism, do not generally become defensive, taking exclusivist theological positions. Instead of anxiously trying to clinch the argument in favor of religion and rubbing science's nose in the dirt, they suggest the need for a serious and responsible dialogue between theology and science. Here it may be helpful to refer to Ted Peters' notion of "hypothetical consonance" between science and theology. Hypothetical consonance requires that both theology and science, each in search of greater illumination, be open to comment and correction by each other.[42] Peters illustrates the concept of hypothetical consonance by reference to the God question, which we have been discussing. "[T]his method", he writes, "does not constitute a proof for the existence of God. Rather, by working with the idea of God, we ask whether theology and science in concert provide greater illumination and understanding of the reality in which we live than we would have if we worked with one or the other discipline alone or with the two independently".[43] In its essential form, this method seems to be correct, though it remains up to Muslim scholars to work out its details in responsible consideration of the prospects opened up and constraints imposed by the normative Islamic worldview and historical Muslim tradition.

The Task Ahead

First, let me say a word about the task that does not – or ought not to – lie ahead. One of the current movements of thought in the Islamic world goes by the name of Islamization of knowledge. This movement seeks to Islamize the various disciplines of knowledge, most of them developed in the West, by injecting into them Islamic modes of thought and analysis. I am not convinced that this is a good idea. Restricting myself to the subject of my paper, I would submit that, while it makes sense to use the phrase "Islam and science" indicating that Islam takes a certain view of science or scientific activity, or that the relationship between Islam and science is a subject worthy of study, the phrase "Islamic science" is of doubtful validity for the simple reason that to speak of Islamic science is to provincialize science; it is to grant that there can be Christian, Hindu, Taoist, and other brands of science. Furthermore, it suggests that there can be, for example, Catholic science, Methodist science, and Southern Baptist science–and one can go on with the subdivision. But, it may be asked, do we not speak of Islamic architecture, Christian architecture, and Hindu architecture? We do – but in a very different sense. A term like "Islamic architecture" stands for an "Islamic *style* of architecture"; it does not imply that, when at work, Muslim architects sublimely disregard the established principles of construction and yet succeed in building magnificent monuments, but only that they weave Islamic religious motifs into their products, which consequently become representative of an Islamic worldview and an Islamic lifestyle. But can we then speak of an Islamic style of physics? In light of the above comment, it would be more appropriate to speak of an Islamic *interpretation* of the data of physics or, for that matter, of any other science, or of science in general. In other words, instead of asking whether there can be Islamic, Christian, or any other such science, we should ask: How do the followers of a certain religion interpret the data of science? It is at this point that we can ask: How do Christian scholars interpret scientific data and, given the affinities between the theistic worldviews of Christianity and Islam, what lessons can Muslim scholars draw from Christian interpretations of those data?

There is a definite need for Muslims to engage with science – with both scientific method and the scientific worldview – with a view to: first, determining the role of science in modern Islamic society; second, establishing principles for the conduct of scientific activity in society; and third, relating science to society's other, non-scientific activities. But important questions – such as: What is the Islamic view of science? How can Muslims engage in scientific activity while remaining true to their faith? How can science contribute to the purposes for which an Islamic society exists? Is science a friend or a foe of Islam? – cannot be answered through a cerebral exercise conducted fitfully under adverse circumstances by a handful of isolated individuals. These and other questions cannot properly be treated until there comes into existence, in the Muslim world, an academic culture that recognizes the importance of these questions and resolves to do what it takes to deal with them. Such a culture will not come into being until we train a large number of young minds in religion and theology on the one hand, and in science and scientific method on the other, and then give them the freedom and support they need to chart a bold course through a challenging terrain.

Notes

[1] I would like to acknowledge the crucial help of Dr. Muzaffar Iqbal. Any merit this paper has is due to the ruthless, but entirely justified, criticism he offered on an earlier draft.

[2] In this paper, "religion" stands for theistic religion – the three great theistic religions being Judaism, Christianity, and Islam. At times, "religion" will include or imply theology. Cf. John Haught, *Science and Religion: From Conflict to Conversation* (New York and New Jersey: Paulist Press, 1995), 4-5.

[3] Ibid., 5. "For although there are obvious differences among the Abrahamic faiths, today they all have to face the same question together: is modern science compatible with what they call 'God'? Put otherwise, can the concerned, creative, salvific deity depicted in their scriptures and theologies survive the challenges of modern science?"

[4] In numerous other verses, the Qur'ān says that the kingdom of God extends over the heavens and the earth, implying – and in several other verses stating – that such natural phenomena as the wind and the rain are products of the operation of a system that gives evidence of the integration of various sectors of the physical world. To this physical order, furthermore, there is a moral analogue, which is described in terms of the *sunna*, "law", of God (e.g., 17:17).

[5] I realize that the use of the phrase "Christian writers" can be problematic. I will use the designation to mean those who express in their works some kind of commitment to the Christian theistic worldview.

[6] The analogy cannot, of course, be pressed too far. The thrust of the analogy is the perception of a unity of Christian-Muslim causes, not the taking of the Sasanians – or of science – as a common foe!

[7] W.R. Inge, "Untitled", in British Broadcasting Corporation, *Science and Religion* (New York: Books for Libraries, 1931; reprint, 1969), 143.

[8] Some modern Buddhist writers, likewise, invoke science to prove the validity of an atheistic worldview.

[9] Ted Peters, "Science and Theology: Toward Consonance", in Ted Peters, ed., *Science and Theology: The New Consonance* (Boulder: Westview, 1998), 15.

[10] Ibid., 13. Peters distinguishes between scientism from scientific imperialism. Whereas, "[i]n the warfare between science and theology, scientism demands elimination of the enemy, scientific materialism seeks to conquer the territory formally possessed by theology and claim it as its own. Whereas scientism is atheistic, scientific imperialism affirms the existence of something divine but claims knowledge of the divine comes from scientific research rather than religious revelation" (13–14). Notwithstanding scientism's dismissive, and scientific materialism's patronizing, attitude toward religion, the two views – one baring its tooth and claw, the other sporting kid gloves – are essentially similar. Cf., John Haught, who stresses that scientism is a philosophical belief: Scientism is "the *belief* [Haught's emphasis] that science is the only reliable guide to truth"(*Science and Religion*, 16). The term "scientism" is fairly old. John Wellmuth in his 1944 Aquinas Lecture, published as *The Nature and Origins of Scientism*, defines scientism as "meaning the belief that science, in the modern sense of that term, and the scientific method as described by modern scientists, afford the only reliable natural means of acquiring such knowledge as may be available about whatever is real" (1–2). He lists three characteristics of scientism: "the fields of the various sciences ... are taken to be coextensive, at least in principle, with the entire field of available knowledge" (2); "the scientific method ... is the only reliable method of widening and deepening of our knowledge ..." (3); philosophy should either adopt scientific method or integrate the other sciences on the basis of the findings of those sciences, "after having rid itself of outworn metaphysical notions" (4–5); John Wellmuth, *The Nature and Origins of Scientism* (Milwaukee: Marquette University Press, 1944).

[11] Wolfgang Smith, *Cosmos and Transcendence: Breaking Through the Barrier of Scientistic Belief* (Peru, Illinois: Sherwood Sugden, 1984), 9-10.

[12] For example, see Richard Lewontin, *Biology as Ideology: The Doctrine of DNA* (New York: HarperPerennial, 1991). Lewontin shows how science can be used for purposes of legitimation. In fact, science has "replace[d] religion as the chief legitimating force in modern society" (8). Citing the human genome sequencing project as an example, Lewontin delivers the damning verdict that many scientists' evaluations of the project are determined by the opportunities they have of benefiting from it financially. The project is "a multibillion dollar program of American and European biologists that is meant to take the place of space programs as the current great consumer of public money in the interest of conquering nature" (46); the project, with all its erroneous assumptions, is popular with many scientists

because it has "straightforward economic and status rewards" (51); "the human genome sequencing project is big business" (52; for more details, see Chapter 4, "The Dream of the Human Genome"). After citing another example, that of the hybrid corn (53 ff.), Lewontin concludes: "what appears to us in the mystical guise of pure science and objective knowledge about nature turns out, underneath, to be political, economic, and social ideology".

[13] "To mention Science and Religion in the same sentence is, as we are all well aware, to affirm an antithesis and suggest a conflict." Charles Raven, *Science, Religion, and the Future* (Cambridge: Cambridge University Press and New York: Macmillan, 1944), 1.

[14] Albert Einsten, *Ideas and Opinions*, ed. Carl Seelig and trans. Sonja Bargmann (New York: Crown, 1952; reprint, 1984), 49. It is true that Einstein believes that religion and science can be reconciled – he famously remarked that "science without religion is lame, religion without science is blind" (55). But, in his view, true religion is no more than a "cosmic religious feeling" (47), "which knows no dogma and no God conceived in man's image" (48; cf., 59). He holds that science and religion have distinct realms of operation – science supplying knowledge of the objective world and religion furnishing ideals and values (51, 54). But it is not clear how a stripped-down Einsteinian version of religion – i.e., how "religious feeling [that] takes the form of a rapturous amazement at the harmony of natural law" (50) – can serve as a source of ideals and values.

[15] Raven, 24. Raven comments similarly on two of the well-known 19th century books on the conflict between science and Christianity – John William Draper's *History of the Conflict Between Religion and Science* and Andrew Dickson White's *A History of the Warfare of Science with Theology in Christendom*. These books, Raven says, "can hardly claim to be impartial, and in fact read back the struggle of [the] last century into earlier times" (11, n. 1).

[16] Frederick Copleston, *A History of Philosophy*, 9 vols. (New York: Image/Doubleday, 1962-1977), 3:262.

[17] William R. Shea, "Galileo and the Church", in David C. Lindberg and Ronald L. Numbers, eds., *God and Nature* (Berkeley: University of California Press, 1986), 114.

[18] Ibid., 132.

[19] Ibid., 127-128.

[20] Ibid., 132. It is not irrelevant to note that Galileo's *Dialogue on the Two Chief World Systems* was taken off the Index of Proscribed Books in 1832 (ibid., 133).

[21] Edward Grant, "Science and Theology in the Middle Ages", in David C. Lindberg and Ronald L. Numbers, *God and Nature*, 49.

[22] Cf., ibid., 63 and elsewhere.

[23] As Raven says: "[T]he early scientists, whether in Europe generally or in this country [Britain], were Christians and in many cases clergy; they proclaimed that the study of nature was in itself a religious duty; and they challenged the old system of belief

and education because it was concerned with dry-as-dust conventionalities instead of with the manifold and fascinating works of the living God. ... Men turned to the study of science not as rebels against Christianity but as dedicating themselves to a new and more plainly Christian crusade". *Science, Religion, and the Future*, 24-25.

[24] Maintaining that "the Church has a magnificent record in the realm of scientific achievement", Arnold Lunn cites the names of a few "eminent Catholic scientists" – Copernicus, Pope Gregory, Galvani, Ampère, Volta, Coulomb, Mendel, Pasteur, Röntgen, and Marconi – and adds: "Modern astronomy is Copernican, our calendar is Gregorian; iron is galvanised; electricity is measured by amps, volts, and coulombs; cattle breeding is conducted on Mendelian principles; milk is pasteurised; scientists make use of the Röntgen rays for their experiments; and Marconi has provided scientists with the chance of informing hundreds of thousands of unseen listeners that the Church to which the inventor of this medium of communication belongs is an enemy of science". Arnold Lunn, *The Revolt Against Reason* (London: Sheed and Ward, 1951), 214. Cf.: "More than a dozen Jesuits have their names printed on the map of the moon" (215). Cf., Arthur Peacocke, *Science and the Christian Experiment* (London: Oxford University Press, 1971), 11: "Indeed, it is likely that the proportion of practicing, convinced Christians among scientists is no less, and, to my observation, possibly larger than in the population as a whole".

[25] Ian Barbour, *Religion and Science: Historical and Contemporary Issues* (San Francisco: HarperSanFrancisco, 1997), 77.

[26] Cf., Haught, 19-20: "Science no longer appears quite so pure and objective as we used to think, nor theology so impure and subjective. Both science and theology generate imaginative metaphors and theories to interpret certain kinds of 'data', but in neither case is it always clear just where metaphor or theory leaves off and 'fact' begins. Indeed the consensus of philosophers today is that there are no uninterpreted facts. And so we are now more aware than ever before that in both science and theology there is an aspect of human 'construction' which we previously failed to notice". See also note 27.

[27] Peacocke cites historical instances of the role of the imagination in making major scientific discoveries possible: "as, for example, Kekulé's half-dreaming of the ring form of benzene, Darwin's reading of Malthus and joining this with the *idea* of natural selection to provide the key to understanding evolution, and Watson and Crick's realization that DNA is a double helix" (17). Author Peacocke, *Science and the Christian Experiment* (London: Oxford University Press, 1971). In Thomas Torrance, *Christian Theology and Scientific Culture* (New York: Oxford University Press, 1981), Torrence talks about the priority of belief in scientific work. Discussing the work of James Clerk Maxwell (1831-1879), the Scottish physicist who propounded the electromagnetic theory, he observes that Maxwell's "idea of the relational character of the real world and of the need for relational thinking was not derived from his scientific reasoning but was brought to bear upon his scientific reasoning from a

prior stock of theological and metaphysical convictions which had come to exercise a regulative role in his outlook upon the universe" (50). And: "The regulative role of fundamental belief and intuitive insight also characterised the scientific outlook and thought of Albert Einstein" (56). Torrance also cites the work of the Oxford scientist and social theorist Michael Polanyi on "the priority of belief in rational knowledge" (62); "Polanyi went beyond Maxwell and Einstein in showing that there can be no knowledge even of material realities apart from the personal activity of a knower and demanding that this personal factor in scientific inquiry be brought out into the open and be given its due place in the philosophy of science" (62). For a convenient introduction to Polanyi's thought, see Michael Polanyi, *The Study of Man: The Lindsay Memorial Lectures given at the University College of North Staffordshire, 1958* (Chicago: University of Chicago Press, 1959).

[28] Peacocke, *Science and the Christian Experiment*, 12 ff.

[29] Introduction to A.R. Peacocke (ed.), *The Sciences and Theology in the Twentieth Century* (Notre Dame: University of Notre Dame Press, 1981), xiii–xiv.

[30] See the concluding paragraph of the present section.

[31] John Haught, in Chapter 1 of *Science and Religion*, offers a four-fold scheme for studying issues in religion and science. He discusses a number of issues, each under the following heads: conflict, contrast, contact, and confirmation. Ian Barbour, in *Religion and Science*, uses a similar scheme; his categories are: conflict, independence, dialogue, and integration.

[32] The attempts made by certain medieval Muslim philosophers to promote this fourth view did not ultimately succeed, and are not likely to succeed today either.

[33] Cf., part III ("Religion and the Theories of Science") of Ian Barbour, *Issues in Science and Religion* (Englewood Cliffs, New Jersey: Prentice-Hall, 1966).

[34] Robert John Russell, "Does the 'God Who Acts' Really Act in Nature?," in Ted Peters (ed.), *Science and Theology*, 83.

[35] Ibid.

[36] Ibid., 85-86.

[37] Ibid., 94.

[38] Donald M. MacKay, *Science, Chance, and Providence* (New York: Oxford University Press, 1978), 52.

[39] Ibid., 54-55.

[40] MacKay illustrates this further by offering and discussing a modified version of Newcomb's Paradox (Ibid., 55-60). Perhaps a simpler example will explain the point. Suppose you have a house to rent, but it remains vacant for three months, causing you a financial loss of $3,000. Suppose, further, that during these three months you are invited to give three lectures, each of which earns you $1,000. You could interpret the situation in one of several ways: (1) That you have suffered a loss of $3,000, for you were set to receive the money from the talks anyway; or (2) that your gain of $3,000 from the lectures has been cancelled out by the loss of $3,000

in unearned rent – that it was an accident that you made the gain, and another accident that you incurred the loss; or (3) that your earning of $3,000 from the speeches was somehow *causally* connected with your loss of $3,000, such that you could not have earned the $3,000 from the speeches had you not lost $3,000 on the unrented house – or vice versa. MacKay would seem to favor the third interpretation.

[41] Ibid., 55.

[42] Peters, *Science and Theology*, 1 ff.

[43] Ibid., 2. This method, as Robert Russell aptly remarks, is "rooted in the ancient formula *fides quaerens intellectum*, which we take to be in an implicit dialectical relation to its converse formula, *intellectum quaerens fides*" (Peters, *Science and Theology*, 89).

Chapter 5

The Anthropocosmic Vision in Islamic Thought

William C. Chittick

I take the expression "anthropocosmic vision" from Tu Weiming, Director of the Harvard-Yenching Institute, and Professor of Chinese History and Philosophy and Confucian Studies at Harvard University. Professor Tu has used this expression for many years to encapsulate the East Asian worldview and to stress its salient differences with the theocentric and anthropocentric worldviews of the West.[1] By saying that the Chinese traditions in general and Confucianism in particular see things "anthropocosmically", he means that Chinese thinkers and sages have understood human beings and the cosmos as a single, organismic whole. The goal of human life is to harmonize oneself with heaven and earth and to return to the transcendent source of both humans and the world. As long as Chinese civilization remained true to itself, it could never develop "instrumental rationality", the Western Enlightenment view that sees the world as a conglomeration of objects and considers knowledge as a means to manipulate and control the objects. In the anthropocosmic vision, the world as object cannot be disjoined from the human as subject. The purpose of knowledge is not to manipulate the world but to understand the world and ourselves so that we can live up to the fullness of our humanity. The aim, to use one of Tu Weiming's favorite phrases, is "to learn how to be human". As he writes, "[t]he Way is nothing other than the actualization of true human nature".[2]

With slight revisions in terminology, Tu Weiming's depiction of the Confucian anthropocosmic vision could easily be employed to describe the overarching worldview of Islamic civilization in general and Islamic thought in particular.[3] By "Islamic thought" I do not mean the many scholarly disciplines that developed in the Islamic world, but rather those specific schools that asked and answered the deepest human questions about ultimacy and meaning. These are the questions that great thinkers, philosophers, and sages have addressed in all civilizations. Specifically, I have in mind the Islamic wisdom tradition. I understand the word "wisdom" in the broad sense of the Arabic word ḥikmah, which embraces both Hellenized philosophy and various other perspectives, in particular theoretical Sufism (what is often called ʿirfān or "gnosis"). As I understand it, ḥikmah excludes the juridical tradition (fiqh) and much of Kalam (dogmatic theology), both of which focus on narrower issues.

For the purposes of this chapter, I will focus on the more philosophical side of the wisdom tradition, ignoring the Sufi dimensions, to which I have devoted a great deal of attention elsewhere. I do so for two reasons. First, among all the Islamic approaches to knowledge, this discipline alone has produced figures who have been looked upon by Western historians and modern-day Muslims as "scientists" in something like the current meaning of the word. And second, only this approach has discussed the significance of being and becoming without presupposing faith in Islamic dogma, so its language can more easily be understood outside the context of specifically Islamic imagery.

In the technical terminology of the Islamic sciences, the wisdom tradition is commonly classified as "intellectual" (ʿaqlī) rather than "transmitted" (naqlī). Transmitted learning is all knowledge that has been passed down from previous generations and that cannot be gained by the human mind functioning on its own. Typical examples are language, divine revelation, and law. "Intellectual" learning is all knowledge that can, in principle, be acquired by the human mind without help from past generations or divine revelation. Salient examples are mathematics and astronomy. However, intellectual learning also includes what can be called "metaphysics", "cosmology", and "psychology". It is these three domains that are most explicitly informed by the anthropocosmic vision about which I wish to speak. It is obvious, however, that I will be speaking in general terms; there are many significant variations on the main themes, even within the philosophical tradition itself.

Universal and Eternal Truth

In Western civilization, it has been common to draw a sharp distinction between reason and revelation, or between Athens and Jerusalem. In order to understand the role that the "intellectual" sciences have played in the Islamic tradition, it needs to be understood that the predominant Islamic perspective sees reason and revelation as harmonious and complementary, not antagonistic. The very content of the Qur'ānic message led to a viewpoint that diverges sharply from what became normative in the Christian West. Without understanding the divergence of viewpoint, it will be difficult to grasp the role that the wisdom tradition has played in Islam.

If Christianity is considered in terms of the dichotomy between intellectual and transmitted knowledge, what immediately strikes the eye is that the first truths are indebted to transmission, not intellection. The defining notion of the Christian worldview – to the extent that it is meaningful to generalize about a diverse tradition – is the incarnation, a historical event that is known to have occurred on the basis of transmitted knowledge. To be sure, the incarnation was seen as a divine intervention that transmuted history, but it was also understood as occurring in the full light of historical actuality. In order to know about it, people needed the transmission of knowledge within history. Once the incarnation was acknowledged, it becomes possible to see how it is prefigured in the unity of God, through the logos and the trinity. Even though a whole tradition of thinking developed that can be called "Christian Platonism", a tradition that began with ideas in the divine Mind, the specifically Christian content of this tradition depended upon the historical fact of the incarnation.

The Islamic tradition has a very different starting point. It is often assumed by both Muslims and non-Muslims that Islam began with the historical event of Muhammad and the Qur'ān. Of course, there is some truth in this, but this is not the way the Qur'ān presents the picture, nor is it the way more reflective Muslims have understood their religion. Rather, Islam began with the creation of the world. In its broadest Qur'ānic meaning, the word islām ("submission, submittedness, surrender") designates the universal and ever-present situation of creatures in face of the Creator.[4] This helps explain why the first and fundamental dogma of the religion has nothing to do with the historical facts of Muhammad and the Qur'ān. It is simply the acknowledgment of a universal truth, a truth that expresses the nature of things for all time and all eternity.[5]

This primary truth upon which the Islamic tradition is built is stated most succinctly in the first half of the Shahadah, the assertion of faith that is the basis for all Islamic teaching and practice. This assertion, lā ilāha illa'llāh – "(There is) no god but God" – is known as kalimat al-tawḥīd, "the word that declares unity". It is understood as a declaration of the actual situation of all things, since everything submits to God's Unity by the very fact of its existence. Among all creatures, only human beings have the peculiar status of being able to accept or reject this truth. To accept it freely is to utter the first half of the Shahadah and thereby give witness to the unique reality of God. The Qur'ān attributes tawḥīd, this acknowledgment of God's unity, and the free acceptance of its consequences to all rightly guided human beings, the first of whom was Adam. Included here are all the prophets – who are traditionally said to number 124,000 – and all those who correctly and sincerely followed them.[6]

In the Islamic perspective, tawḥīd stands outside history and outside transmission. It is a universal truth that does not depend upon revelation. So basic is the recognition of this truth to the human situation that it is typically said to be an inherent quality of the original disposition (fiṭrah) of Adam and all his children. Remember here that in the Islamic view, the fall from the Garden does not represent a serious shortcoming. Rather, it signifies a temporary lapse, a single act of forgetfulness and disobedience. The lapse had repercussions to be sure, but it was immediately forgiven by God, and Adam was designated as the first prophet. God had created Adam in his own image, and this image was in no way blemished by the fall, even if the divine image does indeed become obscured in many if not most of Adam's children.[7]

As for the historical tradition of Islam, that began in the 7th century with the revelation of the Qur'ān, the testimony of faith does not acknowledge the importance of this tradition until its second half, the statement "Muhammad is the messenger of God". Tawḥīd precedes Muhammad and his revealed message, because it does not pertain to history. Rather, it pertains to the nature of reality and the substance of human intelligence.

In this perspective, tawḥīd informs all true knowledge in all times and all places. Every one of the 124,000 prophets came with a message based upon tawḥīd, and each of them taught it explicitly. However, they did not teach it because people could not know it without being told. They taught it because people had forgotten it and needed to be "reminded". The Arabic word used here, dhikr (along with its derivatives tadhkīr, tadhkirah, and dhikrā) designates one of the most important concepts in the Qur'ān. It informs Islamic religiosity on every level of faith and practice. The word means not only "to remind", but also "to remember". In the sense of reminder, it indicates the primary function of the prophets, and in the sense of remembrance it designates the proper human response to the prophetic reminder. The whole process of "learning how to be human" depends first upon being reminded of tawḥīd, and second upon the active and free remembrance of tawḥīd, the acknowledgment that asserting God's unity is innate to the human soul.

In short, tawḥīd, the foundational teaching of Islam, stands outside history because it is woven into the deepest nature of every human being. With rare exceptions, however, coming to understand it will depend upon being reminded of it by someone who knows it. Once it is understood, it is recognized as self-evident and without any essential connection with historical revelation. The Islamic doctrine that Adam was the first prophet suggests in mythic form the idea that to be human is to have present within oneself, as a direct consequence of being created in the image of God, the recognition of God's unity.

Given that the Islamic testimony of faith differentiates between a universal, ahistorical truth and a particular, historically conditioned truth, it already distinguishes implicitly between knowledge that is intellectual and knowledge that is transmitted. The first half of the Shahadah declares tawḥīd, a knowledge innate to the original human disposition and free of historical particularity. The second half of the Shahadah designates the specific, historical fact of the coming of Muhammad and the revelation of the Qur'ān. This second knowledge cannot be gained without historical transmission.

Although intellectual knowledge is implicitly differentiated from transmitted knowledge in the first principles of the religion and explicitly differentiated by the later tradition, this does not mean that the two sorts of knowledge can be considered independent. It is obvious that all understanding depends upon transmission, if only the transmission of language. And it is also obvious that transmission alone is no guarantee of understanding. The relationship between the two modalities of knowing can perhaps best be understood as complementary, in something like the yin-yang manner. Transmission is needed to actualize understanding, and understanding is needed to grasp the full significance of transmission.[8]

Transmitted Knowledge and Intellectual Learning

Among all the schools of Islamic thinking, the philosophers were the most careful to distinguish between transmitted and intellectual learning. They themselves were not primarily interested in transmitted knowledge. Compared to Kalam and jurisprudence, or to the other intellectual approach to Islamic learning, that is, theoretical Sufism, the philosophers paid relatively little attention to the Qur'ān, Hadith, and the religious sciences. This is not to deny that most of them were well versed in these sciences, or that some of them even wrote Qur'ānic commentaries and juridical works. Despite the suggestions of some historians, they were not hostile to the transmitted learning. Rather, they focused their primary attention elsewhere. They wanted to develop their own intellectual vision, and they saw this as the task of working out all the implications of tawḥīd, first in theory and then in practice.[9] If they were to understand the full significance of the transmitted knowledge, they needed to investigate the nature of the Ultimate Reality, the structure of the cosmos, and the reality of the human soul. These are the three domains of metaphysics, cosmology, and psychology mentioned earlier. However, in the quest for understanding, tawḥīd was always the underlying axiom. The philosophers took it for granted that anyone with a healthy mind would see the unity of God as a self-evident truth. Even so, they provided numerous proofs to help human intelligence remember what is latent within itself.

My basic point here is that Muslim "intellectuals" – in the specific sense of the term *intellectual* that I have in view – always saw themselves as investigating things in the context of the most fundamental declaration of the Islamic tradition, which is the unity of God, the Ultimate Reality that rules all things. They never saw their efforts as opposed to the goals and purposes of the religious tradition. They accepted that the prophets came to remind people of tawḥīd and to teach them how to be human. However, they also believed that the commoners had one path to follow, and those drawn to intellectual pursuits had another path, because of their specific gifts and aptitudes.

In the view of all branches of the wisdom tradition, seekers of intellectual knowledge were trying to learn how to be human in the fullest sense of the word *human*. Their primary focus was always on the transformation of the soul. As Tu Weiming says of the Confucian anthropocosmic vision, "The transformative act is predicated on a transcendent vision that ontologically we are infinitely better and therefore more worthy than we actually are".[10] This is a "humanistic" vision, but the humanism is elevated far beyond the mundane, because the "measure of man" is not man or even rational understanding, but rather the transcendent source of all. As Tu puts it:

> Since the value of the human is not anthropocentric, the assertion that man is the measure of all things is not humanistic enough. To fully express our humanity, we must engage in a dialogue with Heaven because human nature, as conferred by Heaven, realizes its nature not by departing from its source but by returning to it. Humanity, so conceived, is the public property of the cosmos, not the private possession of the anthropological world, and is as much the defining characteristic of our being as the self-conscious manifestation of Heaven. Humanity is Heaven's form of self-disclosure, self-expression, and self-realization. If we fail to live up to our humanity, we fail cosmologically in our mission as co-creator of Heaven and Earth and morally in our duty as fellow participants in the great cosmic transformation.[11]

For the Islamic wisdom tradition, grasping the full nature of our humanity necessitates investigating the nature of things and the reality of our own selves. This means that intellectuals could not limit themselves to the mere acceptance of transmitted learning. They could not ignore the human imperative to search for knowledge in every domain, especially not when the Qur'ān explicitly commands the study of the universe and the self as the means to know God. Although some philosophers paid relatively little attention to the transmitted learning and had no patience with the quibbling of the dogmatic theologians, they did not step outside of the Islamic tradition, because they could not doubt the universal and ahistorical axiom upon which it is built. In other words, there was no historical chink in their intellectual armor. Historical contingencies cannot touch tawḥīd, because, once it is grasped, it is seen as a self-evident truth so foundational that it becomes the unique certainty upon which the soul can depend.[12]

As for the theologians and jurists and their claims to authority in all religious matters, the representatives of the wisdom tradition saw their positions as pertaining to transmitted learning, not to intellectual learning, and they found no reason to submit themselves to the limited understandings of pious dogmatists. To a large degree they kept themselves apart from theological and juridical bickering, and this helps explain why the philosophers among them (in contrast to the Sufis) preferred to employ a language colored more by Greek models than the imagery and symbols of the Qur'ān.

Instrumental Rationality vs. Dogmatic Givens

Once we recognize that Islamic "intellectual" learning stands aloof from transmitted learning, we can begin to understand why the modern scientific enterprise could never have arisen in Islam. Science gains its power from the rejection of any sort of teleology, the brute separation of subject and object, the refusal to admit that consciousness and awareness are more real than material facts, the exclusive concern with the domain of the senses, and the disregard for the ultimate and the transcendent. The instrumental rationality of scientific knowledge could appear in the West only after the baby had been thrown out with the bath water. Having rejected the bath water of theology – or at least the relevance of theological dogma to scientific concerns – Western philosophers and scientists also rejected the truth of tawḥīd, the bedrock of human intelligence. Once tawḥīd was a dead letter, each domain of learning could be considered as independent from the others.

Instrumental rationality did not appear suddenly in the West, of course. A long and complex history gradually brought about an ever more severe separation between the domain of reason and that of revelation. Many scientists and philosophers remained practicing Christians, but this did not prevent them from coming to consider the rational domain as free from the trammels of revelational givens. It is precisely because these givens were posed in the dogmatic and historical terms of transmitted learning that the separation between reason and revelation could occur. In contrast, the Islamic intellectual tradition was always rooted in the vision of tawḥīd, never in historically conditioned theological dogma. No matter what sort of misgivings certain Muslim thinkers may have entertained about the historical contingency of the Arabic language, the events surrounding the coming of Muhammad, the transmission of the Qur'ānic revelation, and the interpretation of the revelation by the theologians and dogmatists, these misgivings could not impinge on the fundamental insight of tawḥīd, which to them was utterly transparent.

My first conclusion, then, is this: Many historians have suggested that medieval Islamic learning declined when Muslim scientists neglected to build on their early discoveries. But this is to read Islamic history in terms of the ideology of progress, which in turn is rooted in contemporary scientism – by which I mean the belief that science has the same sort of unique reliability that was once reserved for revealed truth. Scientism gives absolute importance to scientific theories and relativizes all other approaches to knowledge, if it considers them in any way legitimate.

Moreover, historians who talk in broad terms of the decline of Islamic "science" ignore two historical contexts.[13] The first is the Islamic, in which the axiom of tawḥīd infused all intellectual endeavor. Tawḥīd declares the interrelatedness of all things, because it asserts that everything comes from the First Principle, everything is constantly sustained and nourished by the First Principle, and everything returns to the First Principle. Given that Muslim intellectuals saw all things as beginning, flourishing, and ending within the compass of the One Source, they could not split up the domains of reality in any more than a tentative way. They were not able to disengage knowledge of the cosmos from knowledge of God or from knowledge of the human soul. It was impossible for them to imagine the world and the self as separate from each other and from the One Principle. Quite the contrary, the more they investigated the universe, the more they saw it as manifesting the principles of tawḥīd and the nature of the human self. They could not have agreed more with Tu Weiming, who writes, "To see nature as an external object out there is to create an artificial barrier which obstructs our true vision and undermines our human capacity to experience nature from within".[14]

The second context that people ignore when they claim that the Muslim intellectual tradition declined is the Christian. Christian civilization, qua *Christian* civilization, did in fact decline, because it experienced the breakdown of a synthetic worldview and the eclipse of Christian Platonism. One could easily argue that its decline has been far more serious than that of Islamic civilization. Part of the reason for its decline and the concurrent rise of a secular and scientistic worldview was that the transmitted nature of the basic religious givens was not able to withstand the critical questioning of non-dogmatic thinkers. In the Islamic case, the Muslim intellectuals did not depend on revelation and transmission for their understanding of tawḥīd, so theological squabbles and historical uncertainties could not be taken as impinging upon the basic vision of reality.

To forestall misunderstanding, perhaps I need to insist here that I do wish to imply that the Muslim philosophers rejected Muhammad as their prophet and the Qur'ān as their book of guidance. Generally speaking, they saw no reason to question the dogmatic basis of the transmitted knowledge, because they considered religious teachings to be beneficial for everyone, and certainly so for the masses. However, wisdom – true intellectual learning – was by its nature reserved for the qualified, who are few and far between. This "undemocratic" and "elitist" position goes back to the fact that political ideology does not color their view of social reality. They took human beings as they were, not as they wished them to be.

Scientific Verification vs. Theological Verification

In order to suggest some of the implications of the anthropocosmic vision, I need to expand on the distinction between intellectual and transmitted. The ulama, by whom I mean the experts in transmitted learning, claimed authority for their knowledge by upholding the authenticity of the transmission and the truthfulness of those who provided the knowledge – that is, God, Muhammad, and the pious forebears. They asked all Muslims to accept this knowledge as it was received. The basic duty of the Muslim believer was taqlīd, that is, "imitation", or submission to the authority of the transmitted knowledge. In contrast, the intellectual tradition appealed to the relatively small number of people who had the appropriate aptitudes. The quest for knowledge was defined not in terms of taqlīd or "imitation" but in terms of taḥqīq, "verification" and "realization".

It is important here not to confuse taḥqīq with ijtihād. Both these words are used as opposites of taqlīd. However, taḥqīq pertains to the intellectual sciences, and it means to find the truth and reality of all things by oneself and in oneself. Ijtihād is employed in reference to the transmitted sciences, specifically fiqh or jurisprudence. Ijtihād is to gain such a mastery of the Shariah that one does not need to follow the opinions (taqlīd) of earlier jurists. For centuries, many legal experts have considered "the gate of ijtihād" to be closed. But the "gate of taḥqīq" can never be closed, because it is mandatory for all Muslims to understand God and the other articles of faith for themselves. "Faith in God" by imitation is no faith at all.

An important key to understanding the different standpoints of modern science and the Islamic intellectual tradition lies in these two concepts – taḥqīq and taqlīd. Unless we understand that knowledge attained by verification and realization is not of the same sort as that received by imitation, we will not be able to understand what the Muslim intellectuals were trying to do and what modern scientists and scholars are trying to do. We will then continue to falsify the position of the Muslim philosophers by making them precursors of modern science, as if they were trying to discover what modern scientists try to discover, and as if they accepted the findings of their predecessors on the basis of imitation, as modern scientists do.

Given that *scientism* – belief in the unique reliability of scientific, empirical knowledge – infuses modern culture, it is difficult for moderns to remember that the whole scientific edifice is built on transmitted learning. Despite all the talk of the "empirical verification" of scientific findings, this verification depends on assumptions about the nature of reality that cannot be verified by empirical methods. Even if we accept for a moment the scientistic proposition that scientific knowledge is uniquely "objective", it is in fact verifiable only by a handful of specialists, since the rest of the human race does not have the necessary training. In effect, everyone has to accept empirical verification on the basis of faith (taqlīd).

The tiny amount of verification that any individual scientist might be able to accomplish follows the scientific method, which is to say that it is based on instrumental rationality. The experiments show that, given certain conditions and certain goals, *y* will follow from *x*. There is no question of discovering the ultimate truth of things because the means are inadequate, and no scientist, qua scientist, can claim that the means are adequate. If he or she does claim that they are adequate, he or she does so as a believer in scientism or as a philosopher, not as scientist. It is in terms of scientism, not science, that people declare that there is no such thing as "the soul" or "absolute reality". Neither science nor scientism would dream of acknowledging what appeared as a simple fact to the wisdom traditions in all pre-modern civilizations: Human possibility transcends time, space, history, physicality, energy, ideation, the angels, and even the gods (though certainly not "God" in the proper meaning of the word).

To come back to the quest for the issue of taḥqīq or verification/ realization, we need to remember that the Arabic expression derives from the word ḥaqq. Ḥaqq is both a verbal noun and an adjective meaning true, truth, to be true; and, with similar permutations, real, right, proper, just, and appropriate. The word plays an important role in the Qur'ān and in all branches of Islamic learning. Its first Qur'ānic meaning is as a name of God. God as ḥaqq is absolute truth, rightness, reality, properness, justness, and appropriateness.

Taḥqīq is a transitive and intensive verbal form derived from ḥaqq. It means to ascertain the truth, the right, the real, the proper. Ascertainment is to know something for certain. The only place where certainty can be found is within the human self, not outside of it. Taḥqīq is to understand and actualize truth, reality, and rightness within oneself, to "realize" it and to make it actual for oneself and in oneself.

If the word ḥaqq is applied to God, this is because God is the absolutely true, right, real, and proper. But it is also applied to everything other than God. This secondary application of the word acknowledges that everything in the universe has a truth, a rightness, a realness, and an appropriateness. If God is ḥaqq in the absolute sense, everything other than God is ḥaqq in a relative sense. The task of taḥqīq is to build on the knowledge of the absolute ḥaqq, beginning with the axiom of tawḥīd, and to grasp the exact nature of the relative ḥaqq that pertains to each thing, or at least to each thing with which we come into contact, whether spiritually, intellectually, psychologically, physically, or socially.

The formula of tawḥīd can help us to understand the goal of taḥqīq. If "There is no god but God", this means, "There is no ḥaqq but the absolute ḥaqq". The only true and real ḥaqq is God himself. This Ḥaqq is transcendent, infinite, and eternal. In face of it, there is no other ḥaqq. At the same time, all things are God's creatures, and they receive what they have from God. God creates them with wisdom and purpose, and each has a role to play in the universe. Nothing that exists is inherently bāṭil – the opposite of ḥaqq, that is, false, vain, unreal, inappropriate.[15] The ḥaqqs of the individual things are determined by God's wisdom in creation. It is in respect to these individual ḥaqqs that the Prophet commanded people "to give to each that has a ḥaqq its ḥaqq" (ītā' kull dhī ḥaqq ḥaqqahu). "Giving each thing its ḥaqq" is often taken as a nutshell definition of taḥqīq.

To give things their ḥaqqs is obviously more than a simple cognitive activity. We cannot give things their rightful due simply by knowing their truth and reality. Over and above knowing, taḥqīq demands acting. It is not simply to verify the truth and reality of a thing; it is also to act toward that thing in the appropriate and rightful manner. The intellectual tradition always considered morality and ethics as an integral part of the quest for wisdom, and many of its representatives made a conscious effort to synthesize Greek ethical teachings and the moral and practical teachings of the Qur'ān.

The task of the seeker of wisdom, then, was to verify and realize things. This could not be done by quoting the opinions of Aristotle or Plato, or even by citing the words of the Qur'ān and Muhammad. One verified and realized things by knowing them as they truly are and by acting appropriately. More than anything else, the intellectual quest was a rigorous path of self-discipline, and the goal was to achieve true knowledge of self and appropriate activity on the basis of this knowledge. Nothing encapsulates the spirit of the quest as well as the famous maxim attributed to the Prophet, "He who knows himself knows his Lord". Historians have considered this statement to be an Islamic version of the Socratic maxim, "Know thyself". Certainly, the fact that this version of the maxim links knowledge of self with knowledge of God is indicative of the primary importance that is always given to tawḥīd.

It should be obvious to everyone that one cannot know oneself and one's Lord by memorizing the opinions of Avicenna. One can surely take the prophets and the great philosophers as guides on the path to self-knowledge, but one cannot claim to know what they knew unless one discovers it for oneself and in oneself. The quest for wisdom was an intensely personal activity, a spiritual discipline that demanded the training of one's mind and the honing of one's soul. To verify and realize things was to achieve an authentic vision of reality, a correct perception of the world, a sound understanding of the self, and a true knowledge of the First Principle. At the same time, it was to act in keeping with what one had come to know. It demanded an ethical vision and virtuous activity.

Soul, Cosmos, God

In order to grasp the purpose of taḥqīq, it is useful to reflect on how
the philosophers understood the word ʿaql, the noun that gives us the
adjective form ʿaqlī – which I have been translating as "intellectual".
ʿAql means intellect, intelligence, reason, mind, *nous*. To understand
what is meant by the word, we need to review a few of the basic
teachings of the intellectual tradition. These teachings provide pointers
toward the knowledge that Muslim intellectuals were trying to verify
and realize. The teachings should not be taken as dogma, because no
one can realize anything by memorizing catechisms. One has to find
out for oneself.

The underlying substance of a human being is called nafs, a
word that functions as the most important reflexive pronoun in the
Arabic language. Nafs is typically translated as both "self" and "soul".
In its philosophical sense, it designates the invisible something that
makes its appearance in the cosmos wherever there is life, and hence
it can be ascribed to any living thing.

Verifying the nature of soul was one of the foundational
activities of the Muslim intellectual. A standard way to do so was to
begin by investigating the apparitions of soul in the visible world. The
visible realm is a conglomeration of bodily appearances, yet we
instinctively differentiate among things in terms of their modality of
appearance. We know the difference between living things and dead
things precisely by their appearance. "Soul" is a generic name for the
invisible power that shows itself when we recognize life and awareness.
Moreover, when we recognize soul in other things, we are
simultaneously recognizing it in ourselves. To see the apparitions of
soul in the outside world is to experience the presence of soul in the
inside world. Life and awareness are precisely the properties that we
find in ourselves in the very act of seeing them in others.

There are degrees of soul, which is to say that this invisible
power is more intense and influential in some things than in others.[16]
The classification of creatures into inanimate, plant, animal, human,

and angel is one way of acknowledging the different degrees. The most intense and at the same time the most complex and layered soul is found in human beings. Outwardly, this appears in the indefinite diversity of their activities, which clearly has something to do with vast differences in aptitude and ability. Because of the diverse and comprehensive powers of their souls, human beings can grasp and replicate all the activities that appear in the world by means of other modalities of soul.

In discussing the human soul, the texts frequently elaborate upon the intimate relationship between it and the cosmos. So similar are soul and world that they can even be considered mirror images. As two mutually reflecting images, they are often called "microcosm" and "macrocosm".

The correspondence between microcosm and macrocosm was understood as something like a subject-object relationship. The human soul is an aware subject that can take as its object the whole universe. So closely intertwined are soul and universe that, using Tu Weiming's term, their relationship can properly be called "organismic". The human soul and the world can be seen as one organism with two faces. It follows that there can be no microcosm without macrocosm, and no macrocosm without microcosm. The vital cosmic role of human beings was always affirmed. It was recognized that the macrocosm appears in the visible realm before human beings, but it was also understood that the macrocosm is brought into existence precisely to make it possible for human beings to appear and then to learn how to be human. Without human beings (or, one can guess, analogous beings), there is no reason for a universe to exist in the first place. The teleology was always acknowledged.

In the more religious language, this is to say that God created the world with the specific aim of crowning his achievement with human beings, who alone are made fully in his image and are able to function as his vicegerents (khalīfah). They alone can love God, because true love demands loving the Beloved for himself. If one loves God with the aim of receiving some gift or benefit, one has not in fact loved God, but the gift or benefit.[17] Nothing can love God for God's sake alone and without any ulterior motive except that which is made in his image. God created human beings precisely so that they could verify and realize their own divine images and love their Creator, thereby participating in his infinite and never-ending bounty.

For the intellectual tradition, the ultimate purpose of studying the macrocosm is to come to understand the powers and capabilities of the microcosm. By understanding the object, we simultaneously come to understand the capacities and potentialities of the subject. We cannot study the natural world without learning about ourselves, and we cannot learn about ourselves without coming to understand the wisdom inherent in the natural world.

Social reality was often studied for the same purpose – as an aid to understand the human soul. It was not uncommon for Muslim philosophers to provide descriptions of the ideal society. But they were not interested in the utopian dreams that have so often preoccupied modern political theorists. Rather, they wanted to understand and describe the various potentialities of the human soul that become manifest through social and political activity. They did not want to set down a program, but rather to illustrate to aspiring philosophers that every attribute and power of the soul, every beautiful and ugly character trait, can be recognized in the diversity of human types. When seekers of wisdom recognize their own selves as microcosms of society, they can strive to know and realize the true sovereign of the soul, the real philosopher-king, which is the intellect whose duty is to govern both soul and body with wisdom and compassion.

If the philosophers analyzed the souls of plants, animals, humans, and even angels, and if they described all the possibilities of human becoming in ethical and social terms, their purpose was to integrate everything in the universe into the grand, hierarchical vision of tawḥīd. It was self-evident to them that the intellect within us – the intelligent and intelligible light of the soul – is the highest and most comprehensive dimension of the human substance. The intellect alone can see, understand, verify, and realize. The intellect alone gives life, awareness, and understanding not only to our own souls, but to all souls. The intellect alone is able to grasp and realize the purpose of human life and all life.

Returning The Intellect to God

What then is this intellect that is the fountainhead and goal of intellectual learning? To define it is impossible, because it is intellect that is the very understanding that allows for definitions. It cannot be limited and confined by its own radiance. However, we can describe it in terms of its role in cosmogenesis, whereby all things are created through it. And we can also depict it in terms of the human return to God, which can be experienced in its fullness only by the actualized intellect, which is the self-aware image of God. Let me deal with cosmogenesis first.

The wisdom tradition typically discussed the birth of the cosmos beginning with God's creation or emanation of the first creature, which is given many names in the texts, such as intellect, spirit, word, pen, and light. Things appear from the One Principle in a definite, intelligible order and in keeping with a fixed and known hierarchy (known, that is, to God and the intellect, but not necessarily to us). It was obvious to Muslim thinkers that the One God creates intelligently, and that the first manifestation of his reality, the contingent being closest to his unity, the stage of created actuality nearest to his utter and absolute simplicity, is pure intelligence and awareness. Within this awareness is prefigured the universe and the human soul.

This living intelligence is the instrument with which God planned, ordered, arranged, and established all creatures, and it lies at the root of every subject and every object. It is a single reality that is the self-aware and self-conscious principle of the universe and the human soul. Among all creatures, humans alone manifest its full and pure light, a light that in Qur'ānic language is called "the spirit blown into Adam by God". The "fall" of Adam is nothing but the obscuration of this light.

When we look at the intellect from the point of view of the human return to God, we see that the goal of human existence is to remember God and to recollect our own divine images by awakening the intellect within. The task of seekers of wisdom is to recover within themselves the luminous consciousness that fills the universe. This recovery is the fruition and fulfillment of human possibility. Although the intellect is already dimly present in every soul, human or otherwise, in human beings alone is it a seed that can sprout and then be cultivated, nourished, strengthened, and fully actualized.

The human soul is a knowing and aware subject that has the capacity to take as its object the whole universe and everything within it. However, it is typically blind to its own possibilities, and it takes on the color of souls that are not fully human. The soul needs to learn how to be human, and being human does not come easy. Most of us have to be reminded by the prophets about what being human implies, and even budding "intellectuals", with all their gifts, have a steep and rocky road ahead to them if they are to achieve the goal.

The intellectual tradition held that one of the best ways to begin learning how to be human was to differentiate the qualities of the human soul from the qualities of other souls. Here we come back to a discussion of plants and animals, which represent limiting and confining possibilities of soulish existence. All the moral injunctions to overcome animal instincts rise up from the understanding that animals cannot manifest the fullness of intellectual and ontological possibility. This is not to denigrate animal qualities, since they also play important roles in the human soul. The issue is rather one of priorities. People need to put things in their proper places. They must order the world and their own goals in an intelligent manner, and this means that they must understand everything in terms of the ruling truths of the cosmos, the first of which is tawḥīd.

The soul, then, is the subjective pole of manifest reality, and its counterpart is the universe, the objective pole. The soul in its human form has the unique capacity to know all things. However, the soul is only the *potential* to know all things. It is not the actuality of knowing. Actuality is a quality of intellect. Every act of knowing actualizes the soul's potential to know and brings it closer to the intelligent and intelligible light at its core. But what exactly is the limit of the soul's potential? What can it know? What should it strive to know? The intellectual tradition answers that there is no limit to the soul's potential because nothing exists that the soul cannot know. The goal of learning is to know everything that can possibly be known. However, knowable things need to be prioritized. If we do not search for understanding in the right manner and the correct order, the goal will remain forever unattainable.

As long as the soul remains occupied with the search for wisdom and has not yet actualized its full potential, it remains a soul – that is, an aware self with the possibility of achieving greater awareness. Only when it reaches the actuality of all-knowingness in the inmost center of its being can it be called an "intellect" in the proper sense of the word. At this point it comes to know itself as it was meant to be. It recovers its true nature, and it returns to its proper place in the cosmic hierarchy. The philosophers frequently call the human soul a "potential intellect" (ʿaql bi'l-quwwah) or a "hylic intellect" (ʿaql hayūlānī), which is to say that it has the capacity to know all things. Once the soul ascends through the stages of actualizing its own awareness and achieving its own innate perfection, it is called an "actualized intellect" (ʿaql bi'l-fiʿl).

Often, philosophers refer to the actualization of the intellect by the Qurʾānic terms "salvation" (najāt) or "felicity" (saʿādah). They would agree with Tu Weiming, who writes, "Salvation means the full realization of the anthropocosmic reality inherent in our human nature".[18] For them, this anthropocosmic reality is the intellect that gave birth to macrocosm and microcosm and that is innate to human nature, a nature that is made in the image of God and identical with his intelligent and intelligible light.

The Quest for Omniscience

If the Muslim philosophers saw the quest for wisdom as the search to know all things, can we conclude that they are simply following Aristotle, who says as much at the beginning of the *Metaphysics*? I think not. They would say that they are trying to live up to the human potential, and Aristotle also understood the reality of human potential, that is precisely why they respect him and call him "The First Teacher" (al-muʿallim al-awwal). They would remind us that the Qurʾān discusses the human potential in rather explicit terms. It tells us, after all, that God taught Adam *all* the names (al-Baqarah 2:31), not just some of them. They might also point out that this quest for omniscience is implicitly if not explicitly acknowledged not only by all the world's wisdom traditions, but also by the whole enterprise of modern science. But, from their perspective, omniscience can only be found in the omniscient, and the only created thing that is omniscient in any real sense is the fully actualized intellect, the radiance of God's own Ipseity. Omniscience, in other words, can never be found in the compilation of data, the collections of facts, and the spinning of theories. It is not an "objective" reality, but a "subjective" experience – though no distinction can be drawn between subject and object when one has actualized the very being of the omniscient.

Nothing differentiates the Islamic intellectual quest from modern scientific and scholarly goals more clearly than the differing interpretations of the quest for omniscience. Both the Muslim intellectuals and modern scientists are striving to know everything, but the Muslim intellectual does so by looking at roots, principles, and *noumena*, and by striving for a synthesis of all knowledge and unification of the knowing subject with its object. In contrast the modern scientist looks at branches, applications, and phenomena and strives to analyze objects and multiply data.

The traditional intellectual undertakes the quest for omniscience as an individual. He or she knows that this is a task that can only be accomplished within, and that it can only be done by achieving the fullness of humanity, with everything that this demands ethically and morally. The modern scientist undertakes the quest for facts and information as a collective undertaking, knowing that he or she is one insignificant cog in an enormously complex apparatus. The modern scientist sees omniscience as something that can be achieved only by the sacred enterprise of Science, for Science alone has uniquely privileged methodologies and brilliantly sophisticated instruments. He or she rarely gives a thought to the possibility that all knowledge makes ethical demands upon the knower. If a thought is given to it, it is done not as a scientist, but as an ethicist or a philosopher or a religious believer. There is no room in Science for ethics.

Traditional seekers of wisdom aim to actualize the full potential of intelligence in order to understand everything that is significant for human ends, and these ends are defined in terms of a metaphysics, a cosmology, a psychology, and an ethics that takes Ultimate Reality as the measure of humanity. Modern seekers of facts aim to accumulate information and to devise ever more sophisticated theories in order to achieve what they call "progress". In other words, they want to achieve a transformation of the human race on the basis of scientific pseudo-absolutes if not political ideology.

The quest for wisdom is qualitative, because it aims at the actualization of all the qualities present fully in the divine image and named by the names of God. The scientific quest for knowledge and theoretical prowess is quantitative, because it aims to understand and control an ever-proliferating multiplicity of things.

The more the traditional intellectual searches for omniscience, the more he or she finds the unity of his or her own soul and organismic interrelationship with the world. The more the modern scientist searches for data, the more he or she is pulled into dispersion and incoherence, despite the claims that overarching theories will one day explain everything.

The traditional quest for wisdom leads to integration, synthesis, and a global, anthropocosmic vision. The modern quest for information and control leads to mushrooming piles of facts and the proliferation of ever more specialized and narrower fields of learning. The net result of the modern quest is particularization, division, partition, separation, incoherence, mutual incomprehension, and chaos. No one knows the truth of this statement better than university professors, who are often so narrowly specialized that they cannot explain their research to their own colleagues in their own departments – much less to colleagues in other departments.

Conclusion

Let me recapitulate as follows.

For the Islamic intellectual tradition, the study of the universe was a two-pronged, holistic enterprise. In one respect its aim was to depict and describe the world of appearances. In another respect its goal was to grasp the innermost reality of both the appearances and the knower of the appearances. The great masters of the discipline always recognized that it is impossible to understand external objects without understanding the subject that understands. This meant that metaphysics, cosmology, and psychology were essential parts of the intellectual quest. The goal was to see earthly appearances, intelligible principles, and the intelligent self in one integrated and simultaneous vision. It was understood that intelligence is not only that which grasps and comprehends the real nature of things, but also that which gives birth to things in the first place. Everything knowable is already latent within intelligence, because all things appear from intelligence in the cosmogonic process.

The anthropocosmic vision allowed for no real dichotomy between the subject that knows and the object that is known. The structure and goals of the intellectual enterprise precluded losing sight of the ontological link that binds the two. To do so would be to forget tawḥīd and to fall into the chaos of dispersion and egocentricity. Ignorance of the reality of the knower leads to using knowledge as a means to achieve illusory ends, and ignorance of the reality of the known turns the world into things and objects that can manipulated for goals cut off from any vision of true human nature. The possibilities of human understanding define the possibilities of human becoming. To know is to be. To ignore the reality of either the object or the subject is to fall into foolishness, error, and superstition. An impoverished and flattened universe is the mirror image of an impoverished and flattened soul. The death of God is nothing but the stultification of the human intellect. Ecological catastrophe is the inevitable consequence of psychic and spiritual dissolution. The world and the self are not two separate realities, but two sides of the same coin, a coin that was minted in the image of God.

Notes

1 Tu in turn takes the word "anthropocosmic" from Mircea Eliade. Tu, *Centrality and Commonality: An Essay on Confucian Religiousness* (Albany: SUNY Press, 1989), 126. The present paper is partly an offshoot of an on-going "Islamic-Confucian Dialogue" begun five years ago by Tu and Seyyed Hossein Nasr, in which I have been a regular participant. It is also the fruit of an in-house dialogue with my wife, Sachiko Murata, which has been going on for many more years than five. I do not mean to suggest that I want to interpret the Islamic tradition in Chinese categories. I cite Tu Weiming to acknowledge a certain influence on my own conceptualization of things and to point out that there is nothing unusual about the Islamic worldview. One can even argue that the anthropocosmic vision I discuss here is the Islamic version of a perspective that is normative for the human race. If there is an incongruity, it is Western natural science and, following in its wake, the other disciplines of the modern academy. The real question is not why Confucianism and Islam share a common vision, but why the West has broken from the perennial pattern. The oddity is modern science and thought, not the holistic visions of pre-modern civilizations and cultures.

2 Ibid., 10.

3 Western scholars have rarely looked to East Asia for help in interpreting Islamic thinking. One reason for this is that we are talking about "Western" scholarship, with all the presuppositions and interpretive biases that this implies. Moreover, Western scholars have been primarily concerned with situating Islamic thinking in its historical context, not with understanding what Muslim thinkers were trying to say, and this context is largely the same as that of the Judeo-Christian and

Hellenistic West. I am not denying the great value of such research, but this approach has meant that interpreters of Islamic intellectuality have been peculiarly insensitive to certain dimensions of Islamic thinking that happen to have a deep resonance with the East Asian traditions. Most modern-day Muslim scholars follow Western models or assume an apologetic and reactive stance vis-a-vis Western scholarship, so they also have not looked to East Asia. Nonetheless, there is no reason to suppose that Islamic thought is in any essential way uncongenial with the East Asian traditions, as Sachiko Murata has illustrated in her study, *The Tao of Islam* (Albany: SUNY Press, 1992). Her more recent research has shown that Muslim scholars in China were at home in the Neo-Confucian worldview, which is eminently anthropocosmic, and that they employed its technical terminology to express an Islamo-Confucian vision of reality. See Murata, *Chinese Gleams of Sufi Light* (Albany: SUNY Press, 2000).

4   Take, for example, this verse: "What, do they desire other than the religion of God, while to Him has submitted [islām] everything in the heavens and the earth, willingly or unwillingly?" (Āl 'Imrān 3:83). On the different meanings of the word islām in the Qur'ān and the Islamic tradition, see Sachiko Murata and William C. Chittick, *The Vision of Islam* (New York: Paragon, 1994), 3-7.

5   Except, of course, in the sense that there must first be a contingent reality for the truth to find expression in the universe. Muslim thinkers often say that God's unity (waḥdah or aḥadiyyah) pertains to God alone, transcending all contingency and all creaturely attributes, whereas tawḥīd is the human response to that unity. It is also pointed out that the human response is only possible because God's own reality declares its own unity – as the Qur'ān puts it, "God bears witness that there is no god but He", (Āl 'Imrān 3:18). This is why it is sometimes said that no one truly voices tawḥīd but God himself, and every human assertion of God's unity can only be a pale reflection made possible by the human image of God.

6   The specific verse I have in mind is al-Anbiyā' 21:25: "And We never sent a messenger before thee save that we revealed to him, saying, 'There is no god but I, so serve Me'". Lest someone claim that the statement of tawḥīd is itself historically particular, we need to remember that the linguistic formulation is not at issue, but rather the unique, unitary reality that gives rise to the universe. Note also that the Qur'ān says that God sends every prophetic message in the language of the messenger's people (Ibrāhīm 14:4), thereby acknowledging that God speaks every language, for "Each community has a messenger" (Yūnus 10:47). In this way of looking at things, what was different about each revelation was not tawḥīd, but rather the specific teachings and practices necessitated by the historical context of the people to whom the message was revealed. Of course, it can also be objected that this unitary reality is itself historically particular, because it was invented by human minds. People who hold this position still have to justify it, and that demands a

metaphysics: On what basis do we declare history, language, politics, gender, atoms, energy, the human mind, the brain, or whatever "foundational"?

[7] This is why certain Muslim thinkers can maintain that even Adam's "forgetfulness" (nisyān), which caused his fall, pertains to the divine image that is the defining characteristic of the human race. The transmitted support for this idea is the Qur'ānic verse, "They forgot God, so God forgot them" (al-Tawbah 9:67). If God "forgets", then "forgetfulness" is a divine attribute. See Ibn al-ʿArabī, as cited in Chittick, *The Sufi Path of Knowledge* (Albany: SUNY Press, 1989), 296.

[8] Some of the discussions concerning the relationship between the two sorts of knowledge might remind us of the constant battles that go on among educational theorists about the relative merit of rote learning or cultural literacy (transmitted knowledge) and critical thinking or creativity (intellectual knowledge). Like other traditional civilizations, Islam stressed that transmitted learning was the foundation for all real understanding. This explains why the process of learning began at a very young age, typically with the memorization of the Qur'ān.

[9] I am focusing on tawḥīd, the first principle of Islamic faith. It should be noted that the philosophers also investigated the other two principles of Islamic faith – "prophecy" (nubuwwah) and the "return" to God, or eschatology (maʾād) – as intellectual rather than transmitted issues. They were not especially interested in the historical events surrounding Muhammad and other prophets, or in the details of revealed scripture. Nor, in the earlier period, did they defend the graphic Qur'ānic depictions of the afterlife as anything more than a rhetorical necessity. However, they were extremely interested in "prophecy" as the highest form of human perfection, and they were especially concerned with the immortality of the soul, an immortality that is achieved through intellectual perfection. Because they discussed the three principles of the faith with little explicit reference to the transmitted learning and much mention of Greek antecedents, some historians have found it easy to ignore the thoroughly Islamic character of their writings. If the philosophers were often criticized by other Muslim scholars for the positions they took on the principles of faith, it was because their interpretations did not coincide with the theological and dogmatic readings. Given the nature of theological polemic, the criticism often took the form of accusations of unbelief. But, in a broader view, philosophy and theology were largely in agreement, especially if we compare their positions with the beliefs that infuse most modern scholarship.

[10] Tu Weiming, *Confucian Thought: Selfhood as Creative Transformation* (Albany: SUNY Press, 1985), 137.

[11] Tu Weiming, *Centrality and Commonality*, 102.

[12] I am not suggesting, of course, that it is self-evident to everybody, any more than mathematical truth is self-evident to everybody. My point is rather that the position of the intellectual tradition on tawḥīd was that once it is understood, it cannot be

denied. Its truth is such that, once one understands it, one knows that it has always lurked in one's soul. This is precisely the sense of "remembrance".

[13] I am not denying that there was a decline. I am simply saying that by making the criterion for measurement "scientific progress" or the lack thereof, we are accepting the ideological presuppositions of modernity and scientism. Why should these historical oddities be considered the universal criterion by which all civilizations must be measured? If we keep in view Islamic criteria (e.g., adherence to tawḥīd, the Qur'ān, and the Sunnah), there was certainly a serious decline, but that decline cannot be measured by the "scientific" criteria that are normally applied.

[14] Tu Weiming, *Confucian Thought*, 46-47.

[15] This is not to say that there is no such thing as "evil". The issue of discerning the ḥaqq of "evil" things is one of the more subtle dimensions of taḥqīq. Recognizing a thing's ḥaqq may entail acknowledging that part of its proper role is to be the occasion for evil and that the appropriate human response is to avoid it. This very need to avoid it alerts us to something of its cosmic role. Without evil, human freedom of choice is meaningless.

[16] Compare Tu Weiming's description of the degrees of spirituality as viewed by the Confucian vision: "Rocks, trees, animals, humans, and gods represent different levels of spirituality based on the varying compositions of ch'i", *Confucian Thought*, 44. In the typical Islamic version, the ch'i or invisible power that animates rocks is called "nature" (ṭabī'ah). Only at the plant level is a second modality of ch'i, called "soul", added to the first. Rocks are by no means "only matter". In the hylomorphism adopted by the intellectual tradition, the role of matter (mādda) is largely conceptual, because there is no such thing per se. "Matter" is simply the name that is given to an observed receptivity for the apparition of "form" (ṣūrah). Form itself is an intelligible and spiritual reality that descends into the domain of appearances from the spirit or intellect and ultimately from God, who is, in Qur'ānic language, "the Form-giver" (al-muṣawwir). Since all things are "forms", there is nothing in the universe that does not manifest the living presence of the intelligent and the intelligible.

[17] To those who know the Islamic tradition, this will sound like a "Sufi" idea rather than a philosophical position. Notice, however, what Avicenna says: "The knower ['ārif] desires the Real, the First, only for His sake, not for the sake of anything else. He prefers nothing to true knowledge of Him. His worship is directed only to Him, since He is worthy of worship and because worship is a noble relationship with Him. At the same time, the knower has neither desire nor fear. Were he to have them, the object of his desire or fear would be his motive, and it would be his goal. Then the Real would not be his goal but rather the means to something else, less than the Real, which would be the goal and the object". *Al-Ishārāt wa'l-tanbīhāt*, edited by S. Dunyā (Cairo, 1947), 3:227.

[18] Tu Weiming, *Confucian Thought*, 64.

Chapter 6

Moments in the Islamic Recasting of the Greek Legacy: Exploring the Question of Science and Theism

S. Nomanul Haq

> Islamic philosophy is Greek philosophy, but it is not Greek philosophy
> studied for scholarly reasons nor for the satisfaction of scholarly curiosity. It
> is meant primarily to serve the needs of the new religion of Islam: it is an
> attempt at a Muslim natural theology, and the greatest representatives of this
> theistic Islamic philosophy went so far as to see the only valid interpretation
> of Islam in following the ways of the philosophers ...[1]

The story of what we call Arabic or Islamic science is largely, though neither exclusively nor simply, the story of the Islamic career of Hellenism. To be sure, there exists pressing evidence that many currents other than the Greek were flowing into the reservoir of the Islamic culture in its heyday; and yet it is also true that the metaphysical and cosmological framework of Arabic science in general arose out of a process of a uniquely Islamic appropriation of the received Greek legacy – a legacy in which Neoplatonism loomed large. In the hands of the scientists of Islam, a large number of whom were also philosophers in the sense of philosophy proper, this legacy underwent such fundamental transformations as to transcend itself. Here it should be added that the growth of science from the European Middle Ages down to what we call the Scientific Revolution cannot be explained if the history of these fateful transformations is absent from our perspective.

It has been plausibly claimed that in the history of civilization the fundamental contribution of the classical Greek tradition is its confidence in human reason – this was something essentially new, even though Greek philosophy never discarded from its chambers the irrational element altogether, and this is particularly true of Plato and the Neoplatonic school of Athens. Note that for the Greeks, philosophy was not merely a disembodied rational preoccupation; rather, it was a way of life, the road leading to the ultimate perfection and happiness of the soul – and it is for this reason that Plato has been called the founder of a "natural theology",[2] and Greek philosophy characterized as the "Greek philosophical religion",[3] and Platonism declared to be "the spiritual religion of the Greeks".[4] In this context, the case of the Pythagoreans is much too familiar to be rehearsed here.

In the centuries before the historic rise of Islam, both Greek and Latin Christians had accepted Greek philosophy. For them, it provided a theory of the divine as revealed in the nature of reality and as accessible to human reason – in other words, it provided a *natural* rather than a *revealed* theology. The Neoplatonic philosopher John Philoponus (d. *c.* 570s), a monophysite Christian known to Islam as Yaḥyā al-Naḥwī, was one of the pioneers who attempted to harmonize Aristotelian philosophy and Christian theology, defending *formatio mundi* against Aristotle, and studying the relation between faith and reason. In the same spirit, Greek philosophy was cultivated by Muslims for whom, like their Hellenistic predecessors, it constituted a search for the universal in contrast to the mere transient particular; it was a search at once requiring and generating a purification of the soul (*nafs*) which made rational inquiry possible. But more, the way of philosophy was the way, or a necessary precondition to be admitted upon the way, that is bestowed by God for human beings to recognize Him, His messengers, and His design.

By the time Islam emerged on the world scene, it had become a Neoplatonic, philosophical orthodoxy that the two giants of Greek philosophy, Plato and Aristotle, were in agreement. Aristotle's distinction between the highest God and the star-gods gained prominence and was now being viewed in a Platonic mythic perspective. And Aristotle's Unmoved Mover, the First Cause, became in Plotinus (d. *c.* 260) the One (*to hen*), the supreme hypostasis existing beyond the world, from whom in a timeless hierarchical process of emanation the hypostases of Intellect (*noūs*) and Soul (*psyché*) were generated, leading finally to Matter (*hulé*). Thus, admitting the Platonic distinction between the two realms of the intelligible and the sensible, reality was conceived as a hierarchical descent from the One – itself remaining unaltered and undiminished even though it continued in creation eternally. This Plotinian metaphysics of emanation and hypostases was accepted by Christian Neoplatonists for whom it was not a far cry from here to identify the One with the Godhead of their monotheistic religion. And again, with varying details and with significantly different and often fundamental transformations, this type of metaphysics is practically common to all Islamic philosophers, all of whom by the nature of their very trade were involved in the natural sciences.

These philosophers (*falāsifa*, sing. *faylasūf*) typically espoused Aristotle's theory of the four causes and ten categories, remained committed to his *Organon*, and – as it was an integral part of the *falāsifa's* creed in general – took over the Neoplatonic doctrine of hypostases and emanation. But profoundly interesting, both philosophically and historically, is the radical *Islamic* recasting to which the *falāsifa* subjected the complex Greek legacy which they had received – a highly sophisticated recasting that throws Islam's revelationary data themselves into a new perspective, promising to make even these data amenable to a logical demonstration of the Aristotelian kind. One can, in this vein and ironically, say that these Hellenized *falāsifa* have given us a new rational Islamic *theology*.

There exists, however, an important exception to this general description of Hellenism in Islam – indeed, a monumental exception: that embodied in the cosmology of Abū Bakr Rāzī (the Rhazes of the Latin West, d. *c.* 925), a towering giant both in the history of medicine and of natural philosophy. It is difficult to classify Rāzī's thought; his own claim is that he is simply a follower of Plato, but his atomistic natural philosophy shows, *inter alia*, Indian and Harranian elements integrated into a framework of a non-Aristotelian, non-Neoplatonic, Platonic kind. Rāzī was a freethinker who is known to have dismissed prophecy, exercising this freedom to such a daring extent as to declare all prophets impostors.[5] And yet it is quite remarkable that, as we shall see, he destroyed the ordered cosmos of Aristotle and reintroduced God in a reconstructed metaphysical system based on his five eternal principles – God being the eternal principle of creation, *al-Bāri'* (Demiurgus). Thus, despite his rebellious independence and freethinking, Rāzī transformed Aristotle's cosmology into a thoroughgoing *theistic* system.

In the exploration of the question of science and theism, what follows constitutes a case study. This study takes up, first and in some detail, the case of a typical but outstanding and enduring Hellenized personage: the grand philosopher and sustained medical authority both in Islam and in Europe, Abū 'Alī Ibn Sīnā, Latin Avicenna (d. 1037). Next, it takes up somewhat briefly the exceptional case of Rāzī, who is in many ways closer to Descartes and Newton than to his Greek predecessors, and whose direct influence on European thought is plainly visible in both historical and philosophical evidence.

Reconstructing God and His Angels: Ibn Sīnā's Recasting of the Greek Legacy

Ibn Sīnā's Neoplatonized Monotheism: God Transcendent, God Immanent

Supreme over all else in Ibn Sīnā's entire metaphysical system is God's sovereignty. He teaches that everything derives both its being (*māhiyya*) and its existence (*wujūd*) from God, the Necessary Being (*wājib al-wujūd*) which is pure Perfection and pure Goodness, the source and origin of everything; and that everything other than God is merely contingent (*mumkin al-wujūd*) upon God. The contingent beings are then divided by *al-Shaykh al-Ra'īs* (the Grand Shaykh), as Ibn Sīnā is deferentially referred to in the Arabic sources, into two kinds: (1)

Those which are essentially contingent but receive from the First Cause the quality of necessity – they are, then, necessary in a contingent sense. These were Intellects and angelic substances; and (2) those beings which are only contingent – the non-simple bodies of the sublunary world "which come into being and pass away".

Remaining committed to Aristotle's definition of substance (*jawhar*), Ibn Sīnā tells us that three kinds of substances comprise the first group of beings: (i) that whose being is one, which is completely separate (*mujarrad*) from all matter and potentiality – this is Intellect (*ʿaql, noūs*); (ii) that whose being is one but which accepts the form of other beings, which is indivisible, and needs body in its action – this is Soul (*nafs, psyché*); and (iii) that whose being is one but accepts the form of other beings, that which accepts divisibility and has the three dimensions of length, width, and depth – this is Body (*jism, hulé*).[6] All this is reminiscent of Neoplatonic Aristotelianism – but Neoplatonic Aristotelianism Islamized, as we shall see progressively more clearly.

I shall return to Ibn Sīnā's highly original and fateful distinction between being and existence, but let us here proceed with his cosmology. The fundamental premise of Ibn Sīnā's cosmology is that the supreme and ultimate cause of existence is God's intellection – and the object of God's intellection can be, and here our sage remains true to the uncompromising monotheistic thrust of Islam, none other than God Himself. This radiates forth in Ibn Sīnā's system and develops into a powerful theory of knowledge, reaching out from him to European philosophy, particularly to Descartes and Kant – a theory declaring that nothing is epistemologically more present to the mind than the mind itself and its ideas, paving the way for our modern-day noetics. Here one is also reminded of that untiringly repeated *ḥadīth qudsī* of the Sufis in which God is made to say, "I was a hidden treasure and I longed to be known [to myself], so I created the world".

The First Intellect, by intellection (a) of the Divine Essence, gives rise to the Second Intellect; and by intellection (b) of its own essence it gives rise to the Soul of the first heaven, and its body. By similar intellection, the Second Intellect generates the Third Intellect, the Soul of the second heaven and its body, and so on until we reach the ninth heaven, and the Tenth Intellect. Note how tenaciously the great physician keeps intact God's unity, unicity, and uniqueness, embodied in the concept of *tawḥīd* which is the hallmark of Islam among the three monotheistic faiths. He allows no multiplicity to be generated within God; rather multiplicity arises out of the First Intellect which is a *contingent* being. And again, note that when the Intellect's object of intellection is the Divine Being, it generates only another intellect which is totally *separate* from matter; it does *not* generate the soul which needs and acts upon corporeal matter. In this way, a balance is effected between God's transcendence and His immanence – a balancing act that attempts to meet a challenge posed by none other than the text of the Qur'ān itself. For example, while maintaining, on the one hand, an insistent ontological dichotomy between God and *all else* in the cosmos, the Qur'ān says on the other hand that God is "closer to human beings than their jugular vein" (50:16), or that God breathed His "own spirit" (*rūḥī*) into the human being (15:29; 38:72; 32:9), or that "God's throne (*kursī*) envelopes the cosmos" (2:255). Here, the Qur'ān declares that "God is Light (*nūr*) of the heavens and the earth" (24:35); there, with great intensity that "nothing, but nothing, is like Him" (24:11); it speaks of God's face (*wajh*) at one place (2;115); and emphasizes that "there is none like unto Him" (112: 4), at another.

Angels Hellenized: Archangel Gabriel and Others

Recall that Ibn Sīnā tells us that the first kind of contingent beings were Intellects and angelic substances. Thus, the Souls of the celestial spheres which moved these spheres were angels. But these angels emanated from pure Intellects, and these Intellects were the Archangels. Finally, there were human souls, or terrestrial angels which moved and governed earthly human bodies. So here we have a tri-level angelic hierarchy: archangels, celestial angels, and terrestrial angels, in descending order. Note the equivalence here between the pleroma of Intellects (*'uqūl*) and the angelic pleroma (*malā'ika*); this forms part of the creed of the Hellenized philosophers of Islam. Earlier, we noted that it was intellection (*noésis*) that generated being and substance – from Intellect to Intellect down to the Tenth Intellect which is our (rather familiar) Active Intellect (*al-'aql al-fa''āl*), the originator of our souls, presiding over our world. Islamic philosophers identified the Active Intellect with the Qur'ānic Spirit of Holiness (*Rūh al-Quds*), *sc.* Gabriel, the Archangel of revelation.

The theory of the Active Intellect has exercised several generations of historians of philosophy. While it may be possible to find some Greek precursor or germs of this theory (for example, Aristotle says in *De Anima* that mind is in its essential nature activity, 430a:15-20), it seems that it is essentially an Islamic metaphysical innovation in a Neoplatonic mode. The Active Intellect was an intermediary between the celestial world above the moon and the human soul, through which the latter was linked to the divine. To this Archangel the human souls were in the same relation as was each *Anima coelestis* to its Archangel. The human mind received the intelligibles, the universals, by turning toward the Active Intellect; by doing so, it reversed in its thinking consciousness (*nafs nāṭiqa*) the descent from unity to multiplicity by reascending from multiplicity to ultimate unity. "Prior to any plurality", expounded de Boer, "everything has an existence [better: being] in the mind of God and of the angels; then, ... it enters upon plurality, to be raised finally in the intellect of man to the universality of the Idea".[7] In his more private moments Ibn Sīnā says that in the world beneath the moon, movement is no longer drawing away from the principle but returning to it: not an emanation (*faiḍ*), but love (*'ishq*) which the human soul receives from Divine Command (*amr*). He quotes the Qur'ān: "And unto Him the whole matter will be returned" (11: 123).

*The Fateful Distinction Between Being (Māhiyya) and Existence (Wujūd):
Reintroducing God, Prophecy, and Inspiration*[8]

Ibn Sīnā had said that it was in obeying God that the heavens, which
were made up of separate substances, moved as a unitary living thing.
But this amounts to a philosophical apostasy on the part of a Neoplatonized Aristotelian. Aristotle's separate substances were separate
not only from matter but also from one another; each was self-sufficient
in having eternally its own being; unrelated, these substances were not
subject to any single efficient cause. But more to the point, Aristotle
tells us in *Metaphysics* (3.2.1003b22-33) that a thing, its unity, and its
being are identical; thus, there is no question of looking for a source of
unity outside being. Ibn Sīnā, on the other hand, makes a distinction
between things existing in the real world and their being, what they are
in themselves. This distinction manifests itself, argues Ibn Sīnā, when
things are considered (a) in relation to their real existence in the
sensible world, and (b) in relation to the existence they have in the
mind that knows them. Now neither (a) nor (b), he points out, belongs
to a nature just by itself. If either type of existence did exist by itself, it
would inevitably be found in the nature wherever the nature happened
to be. The same holds, we are told, with regard to unity and
multiplicity.

Thus, a sensible nature in itself has a being of its own – this is
the thing's proper being, a being that of itself is neither one nor many,
neither existent in mind nor existent in reality. All of this simply means
that a thing's existence does not come from its own nature. It has to be
received from something else – ultimately from God, the Necessary
Existent. In contrast to the Platonian One, this ultimate source is not
utterly beyond all being. It is this characteristic Avicennan distinction
between being and existence which became the *esse essentia* and *esse
existentia* of scholastic metaphysics. "From here it was but a step to the
Cartesian 'idea'" and to the notion in modern noetics asserting that
ideas in the mind are the mind's direct object.[9] The immediate objects

of intellectual cognition, for Ibn Sīnā, were *not* what exists in the external world.

Ibn Sīnā here speaks of three distinct kinds of objects: (1) The objects of the real world; (2) intellectual objects, *sc.* the forms in the intellect which have a distinct ontological status of their own; and (3) logically categorized intellectual objects. There was no ontological order among these objects, nor were these objects mutually relational in themselves. Thus the logical objects of thought, even though they arose out of a treatment in the mind of the intellectual objects, were rendered quite distinct from the intellectual objects, and they were also distinct from the external objects of the real world. Now, we are told that the logical categorization of intellectual objects in a particular way is not a representation of any eternal ontological truths concerning the structure of the world; it reflects no inherent code of relations of essences – it was a causal and contingent product of the intellectual efforts to understand the world. The world is the way it is not because of an inner code of essences; it is a contingent product of God's providence. The subsistence of forms in the material or logical world in certain manner and order was, then, not *essentially* necessary; it was only *causally* necessary. And God was the Cause of causes (*'illat al-'ilal*).

Ibn Sīnā is quite clear in his position that forms have no order in the Active Intellect, and that their manifestation in a specific order in the sensible world or their categorization in a particular way is one of *many* logical possibilities – there can be numerous logically possible worlds. As such, forms themselves exist only in the Active Intellect, not in the material world; and this has the drastic consequence that knowledge of forms or essences is *not* abstracted from the external world. We see: this means that the construction of the objects of knowledge, that is, the construction of the logical order which is an utterly intellectual effort, is a non-definitive exercise. Here, as elsewhere too, Ibn Sīnā is close to the professional theologians of Islam, the *mutakallimūn*: knowledge of the world is a form of belief.

Given that there is no eternal or necessary formal order in reality, Ibn Sīnā's system admits in its epistemological repertoire the intuitive human faculty – that faculty which has the capacity to receive *inspiration*. Human intellects vary in their intuitive capability: some of us move quickly from premises to conclusions, some of us lag behind. Indeed, the intellect must apply itself methodically – that is, particularly, conforming to the rules of (Aristotelian) formal logic – but there is no internal or independent mechanism that guarantees the arrival at results. The result must be *inspired*. Methodical reasoning was a necessary precondition for acquiring knowledge, but it was by no means sufficient.

The intuitive faculty when it achieves perfection is a holy prophetic faculty. Indeed, a prophet is even able to perceive particulars from the future. Ibn Sīnā calls the prophet a "sacred intellect" in whom all ideas radiating forth from the Active Intellect (Archangel Gabriel) come together to illuminate the mind, the perfection of whose intuitive powers make it capable of receiving these ideas in the inner depths of its being. Having attained a contact (*ittiṣāl*) with the Active Intellect, the prophet becomes, one may say, a secondary source of illumination. And none of this is amenable to a logical analysis; here one must invoke the concepts of God's grace, His gifts, and His mercy.

There seems to be a complex and highly creative interplay between the great physician and philosopher Abū ʿAlī Ibn Sīnā's Hellenism and his religious convictions. On the one hand, Hellenism is for him the torch which illuminates the articles of his Islamic faith and the data of revelation. But, on the other, one may say with a good deal of justification that it was a need inspired by the inner dynamics and tensions of a theistic Islamic metaphysics that led him to appropriate Hellenism in the first place.

The Cosmos as Given and the Cosmos as Created: A Brief Consideration of the Case of Abū Bakr Al-Rāzī

I shall now turn briefly to Abū Bakr Rāzī who is to be characterized, as has been remarked at the outset, in his own terms for he cannot be described neatly as a Neoplatonist, nor as an Aristotelian; he considers himself a Platonist, but what he represents is a limited and circumscribed Platonism. Indeed, as Pines has pointed out, the intellectual tendency we find in Rāzī may well be characterized as a special kind of anti-Aristotelianism.[10] But what is most interesting is that in his attack on Aristotle's epistemological presuppositions this religious rebel turns an *inert* Aristotelian God, the Prime Mover, into a *functional* God of the kind conceived in the Abrahamic monotheistic theologies. And this is a powerful irony – an irony that constitutes a historical moment.

Aristotle's natural philosophy reigned supreme for numerous centuries due to its robust coherence and its quality of being intellectually satisfying since it presupposed an immutable cosmic order. Indeed, historians have remarked that the system of Aristotle may even appear as more coherent than Newtonian science: note that the Newtonian system had destroyed the ordered cosmos and had engendered "a spate of theistic ... cosmogonies beset with various antinomies".[11] But, as we shall see, some seven hundred years before Newton, the destruction had already been consummated by Rāzī.

An ordered cosmos, taken as given, is both the virtue and serious weakness of Aristotle's natural philosophy when looked at from an epistemological angle. To be sure, the Aristotelian physical theory was most vulnerable to epistemological arguments – and it is precisely this vulnerability which is targeted by Rāzī for an attack. According to Aristotle, both the notion of "place" (*topos*), and this means negation of space, and that of time were bound up with the existence of bodies. Neither was logically separable from body. Space was the limit of the containing body; it was "the innermost boundary of the body contained in it".[12] Indeed, even in its universal capacity as *locus communis*, it was inseparable from the body of the universe at large and was thus finite.[13] As for time, it was conceived as "the number of motion according to prior and posterior"[14] – again, this means that time too was logically inseparable from body. In the final analysis, then, space and time were *functions of* the eternal and orderly cosmos.

Self-Evident Human Certitudes: The Epistemological Question

Rāzī dismisses Aristotle's logical linkage of the notion of space and time with bodies, and does so on epistemological grounds which bear a remarkable resemblance to those on which Descartes built his system several centuries later. The reality of the existence of an infinite three-dimensional space independent of bodies, argued Rāzī, is proven by the fact that those people who have not been corrupted by philosophical quibbles are certain of its existence. As for time, again the same argument applies: one can conceive it clearly and distinctly as a flowing substance not bound up with bodies.[15] Note that manifesting itself in the foundations of Descartes' system later, here we have the epistemological position that the certitude that attaches in the human mind to these concepts is a proof of their external reality. "The epistemological priority of absolute time and space in Rāzī's doctrine carried with it ontological implications."[16]

Rāzī makes a distinction between universal or absolute space and particular or relative space. Absolute space was not a function of bodies, so that the concept of the body occupying it does not enter into its definition; and this opens up the logical possibility of void, contra-Aristotle. Indeed, absolute space being independent of body was, *eo ipso*, independent of magnitude: it was infinite, again contra-Aristotle. But relative space, on the other hand, was the extension of bodies, and could not be conceived in isolation from matter. One may say that all this is reminiscent of Plato who in the *Timaeus* had spoken of space as the receptacle of bodies, as well as the formless matter from which the creator-god fashions the particular object of sense.[17] As for time, Rāzī in a similar vein distinguishes between absolute and limited time: absolute time was not subject to number or measure, whereas limited time was measured by means of the revolutions of the heavenly spheres. For Aristotle, reality of time was logically dependent upon movement in general, and the movement of the heavens in particular. But Rāzī teaches that motion does not *produce*, but simply *reveals* time; time remained distinct from movement.[18]

The Cosmos: Interlude Created by God

For Rāzī, in contrast to Aristotle, the cosmos is by no means a primary datum; it was not the given, unanalyzable primitive entity in terms of which all else in the physical reality had to be explained. The existence and order of the cosmos needed to be *accounted for*. More fundamental than cosmos were space and time; and more fundamental than the cosmos also was matter which was, like space and time, eternal, and which had an atomic constitution and subsisted before bodies were formed in a state of dispersion. And, finally, there were for Rāzī two more eternal primordial principles: Soul and the Creator. Indeed, the common-sense "Aristotelian cosmic order now having been destroyed by a recourse to spontaneous certainties of the human mind, and the cosmic order being no longer a primary datum, the philosopher had to *construct* his universe out of primordial entities".[19]

What does this mean? This means that, as Pines observed, the cosmos and the order prevailing in it is something *derivative* and not self sufficient.[20] And this opens up the question of the creation of the cosmos in time, and obversely, its dissolution in time – a question that would not arise in Aristotle's cosmology. Thus we find the belief in Rāzī that the world was created in time by divine intervention, and that it will come to an end in the fullness of time; note that this is precisely the thrust of the familiar Muslim formula, *Innā li'l-Lāhi wa innā ilayhi rāji'ūn*, "to God we belong and to Him we return!". Put in Rāzīan terms, the cosmos was a mere interlude in the eternal existence of space, time, matter, Soul, and Creator.

Some Reflections: History and Contemporary Concerns

The Question of Religion and Science

Historical evidence teaches us once again that the very doctrinal framework of science, at least during the episodes we have examined, is conceived not in isolation from the religious context but within it; and that it is a framework which integrates theistic elements in its very fundamental conception and construction. In the case of Ibn Sīnā, these elements clearly manifest a peculiarly Islamic monotheistic character. Abū Bakr al-Rāzī, for his part, erected a natural scientific system which would collapse without an eternal and functional God being an integral principle of its foundations. Given the philosophical parallels we have noted between these two figures and Descartes and Newton, we can ambitiously extend the scope of our historical generalization to bring modern science also into its fold.

It appears that the rational inquiry of science cannot possibly operate in a metaphysical vacuum; it must make, or take for granted, certain presuppositions concerning the nature of reality and our encounter with it. But, in a broad sense, any set of metaphysical presuppositions lying at the base of the scientific enterprise can be described as "religious", since they involve an act of faith at the very outset of the process. More important, this act of faith effectively embodies a recognition of an order of reality which transcends empirical investigation and logical demonstration, but without which rational knowledge is impossible. A presupposition of the uniformity of nature, or of knowable universal laws, or of an integrated and regulated cosmic system, or of simplicity, elegance, and beauty in the very essence of natural reality – these are all, one may legitimately say, articles of faith in what constitutes a rational theology, even when the concept of God is not explicitly invoked by the actors; it need not. One thing, then, is abundantly clear: when we speak of science-religion rivalry, we speak politically not substantively, institutionally and sociologically not doctrinally and philosophically; we speak of historical contingencies, not of essences.

But even in the narrower and more strict sense, the scientific systems of both Ibn Sīnā and Rāzī stand upon a religious foundation; these systems are theistic not merely in a broadly generalized perspective. The case of Ibn Sīnā is compelling and clear: the strict Islamic principle of the unity, unicity, and uniqueness of God; the question of reason in the face of revelation; the nature of intuition, inspiration, and prophecy; the non-deterministic doctrine of the Creator's Will; these are all his fundamental concerns. Ibn Sīnā's concerns were specifically Muslim concerns. There is, moreover, a moral dimension to them which generated on his part an ethical attitude to the natural world – indeed, we observe that for Ibn Sīnā there is no dichotomy or discontinuity between the divine environment and the natural environment:[21]

> The Necessary Being – who is most beautiful, perfect, and best, who apprehends this ultimate beauty and goodness and does so in the most complete manner of apprehension, and who apprehends the apprehender and the apprehended as one in reality – is, in essence and by its essence, the greatest lover and beloved and the greatest thing pleased and pleasurable.[22]

As for Rāzī, whom we have briefly examined, it must be admitted that his case is more complex and very difficult to articulate. As much as we know of his ideas, he had rejected all prophecy and thus all revelation claimed by Abrahamic faiths; and given this, we cannot describe his system as Islamic, or even as monotheistic in a historical sense. Rāzī was a freethinker of sorts, but a detailed analysis of his religious beliefs does not concern us here.[23] For our purposes it is sufficient to note that his God was not simply a logical abstraction of a dry as dust philosopher; his was a *personal* and *living* god, a god who was compassionate, kind, and caring; the Creator who was not utterly separate from the world but directly involved in it; and note: he had declared that God was Pure Good. All this means that Rāzī's theism had powerful moral implications – in other words, it had yielded a religious *system* in the full sense of the word. Indeed, it has been said categorically that Rāzī's free thinking was, and this strikes as a paradox, a *religious* phenomenon. But what is profoundly ironic, it has also been observed that this kind of freethinking could have arisen only in an Islamic *religious* milieu. So, Rāzī was, after all, an Islamic *religious* product.[24]

Science in the Contemporary Islamic World

Construction of a historical perspective also dispels a contemporary fallacy: the fallacy insistently espoused in today's Islamic world that science is created in laboratories. This also has a corollary that enjoys general currency: the more sophisticated the machines used in the laboratories, the more certain and quicker will be the scientific growth – a presumption that has far-reaching economic consequences. The aim is to replicate, that is, to reproduce exactly, what is being done in the scientific world of the industrialized western societies, and the belief is that in this way Islamic science will be revived.

But once again we note, first, that what we call Islamic science was a thoroughly *cultural* phenomenon. And, second, that scientific activity in Islam was not an *isolated* activity – it was born in an ocean of philosophical speculations; and it was only one of the numerous manifestations of a sustained process of the unleashing of intellectual energies whose products are to be found in all spheres of knowledge: in natural philosophy as well as medicine, in philology and grammar as well as music and prosody, in jurisprudence as well as architecture and poetry, in astronomy as well as Qur'ānic hermeneutics and ḥadīth authentication.

What do we mean by saying that Islamic science was a cultural phenomenon? Here the operative explanatory category is A.I. Sabra's *appropriation*.[25] By appropriation is meant an active process of assimilation and integration of the legacy of one culture – in this particular case, Greek – into the living matrix of another – in this particular case, the Islamic. Furthermore, our historical data show that for this appropriation to have taken place, the pre-existence of certain cultural conditions was necessary. Thus, we have seen that the questions Ibn Sīnā was exploring were questions that antedate him in the Islamic intellectual history, and that these question were not replicated from foreign sources but arose out of the inner dynamics of the Islamic milieu itself. Indeed, it has been demonstrated by historians that many of the inquires Muslims undertook in what we would call science-proper have their origins in the Islamic *religious* sciences.[26] The fateful Abbasid translation movement which rendered almost *all* non-literary and non-historical Greek secular texts into Arabic, a monumental event in the history of civilization that has been likened to the Italian Renaissance and the Scientific Revolution,[27] was also inspired by the needs arising in the domain of Islam's indigenous religious tradition.[28]

The Islamic appropriation of Greek knowledge involved a massive rearrangement, recasting, selection, rejection, and frequently a total transformation of the received material. It constituted a consciously carried out organic process, organic in the fundamental sense that it introduced transmitted Greek elements into a living body of culture – a living body which would not accept everything offered to it; and whatever entity it did accept, it integrated that entity into the totality of its own system. This is true, on the one hand, of the transmission of Greek knowledge into Islam, and, on the other hand, of the transmission of the Arabic legacy into the mediaeval Latin West. This largely explains why, despite its heavy debt to the Greeks, the Islamic scientific tradition achieved what the Greeks could not; and, at the other end, despite its heavy debt to the Islamic world, the Latin West achieved what Muslims could not.

That cultures are organic systems is a legitimate historical generalization; and this means that when we speak of the health or sickness of a culture, we speak of a coherent totality. Most instructive is the historical fact that burgeoning scientific creation and scientific growth have never been found in a culture that otherwise happens to be intellectually stagnant. Language, philosophy, literature, history, the arts, all of these disciplines have developed hand in hand with science, or rather, science has developed in a very productive reciprocal relationship with these disciplines, forming with them a vital cultural whole. It seems, then, that more important than advanced equipment and massive laboratories is an attention in the contemporary Islamic societies to extra-scientific and meta-scientific questions.

An awareness of the very nature of the scientific enterprise; the distinction, often blurred, between science and technology; the questions: why science? to what end? whose science?; these are all fundamentally decisive issues for urgent reflection. And among a host of these pressing extra-scientific questions, that of religion and science deserves to loom large, given the power and significance of religion for Muslim peoples, and given that it is their faith that makes the cosmos and their relationship with it ultimately meaningful to them. But to undertake an examination of these matters, a degree of intellectual discipline is necessary, that very discipline, let us note, which begets science itself. We learn from history that science arises out of a critical attitude, and scientific activity is in many ways an embodiment of fancy of imagination, but imagination expressed with intellectual control.

Notes

[1] Richard Walzer, "On the Legacy of the Classics in the Islamic World", in *Festschrift Bruno Snell* (Munich: C.H. Beck, 1956).

[2] Richard Walzer, *Greek into Arabic* (Cambridge, MA: Harvard University Press, 1962), 2.

[3] Walzer, *Greek into Arabic*, 8.

[4] Walzer, *Greek into Arabic*, 16.

[5] A recent and thorough study of Rāzī's freethinking is: Srarah Stroumsa, *Freethinkers of Medieval Islam* (Leiden: Brill, 1999); Cf. Rev. S. Nomanul Haq, *Journal of Islamic Studies*, 13, 1(2002): 54-58.

[6] Cf. Seyyed Hossein Nasr, *Islamic Cosmological Doctrines* (Albany: SUNY Press, 1993).

[7] Tj. de Boer, *History of Philosophy in Islam*, trans. E.R. Jones (1933; London: Luzac & Company, 1970), 135, qu. Nasr, *Cosmological Doctrines*.

[8] In the analysis that follows I have drawn particularly upon three sources: (1) J. Owens, "The Relevance of Avicennian Neoplatonism" in P. Morewedge ed., *Neoplatonism and Islamic Thought* (Albany: SUNY Press, 1992); (2) S. Nuseibeh, "Al-'Aql al-Qudsī: Avicenna's Subjective Theory of Knowledge", in *Studia Islamica*, 49 (1989): 39-54; (3) S. Nuseibeh, "Epistemology" in S.H. Nasr and O. Leaman (eds), *History of Islamic Philosophy* (London: Routledge, 1996).

[9] J. Owens, "The Relevance of Avicennian Neoplatonism" in P. Morewedge (ed), *Neoplatonism and Islamic Thought* (Albany: SUNY Press, 1992), 46.

[10] S. Pines, "What was Original in Arabic Science?" in A.C. Crombie (ed.), *Scientific Change* (New York: Basic Books 1963), 192. It ought to be acknowledged that my account is largely developed on the basis of this outstanding work.

[11] Pines, "Arabic Science", 191.

[12] Aristotle, *Physica*, (ed.) W.D. Ross (Oxford: Clarendon Press, 1936), IV. 212a20.

[13] Aristotle, *Physica*, 209a32; 212b13.

[14] Aristotle, *Physica*, 219b2.

[15] See S. Pines, *Beitrage zur islamischen Atomenlehre*, trans. M. Swarz (Jerusalem: Magnes Press, 1977).

[16] Pines, "Arabic Science", 193.

[17] Plato, *Timaeus*, trans. F.M. Cornford (London: K. Paul, Trench, Trubner and Co., 1937), 52 f.; cf. Aristotle, *Physica* IV. 209b11.

[18] Cf. M. Fakhry, *A History of Islamic Philosophy* (New York: Columbia University Press, 1983), 103-104.

[19] Pines, "Arabic Science", 196.

[20] Pines, "Arabic Science", 193.

[21] This is Seyyed Hossein Nasr's general observation, see his "Islam and the Environmental Crisis", *The Islamic Quarterly*, 34:4 (1991): 217-34.

[22] Shams Inati's (slightly amended) translation of a passage from Ibn Sīnā's *al-Najāt*. See: Inati, "Ibn Sīnā" in *History of Islamic Philosophy*, Nasr and Leaman (eds), (London: Routledge, 1996), 241.

[23] The best study of Rāzī's religious ideas is S. Stroumsa, *Freethinkers of Medieval Islam* (Leiden: Brill, 1999).

[24] See Stroumsa, *Freethinkers, passim*.

[25] This was articulated by A.I. Sabra in his classic paper, "The Appropriation and Subsequent Naturalization of Greek Science in Medieval Islam", *History of Science*, 25 (1987): 223-43.

[26] See R. Rashed, "Problems of the Transmission of Greek Scientific Thought into Arabic: Examples from Mathematics and Optics", in *History of Science*, 27 (1989): 199-209.

[27] D. Gutas, *Greek Thought, Arabic Culture* (London: Routledge, 1998), 8.

[28] Cf. Rashed. "Problems of the Transmission".

Chapter 7

Metaphysics and Mathematics in Classical Islamic Culture: Avicenna and His Successors

Roshdi Rashed

For seven centuries, advanced mathematical research was carried out in Arabic in the urban centers of Islam. We are justified in wondering whether philosophers found themes for reflection in this work, and if they were incited to seek models in mathematics for the elaboration of their systems, or if, on the contrary, they fell back upon what historians like to call *falsafa*, that is, a doctrine of Being and of the Soul which was indifferent to other branches of knowledge, and independent of every determination save that of religion (in brief, an inheritance from Late Antiquity under the sign of Islam). Such a question might be of interest both to the historian of philosophy and to the historian of sciences. Indeed, how can we imagine that, in the face of the unprecedented flourishing of mathematical disciplines and results – algebra, algebraic geometry, Diophantean analysis, the theory of parallels, and methods of projection – philosophers could have remained indifferent? It is even more difficult to believe that they could have failed to react when, before their very eyes, brand-new epistemological questions were being raised by the new *mathesis*. Among these was the question of the applicability of mathematics: never before had the mathematical disciplines been applied to one another; never had the need been conceived of applying mathematics to physics, as a condition of the latter's apodicticity; finally, never had it occurred to anyone to invent a discipline able to express its results by positional geometry as well as by metrical geometry; in other words, a topology *avant la lettre*. These epistemic events were far from being the only ones; and it would be astonishing if all of them had escaped the attention of the philosophers, some of whom were themselves mathematicians, and most of whom were up to date in the field. It is not, of course, necessary that a discipline or scientific activity should have the philosophy it deserves, nor that the philosopher should play any kind of a role in the development of mathematics and of science. There is, in other words, no *a priori* necessity in the relations between mathematics and theoretical philosophy; but this is one more reason to raise the question and return to the writings of both philosophers and mathematicians, in order to try to elucidate these relations. One result already seems established: having attacked this task on several occasions, I believe I have shown the hitherto-unsuspected wealth of the philosophy of mathematics in classical Islam in mathematicians such as al-Sijzī, Ibn Sinān, Ibn al-Haytham, etc., and that of philosophers like al-Kindī, al-Fārābī, and Ibn Sīnā.

This time, we intend to examine another aspect of the relations between mathematics and philosophy in classical Islam: the connections which are inaugurated when the philosopher borrows from mathematics an instrument for the solution of a logico-mathematical question. The situation which interests us here has one specific feature: by a backfire effect, this borrowing turns out to be fruitful for the progress of the mathematical domain which furnished the instrument. The exchange between combinatorial analysis and metaphysics is an excellent illustration of this double movement. On the basis of his ontological and cosmogonic doctrines, Ibn Sīnā had given a formulation of the doctrine of emanation from the One. In order to derive multiplicity from the One, Naṣīr al-Dīn al-Ṭūsī glimpsed within Ibn Sīnā's doctrine itself the possibility of providing it with a combinatorial framework, which he then borrowed from the algebraists. Yet, in order for al-Ṭūsī's act to be possible, the algebraists' combination rules had to be interpreted in a combinatorial way, and it was this combinatorial interpretation which, as it were, signed the birth certificate of this discipline called combinatorial analysis, which al-Ṭūsī's mathematical successors, men like al-Fārisī and Ibn al-Bannā', among others, were to exploit. On the basis of this contribution, the late philosopher al-Ḥalabī would try to organize the elements of the new discipline, by designating it with a name in order to mark its autonomy.

Before we examine this movement, however, we must first distinguish it from an itinerary like that of Raymond Lulle. He combined notions according to mechanical rules, the results of which later turned out to be arrangements or combinations. Yet Lulle did not borrow anything from mathematics, and never recognized anything mathematical in his own procedure. Al-Ṭūsī's development, by contrast, is closer to Leibniz's procedure, despite all that separates the two projects. As we have said, the former intended to give a mathematical solution for the problem of the emanation of multiplicity from the One, which lead him to provide the Avicennian doctrine of the creation with a combinatorial framework; the latter wished to construct an *Ars inveniendi* on the basis of combinatorics.

Part II

The emanation of the Intelligences and the celestial orbs, as well as the other worlds – that of nature and that of corporeal things – from the One, is one of the central doctrines of Ibn Sīnā's metaphysics. This doctrine raises a question which is simultaneously ontological and noetic: how, from a unique and simple being, can there emanate a multiplicity that is also a complexity, which, in the last analysis, contains the matter of things as much as the forms of bodies and human souls? This ontological and noetic duality raises the question to the status of an obstacle, or both a logical and metaphysical difficulty which had to be unraveled. From this viewpoint, we can at least begin to understand why Ibn Sīnā, in his various writings, returns tirelessly to this doctrine and, implicitly, to this question.

The study of the historical evolution of Ibn Sīnā's thought on this problem in his various writings would show how he was able to amend an initial formulation as a function of such a difficulty. To restrict ourselves to *al-Shifāʾ* and to *al-Ishārāt wa-al-Tanbīhāt*, Ibn Sīnā sets forth the principles of this doctrine, as well as the rules for the emanation of multiple things from a simple unity. His explication seems to be an articulate, ordered exposition, but it does not have the value of a rigorous proof: for in it Ibn Sīnā does not give the syntactical rules capable of adapting to the semantics of emanation. It is precisely here that the difficulty of the question of the derivation of multiplicity from the One resides; yet this derivation had long been perceived as a problem, and examined as such. Naṣīr al-Dīn al-Ṭūsī (1201-1273), the mathematician, philosopher, and commentator on Ibn Sīnā, not only grasped the difficulty but sought to supply the missing syntactical rules.

In his commentary on *al-Ishārāt wa-al-Tanbīhāt*, al-Ṭūsī introduces the language and procedures of combinations, in order to pursue emanation as far as the third rank of beings. He then stops the application of these procedures, in order to conclude: "if we then go farther than these ranks [that is, the first three], a denumerable multiplicity may exist (*lā yuḥṣā ʿadaduhā*) in one single rank, and so on to infinity".[1] Al-Ṭūsī's intention is thus clear and the procedure applied to the first three ranks leaves no room for doubt: he seeks to provide the proof and the means which Ibn Sīnā lacked. At this stage, however, al-Ṭūsī is still far from his goal. It is one thing to proceed by combinations for a number of objects, but quite another to introduce a language, together with its syntax. Here, the language in question would be that of combinations; and al-Ṭūsī devotes himself to the introduction of such a language in an independent paper,[2] the title of which allows for no ambiguity: *On the demonstration of the mode of emanation of things in infinite <number> from the Unique First Principle*. As we shall see, this time al-Ṭūsī proceeds, generally speaking, with the help of combinatorial analysis. Al-Ṭūsī's text, and the results it contains, were not to disappear with their author; we find them in a late treatise entirely devoted to combinatorial analysis. Thus, not only does al-Ṭūsī's solution distinguish a style of philosophical research, but it represents an interesting contribution to the history of mathematics itself.

In order to understand this contribution, we must return to Ibn Sīnā's writings to retrieve the elements of his doctrine necessary for our exposition. We must also grasp, within his synthetic exposition, to some extent, the formal principle whose principle renders possible the introduction of the rules of combinatorial analysis. In fact, it is this principle which allows Ibn Sīnā to develop his exposition in a deductive way. On the one hand, he needed to ensure the unity of Being, which is thus said of everything in the same sense; on the other, he required an irreducible difference between the First Principle and its creations. He thus elaborates a general, as it were "formal", conception of Being: considered qua being, it is not the object of any determination, not even that of the modalities; it is only being. It is not a genus, but a "state" of all that is, and it lets itself be grasped only in its opposition to not-being, without the latter preceding it in time – this opposition exists only in accordance with the order of reason. Moreover, only the First Principle receives its existence from itself.[3] It is thus the only necessary existence, and it is therefore only in this case that existence coincides with essence. All other beings receive their existence from the First Principle, by emanation. This ontology, and the cosmogony which accompanies it, supply the three viewpoints from which a being is envisaged: qua being, qua emanation from the First Principle, and qua being of its quiddity.[4] Seen from the first two viewpoints, it is the necessity of this being which is most prominent, whereas its contingence is revealed by the third. These, mentioned schematically, are the notions upon which Ibn Sīnā was to establish his postulates, which are:

1. There exists a First Principle, a Being necessary by essence, one and indivisible in every sense, which neither is a body, nor is in a body.
2. The totality of being emanates from the First Principle.

3. This emanation takes place neither "according to an intention" (*'alā sabīl qaṣd*), nor in order to reach a goal, but by a necessity of the First Principle's being; that is to say, His auto-intellection.
4. Nothing emanates from the One but the One.
5. There is a hierarchy within emanation, from things whose being is more perfect (*al-akmalu wujūdan*) to those whose being is less perfect (*al-'akhaṣṣu wujūdan*).

Some contradictions might be perceived between some of these postulates, for instance 2 and 4, or else it might be suspected that some of them entail contradictory consequences. In order to avoid this first impression, Ibn Sīnā introduces some supplementary determinations in the course of his deduction. Thus, from 1, 2, 4, and 5, it follows that the totality of being, outside of the First Principle, is a set ordered by its predecessor-successor relation, both logical and axiological, with regard both to being's priority and to its excellence. With the exception of the First Principle, each being can have only one predecessor, its predecessor only one predecessor, and so forth. Moreover, each being, including the First Principle, can have only one successor, its successor only one successor, and so forth. The philosopher and his commentator, however, realize that if this order is understood in the strict sense, it excludes the existence of multiple beings – that is, their independent coexistence, without some of them being logically prior to the others, nor more perfect. This, as al-Ṭūsī says, makes this order manifestly false.[5] It is therefore necessary to introduce supplementary specifications, as well as intermediary beings.

In turn, 1 and 2 prevent multiplicity from proceeding from the "impulses" (*nuzū'āt*) and "perspectives" (*jihāt*) of the First Principle, for to suppose the existence of impulses and perspectives within it would mean denying its unicity and simplicity. Finally, 3 and 5 imply that emanation, as the act of the First Principle, are not in the likeness of human action, since its Author knows neither intentions nor goals. Everything, therefore, indicates that intermediaries (*mutawassiṭa*) must be introduced, which are hierarchized to be sure, but which allow us to give an account of multiplicity and complexity.

Let us begin, as is appropriate, with the First Principle and let us designate it, as Ibn Sīnā does in his treatise *al-Nayrūziyya*, as 'a', the first letter of the alphabet. The First Principle "intelligizes" itself by essence. In its auto-intellection, it "intelligizes" the totality of being, of which it is the proper principle,[6] without there being any obstacle to the emanation of this totality within it, nor any refusal thereof. Only in this sense can the First Principle be said to be the "agent" (*fā'il*) of the totality of being.

When this much is admitted, however, it remains to be explained how this necessary emanation of the totality of being takes place, without the need of adding anything which might contradict the Unicity of the First Principle. According to 1, 4, and 5, one single entity emanates from the First Principle, and it is necessarily of inferior rank in existence and perfection. Since, however, it emanates from a being which is unique, pure, and simple, and simultaneously pure truth, pure power, and pure goodness – without any of these attributes existing in it independently, so that the First Principle's unity may be guaranteed – this derived being can only be a pure Intellect. This implication concerns 4, because if this intellect were not pure, we could conclude that more than one thing emanates from the One. The being in question is the first separate Intellect, first effect (*ma'lūl*) of the First Principle. Like Ibn Sīnā, let us designate it as 'b'.

All is now in place to explain multiplicity-complexity. By essence, this pure Intellect is an effect; it is therefore contingent. As an emanation of the First Principle, however, it is necessary, since it has been "intelligized" by the latter. A noetic multiplicity is superposed upon this ontological duality: the pure Intellect knows itself, and knows its own being, as a contingent being; in other words, its essence is different from that of the First Principle, which is necessary. On the other hand, however, it knows the First Principle as a necessary Being. Finally, it knows the necessity of its own being as an emanation from the First Principle. I have just paraphrased Ibn Sīnā's own words in *al-*

Shifā.[7] He responds in advance to a potential detractor, by remarking that this multiplicity-complexity is not, as it were, a hereditary property: it is not from the First Principle that the pure Intellect receives it, for two reasons. First, the contingency of its being belongs to its own essence, not to the First Principle, who gave it the necessity of its being. Moreover, the knowledge it has of itself, as well as the knowledge it has of the First Principle, is a multiplicity, which results from the necessity of its being from the First Principle. Under these circumstances, Ibn Sīnā can reject the accusation of attributing multiplicity to the First Principle.

Ibn Sīnā then describes how, from this pure Intellect, there emanate the other separate Intellects, the celestial Orbs, and the Souls which allow the Intellects to act. Thus, from the pure Intellect 'b' there emanates, through its intellection of 'a', a second Intellect, 'c'; and through its intellection of its essence, the Soul of the ninth celestial Orb; and through its intellection of its being as contingent being, the body of this ninth Orb. Let us designate the Soul of this Orb, and its body, as 'd'.

Ibn Sīnā thus continues the description of the emanation of the Intellects and celestial Orbs with their Souls and their bodies. From each Intellect, there henceforth emanates the matter of sublunary things, the forms of bodies, and human souls. Yet Ibn Sīnā's explanation, although it has the advantage of not separating the question of multiplicity deriving from the One, from that of complexity – that is, from the ontological contents of multiplicity – nevertheless does not allow rigorous knowledge of the latter, in so far as no general rule is given. Ibn Sīnā merely reduces the elements to the Agent Intellect.

This is where al-Ṭūsī steps in. He was to demonstrate that indeed, from the First Principle, there emanates a multiplicity, according to Ibn Sīnā's rules, and with the help of a limited number of intermediaries, such that each effect has only one cause, which exists independently. As we shall see, the price of this definite progress in the knowledge of multiplicity is the impoverishment of ontological content; indeed, of multiplicity-complexity, only multiplicity was to remain.

Al-Ṭūsī's idea was to submit this problem to a combinatory study. In order for the intervention of combinatorics to be possible, however, we must be assured that the variable *time* is neutralized. In the case of the doctrine of emanation, this translates either into setting aside the realm of becoming, or else at the very least, to interpreting it in a purely logical manner. As we have seen, Ibn Sīnā himself provided this precondition. As has rightly been noted, emanation does not develop within time,[8] and priority and posteriority must be understood in an essential, not a temporal sense. This interpretation, which is, in our view, of capital importance within the Avicennian system, refers us to his own conception of the necessary, the possible, and the impossible. Let us briefly recall that Ibn Sīnā takes up this ancient problem again in *al-Shifā*,[9] in order to reject all ancient doctrines at the outset. According to him, they are circular: in order to define one of the three terms, they have recourse to one or the other of the two remaining ones. In order to break this circle, Ibn Sīnā seeks to limit the definition of each term, by reducing it to the notion of existence. He then distinguishes that which is considered in itself to be of necessary existence, from that which – also considered in itself – may exist and may also fail to exist. For him, necessity and contingency are inherent within beings themselves. With regard to possible being, its existence as well as its non-existence depends upon a cause which is external to it. Contingency thus does not appear as "fallen" necessity, but as another mode of existence. It might even be the case that possible being, while remaining such in itself, might exist of necessity under the action of another being. Without wishing to follow the subtleties of Ibn Sīnā's developments here, let us merely remark that, from this particular definition of the necessary and the possible, Ibn Sīnā founds the terms of emanation within the nature of beings, thereby neutralizing immediately, as we emphasized above, the variable *time*. From these definitions, he deduces a series of propositions, most of which are established by reduction to absurdity. He shows that what is necessary cannot not exist; that it cannot, by essence, have a cause; that its necessity involves all its aspects; that it is one and cannot in any way admit multiplicity; that it is simple and without any composition, etc. On all these points, it is opposed to the possible. It is thus in the very definition of the necessary and the possible, and in the dialectic engaged between them, that the priority of the First Principle, as well as its relations with the Intelligences, are fixed for ever.

If, then, we can describe emanation without having recourse to time, it is in so far as its own terms are given within a logic of the necessary and the possible. It does not matter here that this doctrine is not without difficulties. Nevertheless, we know that the conditions for the introduction of combinatorics were already well set in place by Ibn Sīnā himself.

We said that 'b' emanates from 'a'; 'b' is thus at the highest rank of effects. From 'a' and 'b' together emanates 'c' – the second intellect; from 'b' alone emanates 'd' – or the celestial Orb. At the second rank, we thus have two elements, 'c' and 'd', neither of which is the cause of the other. So far, we have a total of four elements: the first cause, 'a', and three effects, 'b', 'c', and 'd'. Al-Ṭūsī calls these four elements the *principles*. Let us now combine these elements two by two, then three by three, and finally four by four. We thus obtain, successively, six combinations: ab, ac, ad, bc, bd, cd; four combinations: abc, abd, acd, bcd; and one four-element combination: abcd. If we take up the combinations of these four elements one to one, we have a sum of 15 elements, 12 of which belong to the third rank of effects, without some being intermediary elements in order to derive from the others. This is what al-Ṭūsī sets forth in his commentary on *al-Ishārāt wa-al-Tanbīhāt*, as well as in the treatise we mentioned. As soon as we go beyond the third rank, however, things quickly get more complicated, and al-Ṭūsī must introduce the following lemma into his treatise.

The number of combinations of n elements is equal to:

$$\sum_{k=1}^{n}\binom{n}{k}.$$

In order to calculate this object, al-Ṭūsī uses the equality:

$$\binom{n}{k}=\binom{n}{n-k}.$$

Thus, for $n=12$, he obtains 4095 elements. Let us note that here, in order to deduce these numbers, he shows the expressions of the sum by combining the letters of the alphabet.

Al-Ṭūsī then returns to the calculation of the number of elements of the fourth rank. He then considers the four principles with the twelve beings of the third rank: he obtains 16 elements, from which he obtains 65,520 effects. In order to reach this figure, Al-Ṭūsī proceeds with the help of an expression equivalent to:

(*) $$\sum_{k=0}^{m}\binom{m}{k}\binom{n}{p-k},\qquad \text{for } 1\le p \le 16,\ m = 4,\ n = 12,$$

the value of which is the binomial coefficient:

$$\binom{m+n}{p}.$$

None of these elements – with the exception of 'a', 'b', and 'ab' – is an intermediary for the others. Thus, al-Ṭūsī's response is general, and (*) gives a rule which allows us to know the multiplicity within each rank.

After establishing these rules, and giving the example of the fourth rank with its 65,520 elements, al-Ṭūsī can affirm that he has replied to the question "of the possibility of emanation of denumerable multiplicity from the First Principle, under the condition that only one can emanate from the one, and that the effects be successive (in a chain). This is what had to be demonstrated".[10]

Al-Ṭūsī's success in making Ibn Sīnā's ontology speak the language of combinatory analysis was the motive force for two important evolutions: in Ibn Sīnā's doctrine, and in combinatorics. It is clear that this time, the question of multiplicity is maintained at some distance from that of the complexity of being. Al-Ṭūsī is not really concerned with the ontological status of each of the thousands of beings which compose the fourth rank, for example. Nor is this all: metaphysical discourse now permits us to talk about a being, without being able to represent it with exactitude. This "formal" evolution of ontology, which is flagrant here, only amplifies a tendency already present in Ibn Sīnā, which we have emphasized elsewhere, in his considerations on "the thing" (*al-shay'*).[11] This "formal" movement is accentuated by the possibility of designating beings by the letters of the alphabet. Not even the First Principle escapes this rule, since it is designated by the letter 'a'. Here again, al-Ṭūsī amplifies an Avicennian practice, but he modifies its sense. In the epistle *al-Nayrūziyya*, Ibn Sīnā had had recourse to this symbolism but with two differences: first, he had attributed to the succession of the letters of the Arabic alphabet in the *abjad hawaḍ* order the value of an order of priority and logical anteriority; secondly, he used the numerical values of the letters (a=1, b=2, etc.). Although al-Ṭūsī implicitly maintains the order of priority, by designating, like Ibn Sīnā, the First Principle by 'a' and the Intellect by 'b', he has abandoned this hierarchy in favor of the symbol's conventional value, and the numerical value has disappeared. This was, moreover, necessary, in order for these letters to become the object of a combinatorics. As a mathematician and a philosopher, al-Ṭūsī thought through the Avicennian doctrine of emanation in a formal sense, thereby favoring a tendency already present in the ontology of Ibn Sīnā.

The historian of mathematics cannot remain insensitive to the second evolution: that of combinatorial analysis itself. In order to measure its importance, let us briefly recall two historical facts. The first one goes back to the end of the 10th century, when al-Karajī conceived of the arithmetical triangle, the law of its formation, and the formula of binomial development. Al-Karajī established these expressions with the help of an archaic finite mathematical induction. These are algebraic formulae, which certainly, albeit only implicitly, contain a combinatoric meaning. Al-Karajī's successors also had recourse to this combinatorial meaning but without exhibiting it to any greater extent. In his arithmetical book *Jawāmiʿ al-ḥisāb*, al-Ṭūsī himself gives these rules as obtained by al-Karajī, without lingering over this implicit signification. We know, moreover, that since al-Khalīl ibn Aḥmad in the 8th century, lexicographers and linguists had utilized combinatorial procedures, which they had no interest in demonstrating. Yet, unlike the mathematicians, they insisted on the combinatorial nature of these procedures. These two currents flow together in al-Ṭūsī's text, thereby founding combinatorial analysis by conferring upon it the status of a fully-blown chapter in the history of mathematics. This time, algebraic formulas are explicitly given a combinatorial meaning, and are illustrated by calculations upon letters. Thus, it is as if the application of this calculus to fields like the one which interests us had been revelatory, inciting the mathematician to exhibit the subjacent combinatory meaning, and to fuse together two currents which had previously been independent. Whether this unifying act was due to al-Ṭūsī or suggested to him by a predecessor, likewise a mathematician and philosopher who is now unknown to us, is a historical detail which need not matter much to us here. In any event, this act allowed the language of combinations to adapt itself to that of Ibn Sīnā, arming it with the syntactical rules which it initially lacked. As we have seen, the doctrine was not to emerge intact, for this gain was at the cost of intuitive richness.

Part III

A return to the history of mathematics will allow us to verify the validity of our analyses if we follow, at least partially, the destiny of al-Ṭūsī's text. Here once again, good fortune has presented us with a philosopher-mathematician who has never been studied and has placed in our hands a treatise composed by him but unknown until now. The author is a late mathematician-philosopher of the second rank named Ibrāhīm al-Ḥalabī,[12] and his treatise is the first we know of to be entirely devoted to combinatory analysis. In it, in fact, the rules of this analysis no longer appear simply when they are applied algebraically, linguistically, or philosophically, but for themselves, in a principal chapter entitled "Combinable Eventualities". This title is a generic designation, which refers to permutations just as much as to arrangements, combinations, etc., in other words, to all the combinations studied at the time. In this treatise, al-Ṭūsī's text is taken up and amplified, and it occupies a prime position: it fulfills the function of a method for determining and establishing combinations.

Let us quickly consider this treatise by al-Ḥalabī; in the process, we will understand what place is reserved, in a treatise on combinatory analysis, for the solution of a metaphysical problem. Al-Ḥalabī starts by wondering about the various possible methods for analyzing the "combinable eventualities" (*al-iḥtimālāt al-tarkībiyya*). Al-Ḥalabī's goal is clear: "to determine the number of combinable eventualities for any number of objects".[13] He rejects the empirical method of enumeration, which offers no general rule despite its efficacy in simple cases. This method consists in enumerating, for instance for a set of three elements (a, b, c), the seven "combinable eventualities" (a, b, c, ab, ac, bc, abc). The difficulty is obvious in the case of a set with n elements.[14]

The second method,[15] by contrast, supplies a general rule of which al-Ḥalabī is proud. This is an expression equivalent to $u_n = 2u_{n-1} + 1$, where u_n is the set of "combinable eventualities" with n elements. In our language:

$$u_n = \sum_{k=1}^{n} \binom{n}{k} \text{ with } \binom{n}{k} = \frac{n!}{k!(n-k)!} \text{ for } 1 \leq k \leq n$$

This method has probably been established on the basis of a rule known since the end of the 10th century:

$$\binom{n}{k} = \binom{n-1}{k-1} + \binom{n-1}{k}.$$

By addition, we get:

$$u_n = \sum_{k=1}^{n} \binom{n-1}{k-1} + \sum_{k=1}^{n} \binom{n-1}{k}$$
$$= \sum_{k=0}^{n-1} \binom{n-1}{k} + \sum_{k=1}^{n} \binom{n-1}{k}$$
$$= 2u_{n-1} + 1$$

Al-Ḥalabī also departs from this method, which requires a complex calculation of all u_i for $1 \leq i \leq n-1$. In order to define a better method, al-Ḥalabī first begins with the expression:

$$\binom{n}{k} = \binom{n}{n-k}.$$

and that:

$$\binom{n}{n+r} = 0 \quad ; \quad \binom{n}{n} = \binom{n}{0} = 1.$$

He then defines several "combinable eventualities", with the corresponding rules of calculus. Thus, we have:

1. The matter (*al-mādda*)[16] of the eventualities of kind k – that is to say, the non-repeating combinations given by the preceding formula:

$$\binom{n}{k}.$$

2. Matter and form (*majmūʿ al-mādda wa-al-ṣūra*)[17] of eventualities of kind k – that is, the arrangements without repetition:

$$A_n^k = k! \binom{n}{k} = \frac{n!}{(n-k)!}.$$

3. The form (*al-ṣūra*)[18] of the eventualities of kind k: it is enough to subtract matter from matter and form (2).

$$k\binom{n}{k} - \binom{n}{k} = \binom{n}{k}(k! - 1).$$

4. The form of the eventualities, independently of the kind; that is to say, the permutations of n objects, or:

$$n! = n\,(n-1)\,\ldots\,1.$$

5. Matter, form, and the repetitions of the eventualities of kind k,[19] that is, arrangements with repetition of n objects taken k to k; that is, n^k.

Let us note that the technical lexicon of the language of combinatory analysis which al-Ḥalabī uses in this treatise is made up of terms already employed by al-Ṭūsī *(tarkība)*, of terms which are peculiar to him, such as *iḥtimālāt* (eventuality), and *tikrār* (repetition), but also of loan-words from Aristotelian vocabulary, such as *mādda* (matter) et *ṣūra* (form). These two terms oblige him, moreover, to introduce problems foreign to his theme, which may be superfluous in this context, and which at any rate damage the clarity of the exposition. For instance, he asks himself if matter and form can be separated.

Once these rules have been laid down, al-Ḥalabī writes: "In order to determine the material eventualities *(al-iḥtimālāt al-māddiyya;* that is, combinations without repetition), there is another method which has been mentioned to determine the Accidental Intellects *(al-ʿuqūl al-ʿaraḍiyya).*" It is here that he integrates the text by al-Ṭūsī, sometimes *in verbis*, sometimes by developing its calculus. Thus, he traces the arithmetical triangle as far as 12, and adds the elements of the diagonal, which he calls "simple combinations" *(al-iḥtimālāt al-basīṭa)* in order to obtain the number 4095, mentioned by al-Ṭūsī. The following are what he calls "composite combinations" (*al- iḥtimālāt al-murakkaba*):[20]

$$(**) \qquad \left(\sum_{k=1}^{m} \binom{m}{k} \right) \left(\sum_{j=1}^{n} \binom{n}{j} \right) \qquad \text{for } m = 4,\ n = 12,$$

He shows that the expression (*) is the sum of the simple and the complex combinations. In other words, we have:

$$(***) \qquad \sum_{p=1}^{m+n} \left(\sum_{k=0}^{m} \binom{m}{k} \binom{n}{p-k} \right) = \sum_{k=1}^{m} \binom{m}{k} + \sum_{j=1}^{n} \binom{n}{j} + \left(\sum_{k=1}^{m} \binom{m}{k} \right) \left(\sum_{j=1}^{n} \binom{n}{j} \right)$$

$$= \sum_{k=1}^{m} \binom{m}{k} + \left(\sum_{k=0}^{m} \binom{m}{k} \right) \left(\sum_{j=1}^{n} \binom{n}{j} \right).$$

When we subtract 1 from both sides, we obtain:

$$\sum_{p=0}^{m+n} \left(\sum_{k=0}^{m} \binom{m}{k} \binom{n}{p-k} \right) = \left(\sum_{k=0}^{n} \binom{m}{k} \right) \left(\sum_{j=0}^{m} \binom{n}{j} \right),$$

whence, from the equivalence with the formula (*):

$$2^{m+n} = 2^m 2^n.$$

Al-Ḥalabī proceeds to give still more calculations on the data supplied by al-Ṭūsī, and he indulges in some reflections on his predecessor's text, all of which have to do with combinatory properties. We are very far from the problem of the emanation of multiplicity from the One, of which there remains only a pale shadow. The ontological content, already blurred in al-Ṭūsī, vanishes completely in this treatise on combinatory analysis, leaving behind only the methods and results necessary or useful for the body of this mathematical discipline. If, then, the "axiomatic" flavor of Ibn Sīnā's doctrine, and his penchant towards formal ontology, made the hope of a mathematical solution for this metaphysical problem conceivable for al-Ṭūsī, this solution was then itself integrated with the mathematical works, independently of the metaphysical problem which it inspired. This was possible in so far as the beings of combinatorics may be Intellects or any kind of objects, as long as they are separate and in a number which may be as large as is wished, but must be finite.

From Ibn Sīnā to al-Ḥalabī, we have witnessed the disappearance of the ontological contents of a doctrine, to the profit of the combinatory methods, the intervention of which was nevertheless initially in the service of this ontology. Unifier of two separate currents of research – that of the linguists and that of the mathematicians – al-Ṭūsī's act was the founder of this movement, and thereby of combinatory analysis. Although a second-rate mathematician, al-Ḥalabī assured the chapter an autonomous existence, by baptizing it with a name. Between al-Ṭūsī and al-Ḥalabī, however, there are many others who also seem to have been under the influence of al-Ṭūsī; one thinks in particular of al-Fārisī and Ibn al-Bannā'.[21]

This example, together with others, is a witness to the importance of the philosophy of mathematics in classical Islam. It also shows that mathematics played a genuine role in philosophy; which is scarcely surprising. It also shows, however, that the role of philosophy in the progress of this branch of mathematics is no less real. As historians of science, we cannot turn our backs on the history of philosophy; but as historians of Islamic philosophy, it would be fatal for us to ignore the role of the new domains of knowledge.

Notes

[1] Ed. Saʿīd Dunyā, vol. 3 (Cairo: 1971), 217-218.

[2] This paper was first established by Mohammad Danesh Pajouh, and was published in *Intishārāt Dānishkā Tehrān* 296, 13-20; it was then established by ʿAbd Allāh Nūrānī and published, together with other papers by al-Ṭūsī at the end of his edition of the *Talkhīṣ al-muḥaṣṣal* (Tehran, 1980), 509-515. These two publications followed the manuscript Danishka 1079/12. We have established the text [in "Combinatoire et métaphysique: Ibn Sīnā, al-Ṭūsī et al-Ḥalabī", *Les Doctrines de la science de l'Antiquité à l'Age classique*, Roshdi Rashed and Joel Biard (eds), *Ancient and Classical Sciences and Philosophy* (Leuven: Peeters, 1999), 61-86, on p. 77-86], on the basis of the following manuscripts: Istanbul, Aya Sofia 4855, fol. 203ʳ-207ʳ; Teheran, Dānishkā 1079/12, fol. 16-31; Marʿashī 7036, fol. 193ᵛ-195ʳ; Āstān Quds 2798, fol. 49-51.

[3] Ibn Sīnā distinguishes existence and essence for all other beings. On this point, see Amelie-Marie Goichon, *La Distinction entre existence et essence* (Paris, 1957) and Michael B. Marmura, "Quiddity and Universality in Avicenna", *Neoplatonism and Islamic Philosophy*, Parviz Morewedge (ed.), (Albany: State University of New York Press, 1992), 77-87. See also Djémil Saliba, *Sur la Métaphysique d'Avicenne* (Pau, 1926); G. Verbeke, "Le statut de la métaphysique"; introduction to *Avicenna Latinus, Liber de Philosophia Prima*, by Simone Van Riet (Louvain-Leiden, 1977).

[4] On Ibn Sīnā's doctrine of emanation, cf. Louis Gardet "En l'honneur du millénaire d'Avicenne", *Revue Thomiste*, LIXᵉ année, t. LI, no 2 (1951): 333-345, Nicholas Heer, "Al-Rāzī and al-Ṭūsī on Ibn Sīnā's Theory of Emanation", *Neoplatonism and Islamic Philosophy*, ed. Morewedge, 111-125; and in particular the article by Ahmad Hasnawi, "Fayḍ", in *Philosophie Occidentale*, 966-972. One may also consult the contributions by Thérèse-Anne Druart, "Al-Fārābī, Emanation, and Metaphysics", 127-148; Morewedge, "The Neoplatonic Structure of Some Islamic Mystical Doctrines", 51-75; Joseph Owens, "The Relevance of Avicennian Neoplatonism", 41-50, in *Neoplatonism and Islamic Thought*, cited above.

[5] Op. cit., 216.

[6] Ibn Sīnā, *al-Shifāʾ, al-Ilāhiyāt*, eds. Muhammad Y. Mūsā, Sulaymān Dunyā, and Saʿīd Zāyed, revised and introduced by Ibrahim Madkour (Cairo, 1960), 2:402, 1. 16.

[7] Ibid., 405-406.

[8] See Hasnawi, "Fayḍ", and Gardet, who writes: "The process described by Ibn Sīnā does not develop within time. The priority of the First Principle over the Intelligences, and, more generally, over the All, is an *essential* anteriority, not a temporal one", *Al-Shifā*, VI, 2, 266. On these questions, see also Herbert A. Davidson, *Proofs for Eternity Creation and the Existence of God in Medieval Islamic and Jewish Philosophy* (New York / Oxford, 1987); Thérèse-Anne Druart, "Al-Farabi and Emanationism", *Studies in Medieval Philosophy*, John F. Wippell (ed.), (Washington: The Catholic University of America Press, 1987), 23-43; and Parviz Morewedge,

"The Logic of Emanationism and Ṣūfism in the Philosophy of Ibn Sīnā (Avicenna), Part II", *Journal of the American Oriental Society* 92 (1972): 1-18.

[9] Cf. in particular book 3, chapter 4 of the *Syllogism*, vol. IV, Saʿīd Zāyed (ed.), introduction and revision by Ibrahim Madkour (Cairo, 1964).

[10] Rashed, "Combinateire et métaphysique", 86.

[11] *Éttudes sur Avicenne*, dirigées par Jean Jolivet et Roshdi Rashed, Collection sciences et philosophie arabes. Études et reprises (Paris: Les Belles Lettres, 1984).

[12] *Risāla fī istikhrāj ʿiddat al-iḥtimālāt al-tarkībiyya min ayy ʿadad kāna*, ms Istanbul, Süleymaniye, Hamidiye 873, fol. 69ᵛ-86ʳ.

[13] Ibid., fol. 69ᵛ.

[14] Ibid., fol. 70ʳ.

[15] Ibid., fol. 70ʳ-71ᵛ.

[16] Ibid., fol. 71ᵛ.

[17] Ibid., fol. 72ʳ.

[18] Ibid., fol. 72ᵛ-73ʳ.

[19] Ibid., fol. 73ᵛ-74ʳ.

[20] Ibid., fol. 81ʳ.

[21] Roshdi Rashed, "Nombres amiables, parties aliquotes et nombres figurés", in *Entre arithmétique et algébre. Recherches sur l'histoire des mathématiques arabes* (Paris: Les Belles Lettres, 1984), 259-299.

Part II

Cosmological Issues

Chapter 8
Islamic Paradigms for the Relationship between Science and Religion
Ahmad Dallal

Modern studies in the history of science show that productive, original scientific research persisted into the 16th century A.D. in the Islamic world. Yet, histories of Islamic civilization consistently repeat and expand an influential theory which maintains that the consolidation of an Islamic worldview already in the 11th century caused the rational sciences to stagnate. This theory even posits an essential contradiction between science and Islam, and is part of a larger contention in post-Enlightenment historiography that opposes science and religion in general in post-medieval civilizations. Thus, according to various accounts based on this theory, scientific activities in Muslim societies were consistently opposed (ostensibly by religious authorities of Islam), and they survived despite, and not as a result of, Islamic culture.[1] Yet, in addition to its apparent counter-intuitiveness, this theory fails to explain the growing body of evidence which confirms the rise, rather than decline, of science in the Islamic world after the 11th century.[2] Further evidence suggests that scientific activity was integrated with, rather than marginal to mainstream intellectual life in Muslim societies.[3] A different approach to the study of the relationship between science and religion in Islam is clearly needed, one that examines both the cultural environment, and the interaction among different cultural dynamics at work.

In the last few decades, a critical mass of excellent studies by competent historians of Islamic science has led to a qualitative shift in our understanding of this history.[4] Yet despite this shift, an integrated approach to the study of the history of science in Muslim societies still needs to overcome some real hurdles. To start with, such an undertaking calls for an examination of wide-ranging cultural activities, in a vast geographical area, under different historical conditions, and for a period of at least seven centuries. Moreover, the sources for the study of this subject are daunting, and they include, in addition to material evidence, thousands of scientific manuscripts, most of which remain unexamined. The abundance of evidence also gives rise to a number of methodological difficulties: earlier surveys of the history of Islamic science were based on a handful of random studies of scientific treatises. Some of the actual studies were of a high quality; yet ironically, the paucity of hard evidence available to early scholars often enabled them to cover all the fields of science in all-inclusive, and often reductive, narratives. In the last few decades, many more scientific treatises have been critically examined, with the dual effect of providing detailed information about the various scientific disciplines, and highlighting the peculiarity of the history of each separate discipline or even fields within disciplines.

In the absence of thorough and exhaustive accounts for developments in the various scientific disciplines as well as accounts for the epistemological foundations of these sciences, it only stands to reason that attempts to provide general characterizations of science in Muslim societies and its relation to religion can only be provisional and subject to scrutiny. Even such seemingly straightforward character-izations of the scientific activity in Muslim societies as Islamic or Arabic cannot be taken for granted, and the same applies to the assertion that Islam has either a positive or a negative attitude towards science. I do not mean here to deny the validity of using terms such as "Islamic science", but simply to stress the importance of addressing the question of methodology before venturing such general characterizations.[5]

Due to the extent of the scientific enterprise in classical Muslim societies, the question of the relationship between science and religion in Islam can be approached from many different perspectives, and may vary according to, and within, the region, period, or discipline under consideration. For example, one may look at standard discussions among religious scholars and theologians. Alternatively, the classifications of the sciences provide an epistemological perspective which pertains to theories of knowledge. One can also examine and attempt to classify the manifold views of scientists as well as religious scholars on the relationship between science and religion. In this essay, I will restrict myself to the field of astronomy; in particular, I will compare two important trends of research in theoretical astronomy. Astronomy, I should add, is especially relevant to the question of the relationship between science and religion because of its cosmological dimension and the relative ease with which it can be invoked in connection with metaphysical questions. The main focus in this paper is on the way communities of scientific knowledge conceived of their profession and research within the larger context of religion. However, I will first say a few words about religious scholars who discussed science and proposed "Islamic" assessments of the various sciences.

Almost invariably, discussions of the Islamic attitude toward science invoke the works of al-Ghazālī (d. 505/1111). I will not attempt to summarize Ghazālī's views on the various sciences; these views have received more scholarly attention than those of any other Muslim scholar who had written on the subject. It is important to note, however, that the debate regarding Ghazālī's true attitudes and views continues among contemporary scholars, and there seems to be no consensus even over the interpretation of his most obvious work, *Tahāfut al-Falāsifa* (*The Incoherence of the Philosophers*), let alone an integrated assessment of his whole oeuvre, including such relevant works to our subject as *al-Iqtiṣād fi al-I'tqād, Mi'yār al-'Ilm, al-Qusṭās al-Mustaqīm, Maqāsid al-Falāsifa*, and *al-Mustasfā min 'Ilm al-Uṣūl*.[6]

Aside from al-Ghazālī and whether he actually condoned, neglected, or opposed the sciences, there are, to be sure, some radical and credible traditionalists, such as Ibn Taymiyya (d. 1328), who attacked some of the fields of knowledge that Ghazālī condoned, but in the face of these there are equally radical and popular traditionalists, such as Ibn Ḥazm (11th century), who defended logic and argued for the interconnection between the various sciences.[7] What is more important about the provocative writings of Ibn Taymiyya with such titles as "The Rebuttal of Logic" and "The attack on Logicians", is that Ibn Taymiyya employed the discourse of formal logic and, rather than deny the validity of logic, he only denies the claim by a professional group of logicians to have an exclusive monopoly over methods of arriving at Truth. Moreover, Ibn Taymiyya questioned the validity of some of the propositions and syllogisms of certain kinds of formal logic, and not all kinds of logic. Furthermore, Ibn Taymiyya criticized Ghazālī's denial of causality and was a strong believer in physics and the natural laws.[8] Again, the purpose of citing these authors here is not to provide an exhaustive analysis of their views, but simply to point out the diversity as well as complexity of the views of traditional Muslim scholars on science and scientific knowledge.

The differences between these traditional religious scholars highlight the difficulty of identifying a unified, traditional Islamic attitude toward science. It is clear, however, that the overall outcome of the religious debates over scientific knowledge was to naturalize some of the exact sciences and to provide Islamic justifications for certain kinds of scientific knowledge. Such was the assessment of the famous 14th century historian Ibn Khaldūn who remarks in his *Muqaddima* that after Ghazālī all religious scholars studied logic, but they studied it from new sources, such as the works of Ibn al-Khaṭīb and al-Khunjī (13th century), and that people stopped using the books of the ancients;[9] "the books and the methods of the ancients", says Ibn Khaldūn, "are avoided, as if they had never been". Later he adds (on page 143):

> It should be known that the early Muslims and the early speculative theologians greatly disapproved of the study of this discipline [logic]. They vehemently attacked it and warned against it... Later on, ever since al-Ghazālī and the imām Ibn al-Khaṭīb, scholars have been somewhat more lenient in this respect. Since that time, they have gone on studying (logic) ...

Generally speaking, therefore, religious assessments of the epistemic value of various kinds of scientific knowledge were nuanced and diverse. And although one cannot adduce a direct and mechanical correlation between the religious arguments and the ways in which scientists perceived of and theorized their own scientific disciplines, it is abundantly clear that the views of scientists were also manifold. Furthermore, since they were inspired by a variety of cultural factors, these articulations by scientists are obvious and tangible expressions of what "Islamic" science meant in actual history, and are as indicative of the Islamic dimension as the views expressed by religious scholars. In what follows, I will approach the question of the relationship between science and religion by focusing on two particular traditions of astronomical research, one in the Muslim east and the other in the Muslim west. My interest is in charting out the peculiar modes of thinking that provided the epistemological and methodological conditions for the formation of these two traditions, and the diverse conceptual frameworks that informed the different planetary theories proposed in each.

Ever since Sarton's attempt to write a universal history of science, the Islamic sciences have had a considerable presence in various accounts of this history. Despite their large quantitative presence, however, Islamic sciences are all too often absent from grand, integrative narratives of the history of science. When historians offer conceptual analysis of epochal changes in the history of science (which is something they often do), the cumulative legacy of the Islamic sciences is simply overlooked. Conceptually, the Islamic scientific legacy is seen as a rather mechanical continuation of the Greek one: the Islamic sciences expanded and refined the Greek sciences without departing from them conceptually.[10] A justification of this oversight is seldom provided, but when it is, it usually has to do with the role of philosophy or theory in science. In the field of astronomy in particular, theoretical considerations were often overlooked on the basis of a widely held assumption that Islamic science was practical and hence theoretically or philosophically shallow.[11] The decline of Islamic science, according to this view, was a result of the lack of theoretical rigor. In the last few decades, however, an alternative view has been proposed, often by competent historians of science. In contrast to the notion that the Islamic sciences declined because of their feeble philosophical foundations, historians of astronomy now argued that the motivation for the most important tradition of astronomical reform in the Muslim world was philosophical.[12] Despite its different understanding of the role of philosophy in connection with the science of astronomy, this thesis often served to undermine the "scientific" value of these astronomical reforms.

In a sense, the two different views regarding the role of philosophy in Islamic science echo a fundamental debate over the function of scientific theory. Simply put, scientists and philosophers (as well as historians of science) differ over whether the primary role of scientific theory is to explain nature as it exists in reality or simply describe and predict its appearance as we perceive it. In the latter case (description and prediction), the quest of science is to "save the phenomena", whereas in the former case, science goes beyond appearance to explore causal connections or, in the language of philosophers, "first causes".[13] This philosophical controversy, and many variations of it, is at the roots of the emergence of what is commonly called "modern science", and it continues to inform modern and postmodern debates on the relationship between scientific knowledge and others forms of knowledge. This controversy has also influenced readings of the history of "non-western" science. Before examining the question of the role of theory in science as reflected in the two Islamic traditions of astronomical reform, a few words on the early developments in Islamic astronomy that provided the background for the latter reform traditions are necessary.

Astronomy was one of the oldest, most developed and most esteemed exact sciences of antiquity.[14] Many of the mathematical sciences were originally developed to facilitate astronomical research. Various disciplines and belief systems intersected and interacted in astronomy, including physics and metaphysics, as well as mathematics and religion. Islamic/Arabic astronomy was also culturally a hybrid (Babylonian, Indian, Persian, and Greek),[15] and intimately connected to politics (astrology, dynastic legitimization).[16] Finally, practical considerations such as finding one's direction during night travel, and the correlation between the seasons of the year and the positions of the planets provided additional incentives for the study of astronomy. For all of these reasons, astronomical research was hybrid and spirited, and the field of astronomy provided fertile grounds for questioning old conceptions and developing and testing new ones.

The first astronomical texts that were translated into Arabic in the 8th century were of Indian and Persian origin. The real emergence of Arabic astronomy, however, occurred in the 9th century at which time the major Greek astronomical texts were translated. Right from its very beginnings in the 9th and all the way until the 16th century, astronomical activity was widespread and intensive. This activity is reflected in the large number of scientists working in practical and theoretical astronomy, the number of books written, the active observatories, and the new observations.[17]

Arabic astronomy was first exposed to Persian and Indian astronomy, and it continued to use some of the parameters and methods of these two traditions, yet the greatest formative influence on Arabic astronomy is undoubtedly Greek. Early in the 9th century, astronomers realized that the Greek astronomical tradition was far superior to the other two, both in its comprehensiveness and its use of effective geometrical representations. One particular Greek author, and more specifically one work by this author, exerted a disproportionate influence on all of medieval astronomy through the whole of the Arabic period and until the eventual demise of the geocentric astronomical system. This is the *Almagest* of Ptolemy (2nd century AD). That this text should exert so much influence is neither accidental nor surprising, for it is the highest achievement in Hellenistic mathematical astronomy, and one of the greatest achievements of all of Hellenistic science.[18]

The *Almagest* was rightly considered the main authoritative work of antiquity on Astronomy. In this book, Ptolemy synthesizes the earlier knowledge of Hellenistic astronomy in light of his own new observations. The main purpose of the book is to establish the geometric models which would accurately account for observational phenomena. A large part of the book is dedicated to the methods for constructing various models and for calculating the parameters of these models. Ptolemy also provides tables for planetary motions to be used in conjunction with his models. Of all the books of antiquity, the *Almagest* represents the most successful work of mathematical astronomy: its geometric representations of the universe provided the most accurate and best predictive accounts for the celestial phenomena. A Greek tradition of physical astronomy is also reflected in the *Almagest* and in Ptolemy's other influential work, the *Planetary Hypothesis*.[19] According to this predominantly Aristotelian tradition, the universe is organized into a set of concentric spheres, each carrying a star and rotating around the stationary earth at the center of the universe. In contrast to sublunary rectilinear motion, the heavenly bodies move in perfect uniform circular motions. Ptolemy adopted, at least in theory, the two basic Aristotelian principles: that the earth is stationary at the center of the universe, and that the motion of heavenly bodies ought to be represented by a set of uniform circular motions. In practice, mathematical considerations often forced Ptolemy to disregard the second of these principles. However, against his better "mathematical" judgement, the only physical theory or cosmology available to Ptolemy was that of Aristotle. Ptolemy thus had no other option but to profess his adherence to this cosmology, an adherence which gave rise, in the Islamic period and later in Europe, to a long and fruitful tradition of astronomical reform.

Astronomical reform in the Islamic period took different forms. Under the Caliph al-Ma'mūn, a program of astronomical observations was organized in Baghdad and Damascus.[20] Like any organized research project, this program endowed astronomical activity in the Islamic world with formal prestige. The professed purpose of this program was to verify the Ptolemaic observations by comparing the results derived by calculation, based on the Ptolemaic models, with actual observations conducted in Baghdad and Damascus some 700 years after Ptolemy. The results were compiled in *al-Zīj al-Mumtaḥan* (*The Verified Tables*), which is no longer extant in its entirety, but is widely quoted by later astronomers.[21] The most important correction introduced was to show that the apogee of the solar orb moves with the precession of the fixed stars. On a more general note, this program stressed the need for continuing verification of astronomical observations, and for the use of more precise instruments.[22]

Thus, right from its beginnings, Arabic astronomy set out to rectify and complement Ptolemaic astronomy. Having noted several discrepancies between new observations and Ptolemaic calculations, astronomers then proceeded to reexamine the theoretical basis of Ptolemy's results. This critical reexamination took several forms. Although the general astronomical research of this period (9th century) is conducted within the framework of Ptolemaic astronomy, this research reworked and critically examined the observations and the computational methods of this astronomy and, in a limited way, was able to explore problems outside its set frame. The application of diverse mathematical disciplines to each other also had the immediate effect of expanding the frontiers of disciplines and introducing new scientific concepts and ideas. The use of systematic mathematization transformed the methods of reasoning and enabled, in turn, further creative developments in the branches of science.[23]

In the 10th and 11th centuries, the earlier examinations of Ptolemaic astronomy led to systematic projects which, rather than addressing the field in its totality, focused on specific aspects of astronomy. One of the main characteristics of this period was the tendency to provide exhaustive synthesizing works on particular astronomical topics, culminating in Bīrūnī's (973-c. 1048) *al-Qānūn al-Mas'ūdī*,[24] a synthesis of the Greek, Indian, and Arabic astronomical traditions. It is with Bīrūnī that we have the first systematic discussion, by a scientist (astronomer), of the relationship between science and philosophy. A book entitled *al-As'ila wa'l-Ajwiba* (*Questions and Answers*) preserves an exchange between Bīrūnī and his contemporary Ibn Sīna, the most celebrated Muslim philosopher of all time.[25] Bīrūnī presents Ibn Sīna with a set of questions in which he criticizes Aristotle's physical theory, especially as it pertains to astronomy. Ibn Sīna then responds, and a lively debate ensues. In the course of this exchange, Bīrūnī questions almost all of the fundamental Aristotelian physical axioms: he rejects the notion that heavenly bodies have an inherent nature, and asserts that their motion could very well be compulsory; he maintains that there is no observable evidence that rules out the possibility of vacuum;[26] he further asserts that, although observation corroborates Aristotle's claim that the motion of heavenly bodies is circular, there is no inherent "natural" reason why this motion cannot be, among other things, elliptical.[27] What is more significant than the actual objections raised by Bīrūnī is the argument he employs in the course of the debate. Bīrūnī draws a distinction between his vocation and that of Aristotle and Ibn Sīna. He seems to argue that the metaphysical axioms on which philosophers build their physical theories do not constitute valid evidence for the mathematical astronomer.[28] In other words, Bīrūnī clearly distinguishes between the philosopher and the mathematician, the metaphysician and the scientist. He conceives of himself as a mathematical astronomer for whom the only valid evidence is observational or mathematical. Bīrūnī's example illustrates how the systematic application of rigorous mathematical reasoning led to the mathematization of astronomy and, by extension, to the mathematization of nature. Rather than subsuming the various sciences under the all-encompassing umbrella of philosophy, many scientists considered their professions as autonomous mathematical enterprises, separate from, and on par with philosophy.

　　As I noted earlier, Ptolemy had taken the liberty to propose models that did not conform to Aristotelian cosmology; so how does Bīrūnī's example differ from that of Ptolemy? Put differently, can we think of both Ptolemy and Bīrūnī as prototypes for scientists that are interested in the descriptive functions of science, in "saving the phenomena", as opposed to scientists seeking to explain and not just describe? I will try to answer this question by comparing two traditions of astronomical reform in the Muslim east and west.

Traditions of Astronomical Reform in the Islamic Period

Building on the cumulative achievements of Arabic astronomy, the 11th century witnessed the emergence of a new tradition of astronomical research. After the 11th century, the efforts of most theoretical astronomers were directed towards providing a thorough evaluation of the physical and philosophical underpinnings of Ptolemaic astronomy, and proposing alternatives to it.[29] It should be noted here that the emergence of this tendency in astronomical research does not represent a move away from the thorough mathematical examination of astronomy, but is an outcome of this increasing mathematization. This line of research was pursued by several 11th century scientists. In a book entitled *Tarkīb al-Aflāk*, Abu 'Ubayd al-Jūzjānī (d. c. 1070) indicates that both he and his teacher, Ibn Sīna, were aware of the so-called equant problem of the Ptolemaic model. Jūzjānī even proposes a solution for this problem. The author of an anonymous Andalusian astronomical manuscript refers to another work which he composed under the title *al-Istidrāk 'alā Baṭlamyūs* (*Recapitulation Regarding Ptolemy*), and indicates that he included in this book a list of objections to Ptolemaic astronomy. The most important work of this genre, however, was written in the same period by Ibn al-Haytham (d. 1039). In his celebrated work *Al-Shukūk 'alā Baṭlamyūs* (*Doubts on Ptolemy*),[30] Ibn al-Haytham sums up the physical and philosophical problems inherent in the Greek astronomical system and provides an inventory of the theoretical inconsistencies of the Ptolemaic models. The tradition of astronomical reform thrived in the 13th century, climaxed in the 14th, and continued well into the 15th and 16th centuries. Most astronomers of this period took up the theoretical challenge outlined by Ibn al-Haytham, attempted to rework the models of Ptolemaic astronomy and to provide, with varying degrees of success, alternatives to these models. The list of astronomers working within this tradition comprises some of the greatest and most original Muslim scientists. The astronomers who have received modern scholarly attention include: Mu'ayyad al-Dīn al-'Urḍī (d. 1266), Naṣīr al-Dīn al-Ṭūsī (d. 1274), Quṭb al-Dīn al-Shīrāzī (d. 1311), Ṣadr al-Sharī'a al-Bukhārī (d. 1347), Ibn al-Shāṭir (d. 1375), and 'Alā' al-Dīn al-Qushjī (d. 1474).[31]

To appreciate the technical aspects of these astronomical reforms,[32] a quick overview of some aspects of Ptolemaic astronomy is in order. In his *Almagest*, Ptolemy used the results of earlier Hellenistic astronomy and incorporated them into one great synthesis. Of particular geometrical utility was the concept of eccentrics and epicycles developed by Hipparchus (2nd century BC) and adopted by Ptolemy. In an astronomical representation employing the eccentric model (Figure 8.1), a planet is carried on the circumference of an eccentric circle which rotates uniformly around its own center G. This center, however, does not coincide with the location O of an observer on the earth. As a result, the speed of the planet appears to vary with respect to the observer at O. In an epicyclic model, the planet P is carried on the circumference of an epicycle, whose center is in turn carried on a circle called the deferent, which rotates uniformly around the center of the universe, the earth. Viewed by an observer at point O, the combination of the two uniform motions of the deferent and the epicycle produces a non-uniform motion which is mathematically equivalent to the motion of the eccentric model.

The Ptolemaic model for the motion of the sun utilized either a simple eccentric or the equivalent combination of a deferent and an epicycle. All the other Ptolemaic models for planetary motions were considerably more complex. For example, in the model for the longitudinal motion of the upper planets Mars, Jupiter, and Saturn (Figure 8.2), the center G of the deferent circle no longer coincides with the earth O; moreover, the uniform motion of the center of the epicycle on the circumference of the deferent is measured around the point E, called the equant center, rather than the center G of the deferent. Ptolemy proposed this model because it allowed for fairly accurate predictions of planetary positions. However, circle G in this model is made to rotate uniformly around the equant E which is not its center. This represented a violation of the Aristotelian principle, adopted by Ptolemy, of uniform circular motion around the Earth, the stationary center of the universe. In other words, for the sake of observation, Ptolemy was forced to breach the physical and philosophical principles on which he built his astronomical theory.

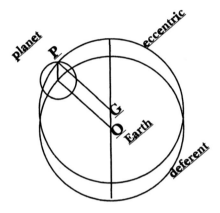

Figure 8.1   The Eccentric Model

Other Ptolemaic models were even more complex, and with each additional level of complexity new objections were raised against Ptolemaic astronomy.

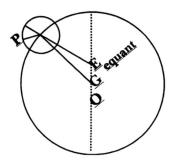

Figure 8.2   Longitudinal Motion

Other objections raised by Ibn al-Haytham and taken up by later astronomers include the problem of the prosneusis point in the model for the longitudinal motion of the moon; the problem of the inclination and deviation of the spheres of Mercury and Venus; the problem of planetary distances, and so on. In the case of the moon, additional difficulties arise because Ptolemy's model has a deferent center which is itself moving; moreover, the motion of the center of the epicycle on this deferent is not uniform around the deferent's center; rather, it rotates uniformly around the center of the world. To complicate matters further, the anomalistic motion on the epicycle is measured away from the mean epicyclic apogee, that is aligned with a movable point called the prosneusis point, rather than being measured from the true apogee, that is aligned with the center of the world. This prosneusis point is the point diametrically opposite to the center of the deferent on the other side of the center of the world. The model for the longitudinal motion of Mercury contained complex mechanisms that were equally objectionable. Additional complications also resulted from the motion of the planets in latitude: the motion in longitude is measured on the plane of the ecliptic which is the great circle of the celestial sphere that traces the apparent yearly path of the sun as seen from the earth. The deferents of the Ptolemaic models, however, did not coincide with this plane. The least problematic is the case of the lunar model, where the deferent has a fixed inclination with respect to the ecliptic, and the epicycle lies in the plane of the deferent. However, the epicycles of the upper planets do not lie in the plane of the deferent, and they have a variable deviation with respect to it. In the case of the lower planets, both the inclination of the deferent with respect to the ecliptic and that of the epicycle with respect to the deferent are variable. Without getting into details, one can easily imagine the complexity and potential problems of the Ptolemaic models which attempted to account for these see-saw and oscillation motions.

The astronomers who attempted to solve the above problems can be classified into two general schools: a mathematically oriented school which was predominantly in the eastern parts of the Muslim world, and a philosophically oriented school based in the western regions of the empire. The name "Marāghā School" is often given to the eastern reformers in recognition of the achievements of a number of astronomers working in an observatory established at Marāghā.[33] Whereas the contributions of these astronomers are no doubt monumental, it should be noted that the reform of Ptolemaic astronomy started before the establishment of the Marāghā observatory in the 13th century and reached its highest point in the 14th. In fact, some of the astronomers of the Marāghā group seem to have started their reform projects even before they joined this observatory; they were perhaps invited to join the observatory team because they were already engaged in such research.[34] The eastern reform tradition, then, was too diffused to be associated with any one geographical area or period; rather, it characterizes several centuries of Arabic astronomical research throughout the Eastern domains of the Muslim world.

Astronomers of the eastern reform tradition adopted several mathematical strategies in their attempts to solve the theoretical problems of the Ptolemaic models.[35] One of their main objectives was to come up with models in which the motions of the planets could be generated as a result of combinations of uniform circular motions, while at the same time conforming to the accurate Ptolemaic observations. Two useful and extremely influential mathematical tools were invented by Ṭūsī and 'Urdī. The first tool, known in modern scholarship as the Ṭūsī couple,[36] in effect produces linear oscillation as a result of a combination of two uniform circular motions. The tool was used in various ways by many astronomers including Copernicus. The 'Urdī lemma is an equally versatile mathematical tool used by 'Urdī and his successors.[37] To produce optimal representations that are physically and mathematically sound, other astronomers used various combinations of these two tools, and devised additional tools of their own invention. In addition, other mathematical solutions were proposed to resolve the contradictions inherent in the Ptolemaic models. For example, 'Urdī reversed the direction and tripled the magnitude of motion of the inclined sphere in the Ptolemaic lunar model; he was thus able to produce uniform motion around the geometric center of the sphere, while at the same time reproducing the uniform motion around the old Ptolemaic center. The most comprehensive and successful models were introduced in the 14th century by the Damascene astronomer Ibn al-Shāṭir; his models for all the planets utilize combinations of perfect circular motions where each circle rotates uniformly around its center. Ibn al-Shāṭir was also able to solve problems of planetary distances, and to provide more accurate accounts for observations.

The development of Arabic astronomy in al-Andalus and North Africa followed different routes. The beginnings of significant scientific activity in al-Andalus started in the 9th century; yet this activity was almost completely dependent upon and lagging behind the sciences of the eastern part of the Muslim world. Between the 9th and 11th centuries, however, a full-fledged scientific tradition emerged. Many scientists traveled east to study science; scientific books were systematically acquired and large private and public libraries were established. A solid familiarity with the eastern astronomical tradition led, in the 11th century, to an intensive and at times original astronomical activity. The emphasis of the activity of these and other astronomers was focused on the compilation of tables and on spherical astronomy. Their primary original contributions were limited to some new observations, but mostly to the mathematics of the trepidation movement of the stars, as well as to the invention of highly sophisticated astronomical instruments. During this entire period, however, little work of significance was devoted to planetary theory.[38]

In contrast to the earlier period, the focus of astronomical research in al-Andalus and North Africa in the 12th century shifted to planetary theory.[39] The names associated with this research tradition include Ibn Bāja (d. 1138), Jābir Ibn Aflaḥ (fl. 1120), Ibn Ṭufayl (d. 1185), Averroes (d. 1198), and Al-Bitrūjī (fl. 1200). Of these, Al-Bitrūjī was the only one to formulate an alternative to Ptolemaic astronomy, while the others produced philosophical discussions of this astronomy. Both the discourses on Ptolemaic astronomy, as well as the actual proposed model of al-Bitrūjī, conceived of astronomical reform in reactionary terms – that is, in terms of adopting older and mathematically inferior models in place of the ones used since Ptolemy. The aim of the western school was to reinstate Aristotelian homocentric spheres, and to completely eliminate any use of eccentrics and epicycles. In accordance with the most stringent and literal interpretations of Aristotelian principles, the western researchers demanded that the heavens be represented exclusively by nested homocentric spheres and perfect uniform circular motions. Even epicycles and deferents that rotated uniformly around their centers were not tolerated because their use entailed an attribution of compoundedness to heavenly phenomena; according to Aristotelian principles, the heavens are perfectly simple. However, since the predictive power of the Ptolemaic models and their ability to account for the observed phenomena relied on the use of epicycles and eccentrics, the western models were strictly qualitative and philosophical, and were completely useless from a mathematical point of view. These models were neither numerically verifiable, nor could they be used for predicting planetary positions. It is no wonder, therefore, that all but one of the western philosophers did not bother to produce actual geometrical models.

The significance of the difference between the eastern and western reform traditions of Arabic astronomy cannot be overemphasized. The prevalent view in contemporary scholarship attributes the steady decline of the intellectual sciences in al-Andalus and North Africa to the rise of the so-called "fundamentalist" states of the Almoravids (1091-1144) and Almohads (1147-1232). It was precisely during this period, however, that the greatest Andalusian philosophers worked under the patronage of the rulers of these two states. What we have, therefore, is not a steady decline of the intellectual disciplines, but the rise of some at the expense of others. The decline of mathematical astronomy has nothing to do with the Almoravids or the Almohads, nor with an alleged theological counter-revolution. Rather, the decline is a result of the adoption of a specific research program of astronomical research, a program which is driven by the untenable, and by then outdated, Aristotelian philosophical concerns that proved incompatible with the advanced mathematical and scientific aspects of astronomy.

In sharp contrast with the western school, the eastern school of Arabic astronomy did not favor philosophy at the expense of mathematics. The objections of this school were mathematical and physical and, as the comparison with their western counterpart clearly illustrates, these objections were certainly not philosophical. A common view which is prevalent in earlier studies maintains that the eastern reform tradition of Arabic astronomy was driven by philosophical considerations, a notion which is often used to undermine the mathematical and scientific significance of this tradition. Given the overwhelming evidence of detailed research on this tradition, such a view is no longer tenable. The alternative solar model proposed by Ibn al-Shāṭir is an example in which reform was motivated by purely observational considerations, even though the Ptolemaic model was completely unobjectionable from a physical or philosophical point of view. More generally, the eastern tradition of astronomical reform has its roots in the systematic mathematization of astronomy and, to some extent, even of nature itself. A recent study of the *al-Takmila fī Sharḥ al-*

Tadhkira of al-Khafrī (d. 1525) clearly illustrates one of the main characteristics of this tradition.[40] Al-Khafrī was primarily a religious scholar who wrote a highly sophisticated commentary on the *Tadhkira* of Naṣīr al-Dīn al-Ṭūsī, one of the classics of the eastern reform tradition. Al-Khafrī presents in this work thorough accounts for the various alternative models proposed by earlier astronomers. The purpose of this presentation, however, is not to look for a correct model, nor to decide which one conforms with an ideal or preferred cosmology, but to establish the mathematical equivalence of all of these models.

Now to go back to the question I raised earlier, namely whether we can think of this tradition of astronomical research as an expansion of the descriptive tendency started by Ptolemy himself. The answer, in my view, is no. To start with, it would be inaccurate to talk of a mathematical school and a philosophical school in Greek astronomy, since the astronomers who provided mathematical models in violation of Aristotelian physics did not theorize the superiority of mathematical principles over philosophical ones. Moreover, this supposed school of mathematical astronomy culminated in Ptolemy, who considered his models defective because they did not conform fully with Aristotelian cosmology. In contrast, in the case of the eastern Islamic astronomical tradition, the proposed mathematical models were deliberate theoretical and epistemological choices that were conceived as alternatives to the philosophical choice. This reform tradition thus shifted the understanding of physics from metaphysics to mathematics. In turn, this shift laid the foundation for the demise of Aristotelian physics and for the emergence of the new sciences. Despite the diversity of their proposed solutions, a shared, fundamental change introduced by the astronomers of the Muslim east is in the under-standing of what constitutes a principle. The principles employed by these astronomers did not derive from philosophical speculation about the nature of heavenly bodies (as in the case of the principles adopted by Ptolemy), but from mathematics. Such is, for example, the principle that the uniform motion of a sphere can only be around an axis passing through its center, since any other rotation is, by definition, non-uniform. At the same time, 'Urḍī, for example, does not hesitate to reverse the direction of the motion in his proposed model, simply because he can reproduce the Ptolemaic observations while employing spheres that rotate uniformly around their own centers; 'Urḍī could not have possibly conceived of this reversed motion as one that corresponds to reality, but only as one that allows accurate predictions of planetary positions. Likewise, Ṭūsī's couple and 'Urḍī's lemma were pure mathematical tools that had no physical counterpart. While the objective of the western Islamic astronomical tradition was to save the (meta-)physical theory, that of the eastern tradition was to save the phenomena as well as the newly constituted physics. In this physics, mathematical principles were not just tools or vehicles for studying nature but also for conceptualizing it.

Philosophy, the overarching discipline in the Greek classifications, was gradually relegated in the Islamic hierarchy of knowledge to one subdivision among many other sciences. Having isolated philosophy, Muslims could then single it out as a potential source of conflict with religion without jeopardizing the other demonstrable sciences. The western (Islamic) tradition of astronomical research subscribed to the older Greek metaphysics, whereas the eastern tradition did not. It is thus legitimate to think of this latter tradition of astronomical reform as a specific Islamic development, and of the views espoused in the formulations of members of this tradition as indications of what is "Islamic" about Islamic science. A notable characteristic of this tradition of astronomical reform is the development of mathematical principles to replace the older physical, or rather metaphysical principles of astronomy. Thus conceived, the areas in which science and religion overlap are reduced, and scientific knowledge is separated from religious knowledge. In other words, one of the consequences of the separation of science and philosophy was the separation of religion and science. To a certain extent, therefore, the Islamization of science in the practice of medieval Muslim astronomers actually meant its secularization.

Notes

[1] The classic formulation of this view is Ignaz Goldziher, "The Attitude of Orthodox Islam Toward the 'Ancient Sciences'", in *Studies in Islam*, M. Swartz (ed.) (Oxford: Oxford University Press, 1975), 185-215. For the most recent and most systematic critique of Goldziher's views see Dimitri Gutas, *Greek Thought, Arabic Culture* (London and New York: Routledge, 1998), 165-175. Despite this and several other critiques, general cultural histories of Islam, as well as general histories of sciences with their occasional chapter on Islamic science still subscribe to some version of Goldziher's thesis. See for example, David Lindberg, *The Beginnings of Western Science* (Chicago: University of Chicago Press, 1992), especially the chapter "Science in Islam", 161-182.

[2] In theoretical astronomy, for example, E.S. Kennedy, George Saliba, F.J. Ragep, and others have documented the highly original contributions of Mu'ayyad al-Dīn al-'Urḍī, Naṣīr al-Dīn al-Ṭūsī, Quṭb al-Dīn al-Shīrāzī, Ibn al-Shāṭir, Ṣadr al-Sharī'a al-Bukhārī, and al-Khafrī, in the period between the 13th and 16th centuries. The studies of Roshdi Rashed on mathematics also confirm the existence of a wide range of original scientific production way beyond the 11th century. Other examples of original scientific research include the contributions of Ibn al-Nafīs (d. 1288) in medicine and Kamāl al-Dīn al-Fārisī (d. 1319) in optics. See, for example, E.S. Kennedy, colleagues, and former students, *Studies in the Islamic Exact Sciences* (Beirut: AUB Press, 1983), especially the section on planetary theories, 50-107; George Saliba, *Kitāb al-Hay'ah; the Astronomical Work of Mu'ayyad al-Din al-'Urḍi* (Beirut: Center for Arab Unity Studies, 1990); George Saliba, *A History of Arabic Astronomy. Planetary Theories during the Golden Age of Islam* (New York: New York University Press, 1994); George Saliba, "A Redeployment of Mathematics in a Sixteenth-Century Arabic Critique of Ptolemaic Astronomy", *Perspectives arabes et medievales sur la tradition scientifique et philosophique grecque*, A. Hasnawi, A. Elamrani-Jamal, and M. Aouad (eds) (Leuven: Peeters, 1997); F.J. Ragep, *Naṣir al-Din al-Ṭūsi's Memoir on Astronomy*, 2 vols. (New York: Springer-Verlag, 1993); Roshdi Rashed, *The Development of Arabic Mathematics: Between Arithmetic and Algebra*, trans. Angela Armstrong (Dordrecht; Boston: Kluwer Academic, 1994); Roshdi Rashed, *Sharaf al-Din al-Ṭūsi: Oeuvres mathematiques. Algebre et geometrie au XIIe siecle* (Paris: Les Belles Lettres, 1986). On Ibn al-Nafīs see Max Meyerhof, "Ibn al-Nafīs and his theory of the lesser circulation", *Isis*, 23 (1935): 100-120. On Fārisī see Roshdi Rashed, "Kamāl al-Dīn Abū'l Ḥasan Muḥammad Ibn al-Ḥasan al-Fārisī", in *Dictionary of Scientific Biography*, 212-219.

[3] This integration is reflected in the large number of religious scholars who were also competent and original scientists; these include, among others, Ibn al-Nafīs, who was a physician and muḥaddith, Ṣadr al-Sharī'a al-Bukhārī (d. 1347) who wrote on the various religious disciplines as well as theoretical astronomy, and al-Nīshābūrī

(d. 1329), who wrote on astronomy and tafsīr. On Ibn al-Nafīs see above reference by Meyerhof. On Ṣadr al-Sharī'a see Ahmad Dallal, *An Islamic Response to Greek Astronomy: the Astronomical Work of Ṣadr al-Sharī'a al-Bukhārī* (Leiden: E.J. Brill, 1995). On Nīshābūrī see Robert Morrison, *The Intellectual Development of Nizām al-Dīn al-Nīshābūrī* (PhD dissertation, Columbia University, 1998). Further indication of the integration of scientific education into the larger intellectual activities can be deduced from the use of the traditional didactic format of *matn* and *sharḥ* (text and commentary) in many scientific texts.

[4] A significant number of critical editions and studies of several important scientific texts were produced in the last three decades. For specific references see note 2 above and the footnotes below for additional references to contributions in other scientific disciplines.

[5] For example, the qualifier "Arabic" can be used to refer to scientific works written in Arabic and, especially in the earlier periods, often composed by non-Muslims. On the other hand, the adjective "Islamic" may be used to characterize the production of scientific works within Islamic societies, whether or not the authors of these works were Muslims. Alternatively, the term "Islamic" may be used to refer to the characteristic imprints of an Islamic worldview on scientific thought. These different usages, though not necessarily mutually exclusive, underscore the fact that none of these terms can be taken for granted.

[6] For two different assessments of Ghazālī's attitude toward the natural sciences see, for example, Michael Marmura, "Ghazālī's Attitude to the Secular Sciences and Logic", *Essays on Islamic Philosophy and Science*, G. Hourani (ed.) (Albany: SUNY Press, 1975), 185-215; and Richard Frank, *Al-Ghazālī and the Ash'arite School* (Durham and London: Duke University Press, 1994).

[7] See Ibn Ḥazm, "Risālat Marātib al-'Ulūm", in *Rasā'il Ibn Ḥazm al-Andalusī*, ed. Ihsan Abbas, 4 vols.(Beirut: Al-Muassasa al-'Arabiyya lil-Dirāsāt wal-Nashr), vol. 4, 61-90. See in particular page 72, where Ibn Ḥazm maintains that logic is needed in all the sciences to distinguish between what is true and what is not.

[8] See for example, Taqī al-Dīn Aḥmad Ibn Tayimyya, *Al-Radd 'alā al-manṭiqiyyīn* (Lahore: Idarat Tarjamān al-Sunna, 1977).

[9] Ibn Khaldūn, *The Muqaddimah*, trans. Franz Rosenthal, abridged N.J. Dawood (Princeton: Princeton University Press, 1967), 143.

[10] For an example of the interest in Islamic science merely on account of its preservation of the Greek scientific legacy see David Lindberg, *The Beginnings of Western Science* (Chicago: University of Chicago Press, 1992). Lindberg's chapter on "Science in Islam" (161-182) is divided into subsections with the following titles: "Learning and Science in Byzantium"; "The Eastward Diffusion of Greek Science"; "The Birth, Expansion, and Hellenization of Islam"; "Translation of Greek Science into Arabic"; "The Islamic Response to Greek Science"; "The Islamic Scientific Achievement"; and "The Decline of Islamic Science".

[11] See for example C.H. Becker, "Turāth al-Awā'il fī al-Sharq wal-Gharb", *Al-Turāth al-Yūnānī fī al-Ḥaḍāra al-Islāmiyya*, 'Abd al-Raḥman Badawi (ed.) (Beirut: Dār al-Qalam, 1980), 3-33. Becker's article is a translation of "Das Erbeder Antike in Orient und Okzident" (Leipzig: Verlag von Quelle and Meyer, 1931). For later formulations of similar views, and the argument that Islamic cultural imperatives militated against the development of science and eventually led to its decline, see G.E. von Grunebaum, *Islam: Essays in the Nature and Growth of a Cultural Tradition* (London: Routledge and Kegan Paul, 1961), especially chapter 6; and F.E Peters, *Aristotle and the Arabs: The Aristotelian Tradition in Islam* (New York: New York University Press, 1968), chapter 4.

[12] For example, Kennedy maintains that "It is well to stress at the outset that the impulse behind the activity we describe was theoretical, and in some sense philosophical, rather than an attempt to improve the bases of practical astronomy". See E.S. Kennedy, "Late Medieval Planetary Theory", *Studies in the Islamic Exact Sciences*, 85. Although Kennedy does not make this observation to question the scientific value of the Islamic contributions in planetary theory, other historians of science derive such conclusions from this observation.

[13] Of many famous proponents of the view that scientific theories do not represent reality and that its main objective is to "save the phenomena", perhaps the most famous is Pierre Duhem (d. 1916). See, for example, Pierre Duhem, *To Save the Phenomena, an Essay on the Idea of Physical Theory from Plato to Galileo*, trans. Edmund Doland and Chaninah Maschler (Chicago: University of Chicago Press, 1969).

[14] For a brief overview of early developments in astronomy see, A. Aaboe, "Scientific Astronomy in Antiquity", *Phil. Trans. R. Soc. Lond. A.*, 276 (1974): 21-42.

[15] On some of the earliest astronomical works in Arabic see David Pingree, "The Fragments of the Works of Ya'qūb b. Ṭāriq", *Journal of Near Eastern Studies*, 27 (1968): 97-125; and "The Fragments of the Works of al-Fazārī", *Journal of Near Eastern Studies*, 29 (1970): 103-23. See also David Pingree, "The Greek Influence on Early Islamic Mathematical Astronomy", *Journal of the American Oriental Society*, 93 (1973): 32-43.

[16] See Dimitri Gutas, *Greek Thought, Arabic Culture*, especially Chapter 2, p. 28-60.

[17] For a brief overview of the early developments in the field of astronomy see Regis Morelon, "General Survey of Arabic Astronomy", *Encyclopedia of the History of Arabic Science; Vol. I, Astronomy-Theoretical and Applied*, Roshdi Rashed (ed.) (London and New York: Routledge, 1996), 1-19.

[18] See G.J. Toomer (trans. and annot.), *Ptolemy's Almagest* (New York: Springer-Verlag, 1984). The best study of the Almagest is Olaf Pedersen, *A Survey of the Almagest* (Odense: Odense University Press, 1974). The First chapter of this book, "The Almagest through the Ages", includes a section on "the Almagest among the Arabs". See, in particular, pages 11-25.

[19] See Regis Morelon, "La Version Arabe du Livre des Hypotheses de Ptolemee", *Melanges-Institut dominicain d'etudes orientales du Caire*, 21 (1993): 7-85.

[20] The classic work on observatories and observations remains Aydin Sayili, *The Observatory in Islam* (Ankara: Turk Tarih Kurumu Basimevi, 1960).

[21] On early observational activities see Aydin Sayili, "The introductory Section of Habash's Astronomical Tables known as the 'Damascene' Zij'", *Ankara Üniversitesi Dil ve Tarih-Gografya Fakültesi Dergisi*, 13.4 (1955). See also Ibn Yunus, *Kitāb al-Zij al-Ḥākimī al-Kabīr*, published *as Le Livre De la Grande Table Hakémite*, ed. with introduction and French translation by Caussin, (Paris, 1804). In the same book, Caussin also reproduced useful quotes from a variety of sources on the observational activities in 11th century Cairo; especially useful is the detailed account by the historian al-Maqrīzī on the Afḍal-Baṭā'iḥī observatory. See also Al-Bīrūnī, *Taḥdīd nihāyāt al-amākin li-taṣḥīh masāfāt al-masākin*, P.G. Bulgakov (ed.), (Cairo, 1962). An English translation of this work is Jamil Ali, *The Determination of the Coordinates of Cities, al-Bīrūnī's Taḥdīd al-Amākin* (Beirut: AUB Press, 1967).

[22] For a brief account of some of these early developments see Regis Morelon, "Eastern Arabic Astronomy between the Eighth and the Eleventh Centuries", *Encyclopedia of the History of Arabic Science; Vol. I, Astronomy*, Rashed (ed.), 20-57. In particular, see pages 25 f., on the "Critical analysis of Ptolemy's results", and 34f., on "The mathematization of astronomical reasoning".

[23] The main example of this kind of reform of Ptolemaic astronomy is the work of Thābit ibn Qurra. For editions, translations, and analysis of Thābit's extant astronomical works, see Regis Morelon, *Thābit ibn Qurra, Oeuvres d'astronomie*, Collection Science et Philosophie Arabes: Textes et Etudes (Paris: Société d'édition "Les Belles Lettres", 1987).

[24] Abū al-Rayḥān Muḥammad ibn Aḥmad al-Bīrūnī, *Al-Qānūn al-Mas'ūdī*, 3 vols. (Haydarabad: Dā'irat al-Ma'ārif, 1954).

[25] Al-Bīrūnī and Ibn Sīna, *Al-As'ilah wa'l-Ajwibah (Questions and Answers), Including the further answers of al-Bīrūnī and al-Ma'ṣūmī's defense of Ibn Sīnā*, ed. with English and Persian Introductions by Seyyed Hossein Nasr and Mahdi Mohaghegh (Tehran: High Council of Culture and Art, Centre of Research and Cultural Coordination, 1352 AH).

[26] See Bīrūnī, *Al-As'ilah wa'l-Ajwibah*, 2-3, and passim.

[27] Ibid., 28.

[28] As evidenced by his contention that he does not suggest the possibility of an elliptical orb because he thinks it to be so, but simply because he objects to the reasoning of Aristotle (*ta'ajjuban min sāḥib al-manṭiq*); see *Al-As'ilah wa'l-Ajwibah*, 28.

[29] On the post-11th century developments in Planetary theory see George Saliba, "Arabic Planetary Theories after the Eleventh Century AD", *Encyclopedia of the History of Arabic Science; Vol. I, Astronomy*, 58-127; and George Saliba, *A History of Arabic Astronomy*.

30 Ibn al-Haytham, *Al-Shukūk ʿAlā Baṭlamyūs*, A. Sabra and Nabil Shehaby (eds), (Cairo: Dar al-Kutub Press, 1971).

31 For references to these works see notes 2 and 3 above.

32 For a detailed account of these problems and the solutions proposed by various Muslim astronomers, see George Saliba, "Arabic Planetary Theories after the Eleventh Century AD", *Encyclopedia of the History of Arabic Science, Vol. I, Astronomy*, 58-127.

33 On the Marāghā observatory see Fadl Allāh Rashīd al-Dīn, *Jāmiʿ al-Tawrīkh*, ed. and trans. E.M. Quatremere, (Paris, 1836); Ṣalāḥ al-Dīn Khalīl Aybak al-Ṣafadī, *al-Wāfī bil-Wafiyyāt*, H. Ritter (ed.), (Leipzig, 1931), vol. 1; and Ibn Shākir al-Kutubī, *Fawt al-Wafiyyāt* (Cairo, 1299 AH), vol. 2. For a detailed account of the design and use of various instruments at Marāghā see Muʾayyad al-Dīn al-ʿUrḍī, *Risāla fī Kayfiyyat al-Arṣād*, in "Al-Urḍī'nin "Risalet-ün Fi Keyfiyet-il-Ersad" Adli Makalesi", ed. with English and Turkish translations Sevim Tekeli, *Arastirma*, 8 (1970). For an earlier German study and translation of ʿUrḍī's work see Hugo J. Seemann, "Die Instrumente der Sternwarte zu Maragha nach den Mitteilungen von al-ʿUrḍī", *Sitzungsberichte der physikalisch-medizinischen Sozietät zu Erlangen*, vol. 60 (1928): 15-126. Also on Marāghā in general see André Godard, *Les Monuments de Maragha* (Paris, 1934).

34 This is equally true of Ṭūsī and ʿUrḍī, both of whom commenced their reformative work before the establishment of the Marāghā observatory. See Saliba, *Kitāb al-Hayʾah; the Astronomical Work of Muʾayyad al-Dīn al-ʿUrḍī*, 31f.; and Ragep, *Naṣir al-Dīn al-Ṭūsī's Memoir on Astronomy*, 65f.

35 For a detailed account of the various models proposed by the astronomers of the eastern parts of the Muslim world to solve the problems of Ptolemaic astronomy see Saliba, "Arabic Planetary Theories after the Eleventh Century AD", especially 86ff.

36 On the Ṭūsī couple see Saliba, "Arabic Planetary Theories after the Eleventh Century AD", 94-5.

37 On the ʿUrḍī lemma see Saliba, "Arabic Planetary Theories after the Eleventh Century AD", 106.

38 For a collection of essays on Astronomy in Islamic Spain and North Africa see Julio Samso, *Islamic Astronomy and Medieval Spain* (Aldershot: Variorum, 1994), especially chapters I, VIII, XII, and XIX.

39 For a brief outline of the proposals of the astronomers/philosophers of the western parts of the Muslim world see Saliba, "Arabic Planetary Theories after the Eleventh Century AD", 84-6. For a fuller account of the philosophical rationale behind these proposed models see A.I. Sabra, "The Andalusian revolt against Ptolemaic astronomy: Averroes and al-Biṭrūjī", *Transformation and Tradition in the Sciences*, E. Mendelsohn (ed.), (Cambridge: Cambridge University Press, 1984), 133-153.

[40] On al-Khafrī see, George Saliba, "A Sixteenth-Century Arabic Critique of Ptolemaic Astronomy: The Work of Shams al-Dīn al-Khafrī", *Journal for the History of Astronomy*, xxv (1994): 15-38.

Chapter 9
Creation in the Islamic Outlook and in Modern Cosmology
Mehdi Golshani

Introduction

The problem of creation has always been one of the major problems of human concern. But, prior to the 20th century it was mostly dealt with by theologians and philosophers. It was during the first quarter of the 20th century that scientific cosmology was developed and the problem of creation became the concern of scientific circles as well.

In this paper, we shall discuss creation from the Qur'ānic outlook and from the viewpoint of Muslim theologians, philosophers, and mystics. Then, we will discuss this problem from the point of view of modern cosmology, describing various schools of thought prevalent there. In this discussion we shall be brief because there are already some excellent reviews available. Finally, we shall have a comparative study between the views of the Muslim theologians, philosophers, and mystics, and the dominant schools of thought in modern cosmology. We will then draw some conclusions from this study and discuss the current state of affairs and cautions to be exercised in future studies.

Creation in the Qur'ān and the Islamic Tradition

According to the Qur'ān, everything is created by God:

God is the Creator of everything; is the One, the Omnipotent. (13:16)

God is not only the Originator of the universe, but is its Sustainer:

> God is the Creator of everything, and He is in charge of everything. (39:62)

The Qur'ān asserts that everything depends on God:

> Mankind, it is you who stand in need of God, and He is the All sufficient, the Praiseworthy. (35:15)

To emphasize this dependence, the next verse mentions that if God willed, He could take us away and bring in some new creation:

> If He so wished, He could take you away and bring some new creation. (35:16)

It is also mentioned in the Qur'ān that God's effusion is never withheld and that His favors are uncountable:

> Each We shall supply, these as well as those, with a gift from your Lord, and your Lord's gift was never withheld. (17:20)
> ... if you counted up God's favors, you would never [be able to] number them. (14:34)

There are verses in the Qur'ān which have been interpreted by some Muslin scholars to indicate continuous creation:

> Everyone in Heaven and Earth asks for something from Him; each day He is at some task. (55:29)
> Were we worn out by the first creation? Yet they are in a quandary about fresh creation. (50:15)

These are in fact, the verses which have been used by the Muslim mystics and Mullā-Sadrā to infer the doctrine of continual creation. In the Qur'ān as well as the Bible (Book of John), the act of creation is identified with the word of God:

> Originator of Heaven and Earth, and whenever He decrees something, He says to it: 'Be' and it is. (2:117)

Another important point is that there are frequent references in the Qur'ān to the multitudes of universes. For example:

> All praise is for God, the Lord of the worlds.(1:2)

Some religious authorities and scholars have interpreted these references to "the worlds" as an indication of the existence of other worlds besides ours. For example, it is narrated from Imām Muhammad al-Bāqhir (A.S.):

> Maybe you see that God created only this single world and that God did not create Homo sapiens besides you. Well, I swear by God that God indeed created thousands and thousands of worlds and thousands and thousands of humankind. You are in the last of these worlds and are the last of those human beings.[1]

In his celebrated commentary on the Qur'ān, Fakhr al-Din al-Rāzī, the eminent Muslim theologian-philosopher, brings up the possibility of multiple worlds:

> It has been proven by evidence that God, the Exalted, is capable of actualizing all possibilities. Thus, be He Exalted is capable of creating thousands and thousands of worlds beyond this world, each of which would be greater and more massive than this world ... and the argument of the philosophers for the uniqueness of this world is weak and poor, being based on invalid premises.[2]

Finally, it is recommended in the Qur'ān that we find out how God initiated the creation:

> Do they not see how God initiates the creation, and then reproduces it? Surely that is easy for God. Say: 'travel in the earth and see how God initiated the creation'. Then God will create another creation; surely God has power over all things. (29:19-20)

Considering the possibility of other worlds – a possibility which can be inferred from the last two verses as well as other verses – this verse implies that we are instructed to find out through observation and reasoning, how our own world originated.

Muslim Theologians

The early Muslim theologians claimed that the world was created in time. Their main argument for this belief was that if the world did not originate in time, then it would be co-eternal with God. Thus, it could not be caused by God. They believed that eternity belonged exclusively to God, that everything else was temporal, and that createdness requires temporality.

Theologians' beliefs in the existence of an absolute beginning for time, requires that time be preceded by its non-existence. Thus, they talked about the world being preceded by an imaginary extension.

In his celebrated book, *The Incoherence of Philosophers*, al-Ghazālī, an eminent Asharite theologian, accused philosophers of infidelity on three accounts, the third one being their belief in the eternity of the world.

> Pronouncing them infidels is necessary in three questions. One of them is the question of the world's pre-eternity and their statement that all substances are pre-eternal ...

These three doctrines do not agree with Islam in any respect. The one who believes them believes that prophets utter falsehood and that they said whatever they have said by way of [promoting common] utility, to give examples and explanation to the multitudes of created mankind. This is manifest infidelity which none of the Islamic sects have believed.[3]

Imām Fakhr al-Din al-Rāzī, another eminent Asharite theologian, differed from al-Ghazālī in this respect. In his view there is nothing in the Sacred books to indicate that the world had a temporal beginning,[4] and he attributes this to the complexity of the problem. He writes, "The Great Prophets (A.S.) abstained from digging into this problem, and this indicates that it is so much difficult that human rationality cannot have access to it".[5]

Some of the later Muslim theologians, however, have supported the view of the Muslim philosophers who believed there was no temporal beginning to the world. In their view, the createdness of the world means its ontological dependence on God. To quote Lahījī:

In the narrations from our infallible Imāms, ... there is no explicit reference to either of the two views [temporality or eternity of the world], but the inferred meaning is that which implies dependence on the Creator alone ... the ancient and recent theologians believe in the temporality of the world. Sometimes, they even claim that there is a unanimous view on the temporal createdness. But the proof of this unanimity is difficult, and if there is a unanimity it is on the absolute createdness, without the condition of temporality or atemporality. Their rational arguments in this domain is quite weak, and the more recent philosophers have insisted on atemporality, and their doubt in this case is not without strength.[6]

Muslim Philosophers

The early Muslim philosophers, led by al-Fārābī and Ibn Sīnā (Avicenna), believed that the world had not originated in time, i.e. it is eternal. In their view the creation in time would have the following implications:

1. It would mean that God is required for the creation of the world, but not for its sustenance.
2. It would necessitate a change in the Divine nature, which is not permissible for an immutable God.
3. It would require an interruption in God's effusion, which is inconsistent with the eternity of God's attributes, such as His creativity.

In this problem, both major schools of Islamic philosophy, Peripatetics and Illuminationists, had the same position. Tūsī, who was a Peripatetic philosopher, says in his commentary on Ibn Sīnā's *al-Ishārāt wa al-Tanbīhāt* that "since the First Principle was for them [i.e. philosophers] eternal and perfect in action, they asserted that the world, which is His action, is eternal ...".[7] As Illuminationist philosopher, Suhrawardī says, "the effusion is eternal because the cause is unchangeable and immutable. Thus the world continues with His endurance".[8]

In their view, creation meant an ontological relationship and createdness meant ontological dependence, which has its roots in the contingency of every existent besides God. Thus, it is contingency, not temporality, that is the prerequisite for createdness. The Necessary Being (God) confers existence upon the contingent beings. Such a process is called creation.

These philosophers believed that there is neither a beginning nor end to time. Theologians, however, believed in the existence of two boundaries for time. Otherwise, they claimed, this would require that time be co-eternal with God. In Tusi's words, "the [temporal] createdness of the world requires its [i.e. time's temporal] createdness".[9] Here, Tūsī speaks as a theologian.

In refuting philosophers' claims, al-Ghazālī pointed out that if philosophers had accepted the finitude of space, there is no reason why they should not have accepted the finitude of time.[10] In response, to al-Ghazālī, the contemporary Persian philosopher M. Mutaharī pointed to the difference between temporal and spatial dimensions: the elements of space can co-exist, but the elements of time are mutually exclusive. There is a relation of potentiality and actuality between the elements of time, but there is no such relation between the elements of space.[11] Einstein, whose special theory of relativity has been used by some people to negate any distinction between space and time coordinates, disapproved the identification of time as a dimension of space. "Time and space are fused into one and the same continuum, but this continuum is not isotropic. The element of spatial distance and the element of duration remain distinct in nature."[12]

What we mentioned above were the beliefs of the major schools of Islamic philosophy. But there were some individual philosophers in the Islamic world whose ideas on the problem of the creation of the world were different. For example, al-Kindī argued that the world is created in time.[13] Similarly, Maimonides claimed that the Aristotelian arguments for the eternity of the world were not conclusive arguments and that temporal creation is a more plausible alternative.[14] On the other hand, Muhammad ibn Zakarīyya al-Rāzī believed in five eternals: God, the universal soul, first matter, absolute space, and absolute time.[15] But, before Mullā-Sadrā, the dominant view was atemporal createdness and it was shared by both Peripatetic and Illuminationist philosophers. Nevertheless, Ibn Sīnā's concluding words on this problem are very cautious and extremely instructive. In his *al-Ishārāt wa al-Tanbīhāt*, which was one of his last books, he describes the views of various schools of thought on the problem of creation. Then, he leaves the choice of which is the correct view to the readers, but gives three recommendations:

1. To be firmly committed to the unity of God
2. To avoid prejudices
3. To use their intellectual capacity

In his words, "thus, the schools of thought on this problem are what we described. You must choose one of them, after you have subscribed to the unity of God, using your faculty of intellect, rather than your prejudices".[16]

Muslim Mystics

Muslim mystics introduced the doctrine of the recreation (or perpetual motion) of the world at every instant. According to this doctrine, the universe is annihilated and recreated at every moment, i.e. there is continuous creation going on. One of the earliest exponents of this doctrine is the Persian mystic – philosopher 'Ayn al-Qudāt Hamadānī of the 12th century. In his view, everything which comes into being is going to be annihilated instantaneously and then it is immediately recreated again. Thus, God is not only the originator of the universe but its constant Creator. Everything derives its existence from Him. But, the ontological relationship between the two must be renewed at every moment.[17] This renewal is due to two facts:

1. The ontological contingency of all things.
2. Constant effusion from God.

Thus, every existent, due to its ontological contingency, takes off the garment of existence once it comes into being. But at the same time, God's effusion confers upon it a new garment of existence. We do not see this renewal, because it takes place instantaneously. Hamadānī offers a good analogy:

> Small children, observing a lamp burning continuously, would naturally think that what they see is one single flame. But the grown ups know very well that it is a series of different flames appearing and disappearing moment by moment. And from the viewpoint of the mystics this must necessarily be the case with everything in the world except God.[18]

Later Mystics, following the lead of Hamadānī and the eminent mystic Ibn Arabī, advertised the thesis of recreation. Here I simply quote two well-known Persian mystic – poets, Shabistarī and Rumi. In Shabistarī's words (1317):

> The world is this whole, and in every twinkling of an eye,
> it becomes non-existent and endures not two moments.
> There over again another world is produced,
> every moment a new heaven and a new earth.
> Things remain not in two moments,
> the same moment they perish, they are born again.

In Rumi's words:

> Every Instant then thou art dying and returning,
> Mustafa [the prophet] declared that this world is (but) a moment.
> Every moment the world is renewed, and we
> are unaware of its being renewed whilst it remains [the same in appearance].
> Life is arriving a new, like a stream,
> Though in the body it has the same semblance of continuity.

Mullā-Sadrā

We have separated the discussion of Mullā-Sadrā's view on this problem from the rest of Muslim philosophers because he established an independent school of thought in which he took some elements from various schools of philosophy – from mystics, the Qur'ān, and the Islamic tradition – and combined them to develop his own school of philosophy, the so-called *al-Hikmat al-Muta'āliyah*.

Mullā-Sadrā's approach to the problem of creation is based on his doctrine of transsubstantial motion. Earlier Muslim philosophers had restricted motion to some categories of accidents (e.g. quantity and quality), but they had denied the possibility of motion in the category of substance. Mullā-Sadrā argued that changes in an accident requires changes in the substance to which the accident belongs, because accidents have no independent existence of their own.

According to Mullā-Sadrā, the essence of everything is continually renewed through the process of transsubstantial motion. In other words, every existent is in constantly renewed creation at every moment.

> There is absolutely no ipseity or individual – be it celestial or elemental, simple or composite, substance or accident – but that its non-existence precedes its being in time, and its being likewise precedes its non-existence in time. In general, every body and every bodily thing whose being is in any way connected with matter is constantly renewed in its ipseity and impermanent in its being and its individuality.[19]

All existents have this constant renewal in their nature. Thus, every existent is different now from what it was before. What it is now was non-existent before. Thus, the doctrine of creatio ex nihilo holds at each instant, i.e. we have a continuous effusion of existence from the ultimate source of existence.

Mullā-Sadrā confirms the doctrine of temporal createdness of the Muslim theologians, but unlike them he does not restrict temporal creation to a specific time in the past. Rather, it is a continual re-creation, without having an absolute beginning in the past. Thus, as earlier Muslim philosophers had emphasized, while nothing is eternal, there is no absolute beginning to time:

> Thus, the continuation of the effusion of the absolute bountiful and the eternity of the creation of the true Creator became clear from what we said … But the continuation of the effusion of the Creator and His creation does not require the eternity of contingents.[20]

In short, in Mullā-Sadrā's view, nothing precedes time and motion but God.

According to Mullā-Sadrā all Divine religions believe in the createdness of the universe, and by that they mean temporal createdness. The creation did not take place in time, but occurred with time. In fact, time is the measure of the universal transsubstantial motion. The universe can be considered as an infinite series of continual creations. In Mullā-Sadrā's view the whole universe is nothing but its parts, and the [temporal] creation really refers to them, rather than to the whole. "The whole has no existence besides the existence of the parts. The parts are numerous. Thus, their [temporal] creation is numerous."[21]

The major difference between Mullā-Sadrā's view and that of Muslim Mystics, in the problem of creation, is that for Mullā-Sadrā the state of the universe at any instant becomes matter for new forms which are conferred upon it by God, while for the Muslim Mystics the universe is annihilated and recreated at every instant. The first is called "dressing after dressing" and the latter is called "dressing after undressing".

Modern Cosmological Models of Creation

Big Bang Model

Scientific Cosmology started with Einstein's 1917 celebrated paper, "Cosmological Considerations on the General Theory of Relativity".[22] In this paper Einstein applied his general theory of relativity to the universe. Einstein's equations have different solutions corresponding to different distributions of fields and matter but the theory by itself cannot select a particular one. Among them, there are solutions that predict an expanding universe from extremely hot and dense conditions at t=0.

From 1917 until the presentation of E. Hubble's results in the 1930's, the dominant view was that our universe is a static one. There were two static models available: Einstein's closed universe and de Sitter's open, infinite, and empty universe.

In 1922 Alexander Friedman, and in 1927 George Lemaitre, presented solutions of Einstein's equations which indicated the expansion of the universe. Einstein first rejected Friedman's solution because of its prediction of singularity but in 1923 he accepted Friedman's solution.

In 1929 Hubble noticed a red shift in the spectra of galaxies, which was proportional to their distance from our galaxy. This was interpreted as a "Doppler effect", which meant that galaxies are receding from our galaxy with a speed proportional to their distances, i.e. the universe is expanding.

In the late 1940s some people including Fred Hoyle, Herman Bondi, and Thomas Gold presented different versions of the so-called "steady state theory", which assumed that the universe is both spatially and temporally homogeneous, i.e. it is external. Hoyle explicitly mentioned that the creation could not be causally explained and that the assignment of a beginning to the universe is against the spirit of scientific enquiry. "It is against the spirit of scientific enquiry to regard observable effects as arising from 'causes unknown to science' and this in principle is what creation-in-the-past implies."[23]

During 1950s both the Big Bang theory and the steady state theory were popular. The discovery of the microwave background radiation in 1965 gave solid support to the Big Bang theory and weakened the steady state theory.

In the late 1960s several people, notably Hawking and Penrose, proved that under some very reasonable assumptions cosmological models governed by general relativity exhibit a singularity at t=0, which means that the universe must have started in a space-time singularity. The Big Bang could be combined with infinite time, leading to an oscillating universe, i.e. an infinite series of expansions followed by contractions. The oscillating universe was popular with some physicists and cosmologists, but it has become less popular on physical grounds.[24]

Reactions to Standard Big Bang Model of Universe

There have been six major reactions to the Big Bang model of the universe.

Creation ex nihilo The theistic interpretation of the standard Big Bang cosmology is, to paraphrase W.L. Craig, the classical doctrine of creatio ex nihilo: that a finite time ago God brought the universe into being with a material cause and fashioned the cosmos according to His design. The argument for the existence of God can be expressed in the forms of the following syllogism: a) whatever begins to exist has a cause; b) the universe began to exist; c) therefore, the universe has a cause.[25] This interpretation of Big Bang was welcome by Pope Pius XII in 1951, and some scientists, philosophers, and theologians throughout the Muslim and Christian world have embraced it with enthusiasm. For example, Ted Peters sees the doctrine of creatio ex nihilo in Christian theology as in "consonance" with the problem of t=0 in Big Bang cosmology. He states, "If we identify the concept of creation out of nothing with the point of temporal beginning or perhaps the source of the singularity, we have sufficient consonance with which to proceed further in the discussion".[26]

Singularity with cause The other prominent reaction to Big Bang has been by those who saw Big Bang as a support for theism. As Paul Davies put it, "a singularity is the nearest thing that science has found to a supernatural agent".[27] These people have tried to eliminate the singularity at t=0 by various physical and mathematical tricks including an appeal to various theories of quantum gravity. Here, there are models with a background space-time in which the universe emerges as a quantum fluctuation of vacuum, and models in which space-time arises out of pure chance from a space with no boundary.

Singularity with no cause Some scholars have accepted the singularity and the existence of temporal beginning to the universe, but they deny that the creation of the universe needs a cause. Q. Smith, e.g. believes that the universe, including the initial singularity sprang into being out of nothing without a cause:

> There is no good reason to believe that there is a sound a posteriori or a priori argument for a cause of the big bang. Thus we reach a general conclusion: there is no philosophy of big bang cosmology that makes it reasonable to reject the fundamental thesis of big bang cosmology: that the universe began to exist without a cause.[28]

Ontological Dependence on God Some scholars believe that the doctrine of creatio ex nihilo does not imply temporal createdness; rather, it implies ontological dependence on God. Thus, the singularity at t=0 should not be identified with the doctrine of creatio ex nihilo. In Arthur Peacocke's words:

> The principal stress in the Judeo-Christian doctrine of creation is on the dependence and contingency of all entities and events, other than God himself: it is about a perennial relationship between God and the world and not about the beginning of the Earth or the whole universe at a point of time.[29]

Ian Barbour has the same view. He writes, "the doctrine of creation is not really about temporal beginning but about the basic relationship between the world and God".[30] J. Polkinghorne also shares this view; he writes, "theology could have lived with either physical theory, for the assertion that God is Creator is not a statement that at a particular time he did something but rather that at all times he keeps the world in being".[31]

Creatio Continua In the last 40 years, the old idea of continuing creation (creatio continua) has been revived in different senses. Creatio continua refers to the idea of change within an already existing matter. In the words of Ian G. Barbour, "continuing creation expresses the theme of God's immanence and participation in the ongoing word. God builds on what is already there; each successive level of reality requires the structure of lower levels".[32]

Creatio continua also means the continuation of the original creation out of nothing. As Wolfhart Pannenberg put it:

> The creatio continua formula presupposes the strict conception of creatio ex nihilo in as much as it characterizes God's preserving activity as the continuation of the creation out of nothing. For this reason alone the idea of a continuing creation cannot be set in opposition to the creatio ex nihilo formula.[33]

For Philip Hefner, creation refers not only to the original creation, but it also includes God's continuing sustenance of the world:

> Creation for Christian theology is by no means limited to protology. It is not limited to what happened at the beginning when time was first created. Creation also refers to God's ongoing sustaining of the world. Every moment of the world's existence depends upon the ongoing grace of God.[34]

The last sentence reminds one of the Muslim mystics and Mullā-Sadrā.

Creatio Continua also means that at every moment the universe depends on God, irrespective of whether there was an absolute beginning. In the words of Keith Ward:

> The Big Bang has not the slightest theological significance. It does not matter whether the world began with a bang or whether it began at all. It might always have been there. Theologians have always agreed that this does not make any difference. When you say that God 'creates' the Universe, you just mean that everything – however long it has been there – always depends, at every moment of time, upon God. That is all you mean. It's a pity that some physicists use the word 'creation' when they actually mean 'origin' of the Universe. Creation isn't at the beginning, it is now and always.[35]

He also states, "but a more satisfactory notion of creation is that God at every moment sustains the universe, so that every moment is a moment of creation".[36]

Creatio continua refers to the continuous creatio ex nihilo. This is exemplified, e.g., by the steady state theory of Hoyle et al., in which there is continual creation of matter out of nothing. As Bondi put it, "there is going on everywhere and at all times a continual creation of matter, the appearance of atoms of hydrogen out of nothing".[37]

Finally, some people admit the temporality of the universe but they believe in the eternity of the laws of physics and think that these laws are enough to put the universe into existence. Paul Davies elaborates on this position:

> The possibility that given the laws of physics, a universe can appear spontaneously, rests on the 'prior' existence of these laws of physics. Given, the laws, the universe can take care of itself. But where do the laws come from?
>
> ... the laws are logically prior to the universe. If this were not so, we should have to suppose that the whole package, the universe plus laws, just popped into existence for no reason. So, I contend that the laws enjoy some sort of timeless transcendent, Platonic existence.[38]

Quantum Cosmological Speculations

As we mentioned, the singularity theorems indicate that all of the models of an expanding universe that satisfy certain reasonable assumptions start with a singularity, at which the density and temperature become infinite and Einstein's equations cease to be valid. Einstein, himself, had the following insight about the initial singularity:

> For large densities of field and matter, the field equations and even the field variables which enter into them have no real significance. One may not therefore assume the validity of the equations for very high density of field and matter, and one may not conclude that the 'beginning of the expansion'

must mean a singularity in the mathematical sense. All we have to realize is that the equations may not be continued over such regions.[39]

To overcome this obstacle, some people have argued that as we go backward toward the singularity, when we go beyond Planck's time, the first 10^{-43} seconds of the early universe, the universe becomes ultra-microscopic and the quantum mechanical effects become important. Thus, we have to use a proper quantum theory of gravity. There is a hope that this theory will not involve singularities.

During the last three decades, the standard Big Bang model has been replaced by models in which the universe arises by pure chance from a quantum mechanical vacuum or from a space-time with no boundary. Here we say a few words about some of these models.

1. In 1973 Edward Tryon suggested that our universe originated as a quantum fluctuation of the vacuum – the vacuum of some larger space in which our universe is embedded.[40]
2. In the early 1980s, Alexander Vilenkin of Tufts university introduced a model in which the universe was created through a quantum tunneling effect – a tunneling from a state with no classical space-time to a de-Sitter space.[41]
3. In 1983, Hartle and Hawking suggested a model in which the initial singularity is avoided by making time less well-defined in the early universe.[42] Starting from the Wheeler-Dewitt equation, they tried to construct the wave function of the universe which represents the amplitude for the creation of the universe from finite quantum fuzz. In their model, the space-time diagram of the universe does not start from a single point, but from a curved surface with no boundary, i.e. their universe has a finite past but no initial singularity. In this no boundary proposal there is no beginning for the universe, and therefore Hawking sees nothing left for the Creator to do. In Hawking's words, "there would be no singularities at which the laws of science broke down, and no edge of space-time at which one has to appeal to God or some new law to set the

boundary conditions for space-time".[43] In another place he states, "but if the universe is really completely self-contained, having no boundary or edge, it would have neither beginning nor end. What place, then, for a Creator?".[44] But, as Don Page pointed out,[45] Hawking's objection does not apply when one holds that God created the universe and sustains it, as it is believed in the monotheistic religions, rather than just interfering at the beginning. Hawking admits that the existence of an edge for space-time implies the existence of God, which is what the early Muslim theologians believed. But he departs from their position, by denying the existence of this edge. Nevertheless, as John Polkinghorne pointed out, the 'no boundary' condition of Hawking is itself a boundary condition.[46] Other cosmologists (e.g. Linde and Penrose) have imposed other boundary conditions.

Islamic Cosmological Doctrine vs. Modern Cosmological Models

The Islamic schools of thought about the creation could be summarized in the following categories:

1. Theologians' beliefs in temporal createdness of the universe.
2. Philosophers' beliefs in the eternity of the world and its ontological dependence on God.
3. Mystics' and Mullā-Sadrā's views about perpetual creation (continual recreation) of the world.

All of these views are present in the current schools of cosmological thought – among cosmologists, theologians, and philosophers. For example, the temporal createdness of the universe was hailed by E. Whittacker, the eminent British physicist in 1951; today, it is seriously defended by physicist H. Ross and philosopher W.L. Craig. It is amusing that even those, like Hawking, who deny temporal createdness of the universe, share Muslim theologians' understandings of a created universe. Similarly, the view of the Muslim philosophers about the ontological dependence of the world on God is shared by some contemporary scientists, theologians, and philosophers (e.g. P. Hodgson and A. Peacocke). Likewise, the doctrine of continual reaction of the Muslim mystics and Mullā-Sadrā is echoed in the thesis of continuous creation of some contemporary Christian theologians, though in different senses. The closest view to Mullā-Sadrā's is that of K. Ward.

Finally, the idea of the existence of multiple worlds suggested by some Qur'ānic verses and Islamic traditions is seen in the work of some modern cosmologists, who are not necessarily theists but believe in this idea either on physical grounds or to remove the need for God. The idea of many worlds has been brought up in modern cosmology in several contexts (the reduction of the wave function of the universe, oscillating model of the universe, anthropic principle, etc.). One of the most recent ones is the chaotic inflationary scenario. In this scenario, the universe started in a chaotic state. Then, some regions underwent inflation and the amount of inflation was different from region to region. Each inflated region resembled a bubble with smooth conditions.[47] The universe we live in is one bubble among other bubbles, with a particular set of fundamental constants. In Andrei Linde's version of chaotic inflation, inflation is a potentially self-reproducing process.[48] The fluctuations produced by inflation induce further inflations in small subregions of the inflating bubbles. The whole network of inflating bubble universes need not have any beginning. Of course, the eternal inflationary scenario is not testable by observations, and in this scenario the universe is different beyond our horizon of possible observations. Thus, it is not possible to answer questions about the origin of the whole universe.

Conclusion

In my opinion, there is a lot of confusion and there are a lot of fallacies concerning the problem of creation, especially among modern cosmologists. This, in my humble view, is the result of their lack of philosophical understanding. The problem of creation is not a matter of physics alone. It needs theological and philosophical reflection as well. Here, I would like to summarize some of the misunderstandings prevalent among the practitioners of modern cosmology.

The use of Big Bang cosmology for the affirmation or the denial of temporal createdness is a clear misunderstanding of both cosmology and creation (as understood in theology and philosophy).

We still do not have a successful unification of quantum theory and general relativity, i.e. a coherent quantum theory of gravity. All of the current works on quantum cosmology are based on assumptions that are thought to be valid when we get that theory. But, as Isham pointed out, it is not obvious that:

> Relativity can be quantized in the way it has been done so far.
>
> A unification of general relativity and quantum theory can be achieved without invoking radical conceptual changes in either.
>
> The prevalent concepts of space, time and matter remain intact in the region of the Planck length.
>
> The concept of probability can be extended to quantum cosmology without getting into conceptual problems.[49]

The beginning implied by the Big Bang models is not necessarily an absolute beginning, because: a) the initial singularity is predicted by present theories, which are not valid at the Big Bang anyhow; and b) even if there were an absolute beginning to the world, science could never reveal it. In Saint Thomas Aquinas' words, "we hold by faith, and it cannot be proved by demonstration that the world did not always exist ... the reason being that the newness of the world cannot be demonstrated by the word itself".[50] And, in the words of J.M.

Zycinski, "there are no physical or philosophical means that would make it possible to prove that at this very moment our universe emerged from ontologically understood nothingness".[51] The reason is that we cannot say what happened before the Planck time (about 10^{-4} seconds after the Big Bang), and we cannot ever get to t=0. So, the identification of the initial singularity with creatio ex nihilo is doubtful. As Hawking and Ellis put it, "the results we have obtained support the idea that the universe began a finite time ago. However, the actual point of creation, the singularity, is outside the scope of presently known laws of physics".[52]

All models of Big Bang assume infinitely dense and hot matter plus certain physical laws. Thus, as Isham pointed out, these models describe "the creation of the universe from an initial point", rather than a "creation from nothing".[53] Thus, the Big Bang is really a change, rather than a creation.

The vacuum that quantum cosmologists talk about is a particular state of quantum fields, subject to many constraints, including the principles of quantum mechanics and the principles of logic. Thus it should not be confused with metaphysical nothingness which is implied in the creatio ex nihilo.

The Big Bang inferred from the present expansion of the universe could indicate only the beginning of one world – our own world. There could have been other worlds before the present one, or there could be others alongside the present one, as some of the inflationary models claim. M. Mutahhari, the eminent Persian philosopher expressed the matter elegantly. He writes, "physicists could be right that 10 billion years ago the world did not exist with the present laws. But, how do we know that there were not other worlds before, with different laws".[54] And, in the words of Peter Hodgson, the British nuclear physicist, "the cosmic singularity seems to be the ultimate limit of science. This singularity is not necessarily the beginning of the universe; there may have been a previous contraction".[55]

Some contemporary cosmologists have been very arrogant in making big claims. For example, some cosmologists claim that they can explain the universe completely through science alone, and that it is self-created. Had we a successful and complete quantum theory of gravity, these claims could, in some sense, be justified. But we do not have such a theory; rather, we have highly speculative sketches of the alleged general features of this theory – features that are based on our present fragmentary knowledge. Chris Isham has put the matter elegantly:

> Major conceptual problems arise when trying to apply quantum theory to the universe as a whole. This problem is so severe that many highly respectable theoretical physicists think that the whole subject of quantum cosmology is misconceived.
>
> It follows that theories of the quantum origination of the universe are highly speculative and do not have anything like the scientific status of, say, even the more exotic branches of modern elementary particle physics.[56]

When our major theories, such as quantum theory, have conceptual problems and we do not have a successful marriage of quantum theory and general relativity, it is unwise to make conclusive inferences from them. The American astrophysicist J. Bahcall has articulated this point:

> I personally feel it is presumptuous to believe that man can determine the whole temporal structure of the universe, its evolution, development and ultimate fate from the first nanosecond of creation to the last 10^{10} years on the basis of three or four which are not very accurately known and are disputed among the experts. That I find, I would say, almost immodest.[57]

The grand masters of physics were very humble and cautious when the problem of the origin of the universe was concerned. For example, in 1930, the eminent physicist J.J. Thomson gave the following warning:

I think this is a warning against taking too seriously speculations about either the remote past or the remote future of the universe, founded as they must on the physics of the moment.[58]

This warning was given at a time that both major theories of physics, general relativity and quantum mechanics, were taken to be beyond any doubt and the end of science seemed to be in sight, and Gödel's incompleteness theorem had not arrived on the scene. According to this theorem, in any axiomatic system which includes arithmetic, there are statements whose truth or falsity cannot be decided within the system. Scientific cosmology is such a mathematical system. Thus, we cannot expect it to answer all of our cosmological questions. Serious conceptual problems of quantum mechanics plus the inability of physicists, so far, to give a coherent formulation of quantum gravity plus the existence of Gödel's theorem make it necessary to avoid any conclusive claims about the origin of universe. Some physicists (among them both theists and atheists) believe that science will finally settle this problem by itself. In the words of Ian G. Barbour:

> It is equally impossible to imagine a beginning of time or an infinite span of time. Both are unlike anything we have experienced. Both start with an unexplained universe. I will agree that the choice of theories could be made on scientific grounds alone, and that the difference between them is only of secondary importance religiously.[59]

However, I do not believe that science alone can ever settle the problem of the absolute beginning of the universe, though I agree with Barbour that either way (temporality or atemporality of the universe) is of secondary importance religiously.

I, personally, recommend the following strategy: we should explore our universe through science as much as we can, but we must avoid making claims about the absolute origination of the universe on physical grounds. Philosophy and theology can save us from making unsound exaggerated scientific claims, and can give us a proper metaphysical framework for our science and a ground for our being. In this framework, the description of the physical aspects of the universe is left for scientific investigation, but the ultimate explanation of the universe is provided by God. Robert J. Russell puts the matter elegantly:

> Whether the origin of the universe as we know it involves a previous quantum superspace, or whether the universe had an absolute beginning 15 billion years ago, the universe is contingent: it does not seem to include the grounds for its own existence, it does not offer an ultimate explanation of why anything at all exists in the first place, and therefore it points to that on which all beings necessarily exist – God.[60]

Notes

[1] al-Saduq, *al-Tawhid* (Qum: Manshourat Jamiah al-Mudarresin fi al Hawzah al-Ilmyyah, 1398 H.) 277.

[2] al-Rāzī, Fakhr al-Din, *al-Tafsir al-Kabir*, vol. 1 (Beirut: Dar Ihy al-Turath al-Arabi, no date specified), 6-7.

[3] al-Ghazālī, Abu Hamid Muhammad, *The Incoherence of the Philosophers*, trans. M.E. Marmura (Provo, Utah: Brigham Young University Press, 1977), 230.

[4] al-Rāzī, F., *al-Matalib al-Aliyah min al-Ilm al-Ilahi*, vol. 4 (Beirut: Dar al-Kitab al-Arabi, 1987), 29.

[5] Ibid., 33.

[6] Fayyaz Lahījī and Abd al-Razzaq, *Gowhar-e Murad* (Tehran: Irshad-e Islami, 1372 H.), 229-230.

[7] Abu Ali Ibn Sīnā, *al-Ishārāt wa al-Tanbīhāt*, vol. 3 (Tehran: Heidari, 1379 H.), 82.

[8] Shahab al-Din Suhrawardī, *Hikmat al-Ishraq* in *Majmouah Mosannefat Sheikh Ishraq*, vol. 2 (Tehran: Moassesah Motaliat we Tahqiqat-e Farhangi, 1372 H.), 181.

[9] Nasir al-Din Tūsī, *Tajrid al-Iateqad* (Qum: Maktab al-Aalam al-Islami, 1407 H.), 185.

[10] al-Ghazālī, op. cit., 32-36.

[11] M. Mutahharī, *Harakat wa Zaman dar Falsafeh-e Islami*, vol. 3 (Tehran: Intesharat-e Hikmat, 1375 H.), 234-235.

[12] W.L. Craig and Q. Smith, *Theism, Atheism, and Big Bang Cosmology* (Oxford: Clarendon Press, 1993), 294.

[13] S.H. Nasr and Leaman, *History of Islamic Philosophy*, vol. 1 (London: Routledge, 1996), 110.

[14] Ibid., 688.

[15] M.M. Sharif, *A History of Muslim Philosophy*, vol. 1 (Wiesbaden: Otto Harrassowitz, 1963), 441.

[16] Ibn Sīnā, op. cit., vol. 3, 138.

[17] T. Izutsu, *Creation and the Timeless Order of Things* (Ashland, Oregon: White Cloud, 1994), 151-158.

[18] Ibid., 167.

[19] J.W. Morris, *The Wisdom of the Throne* (Princeton: Princeton University Press, 1981), 119-120.

[20] Mullā-Sadrā, *al-Hikmat al-Muta'āliyah fi al-Asfar al-Aqliyyah al-Arbaah*, vol. 7 (Beirut: Dar Ihya al-Turath al-Arabi, 1981), 305-306.

[21] Ibid., 297.

[22] A. Einstein, "Cosmological Considerations on the General Theory of Relativity," in *The Principle of Relativity*, eds. W. Perrett and G.B. Jeffery (New York: Dover, 1952).

[23] F. Hoyle, "A New Model for the Expanding Universe", *Monthly Notices of the Royal Astronomical Society*, 108 (1948): 372-382.

[24] W.L. Craig and Q. Smith, op. cit., 47-56.

[25] Ibid, 284.

[26] Ted Peters, "On Creating the Cosmos" in *Physics, Philosophy and Theology*, Bob Russell, William R. Stoeger, and George Coyne (eds), (Vatican City State: Vatican Observatory, 1988), 291.

[27] Paul Davies, *God and the New Physics* (London: Penguin Books, 1988), 55-56.

[28] Q. Smith, "Did Big Bang Have a Cause", *British Journal for the Philosophy of Science*, 45 (1994): 666.

[29] A.R. Peacocke, *Creation and the World of Science: The Bampton Lectures, 1978* (Oxford: Clarendon, 1979), 78.

[30] Ian G. Barbour, *Issues in Science and Religion* (New York: Harper and Row, 1966), 368.

[31] John Polkinghorne, *Science and Creation* (Boston: Shambhala, 1998), 54.

[32] Ian G. Barbour, *Religion and Science: Historical and Contemporary Issues* (San Francisco: HarperSanFrancisco, 1997), 214.

[33] Quoted in Mark Worthing's *God, Creation and Contemporary Physics* (Minneapolis: Fortress Press, 1996), 113.

[34] P. Hefner, "The Evolution of the Created Co-Creator", in *Cosmos as Creation*, ed. Ted Peters (Nashville: Abdingdon Press, 1989), 227.

[35] Quoted in R. Stannard, *Science and Wonders* (London: Faber and Faber, 1996), 16.

[36] K. Ward, *God, Chance and Necessity* (Oxford: One World, 1996), 79.

[37] Quoted in Mark Worthing, *God, Creation and Contemporary Physics*, 116.

[38] Paul Davies, "The Birth of the Cosmos", in *God, Cosmos, Nature and Creativity*, ed. Jill Gready (Edinburgh: Scottish Academic, 1995), 19-20.

[39] A. Einstein, "On the 'Cosmological Problem'", Appendix in *The Meaning of Relativity* (London: Methuen, 1950), 123.

[40] E.P. Tryon, "Is the Universe a Vacuum Fluctuation", *Nature*, 246 (1973): 396-397.

[41] A. Vilenkin, "Creation of Universe from Nothing", *Physical Letters B*, 117:25; *Physical Review D*, 27:12 (1983): 2848.

[42] J. Hartle and S. Hawking, "Wave Function of the Universe", *Physical Review D*, 28 (1983): 2960-2975.

[43] S. Hawking, *A Brief History of Time* (London: Bantam, 1988), 136.

[44] Ibid., 141.

[45] D.N. Page, "Hawking's Timely Story", *Nature*, 332 (1988): 742-743.

[46] J. Polkinghorne, "The Mind of God", *The Cambridge Review*, vol. 113, no. 2316 (1992): 4.

[47] J.D. Barrow and R. Matzner, "The Homogeneity and Isotropy of the Universe", *Monthly Notices of the Royal Astronomical Society*, 181 (1977): 719-28.

[48] A. Linde, "The Inflationary Universe", *Physics Today*, vol. 40, no. 9 (1987): 61.

[49] C. Isham, "Quantum Theories of the Creation of the Universe", *Quantum Cosmology and the Laws of Nature*, R.J. Russell et al. (eds), (Vatican City State: Vatican Observatory, 1993), 77-78.

[50] Quoted in Max Jammer, *Einstein and Religion* (Princeton: Princeton University Press, 1999), 251.

[51] J.M. Zycinski, "Metaphysics and Epistemology in Stephen Hawking's Theory of the Creation of the Universe", *Zygon*, vol. 31, no. 2 (1996): 271.

[52] S. Hawking and G. Ellis, *The Large Scale Structure of Space-Time* (Cambridge: Cambridge University Press, 1973), 364.

[53] C. Isham, "Creation of the Universe as a Quantum Process", *Physics, Philosophy and Theology*, 398.

[54] M. Mutahharī, *Sharh-e Mabsout-e Manzoumah*, vol. 4 (Tehran: Intesharat-e Hekmat, 1369 H.), 109.

[55] P. Hodgson, *Science and Creation* (Oxford: The Farmington Institute for Christian Studies, 1995), 1-3.

[56] C. Isham, *Quantum Cosmology and the Laws of Nature*, 54-55.

[57] E. Regis, *Who Got Einstein's Office?* (London: Simon and Schuster, 1988), 210-211.

[58] Quoted in S. Jaki, *The Relevance of Physics* (Edinburg: Scottish Academic, 1970), 449-450.

[59] Ian G. Barbour, "Creation and Cosmology", *Cosmos and Creation*, ed. Ted Peters, 122.

[60] R.J. Russell, "Cosmology from Alpha to Omega", *Zygon*, vol. 29, no. 4 (1994): 563.

Chapter 10
The Impossible Possibility: Divine Causes in the World of Nature
Philip Clayton

Physical science, it appears, leaves no place for divine action. Modern science presupposes that the universe is a closed physical system, that interactions are regular and law-like, that all causal histories can be traced, and that anomalies will ultimately have physical explanations. But traditional assertions of God acting in the world conflict with all four of these conditions: they presuppose that the universe is open, that God acts from time to time according to his purposes, that the ultimate source and explanation of these actions is the divine will, and that no earthly account would ever suffice to explain God's intentions.

Moreover, one must worry about equivocation: the meanings of the word "cause" used of a chemical catalyst and of God's upholding the universe appear to diverge so widely that perhaps the same appellation should not be used to express both claims. Only if we can give some broader account of what causal features chemicals and providence share in common can we make sense of Jewish, Christian and Muslim claims for divine action in the world.

The problem of divine agency therefore stands on center court for theists today. Christians and Muslims, in particular, have traditionally been committed to a robust account of the actions of Allah or God within the natural order. But how can we attribute events to the causal activity of God when science appears to fully explain each event that occurs within the natural world? What conceptual resources might allow believers to acknowledge the power of science without reducing the divine to a "God of the [few remaining] gaps?". I assume – as one can hardly deny – that science has been massively successful in explaining events in the natural world. We cannot give just any account about what causes chemical and physical events; well-attested scientific explanations are not just "one story among the rest". This is not to deny that scientific theories have a preliminary status, that they are open to change and some of them will be falsified. Still, the fact that a given theory will possibly be revised in the future does not mean that it stands on the same level as any other account of the phenomena in the present.[1]

The Determinist Challenge

The problem is not just that science has a preference for non-divine causes. Far more serious, physical science presupposes the principle of *causal closure*. A physical system must be closed if physical calculation and prediction are to be possible. A core principle of physics is the principle of the *conservation of energy*. If we cannot assume that the total energy of a system remains constant – or at least know the exact quantity of energy that is added at a given time – we can have little or no knowledge of the system.

Put together these various requirements and you have the principle of causal or physical determinism. As William James notes, determinism "professes that those parts of the universe already laid down absolutely appoint and decree what other parts shall be. The future has no ambiguous possibilities hidden in its womb: the part we call the present is compatible with only one totality".[2] This determinism of physical causes involves the claim that the physical state of the world at a given time determines the physical state of the world for all future times. It is thus a *modal* notion, since it denies that it is *physically possible* that the present state of the world should give rise to more than one future state of affairs.[3]

Physical determinism is fundamentally a claim about causality – the claim, namely, that all that happens is a necessary effect of antecedent causes. It entails that the causal chain is all of a piece; no one cause stands out from the others as more fundamental. For example, neither genes in the biological sphere nor intentions in the realm of the psychological can be taken as the "real" determining factors without reference to *their* causal antecedents. At the same time, it claims that all physical occurrences are lawful: the universe is such that a given set of physical events can give rise to only one successor set.

All versions of determinism accept the *ontological* thesis that the state of the universe up to and including the present time *t* determines the universe's state in subsequent moments. But the challenge for theists is compounded by the fact that the ontological thesis usually begets an *epistemological* thesis: that future states could be predicted if one had enough knowledge of the past and present. Its most famous version is expressed by Laplace's thesis that all future and past events could be predicted from a complete knowledge of the present:

> An intelligence which knows at a given instant all forces acting in nature, as well as the momentary positions of all things of which the universe consists, would be able to comprehend the motions of the largest bodies of the world and those of the smallest atoms in one single formula, provided it were powerful enough to subject all data to analysis. To it, nothing would be uncertain; both future and past would be present before its eyes.[4]

By (often tacit) appeal to what I just called the epistemological thesis, debates about determinism often turn into debates about what is physically possible. In a broad sense of the term, it is physically possible that a divine agent exists – a being with no body who is utterly separate from this world. But, it seems, the actions of this agent could not be scientifically discerned, since all the observer would detect would be anomalies in causal sequences in the physical world. Under a stricter interpretation, however, the existence of a divine being might be viewed as physically impossible, since it is not a physical thing. If this interpretation is correct, theism and physical determinism would be incompatible. To be honest, one must admit that modern science has presupposed one of these two interpretations; and by and large it has been the stricter view that has predominated.[5]

It is on these grounds, for example, that the "new synthesis" in evolutionary biology represents a serious challenge to theism. Evolution requires that no outside causal force be responsible for the development of more complex systems and life forms; random genetic variation and selective retention through the environment are the only allowable causal determinants of the evolutionary process. For its part, theism requires that the development be intended by God, so that God is in some sense responsible for the outcome. Some Christian biologists, most notably Arthur Peacocke, have argued that God could have initiated a process of cosmic evolution that God knew would lead to the development of conscious life without any further role being required on God's part.[6] But this viewpoint faces a serious dilemma: either the development of life would have to be a necessary consequence of the Big Bang (which does not seem likely given the quantum uncertainties involved), or God would have had to be ready to intervene, and perhaps actually *has* intervened, in order to bring about conscious life (which would contradict the "hands-off" position). At first blush, at least, it looks like a stand-off, such that evolution is incompatible with theism and divine providence or action in the world is incompatible with evolution.

Needed: A New Theory of Causation

The challenge we have been exploring requires theologians to do some fundamental rethinking on the topic of divine action, since the inherited tools and concepts are no longer adequate to make sense of divine action in an age of science. To put it bluntly, the theologian seems to be faced with a forced choice between two alternatives: either God acts as the Divine Architect only, creating a finely tuned machine and leaving it to function in a consistent manner expressive of its Designer; or God becomes the Divine Repairman, whose imperfect building of the machine in the first place requires him, like a refrigerator repairman, to return from time to time to fix up errors he made the first time around. Though perhaps not impossible, it is certainly difficult to develop an alternative perspective that allows one to speak of a "different but equal" causal system, alongside the network of scientific explanations, that is equally constitutive of physical events in the world.

Many attempts have been made to respond to this challenge. Some have found an opening in quantum indeterminacy. Perhaps, they argue, the physical world is fully lawlike, and even physically closed (i.e., the total amount of energy remains constant). But quantum physics, at least on the Copenhagen interpretation, reveals a world that is both law-governed and essentially indeterminate: unobserved subatomic events do not have a precise location and momentum, and probabilistic laws leave some room for chance. Now it does seem significant that quantum mechanics allows for multiple outcomes given the same initial conditions, since it leaves room for top-down influences (more on this below). Still, "stochastic" or probabilistic laws are still laws: they may not determine the individual case but they do reflect a physical determinism of the overall pattern. Also, the laws say nothing about agents and agents' freedom; hence they do not provide the stronger sense of counterfactual free action that theists appear to need to make their case.

This lack has led some to set strongly dualist notions of mental causation over against the world of physical causes. Among these non-physical types of causation are the "agent causation" of Richard Taylor and the ubiquitous divine causation ("double agency") of Austin Farrer. Such approaches posit mental or divine causes that affect outcomes without introducing new energy into the physical world. Certainly views of this sort leave room for full human and divine agency. Unfortunately, they do not integrate easily with physical science as we now know it, and some versions actually contradict physical descriptions of the world.

But what of human agency? Do humans not have a freedom of the will: "A staff moves a stone, and is moved by a hand, which is moved by a man".[7] Theists have often argued that since humans are free, God could act in the world. After all, if humans can break the chain of physical causality, could not God do so all the more? But free will may be less of a trump card than it appears. The dominant view within philosophy has been *compatibilism*, the view that physical determinism is compatible with human agency and moral responsibility.[8] The American legal system, for example, holds individuals responsible if they will and then carry out an illegal action (say, murder), *even if* the willing was determined by prior causes. According to compatibilism, agents' actions express their character traits; it is thus irrelevant whether these traits, and thus the actions themselves, are determined by antecedent causes. Perhaps the "sense" of being free is mistaken, since even a fully determined will could still (falsely) imagine itself to be free. Finally, many scientists argue that neuroscience presupposes (or more radically: has already proven) that the only causal agency is physical; aside from brain states and the body's responses, there *is* no "actor" to be found.

Clearly, it is an urgent task for the theologian to provide a clear account of what she means by asserting that God continues to be active in the world. To succeed at this task we need nothing less than a new theory of causation. This chapter offers a first sketch of such a theory. The argument divides into three main parts:

1. I first concede that the threat of equivocation cannot be overcome as long as one's theory of causality includes only physical and divine causes; the gap is just too wide. By contrast, if we find evidence within the natural world of vastly different types of causes we can perhaps extend the line to include super-natural causal influences as well. And in fact the study of the natural world *does* reveal rather different types of causal action, from classical Newtonian causality, to gravity, to the influence of quantum fields, to the "holistic constraints" of integrated systems – and on to the pervasive role of

mental causes in human life, as in your comprehension of the sentence, "Please stop reading this sentence!".

2. The objection arises: Are not all these causal forces ultimately explainable in terms of the laws of the underlying physical reality – unlike divine causes, which are said to issue from a transcendent and free source? In the following sections I marshal the diverse evidence and arguments that point beyond classical notions of physical causality. Taken together, they now encourage us to accept (as the medieval Islamic philosophers also urged) that the genus "cause" includes types of influences other than mechanistic ones.

3. The last section then draws together the results of the earlier sections in the direction of a systematic theory of divine action. Emergent causal levels, reflecting the hierarchical structure of the natural world, help to elucidate the nature of divine action, though they are not identical to it. The differences between natural and super-natural causation that remain do represent a continuing burden to Muslim and Christian thinkers in an age of science. Given an adequately broad theory of causation, however, the burden may be bearable.

This is a high-stakes question for Islam and Christianity. Traditional formulations remain attractive, but they face conceptual objections that some fear are insuperable. Can a scientifically acceptable concept of emergence be developed that will re-enchant the world, allowing us to speak of it again as the ongoing handiwork of God? If so, what might this "theology in a new key" look like? Can we again find the divine in "the light of setting suns, / And the round ocean and the living air, / And the blue sky, and in the mind of man" (Wordsworth)?

The Framework of Emergence

For simplicity's sake one could speak of four major transitions in the natural world that evidence the phenomenon of emergence:[9]

1. Fundamental physics to physical systems and chemistry;
2. Biochemistry to complex biological organisms and ecosystems, including the evolution of life;
3. The brain and central nervous system to the phenomena of consciousness or "mind";
4. The emergence of spirit within the natural order, including the question of its ultimate nature and origin.

One can only understand the emergence of life, mind, and spirit when one has developed a broader notion of causal influence based on emergent levels in the natural world. If we are successful, this notion may be broad enough to at least make sense of the idea of God's causal activity in the world.

Before we can proceed to a constructive theory of causality, we must first review the history of the concept of emergence in the disciplines in which it first arose. In the history of Western philosophy the concept goes back at least as far as Aristotle. Aristotle's biological research led him to posit a principle of growth within organisms that was responsible for the qualities or form that would later emerge. Aristotle called this principle the *entelechy*, the internal principle of growth and perfection that directed the organism to actualize the qualities that it contained in a merely potential state. In this sense the adult form of the human or animal *emerges out of* its youthful form. Famously, Aristotle argued that no less than four different types of causes were necessary to explain the full complexity of the natural world running from physics through biology to psychology. One needs not only "efficient" causes, which work from outside to move it or to cause change, but also: "material" causes, which describe the ways that the matter of a thing affects it; "formal" causes, which operate through the form internal to the organism; and "final" causes, which pull the organism (so to speak) toward its final telos or perfection.

Aristotle's influence on Hellenistic, Islamic, and Western medieval philosophy cannot be overstated. Through Thomas Aquinas, who in the 13th century directly adopted Aristotle's theory of the four causes,[10] he was brought into the center of Roman Catholic theology, a place he continues to occupy among conscious and unconscious Thomists to the present day. Thus, Aquinas insisted that every event involved not only the efficient cause (what physicists would speak of today as *the* cause of an occurrence), but also the formal and material causes, that is the influence of the matter and the form on the outcome. Adapting Aristotle's theory of "final causes" to a theistic context, he introduced the notion of the overall purpose of God as one of the causal forces in every event, thereby making divine causal action a component in every earthly occurrence. Aristotle – or, more generally, Greek natural philosophy – also remained surprisingly dominant in early modern medicine, biology, and geology. In fact, biology was to some extent still under the influence of this paradigm when Darwin began his work.

Of the four causes, final causality is particularly important to theology – and its loss particularly damaging. One of the most sophisticated defenders among contemporary theologians is Wolfhart Pannenberg. In chapter 4 of *Theology and the Kingdom of God*, he adopts something like Aristotelian final causality, speaking of the power of the future as a causal constituent in every event.[11] A similar adaptation or version of final causality is visible in Lewis Ford's "lure of the future", a notion that he adapts from Whitehead.[12] One also recognizes Thomistic overtones in theories of divine action that distinguish between primary and secondary causality – indirectly in the work of Austin Farrer, and more directly in the writings of David Burrell.[13] Such defenses of "future causality" in one guise or another cannot be quickly dismissed as metaphysical non-starters.[14] Nonetheless, they have not won broad acceptance, presumably because final or future causes are not among the causal forces accepted by the ruling scientific worldview.

Note that there are ways other than the Aristotelian-Thomist strategy by which one might introduce divine causal influence, for example, theologies of process and theologies of emanation. The doctrine of emanation, at least in its most famous (Neoplatonic) form, defends the emergence of the entire hierarchy of being out of the One and the subsequent movement of finite beings back up the ladder of derivation to their ultimate source. This Neoplatonist model, of which traditional theologians have always been skeptical, allowed both for a *downward* movement of differentiation and causality and an *upward* movement of increasing perfection. Ultimately, diminishing distance from the Source would lead (in principle) to a final mystical (re)unification with the One. Unlike static models of the world, emanation models allowed for a fluid movement downward and upward through the various species, as well as between the physical, psychological, and intellectual spheres. In those cases in which the emanation was understood in a temporal sense, the emanation doctrine provided an important antecedent to doctrines of biological or universal evolution.

When science was still natural philosophy, emergence played a productive heuristic role. After about 1850, however, emergence theories were several times imposed unscientifically as a metaphysical framework in ways that blocked empirical work. Key examples include the neo-vitalists (e.g. H. Driesch's theory of entelechies) and neo-idealist theories of the interconnections of all living things (e.g. Bradley's theory of internal relations) around the turn of the century, as well as the speculations of the British Emergentists in the 1920s concerning the origin of mind. From these mistakes we can derive certain cautionary conclusions and criteria for the use of emergence. Above all, speculation must never *replace* empirical science; rather, it *supplements* science when broader questions are being raised. The concept of emergence is useful not as a metaphysic *imposed* on the sciences from the outside but as an inductive result that emerges out of a careful study of the sciences themselves.

Quantum Mechanics and the Question of Causation

It is often said that the development of quantum mechanics has transformed our understanding of the causal connections in the world. In one sense this is true: quantum physics countenances types of causal influence utterly foreign to Newtonian physics. In another sense, as we will see, quantum physics by itself does not genuinely move beyond the framework of physical causes in a way that helps to solve the puzzle of God's causal action – at least not until it is supplemented by a broader theory of emergence.

Consider, for example, the position of Werner Heisenberg, who explained the Copenhagen interpretation by taking a fundamentally Aristotelian view of quantum mechanics.[15] Heisenberg believed that quantum indeterminacy was like the world that Aristotle described, in which one of the many potential states represented by the wave function becomes actual at the moment of measurement. Under this interpretation of quantum mechanics, the subject acts as a sort of final cause; she pulls a certain potential state into actual existence by means of her observation. Note that this view reverses the stance of classical (Newtonian) physics, which requires that the subject ultimately be explained in terms of physical laws.

For the Copenhagen theorists more generally, when a definite measurement is made of a quantum event, the macrophysical state that results is understood to combine a quantum-physical probability distribution and the scientist's decision of what, when, and how to measure. Indeed, on this view the subject's role is in one sense the primary one: the "world" is merely potential until the moment of observation, when the conscious observer resolves it into an actual state. The most extreme form of this position – the form propounded for instance by John Wheeler – holds that the entire universe may have existed in a state of quantum potentiality until the moment when the first observer emerged, at which point the universe was *retroactively* resolved into macro-physical structures such as stars, planets, and the like. At one point Wheeler even applied this logic backwards as far as the creation of the universe:

> Is the very mechanism for the universe to come into being meaningless or unworkable or both unless the universe is guaranteed to produce life, consciousness and observership somewhere and for some little time in its history-to-be? The quantum principle shows that there is a sense in which what the observer will do in the future defines what happens in the past – even in a past so remote that life did not then exist, and shows even more, that 'observership' is a prerequisite for any useful version of 'reality'.[16]

The debate between the various interpretations of quantum mechanics has not yet been resolved, and there is reason to wonder whether it ever could be resolved in physical terms alone. It includes irreducibly philosophical components, including, as I hope to show, crucial metaphysical assumptions about causality. Those who are committed to explaining the world in terms of physical causes – and thus in terms of Aristotle's efficient causality alone – maintain that they are justified in accepting almost any purely physical explanation over one that appeals to other types of causes. Thus DeWitt postulated an actual branching of the universe into multiple universes every time a quantum indeterminacy is resolved into a distinct macrophysical state of affairs – after all, even this uncountably infinite multiplying of physical universes is better than allowing subjects to introduce a new type of causality (viz. human choice) into science.[17] By contrast, those whose metaphysical commitments allow for the postulation of subject- or intention-based causes (i.e. final causes) will fault DeWitt's "many worlds" strategy for the most egregious of affronts to the principle of parsimony in explanation.

Now there are also serious objections to the subject-based interpretation of quantum mechanics, objections which draw out its counterintuitive nature (the widely cited thought experiment of Schrödinger's Cat being perhaps the most famous). But the fact is that during the last 75 years major physicists have found themselves needing to experiment with other types of causal influences in order to explain the anomalies of the quantum world. Indeed, quantum physics has recently challenged classical notions of causality in yet another way. "Entangled particles" are particles emitted from a common source that preserve certain symmetries even when widely separated in space. For example, measuring the spin of one entangled particle will instantaneously cause the other to exhibit the corresponding spin – even if the two particles are 10 km apart at the instant of measurement. Because standard efficient causation cannot be propagated faster than the speed of light, these results suggest a radically new type of influence or connection.

Note the important conceptual entailment that arises at this point. One's theory of causality and ontology are crucially related: the data that challenge standard efficient causality can be interpreted *either* as revealing a broader type of causal influence, *or* as revealing a more holistic view of the system in question (or both). Empirically, one can account for entanglement phenomena in quantum physics either as expressing a new type of causal influence or as suggesting that the entangled particles in fact represent a single "object", the two parts of which may be some 10 km apart. Thus the entanglement phenomena have also been cited as evidence for holistic conclusions. Even mainline physicists such as Henry Stapp find in them signs of an overarching interconnection of all things. Stapp writes that:

> the principle of local causes asserts that what happens in one spacetime region is approximately independent of variables subject to the control of an experimenter in a far-away spacelike-separated region. ... Bell's theorem shows that no theory of reality compatible with quantum theory can allow the spatially separated parts of reality to be independent.[18]

In a more extreme vein, Stapp's comments have led Ken Wilber to claim that entanglement experiments provide increased justification for the holism of the Eastern traditions *as well as* for an ontology of spiritual consciousness:

It is common among the 'new-paradigm' thinkers to claim that the basic problem with science is that, under the 'Newtonian-Cartesian' worldview, the universe is viewed as atomistic, mechanistic, divided, and fragmented, whereas the new sciences (quantum/relativistic and systems/complexity theory) have shown that the world is not a collection of atomistic fragments but an inseparable web of relations. This 'web-of-life' view, they claim, is compatible with traditional spiritual worldviews, and thus this 'new paradigm' will usher in the new quantum self and quantum society, a holistic and healing worldview disclosed by science itself. ... The problem, in other words, was not that the scientific worldview was atomistic instead of holistic, because it was basically and generally holistic from the start. No, the problem was that it was a thoroughly *flatland holism*. It was not a holism that actually included all of the interior realms of the I and the WE (including the eye of contemplation).[19]

A similar conceptual relation holds in the field of brain research. One thinks, for example, of the neuroscientist John Sperry, who was reticent to speak in a dualistic fashion of mental causes. What dualists speak of as subjectivity he described as a sign of a holistic interconnection within the brain as a whole. Here postulating holistic interconnection (effects of the brain as a whole) helps to reduce the apparent uniqueness of mental phenomena. Still, in all these cases the holistic influences in question cannot quite be contained within the framework of Newtonian efficient causes.

Although the full case cannot be made here,[20] I do take quantum theory as evidence for the need to expand our notion of causality. The Newtonian picture of the world represented the heyday of efficient causality: all dynamics could ultimately be reduced to billiard-ball-like collisions between objects. (Of course, the causal force of gravity remained somewhat mysterious under this model, and Newton still found himself compelled to retain the possibility of divine corrections to the system. But certainly the followers of Newton – most famously Laplace – have taken his physics to represent the final victory for efficient causation.) By contrast, the world of subatomic physics has uncovered phenomena that are inconceivable on the basis of Newton's laws alone. Perhaps phenomena such as the collapse of the wave packet, decoherence, and quantum entanglement will someday admit of explanations in terms of standard (Newtonian) efficient causation. But the evidence at the moment points more naturally in a different direction – namely, that the nature of causal influences in the natural world is much more complex and multi-layered than the framework of efficient or "billiard-ball" causation could ever convey.

At any rate, the founders of quantum mechanics were the first to recognize that whatever ontology finally expresses the quantum physical results, it will be radically different from the causes and ontologies of traditional macrophysics. It may be, as I have suggested, that quantum mechanics provides evidence for the causal role of the intentionality. This was the view of the quantum physicist Eugene Wigner, who concluded that "the minds of sentient beings occupy a central role in the laws of nature and in the organization of the universe, for it is precisely when the information about an observation enters the consciousness of an observer that the superposition of waves actually collapses into reality".[21] But at the very least quantum physics opens up an inquiry into an expanded notion of causality that is certain to lead to new territory.

Psychological Causes

Classical physics (and non-Copenhagen interpretations of quantum mechanics) hold that all causal forces are ultimately explainable in terms of the laws of the underlying physical reality. Were this view true, it would raise insuperable problems for any appeals to divine causes, since they are said to issue from a transcendent and free source. But there is another area of science, in addition to the one just presented, that suggests the inadequacy of the Newtonian view. If there are genuinely psychological causes, then there is at least one type of causality that is distinct from physical causality. If so, it would appear that the genus "cause" can include types of influences other than mechanistic ones.

I have already noted the four major transitions in the natural world that evidence the phenomenon of emergence. In the case of the emergence of consciousness through the human brain and central nervous system the evidence for another type of cause is perhaps the clearest. In contrast to the standard position a decade or so ago, the natural sciences of the human person – neurobiology, primatology, cognitive science, evolutionary psychology – are today acknowledging the realm of the mental as an emergent phenomenon. The difficulty no longer lies in showing the irreducibility of mind, but rather in demonstrating that mind can have "downward" causal effects on the body and the world (which will be necessary if one is to speak of God's effects on the world).

What precisely is it that emerges? What emerges in the human case is a particular psycho-somatic unity, an organism that can do things both mentally and physically. Although mental functions supervene upon a physiological basis,[22] these two sets of attributes are interconnected and exhibit causal influences in both directions. To say that human persons are *psycho-somatic unities* is to say that we are complexly patterned entities within the world who evidence diverse sets of properties and causes operating at different levels of complexity. A living body and a functioning brain are *necessary* conditions for personhood, yet the wide discrepancy in the vocabularies of neuroscience and psychology suggests that they are not *sufficient* conditions. Personhood is not fully translatable into "lower-level" terms; persons evidence causal and phenomenological properties (*qualia*) that are uniquely personal.

Studies of the human person must be multi-dimensional because persons are the result of causal influences that operate at the physical, biological, psychological, and (I believe also) spiritual levels, and because these levels, though interdependent, are not mutually reducible. In particular, psychology cannot afford to dispute the experience of human actors in the world on the question of mental causation. Mental states – wishing, willing, intending, realizing, and the like – exercise a causal influence on the actions of agents and thus on what their bodies do in the world. The causal history of the mental thus cannot be told in physical terms, and the outcome of mental events is not determined by phenomena at the physical level alone. Human talk of the subjective experience of being in love or of the sense of self-awareness is irreducibly mental; mental experiences of these types exercise a type of causal influence of their own.

Now the critic may object that talk of mental causes is like returning to occult causes in the physical world or "vitalist" causes in the biological world. Science stopped appealing to such causes, however, because of the recognition that the realms of physics and biology operate in a fully law-like manner *based on explanatory successes in the relevant sciences.* Is it true that human persons are analogous to rocks and cells in the sense that their behaviors can be exhaustively predicted and explained in a "bottom-up" manner? I have argued that we have good evidence to think not. Indeed, the hierarchy of the sciences itself offers evidence of principles that are increasingly divergent from "bottom-up" physical causality.[23] Functionalist causal explanations play a role in the biological sciences (from cell structures through neural systems to ecosystem studies) that is different from causal explanations in fundamental physics, just as explanations appealing to intentions as causes play a role in explaining human behavior that is without analogy at lower levels.[24] As one moves up the hierarchy of emergence, one finds an increasing role for top-down causal action. Thus, for example, DNA incorporates into its structure the (top-down) influence of the environment on the molecular biology of the human body. In intentional explanations it is even more clear that the goals for which the agent acts, and the broader contexts within which she understands her actions, causally influence her particular thoughts and behaviors.

Note the theological implications of this view. It is easier to maintain that God influenced the convert to bring him to his new religion than it is to argue that God fixed the broken plumbing system in one's house (unless one has *also* had a plumber come to do the repairs!). The reason for the difference is that we do not now possess, and may never possess, laws of human behavior.[25] In contrast to natural scientists, social scientists can at most ascertain broad patterns of human response, and even these evidence a virtually unlimited number of personal and cultural exceptions. Within the human realm, it seems, uniqueness and idiosyncracy are the norm. No laws are broken when we speak of the uniqueness of an individual action; indeed, this is almost what we *mean* by an individual action. "Psychological miracles" – God's causal influence on the thought, will and emotions of an individual person – could therefore occur without overturning natural law; God could thus bring about changes in one's subjective dispositions without causing an affront to natural scientific knowledge of the world.[26]

Double Agency and Divine Persuasion

But what kind of causal influence would this be? The great British philosophical theologian Austin Farrer developed a sophisticated account of divine action which he called the "double agency" view.[27] On this view, every action in the world includes a causal role for one or more agents or objects in the world (the "secondary" causes) and a role for God as the "primary" cause of what occurs. Kathryn Tanner summarizes and defends something like Farrer's position:

> The theologian talks of an ordered nexus of created causes and effects in a relation of total and immediate dependence upon divine agency. Two different orders of efficacy become evident: along a 'horizontal' plane, an order of created causes and effects; along a 'vertical' plane, the order whereby God founds the former. Predicates applied to created beings ... can be understood to hold simply within the horizontal plane of relations among created beings.[28]

Such a view of action implies that God's action in the world should be understood as something more like divine persuasion. Responding to Tanner, Thomas Tracy concludes:

> There are, therefore, important respects in which the free acts of creatures can be regarded as God's acts. If we deny that God is the *sufficient cause* of the creature's free acts, we can immediately go on to affirm that God acts with the infinite resources of omnipotence to *guide* those choices by shaping the orienting conditions under which they are made. In untraceably many, varied, and subtle ways, God continuously brings to bear the pressure of the divine purpose for us without simply displacing our purposes for ourselves. God's action goes before our own, preparing us (in spite of ourselves) for the unsurpassably great good that God has promised us.[29]

This theory does alter how God's causal agency is said to contribute to human actions in the world, at least in comparison to classical views of divine action. On most classical views, God's decision to bring about an effect in the world was taken to be sufficient for that effect to occur; it did not require the concurrence of any finite person or object. On this view, by contrast, God must persuade the agent in question to act in a particular way for the event to occur. Hence, again, the special role for the human psyche: a mind can be convinced or persuaded, whereas (as far as we know) a rock cannot be persuaded to act on its own, no matter how good the arguments. Though it limits the efficacy of the divine will in the world, I nonetheless believe that Tracy's position is sufficient for the theological needs of Muslim, Christian, and Jewish theists today.[30]

Viewed in this way, God's role in interacting with conscious beings becomes the role of one who prepares and persuades, rather than the one who "brings about" human actions by divine fiat alone. This view is also conceptually much neater than the alternatives, since it also attributes basic actions to humans. Like the theist traditions, however, it does continue to ascribe to God a crucial causal role in "luring" humanity and encouraging certain types of actions. Further, according to this model there must be genuine openness in history. The theologian Wolfhart Pannenberg, among others, has made clear that the result is that one cannot *know* in advance that God will bring about the ends that he desires to accomplish.[31] Nonetheless, one *can* know that, if God is God, these ends will in the end be achieved, such that the final state of affairs will be consistent with God's nature.

Evolution as a Test Case

We turn, finally, to evolution as a particularly difficult test case for this theory of divine causal influence. In what follows, I take contemporary evolutionary theory as the starting point: there is no point in "lowering the bar" at the outset in order to make things easier for theists. On the one hand, the standard model requires that the evolution of life be a product of a process of random genetic mutation, where the environment selects for the fittest individuals. On the other hand, any theist who wishes to avoid deism must assert that God in some way guides the process of evolution to bring about the effects he intends (conscious life, persons, salvation history).

During most of the history of biological evolution there were no conscious beings for God to influence, so the type of causality defended in the previous section could not have been employed, at least not directly. But the recent theoretical overlap between biology and information theory does open the door to an at least analogous type of causal influence. The dimension of information became central in biology following the discovery of the genetic code responsible for the informing of the cell and organism as a whole. Recent work has interpreted biological structures (morphology) and the organism's interaction with its environment as processes involving the storage, use, and exchange of information. One might think of this process as a sort of cybernetic or semantic version of Aristotle's formal causes. Even nutrition has been construed as the ingestion of highly structured (informationally rich) matter with low-information energy as a byproduct.[32]

The informational approach clearly suggests parallels with information processing in the sphere of mental activity. As we saw above, no physical laws are broken if there is an exchange of information between a divine source and conscious human agents. The key to reconciling evolution and theism is the recognition that the process of information transfer at the conscious level is anticipated at earlier moments within the evolution of the biosphere. In particular, the introduction of goals – and especially the goal of increasing complexity – could have been held out to evolving life forms as a possibility for their development without contradicting the mechanisms of evolution. Morphological possibilities (formal causes) could have been presented as a type of information that helped pull the evolutionary process toward the outcome of increasing complexity (final cause).

The perspective of information biology has several advantages. For example, it helps resolve the question of how complex organs, which come to have survival value only when they are fully developed and functional, could emerge gradually over many, many generations through a combination of genetic (bottom-up) and environmental (top-down) influences. It is also consistent with the recent emphasis on epigenetic effects – "top-down" causal influences – in cytology (the study of cells). The data now trace the two-way interaction between the DNA of a cell and the cell as a whole. Since particular proteins in the cell function selectively to cause particular segments of the genome (i.e. particular units of genetic information) to be expressed, the determining influences come not only "from below" but also from the broader context of the cell's environment. In a similar manner, social behavioral studies in primatology show how the broader environment deeply influences the development of the organism without superseding genetic mechanisms. The effects of broader systems or wholes are therefore already standard parts of the full explanatory account in biology. Thus Steven J. Gould writes, "Minor adjustment within populations may be sequential and adaptive. ... Evolutionary trends may represent a kind of higher-level selection upon essentially static species themselves, not the slow and steady alteration of a single large population through untold ages".[33]

My suggestion is that the framework of information theory in biology helps to establish enough parallels with psychological causes that one can make sense of claims to a divine causal influence on the evolutionary process. For emergence theorists, it is a matter of extending the spheres of causal influence "upward": through cell, organ, organism, and environment, up to the influence of mental states, and perhaps beyond to the lure of the divine nature. The information model allows for divine causal constraint in a way that remains consistent with the hierarchical structure of the natural world as we know it. If I am right, it allows theists to speak of the sort of divine influence required by the doctrine of divine providence, yet to conceive this influence in a way that does not require the addition of new causes or new energy into the system. A direct divine intervention to change the chemistry of a cell would be a miracle (and a problematic one at that!) in a way that the chemical effects that one might produce by shifting her focus of attention would not be. My argument has been that an information-based "lure" on the evolutionary process construes the divine influence in a fashion much more similar to the latter than to the former.

Toward a Theory of Emergent Causality

Let us now attempt to put these various resources together into a single theory of emergent causality. We have agreed to accept modern natural science as a source of justified explanations of the natural world, and we have conceded that these explanations depend primarily on efficient causation. It certainly does not follow from the fact that pre-modern philosophers utilized three other types of causality that we can simply reintroduce them as equals alongside the efficient causal explanations of physics and chemistry. Critics would rightly point out that the success of modern science seems to have been based on its insistence upon explaining events in terms of traceable and reconstructable series of (efficient) causal histories in the natural world.

The challenge with which philosophers and theologians are faced is nothing less than to sketch a new theory of causation. I have suggested that the resources for this new theory lie in concepts already employed by scientists in various fields: entanglement phenomena in quantum mechanics, mental causes in psychology, information theory and epigenesis in biology, and the structure of emergence that appears again and again as one climbs the ladder of complexity in the natural world.

Causal relations *up* the emergent hierarchy are uncontroversial, since they rely on efficient causality. The slogan of much of modern science might be expressed as "explanation (and therefore ontology) reduces downward; causes propagate upward". The standard model in scientific explanation is to explain complex behaviors, or the behavior of complex bodies, in terms of fundamental forces acting on their constituent parts. On the standard model, it might *look* mysterious that a cell can divide and divide again, suggesting to vitalists the need for a higher and more mysterious "life principle" to explain these actions. But when one has understood the biochemistry of cell division, the catalytic effect of enzymes, and the basic genetic architecture and functioning of the cell, no mysterious forces remain. The compilation of these myriad physical particles and forces, combined with the effects of chemical properties and basic physical laws, tell the whole causal story. With this bottom-up account in place, no other causal story is necessary. Or so it seemed.

But emergence has shown that upward propagation of causes is *not* the whole story. The state of the whole – the whole physical system within which particles interact, the whole cell, the whole organism, the whole ecosystem, the psycho-physical unity that humans are – affects the behavior of the particles and the causal interactions that they have (though these interactions, once so affected, do propagate upwards). Now admittedly some theorists are arguing that no actual causal forces are involved. Arthur Peacocke leaned in this direction when he used to speak of "whole-part constraint" rather than of downward causation.[34] Likewise, certain branches of complexity theory, including complexity theorists such as John Holland who use the word emergence, also allow only upward causation, although they do grant that something new and unpredictable (at least in lower-level terms) emerges.[35] By contrast, I have argued that the phenomena allow for, and may actually require, the notion of a downwardly propagating causal influence. How can this be understood?

After examining the break with Newtonian efficient causality in quantum physics, I moved to perhaps the most compelling area, the relationship of mental states to physical states. To make the position as little controversial as possible, I have not posited a separately existing substance called soul or mind, but only the existence of mental predicates. Physicalists who reject emergence understand these to be mental properties of a physical object, in this case the brain. But I suggested that the strength of our experience of mental causation – the ability of our ideas and thoughts to cause bodily movements such as speaking, walking, or raising an arm – is so great that real mental causation must be taken as the default position. The onus is thus on those who would deny any causal efficacy to ideas and intentions.

I then turned to the question of evolution. At first blush it looked like a stand-off: many claim that Darwinian evolution is incompatible with theism and that divine providence or action in the world is incompatible with evolution. What does one do when encountering a problem that cannot be solved either from the bottom alone (i.e. through genetics and biochemistry), or from the top alone (i.e. by negating biology and imposing a theological answer)? One looks for a way to place several different disciplines together to solve the problem – not as identical (which is false) or as incompatible (which is inadvisable), but in a dialectical relationship. Specifically, I suggested, the contradiction is overcome if what evolution demands and what theology requires are not contradictory but complementary.

This turned out to be the case: evolution forbids both internal purposes and divine causal influences from the outside, whereas theism requires only that the product of the evolutionary process reflect the divine intention to create rational, moral creatures who can be in conscious relationship with the divine. This divine goal *might* have resulted from God's initiating a process that he knew in advance would necessarily produce such creatures without any further guidance on his part, although such pre-determinism now looks unlikely given what we currently know about quantum physics and genetic drift. In the case of evolution, however, it proved possible to find an analog to the downward causation that we experience in conscious volition. Information biology provides us with a way of conceiving the introduction of information into the environment, and such information could guide the development of life forms in a sort of proto-purpose fashion (think of Kant's slogan, "purposiveness without purpose"). Given the analog, God could guide the process of emergence by introducing new information (formal causality) and by holding out an ideal or image that could influence development without altering the mechanical mechanisms of evolution or adding energy from outside (final causality).

Of course certain caveats and limitations must be expressed. The framework of guided emergence does not amount to the sort of control of the evolutionary process traditionally advanced by theists. On this view, the explanations of biological phenomena are indeed given in terms of evolutionary biology, and the conclusions and constraints of that discipline are not short-circuited by this response. Guidance by possibility and by information is not a form of efficient causation; it comes closest to the luring nature of "formal causes" associated with Aristotelian philosophy. But it *is* sufficient to provide the sort of structure traditionally implied by a doctrine of providence. The notion of "purposiveness" I am employing admittedly has a quasi-"as if" status: the biological world develops *as if* it were being guided by a divine hand. It is, as noted above, *purposiveness without purpose*. Still, all that the view needs to do is to show that the biological sciences do not rule out some form of divine lure, and this, I believe, it successfully does.

Panentheism: The Missing Piece

But there is still one missing piece. The theory of causality sketched here is upwardly emergent. It recognizes different kinds of causal influence at the different levels of organization evident in the natural world. By itself, therefore, it does not show whether the entire process is driven "from above" or whether it reflects a law of self-organization immanent in the natural order itself. An emergentist theory of causality does not prove the existence of God.

But theology (or metaphysics) has never been about proof in the first place. In these fields, the goal is to show broad conceptual coherence across vastly diverse areas of natural science and human experience. There is at least one theology that integrates naturally with the sciences, and with the interdisciplinary theory of causality, that we have been exploring. This is the theology of *panentheism*. Panentheism is a theory of the God-world relation, and thus of divine action, that locates the world within God while holding that God is also more than the world.

Panentheism provides a natural interpretation of each of the levels of causality that we have discussed. Its guiding principle is that each level of the natural world reveals its Origin in a manner consistent with its nature and capacities.[36] The physical world reveals the constancy and regularity of the divine nature. God's providence which sustains the universe is expressed here in the lawfulness of the physical world. If we were to introduce the metaphor of the universe as God's body, we could view this lawfulness as a form of autonomic divine action, similar in some respects to the unconscious or autonomic functions of the human body. (Of course, in the divine case we will imagine that God has full awareness of each of these lawlike functions.) The psychological world reveals the person-like nature of divine Spirit, its rationality, will, and goal-directedness. God offers a lure, a call or guidance, to each conscious creature, influencing that creature's consciousness and (depending on the creature's response) possibly altering the future course of events. Continuing the metaphor, we might view this latter as a type of *focal* divine action. And the biological sphere – the sphere of living things that do not clearly reveal conscious influences on their behavior – represents an in-between stage. The most we can say empirically is that the goal-directed behavior of life forms reflect a sort of proto-purposiveness, a forerunner of the conscious, goal-directed action that characterizes conscious agents.

Agenda for the Future

It has been said that we today lack what the medieval Islamic and Christian philosophers had: a unitary theory of causation. The required theory must be comprehensive enough to do justice to the strength of scientific causal explanations *and* be able to integrate them, together with mental and divine causation, into a single causal account of the world. I have sought to outline such a theory in these pages.

As we noted above, and as both Aristotle and the medieval Islamic philosophers already saw, an adequate theory of causation must finally be integrated with an ontology. The doctrine of "efficient causes alone" was a natural expression of the physicalist ontology of Newtonian mechanics, according to which all that exists are bodies and forces within absolute space and time. This view dominated from the foundations of modern physics in Galileo and Newton to the advent of the Copenhagen interpretation of quantum mechanics in the 1920s. Similarly, Aristotle's theory of four causes was fully integrated into a metaphysics in which things were not mere point-masses but actualities that resulted from the striving of prior possibilities to reach their natural *telos*.

The ontology presupposed in this paper is an ontology of emergence, which I have elsewhere called *emergentist monism*.[37] On this view there is only one natural world (hence dualism is false). But as this one "stuff" becomes organized in more and more complicated ways, new properties emerge. Although their manifestation is dependent on the properties of the underlying particles, and thus ultimately on the laws of physics, their behavior is irreducible to any of the underlying levels. Hence the natural world evidences the emergence of genuinely new properties. At each level of emergence, new structures are obtained and new causal forces are at work. We can extend the structure of emergence downward to address questions of fundamental physical law, and we can extend it upwards to come to a better understanding of conscious, and ultimately spiritual, properties. I have therefore argued that emergent causal levels reflect the hierarchical structure of the natural world and may help to elucidate the nature of divine action (though they are not identical to it). The differences between natural and super-natural causation that remain do represent a continuing burden to Muslim and Christian thinkers in an age of science. Given an adequately broad theory of causation, however, the burden is bearable.

This is truly theology in a new key. We may shy away from magical interventions into the physical world and yet still find that world "re-enchanted" as the field of action of the divine. The beauties of our planet and the richness of its life forms are not distant expressions of the providence of God; they continue to manifest the divine presence. We can again look to the structures (and contents!) of individual consciousness, and to the growth and development of culture, for signs of divine guidance and creativity. Think for example of the cultural means by which individuals who are open to the divine lure can influence other individuals. An idea of genius (Einstein's special relativity, Kant's critical philosophy, Ghandi's non-violent resistance) or an artistic genre (classical harmony, Sufi poetry) – which might be a product of divine causal influence – can spread like wildfire through a large number of minds or through human experience in general. Individual minds integrate into groups of minds; individual actions influence other actions.

Of course, one cannot *demonstrate* that a given idea is God-breathed or that either religious groups or human culture as a whole, is progressing toward greater harmony with the divine will; the previous centuries offer too painful a picture of regress in the other direction for such melioristic optimism to be convincing. Still, the "upwardly open" nature of human consciousness, infused as it is with intimations of immortality, offers a powerful model of the integration of mind and spirit. Just as the neurophysiological structure of the higher primates is "upwardly open" to the emergence and causal power of the mental, so the mental or cultural world is upwardly open to the influence of the Creator Spirit.

Notes

1 On the presumption of naturalism, see chapter 6, "The Presumption of Naturalism", in Philip Clayton, *God and Contemporary Science* (Edinburgh: Edinburgh University Press and Grand Rapids: Eerdmans, 1997), 169-187.

2 William James, *The Will to Believe and Other Essays in Popular Philosophy* (New York: Longmans, Green, and Co., 1905).

3 See C. Brighouse, "Determinism and Modality", *British Journal for the Philosophy of Science* 48 (1997): 465-81.

4 Henry Margenau, *Scientific Indeterminism and Human Freedom* (Latrobe, PA: Archabby Press, 1968), 3. In popular writings it is sometimes assumed that scientists, who are *not* omniscient, will be able to predict the future if determinism is true. But chaos theory, the physics of systems far from thermodynamic equilibrium, now suggests that prediction will be impossible even in fully deterministic systems when they are "chaotic".

5 Among many excellent works see especially John Earman, *A Primer on Determinism* (Norwell, MA: Reidell Publishing Co., 1986); Ted Honderich, *A Theory of Determinism: The Mind, Neuroscience, and Life Hopes, II* (New York: Oxford University Press, 1988); Sidney Hook, ed., *Determinism and Freedom in the Age of Modern Science* (New York: Collier Books, 1961); Keith Lehrer, ed., *Freedom and Determinism* (New York: Random House, 1996); Viggo Mortensen, Robert Sorenson et al.(eds), *Free Will and Determinism: Papers From an Interdisciplinary Research Conference, 1986* (Chicago, IL: Aarhus University Press, 1987); M. Targett, "Determinism, Indeterminism, and Explanatory Bias", *Progress in Neurobiology* 53 (1997): 533-45; R. Taylor, *Action and Purpose* (New York: Humanities Press, 1973); Roy Weatherford,

The Implications of Determinism (New York: Routledge Press, 1991); G.H. von Wright, *Causality and Determinism* (New York: Columbia University Press, 1974).

6   Arthur Peacocke, "Science and the Future of Theology: Critical Issues", *Zygon* 35 (2000).

7   Aristotle, *Physica*, 256a. See also Timothy O'Connor (ed.), *Agents, Causes, and Events: Essays on Indeterminism and Free Will* (New York: Oxford University Press, 1995).

8   The position goes back at least to Kant. See Hud Hudson, *Kant's Compatibilism* (Ithaca: Cornell University Press, 1994). Indeterminists, of course, deny this claim, arguing instead for "genuine" or counter-factual freedom: you did this action now, but you might have done something different even in identical circumstances. As Jean-Paul Sartre puts it in a classic phrase, "the indispensable and fundamental condition of all action is the freedom of the acting being", J.P. Sartre, *Being and Nothingness*, trans. Hazel E. Barnes (New York: Citadel Press, 1956).

9   In a new book the biologist Harold Morowitz finds no less than 28 levels of emergence in the natural order; see his *Emergences: Twenty-Eight Steps from Matter to Spirit* (forthcoming).

10   See e.g. Aquinas, *Summa theologica*, I/1, Q. 44, art. 1-4, which demonstrates that God must exercise all four types of causality.

11   See Clayton, "The God of History and the Presence of the Future", *The Journal of Religion* 65 (1985): 98-108, and "Being and One Theologian", *The Thomist* 50 (1988): 645-671.

12   See Lewis Ford, *The Lure of God: A Biblical Background for Process Theism* (Philadelphia: Fortress Press, 1978).

13   See Austin Farrer, *Faith and Speculation* (New York: New York University Press, 1967). Cf. also David Burrell, *Knowing the Unknowable God* (Notre Dame: University of Notre Dame Press, 1986), as well as Burrell, "Divine Practical Knowing: How an Eternal God Acts in Time", in Brian Hebblethwaite and Edward Henderson, eds., *Divine Action: Studies Inspired by the Philosophical Theology of Austin Farrer* (Edinburgh: T. & T. Clark, 1990), pp. 93-102.

14   Thus my critique of Pannenberg's future ontology as "counterintuitive" in "Anticipation and Theological Method", in Carl Braaten and Philip Clayton (eds), *The Theology of Wolfhart Pannenberg: Twelve American Critiques* (Minneapolis: Augsburg, 1988), must be taken as over-hasty. I offer a fuller and more nuanced critique in the article, "Being and One Theologian", cited above.

15   See Werner Heisenberg, *Physics and Philosophy: The revolution in Modern Science* (New York: Harper and Row, 1962).

16   John Wheeler, quoted in P.C.W. Davies, *Other Worlds: A Portrait of Nature in Rebellion–Space, Superspace, and the Quantum Universe* (New York: Simon and Schuster, 1980), p. 126.

[17] See De Witt, quoted in Davies, *Other Worlds*, p. 136. See also Bryce DeWitt and Neill Graham, *The Many Worlds Interpretation of Quantum Mechanics* (Princeton: Princeton University Press, 1973).

[18] Stapp, "Theory of Reality", *Foundations of Physics* 7 (1977): 313-23.

[19] Ken Wilber, *The Marriage of Sense and Soul: Integrating Science and Religion* (New York: Random House, 1998), pp. 38, 57.

[20] See my "Tracing the Lines: Constraint and Freedom in the Movement from Quantum Physics to Theology", in Robert Russell, John Polkinghorne, Philip Clayton and Kirk Wegter-McNelly (eds), *Quantum Physics and Quantum Field Theory: Perspectives on Divine Action* (Vatican City: Vatican Observatory Press and CTNS, forthcoming).

[21] Eugene Wigner, quoted in Davies, *Other Worlds*, pp. 132f. This view has been recently argued by Henry Stapp in *Mind, Matter, and Quantum Mechanics* (Berlin and New York: Springer-Verlag, 1993). Stapp draws on von Neumann rather than Wigner, however.

[22] For an emergentist theory of supervenience see Clayton, "Neuroscience, the Person and God: An Emergentist Account", *Zygon* 35/3 (Sept. 2000): 613-52.

[23] I cannot review the entire argument here. It is powerfully laid out in Arthur Peacocke, *Theology for a Scientific Age: Being and Becoming–Natural, Divine, and Human* (Minneapolis: Fortress Press, 1993).

[24] These emerging orders of explanation may also involve an increasing role for top-down explanations. In intentional explanations it is even more clear that the goal for which the agent acts, or the broader context within which she understands her actions, influences the particular behaviors or thoughts.

[25] Here I follow Donald Davidson in his defense of the anomalous nature of the mental; see e.g. Davidson, *Essays on Actions and Events* (Oxford: Clarendon, 1980).

[26] Perhaps this is why one finds so little resistance to purely "psychological" accounts of Jesus' resurrection. I recall, for example, listening to various conversations within the Jesus Seminar – a group famous for its resistance to supernatural miracles in the New Testament documents – in which the reawakened faith and hope on the part of the disciples was gladly designated as "the resurrection of the Christ". Christian theologians across the liberal/conservative spectrum are willing to speak of the presence of God in individuals' personal experience and of God's providential role in guiding them "toward all truth" (John 16:13).

[27] See Austin Farrer, *Finite and Infinite*, 2nd ed. (Westminster: Dacre Press, 1959); see also Brian Hebblethwaite and Edward Henderson (eds), *Divine Action: Studies Inspired by the Philosophical Theology of Austin Farrer*, cited above.

[28] See Kathryn Tanner, *God and Creation in Christian Theology: Tyranny or Empowerment?* (Oxford: Basil Blackwell, 1988), p. 89, also cited in Tracy, "Divine Action, Created Causes, and Human Freedom", in Thomas F. Tracy (ed.), *The God Who Acts: Philosophical and Theological Explorations* (University Park, PA: Pennsylvania State

University Press, 1994) p. 86. In Tracy's view, only if I am the cause of my action is my responsibility preserved.

[29] See Tracy's own article in Tracy, ed., *The God Who Acts*, pp. 101f.

[30] It remains *metaphysically* possible, of course, that a God who created the universe could bring about any effect within that universe that he might choose to accomplish. The position seeks merely to describe the standard mode of divine influence in the world.

[31] See e.g. Pannenberg "Der Gott der Geschichte", in *Grundfragen systematischer Theologie: Gesammelte Aufsätze*, vol. 2 (Göttingen: Vandenhoeck und Ruprecht, 1980), pp.112-128.

[32] See John C. Puddefoot, "Information Theory, Biology, and Christology", in W. Mark Richardson and Wesley Wildman (eds), *Religion and Science: History, Method, Dialogue* (New York: Routledge, 1996), pp. 301-319.

[33] Stephen J. Gould, *The Panda's Thumb: More Reflections in Natural History* (New York: W.W. Norton, 1980), p. 15.

[34] Fortunately Peacocke has moved beyond his early refusal to use the term "cause" of such influences. See his two important articles: "Biological Evolution – A Positive Theological Appraisal", in Robert J. Russell et al., *Evolutionary and Molecular Biology: Scientific Perspectives on Divine Action* (Vatican City State: Vatican Observatory Publications, 1998), pp. 357-76; and "Chance and Law in Irreversible Thermodynamics, Theoretical Biology, and Theology", in Robert J. Russell et al., *Chaos and Complexity: Scientific Perspectives on Divine Action* (Vatican City State: Vatican Observatory Publications, 1995), pp. 123-43.

[35] See e.g. John H. Holland, *Emergence: From Chaos to Order* (Cambridge, MA: Perseus Books, 1998); Holland, *Hidden Order: How Adaptation Builds Complexity* (Reading, MA: Perseus Books, 1995).

[36] Note that this view also has its roots in Aristotle and became a core principle of medieval Islamic philosophy.

[37] See my "Neuroscience, the Person and God: An Emergentist Account", cited above. The theory of *emergentist monism* has been developed in collaboration with Arthur Peacocke, whose influence on the outcome I happily acknowledge. See Peacocke's article, "The Sound of Sheer Silence: How Does God Communicate with Humanity", in Robert J. Russell et al. (eds), *Neuroscience and the Person: Scientific Perspectives on Divine Action* (Vatican City State: Vatican Observatory Publications, 1999), pp. 215-47.

Chapter 11
Christian Theism and the Idea
of an Oscillating Universe
Mark Worthing

Models of an oscillating universe arising out of Big Bang cosmologies provide an intriguing example of both the interaction between theistic perspectives and scientific cosmologies. These models also draw into sharp contrast the very different reception they have received, respectively, within the Christian and Islamic traditions. From the point of view of the Christian tradition there appears to be a clear instance in which the Islamic tradition can provide insights that serve to aid in overcoming difficulties traditionally associated with incorporating the possibility of an oscillating universe into a Christian worldview. With this in mind, it must be made clear that the intention of this paper is neither to argue for or against cosmological models of an oscillating universe. What is intended is the presentation of a case study in theistic responses to theories arising out of modern scientific cosmology.

But first, we must specify what we mean today when we speak of 'cosmology' and in what particular context Christian and Muslim theism enter into dialogue with scientific cosmologies.

The Necessity of Dialogue Between Theism and Scientific Cosmology

As is the case with Islam, the Christian confession of God as creator of all things, both material and immaterial, commits Christian theology to a necessary dialogue with scientific cosmologies. If God is indeed creator of the heavens and the earth, then no genuine knowledge of anything either in the heavens or upon the earth can be unrelated to our understanding of God. And by the same token, neither can our understanding of God be irrelevant for a genuine knowledge of the cosmos. Wolfhart Pannenberg, a Christian theologian in the Lutheran tradition, put this point well when he wrote:

> If the God of the Bible is creator of the universe, then it is not possible to understand fully or even appropriately the processes of nature without any reference to that God. If, on the contrary, nature can be appropriately understood without reference to the God of the Bible, then that God cannot be the creator of the universe.[1]

Thus committed to a view of God inextricably linked to our understanding of the physical world, the dialogue with the variety of ever-emerging and changing scientific cosmologies is not just an activity of passing interest for Christian theism, it is a necessity.

But just what is cosmology? Seyyed Hossein Nasr, in a recently published article on Islamic cosmology, points to the great diversity of meanings given to the term cosmology, especially between the ancient world and the modern scientific world. He writes:

> Traditional cosmologies deal with cosmic reality in its totality, including the intelligible or angelic, the imaginal or psychic, as well as the physical domains. They are applications of metaphysical principles to the cosmic realm. Modern cosmologies, in contrast, despite all the recent changes in modern science ... are still based on the Cartesian bifurcation, with the concomitant reduction of cosmic reality to *res extensa* and pure quantity.[2]

The recognition of the modern restriction of the meaning of cosmology, which in its fullest sense entails a comprehensive and unified view of all aspects of reality, is of great significance. It reminds all theists that attempts to bring the idea of God into the dialogue with modern cosmologies as something essentially novel or new have already from the start abandoned the basic claims of theism.

Open or Closed Universe?

A significant debate in recent years within cosmology has been over whether the universe is open or closed. This debate forms part of the fundamental scientific background to the discussion of the possibility of an oscillating universe. Is there enough matter in the universe to halt its expansion and eventually bring everything back together in a so-called Big Crunch, or, when less than the critical mass exists, will the universe continue expanding forever? The entire issue rests with the amount of matter that exists in the universe. Calculating the approximate mass of the universe, however, has proven to be no easy task. From what is visible to observation it would appear that there is far too little matter to bring the universe's expansion to a halt. Yet if that were all the matter that there were, the universe would be expanding much more rapidly than it is. It has been deduced, therefore, that an unseen "material" called "dark matter" exists within the so-called empty spaces of the universe. The question is how much so-called dark matter there may be.

Findings from the Hubble space telescope, using its powerful lens to detect gravitational distortions that are tell-tale signs of the presence of significant amounts of dark matter, have initially suggested that there is insufficient matter in the universe to bring its expansion to a halt.[3] Yet this has not been the end of the story. Other investigations have turned up evidence suggesting the contrary. NASA's Cobe space probe, for instance, generated much excitement when an announcement was made at a meeting of the American Physical Society that it had detected fluctuations in the background radiation of the early universe that confirm the predictions of Big Bang theorists as to why the universe is now so "lumpy".[4] The data produced by Cobe, if correct, indicates that the fluctuations in the evenness of the universe first began to form about 300,000 years after the Big Bang. In order for such fluctuations to have developed so quickly, however, as a result of gravitational attraction, the universe must have significantly more mass in it than physicists had previously suspected – quite probably enough to cause its eventual collapse, producing what has been termed the "Big Crunch".

The Possibility of an Oscillating Universe

Yet, within closed universe models an irreversible big crunch is not the only possibility. Another possibility, long despised and often strenuously rejected within the western intellectual tradition has refused to disappear. This, of course, is what is variously known as an eternal return, or a cyclic, oscillating, pulsating, or reprocessing universe. Or, in keeping with the scientific parlance of the Big Bang, what we might call the "Big Bounce". The concept itself is nothing new. In fact it is quite ancient, having been found among most cultures in antiquity. Yet, it was among the Greeks that the idea was most explicitly developed. We might call to mind, for instance, the thought of Empedocles, who contended that the universe is continually being created and destroyed.[5]

In our own era the American physicist John Wheeler has been among a small number of scientists seeking to revive this ancient concept. Wheeler and his colleague C.M. Patton suggest that, keeping in mind the quantum dynamics of the system of the universe, a model of the universe should be set up to run through the phase of a collapse and see what, if anything, happens afterward. But, how could this be done? They suggest that the tiny electron may already provide us with such a model. They write:

The electron traveling towards a point center of positive charge arrives in a finite time at a condition of infinite kinetic energy, according to classical theory, just as the universe arrives in a finite proper time at a condition of infinite compaction. But, for the electron, quantum theory replaces deterministic catastrophe by probabilistic scattering in (x, y, z) space. Why then for the universe should not quantum theory replace deterministic catastrophe by probabilistic scattering in superspace? ... In brief, this picture considers the laws of physics to be valid far beyond the scale of time of a single cycle of the universe, and envisages the universe to be 'reprocessed' each time it passes from one cycle to the next.[6]

Or, as Wheeler has written elsewhere:

Little as one knows the internal machinery of the black box [i.e. the phase of final collapse in which the physics are unknown], one sees no escape from this picture of what goes on: the universe transforms, or transmutes, or transits, or is *reprocessed* probabilistically from one cycle of history to another in the era of collapse.[7]

George Gamow affirmed the possibility of an oscillating universe perhaps most simply when he wrote, "We conclude that our universe has existed for an eternity of time, that until about five million years ago it was collapsing uniformly from a state of infinite rarefaction ... and that the universe is now on the rebound".[8] In addition to Wheeler and Gamow, I.L. Rozental[9] and M.A. Markov[10] have been among the most prominent scientific advocates of the idea of an oscillating universe.

Yet, while the concept clearly has remained for some scientific cosmologists a fascinating possibility, it has also encountered strong opposition.[11] From the perspective of modern physical science the theory of the oscillating universe suffers from one enormous and unrelenting disadvantage. Since earlier than the Planck time (the period between $t = 10^{-43}$ and 5.4×10^{-44} seconds ABB) our physical laws break down and have no meaning, putting forward a scientific theory of an oscillating universe in which the mechanism by which its reprocessing takes place is a virtual impossibility.

Yet we should not hastily conclude that just because as the universe approaches the point of maximum compaction – or infinite density – and the known laws of physics cease to apply, that therefore there are no laws governing the action of physical matter in this phase. In order to be open to all genuine possibilities modern science must overcome its prejudice against its inability to describe the mechanism whereby the universe could be reprocessed using the known laws of physics. There is something profoundly hubristic in the assumption that if we cannot understand or describe something, even theoretically, given our current state of knowledge, then it cannot be a possibility. Others would oppose the idea not because they view it as impossible that there could be some unknown laws governing such a reprocessing, but simply because anything that has happened or will happen in some other possible cycle than our own is beyond the reach of science and therefore pure and inappropriate speculation. Still others point readily to the principle of entropy, which would seem to indicate that an endless succession of cycles, which most oscillating universe models presume, is an impossibility. Yet as Ian Barbour has pointed out, despite the fact that "one would expect from the law of entropy that there could have been only a finite rather than an infinite number of oscillations, ... under such conditions the applicability of this law is uncertain".[12]

Sir Arthur Eddington: An Early Response to the Modern Idea of a Cyclic Universe

But it is not only the prejudices of scientific thought that have worked against the serious consideration of cyclic models of the universe. Much of the opposition, even from some within the scientific community, has been overtly philosophical and even theological in nature. The physicist Sir Arthur Eddington, whose famous 1919 expedition played a vital role in confirming Einstein's theory of general relativity and helped paved the way for the theory of an expanding universe,[13] was uncomfortable with the idea of an eternal cycle of expansion and collapse that the theory had brought into vogue. Writing in 1935 Eddington said:

> From a moral standpoint the conception of a cyclic universe, continually running down and continually rejuvenating itself, seems to me wholly retrograde. Must Sisyphus for ever roll his stone up the hill for it to roll down again every time it approaches the top? That was a description of Hell. If we have any conception of progress as a whole reaching deeper than the physical symbols of the external world, the way must, it would seem, lie in escape from the Wheel of things. It is curious that the doctrine of the running-down of the physical universe is so often looked upon as pessimistic and contrary to the aspirations of religion. Since when has the teaching that 'heaven and earth shall pass away' become ecclesiastically unorthodox?[14]

Eddington expressed a similar opinion, also in 1935, in his book *The Nature of the Physical World.* There he wrote:

> I am no Phoenix worshiper. ... I would feel more content that the universe should accomplish some great scheme of evolution and, having achieved whatever may be achieved, lapse back into chaotic changelessness, than that its purpose should be banalized by continual repetition. I am an Evolutionist, not a Multiplicationist. It seems rather stupid to keep doing the same thing over and over again.[15]

As a leading scientific thinker of his era and a devout Christian, Eddington had no difficulty incorporating a number of scientific theories, including evolutionary theory, into his worldview. Yet the strength of his reaction against the idea of a cyclic universe was most uncharacteristic. So, what concerns laid behind his outbursts against the notion that the universe may oscillate? Eddington has admitted that his dislike of an oscillating universe is based largely on personal, philosophical, and religious grounds rather than on specific scientific concerns with the theory. These concerns merit some comment as they recur in other thinkers who reject the possibility of an oscillating universe.

First, it must be pointed out that Eddington's use of the biblical reference to heaven and earth passing away is problematic. The concept of heaven and earth passing away occurs in biblical apocalyptic texts almost always in connection with the creation of a new heaven and a new earth. An absolute end to everything – that is, an end that can in no way be seen also as a transformation – is foreign to the thought of the Bible.[16] The frequent misunderstanding of these texts has also been noted by the New Testament scholar Rudolf Bultmann, who wrote:

> It is *the paradox* of the Christian message ... that *the eschatological event* is not genuinely understood in its own sense – at least as Paul and John understood it–if it is interpreted as an event that brings an end to the visible world through a cosmic catastrophe rather than as *an occurrence within history*.[17]

It is precisely for this reason that many ecclesiastics have found the scientifically-based prediction of the end of the universe to which Eddington refers problematic, not because they had never heard the verse "heaven and earth will pass away". For this reason also, we must reject Eddington's implication that the hope that the universe will in some way or in some form prove to be eternal is anti-biblical.

Eddington's view that the world must necessarily "escape from the Wheel of things" also merits comment. The concept is perhaps more reminiscent of Buddhist than Christian thought. The suggestion is that the world is somehow irredeemably flawed and only through coming to an absolute end at some point can it escape its torment and fulfil any purpose it may have had. Eddington's comments about the futile repetition of a cyclic universe also reinforce this direction of thought. Yet it is surprising to hear a Christian theist, even though trained in science and not theology, express these views. The implication is that something is fundamentally wrong with God's good creation, something so serious that it cannot be redeemed or resolved. This in turn raises questions about what kind of God would create a universe whose best of all possible destinies is to complete whatever "evolutionary achievement" it is capable of and then to "escape the Wheel of things". Christian thought clearly recognizes the sufferings and groanings of creation (Romans 8:20-22); but, Christian theology also confesses that the "frustration" to which the creation was subjected due to human sin finds its resolution in God's redemption, not its escape from the cycle of existence.

Current Status of Oscillating Universe as Scientific Theory

The reception of oscillating universe theories in more recent times has not been much better than that given by Eddington. John Wheeler has attempted to find a home for the idea with the concept of the anthropic principle. As John Barrow and Frank Tipler write:

> Wheeler has speculated that the Universe may have a cyclic character, oscillating *ad infinitum* through a sequence of expanding and contracting phases. At each 'bounce' where contraction is exchanged for expansion, the singularity may introduce a permutation in the values of the physical 'constants' of Nature and of the form of the expansion dynamics. Only in those cycles in which the 'deal' is right will observers evolve.[18]

Barrow and Tipler, however, are critical of Wheeler's suggestion as being untestable and too speculative and therefore do not explore its implications within the context of the anthropic principle.

Another strong critic has been Steven Weinberg. In his book, *The First Three Minutes*, he rejects theories of an oscillating universe on the grounds that they do not provide the hoped-for eternity that they seem to promise. Weinberg highlights one of the biggest questions hanging over scientific models of a recurrent universe based upon big bang cosmologies when he points to the second law of thermodynamics – which has spelled the end of more than one scientific theory.[19] Weinberg's concern is that unless we wish to say that the second law does not apply to the cycles of recurrence, then they must at some point run down and come to a conclusion. The second law, he contends, would also imply that there must have been a beginning of the series. Weinberg seems to assume that the chief benefit of a theory of an oscillating universe is that it claims to solve the so-called "Genesis problem" and remove the need for God. In this light the application of the second law means that such recurrences do not really bring any substantial benefit. Explains Weinberg:

> Some cosmologists are philosophically attracted to the oscillating model, especially because, like the steady-state model, it nicely avoids the problem of Genesis. It does, however, face one severe theoretical difficulty. In each cycle the ... entropy per nuclear particle is slightly increased by a kind of friction as the universe expands and contracts. As far as we know, the universe would then start each new cycle with a new, slightly larger ratio of photons to nuclear particles. Right now this ratio is large but not infinite, so it is hard to see how the universe could have previously experienced an infinite number of cycles.[20]

Although the oscillating universe model does not have a great deal of support among physicists, it tenaciously remains an intriguing theory with some vocal advocates. If the NASA Cobe discovery, suggesting that the formation of unevenness in the microwave background radiation of the universe occurred early, proves correct, indicating that the universe may be closed, then a resurgence of interest in models of an oscillating universe could well be expected. In such an event theology would have to take seriously the implications of an oscillating universe.

Origen of Alexandria and Cyclic Cosmology

Although cosmological models of an oscillating universe built upon big bang cosmologies are recent, the idea of a cyclic universe itself is very old, going back at least to the ancient Greeks in the 'West' and even earlier, to China and India in the East and Egypt and Babylon in the Middle East.[21] It is therefore not surprising that we find the first (and until now almost the only) serious attempt to integrate the cosmology of a cyclic universe into Christian thought already in the 3rd century CE theologian Origen of Alexandria. The movement toward engagement between Christian theism and contemporary cosmologies, already begun by the Greek-speaking apologists of the 2nd century, reached its pinnacle in the early Christian church with Origen of Alexandria. Origen was not just one of the most learned theologians of the Christian tradition, he was also well versed in the philosophy and natural sciences of his time, especially in the Platonic and Neo-Platonic schools of thought. In an effort to make Christian teaching comprehensible to the Greek mind he integrated many cosmological ideas prevalent in Greek philosophy into his theology. In a key passage of his *De Principiis*, Origen describes his cyclic cosmology.

> Not for the first time did God begin to work when He made this visible world; but as, after its destruction, there will be another world, so also we believe that others existed before the present came into being. And both of these positions will be confirmed by the authority of holy Scripture. For that there will be another world after this, is taught by Isaiah, who says, 'There will be new heavens and a new earth, which I will make to abide in my sight, saith the Lord'; and that before this world others also existed is shown by

Ecclesiastes, in the words: 'What is that which hath been? Even that which shall be. And what has been created? Even this which is to be created: and there is nothing altogether new under the sun. Who shall speak and declare, Lo, this is new? It has already been in the ages which have been before us'. By these testimonies it is established both that there were ages before our own, and that there will be others after it. It is not, however, to be supposed that several worlds existed at once, but that, after the end of this present world, others will take their beginning.[22]

Apart from what would today be considered questionable exegesis by most Christian scholars, Origen's views serve an important function in demonstrating the conceptual possibility of a cyclic universe within Christian thought. Yet the model comes at a price. A cyclic universe raises a number of difficult questions for theism in general and Christian theism in particular. It must be asked, for instance, if everything repeats itself, does this include human actions? And if so, what of human free will? Are these cycles unending? If they are, then in what sense can we speak of God as Creator? And perhaps most significantly for Christian thought, must Jesus die on the cross in each cycle, making his death non-unique? In an extended passage, again in *De Principiis*, Origen addresses precisely these problems. In answer to those of his contemporaries who believed that each cycle of a cyclic universe would be an exact repetition of the one before it, Origen wrote:

I do not understand by what proofs they can maintain their position ... For if there is said to be a world similar in all respects (to the present), then it will come to pass that Adam and Eve will do the same things which they did before ... and everything which has been done in this life will be said to be repeated – a state of things which I think cannot be established by any reasoning, if souls are actuated by freedom of the will, and maintain either their advance or retrogression according to the power of their will. For souls are not driven on in a cycle which returns after many ages to the same round, so as either to do or desire this or that; but at whatever point the freedom of their own will aims, thither to direct the course of their actions. ... So therefore it seems to me impossible for a world to be restored for the second time, with the same order and with the same amount of births, and deaths, and actions.

But this world, which is itself called an age, is said to be the conclusion of many ages. Now the holy apostle teaches that in that age which preceded this, Christ did not suffer, nor even in the age which preceded that again; and I know not that I am able to enumerate the number of anterior ages in which he did not suffer.[23]

For Origen it is clear that a cyclic universe neither destroys free will nor makes the death of Christ a repeatable (or repeating) event. Regarding the question of divine creation, Origen is not so clear. We know from other parts of his writing that he maintained an original creation out of nothing. Hence, he is able to confess that "there is one God, who created all things, and who, when nothing existed, called all things into being – God from the first foundation of the world".[24] What is not entirely clear is whether Origen intends the *creatio ex nihilo* to apply to the creation of this present cycle or to the very first of the sequence. If Origen has in mind the very first in a series of cycles then this is perhaps what he meant when he wrote that "there was one beginning; and ... there spring from this one beginning many differences and varieties".[25] On the other hand, he seems elsewhere to also hint that God creates the world anew, out of nothing, with each new cycle.[26]

Interestingly, recent contributions of quantum theory to the oscillating universe model have supported Origen's view that the cycles of the universe would not simply be "doing the same thing over and over again" as Eddington seems to have held. In fact, not every cycle may be suitable for life – a possibility that may even allow us to consider our present cycle unique in this regard. This would certainly be no more anthropocentric than the common theological (and in some circles scientific) belief that our planet is the only one capable of sustaining life.[27] In regard to the diversity of cycles suggested by the application of quantum theory to the oscillating universe model, Patton and Wheeler write:

> Even without the actual quantum geometrodynamic calculation, ... can one conclude that any given cycle of expansion and contraction is followed, not by a unique new cycle, but a probability distribution of cycles? According to this expectation, in one such cycle the universe attains one maximum volume and lives for one length of time; in another cycle, another volume and another time; and so on. In a few such cycles life and consciousness are possible; in most others, not.[28]

Wheeler, in a manner similar to his participatory universe theory,[29] applies findings from the microscopic world of quantum physics to the macroscopic realm of the entire universe. In this case, Wheeler adopts the picture of the course charted by probabilistic quantum mechanics for the shattered electron to the universe as a whole as it enters and emerges reprocessed from the Big Crunch phase. Thus a unique feature of Wheeler's oscillating universe is that it has a probabilistic variety of new cycles, apparently awaiting the "final observation" of the participatory observer to become "real". Wheeler's model describes "the beginnings of alternative new histories for the universe itself after collapse and 'reprocessing' end the present cycle".[30] Needless to say, Wheeler's model is speculative even by the standards of traditional oscillating universe models. Nevertheless, it serves to demonstrate that the models of an oscillating universe that are currently being proposed and discussed, especially those that take into account quantum theory, represent something far removed from the mere doing of the same thing over and over again of which Eddington complained. In this context Origen's advocacy of the necessary uniqueness of cycles, which he based on theological grounds, would seem to receive support from recent developments in the scientific discussion of an oscillating universe.

Origen's cosmology, while no less speculative than the theory of the oscillating universe, is not without theological value. Just as Origen wrote his theology in the context of a worldview in which a cyclic universe was the dominant cosmology, so also must we write our theologies within the context of the cosmological models that dominate our modern worldview.

As oscillating models of the universe continue to gain acceptance as credible cosmology, modern theologians would be wise to review carefully the work of Origen who, writing more than 1600 years ago, demonstrated that Christian theology and the idea of a cyclic universe need not be seen as incompatible. Origen's view, for instance, that free will prevents the cycles from being exact repetitions would seem to counter Eddington's argument that a universe in which everything repeated itself would be senseless. Origen also demonstrated that the uniqueness of the Christ event cannot be sacrificed in order to suit the needs of a cyclic cosmology. While modern theologians may be uncomfortable with how Origen does this, making our own age a unique culmination of ages because of the Christ event, he has shown at least one possible solution to a problem some have claimed to be unsolvable.

Reasons for Opposition to Oscillating Universe Models

While the arguments for and against scientifically construed models of an oscillating universe are a matter for debate within the scientific sphere, the unusually strong opposition to such models among Western Christian thinkers merits particular attention. Why are scientific models of an oscillating universe so strenuously rejected by many contemporary Christian thinkers when one of the earliest and foundational Christian thinkers embraced cyclic cosmology already in the 3rd century?

1. Any cosmology incorporating the possibility of an oscillating universe comes up against a rather rigidly conceived linear view of history that has become dominant is the Western Christian tradition. The fact that early Eastern theologians such as Origen held to a cyclic view of history demonstrates, however, that a strict linear view is not necessitated by the Christian tradition as such.

2. Some suggest that there is within such models an implicit rejection of an original creation. One could conceive of an original creation referring to the first in a series of worlds, or even to each individual new cycle. One might also suggest, as did Thomas Aquinas, that an original creation is not strictly necessary to maintain the confession of a creation *ex nihilo*.[31] While each of these possibilities present difficulties none can be ruled out on the basis of the foundational teachings of the Christian faith.

3. If an oscillating universe suggests no clear beginning of the universe, as some models clearly do, then it is assumed that this posses irreconcilable difficulties for the doctrine of creation out of nothing. Yet as already mentioned, Thomas Aquinas sought to independently demonstrate the necessity of the *creatio ex nihilo* without reference to an original creation.[32] The point of the *ex nihilo* doctrine is not that there was an absolute beginning to the universe but that every reality within the universe, whether spiritual or physical, depends upon God for its existence in every moment.

4. Western Christian thought seems to have experienced a loss of ability to view cosmology and reality as embracing more than the physical realm. Closely connected with this problem is the tremendous influence of scientific worldviews in the west, including an often un-nuanced view of matter.

5. Perhaps the most obvious difficulty posed by an oscillating universe is that of the Incarnation and the question of the uniqueness of this

event. But this is no new question. It has been raised already through the centuries-old discussion of the possibility of life on other planets. While there has been no agreed solution to this problem a variety of potential solutions have been put forward and have again become the subject of intensive debate within the Christian tradition.[33]

Oscillating Universe in Islamic Tradition

The opposition to the idea of an oscillating universe that is almost programmed into the western Christian tradition is in stark contrast to the situation within the Islamic tradition.[34] The attitude toward such models within the Islamic tradition show how a different line of development to that of the Christian West makes such models far less problematic. Islamic thought can aid Christian theism at this point by holding up a mirror to the development in the West and revealing other possibilities – possibilities in many ways not dissimilar to the line of thought already begun (but not continued) within the Christian tradition by Origen of Alexandria.

Of the several features that one could mention, I would suggest the following elements of the Islamic tradition bear a significant impact on the response within that tradition to models of an oscillating universe.

1. The Qurʾān itself seems to at least hint at the possibility of a series of worlds. The very first Sura of the Qurʾān (1:2) names Allah as "Lord of the Worlds". Significant is the account of the angels questioning God about his announced plans to place humanity on the earth, suggesting that they may do great harm (Sura 2:30). This has been traditionally seen as suggesting the angels have some prior experience of such things. Also, Sura 29:19 says, "See they not how God produces creation, then reproduces it" and 29:20 can be

understood as saying that "God will create another creation" though other translations say "God will bring forth late growth". While all these texts are subject to interpretation, their presence certainly leaves the conceptual door open in Islam to the possibility of a cyclic view of history.

2. There is also a hadith that speaks of an (endless?) series of Adams. Again, a cyclic view of history is implied.

3. Perhaps even more foundational is the distinctive way in which God's sustenance of the universe is understood in the more mystical traditions within Islam. Namely, that God sustains the universe by recreating or "reprocessing" it in every moment.

4. The strong unity between physical and spiritual realities in cosmological models facilitates a greater flexibility of approach in incorporating a diversity of possibilities that more strictly physical cosmologies do not have.

5. The Islamic tradition is clearly not as bound to linear conceptions of history as western thought in general. There appears no natural aversion to such a view of history.

Conclusion

The idea of an oscillating universe raises the question of what really lies behind and is foundational to what modern science terms 'matter', or 'the physical universe'. It is a question that takes us back to Seyyed Hossein Nasr's observation on the necessity of dealing with cosmic reality as a totality and not reducing it to the purely physical. In this sense I believe that both Christians and Muslims alike would point to the dynamic (i.e. non-static) being of God as the foundational and sustaining reality behind all other realities. God is the necessary Being behind all being, all manifestations, all processes, and all potential cycles.

Notes

[1] Wolfhart Pannenberg, "Theological Questions to Scientists", in *The Sciences and Theology in the Twentieth Century*, A.R. Peacocke (ed.), (Notre Dame, Ind.: University of Notre Dame Press, 1981), 3.

[2] Seyyed Hossein Nasr, "Islamic Cosmology: Basic Tenets and Implications, Yesterday and Today", in *Science and Religion in Search of Cosmic Purpose*, John Haught (ed.), (Washington, DC: Georgetown University Press, 2000), 42.

[3] Cf Ron Cowan, "Hubble: A Universe without End and a Search for Dark Matter", in *Science News* 141:5 (1 February 1992): 79.

[4] Cf. the reports by Robin McKie, "Has Man Mastered the Universe?", *The Sunday Observer* (26 April 1992): 8f.; and Andrew Berry, "Scientists Find Holy Grail of the Cosmos in First Sign of Creation", *The Daily Telegraph* (24 April 1992): 1.

[5] Cf. G. Lloyd, "Greek Cosmologies", in *Ancient Cosmologies*, C. Blacker and M. Loewe (eds), (London: George Allen and Unwin Ltd., 1975), 207.

[6] C.M. Patton and John Wheeler, "Is Physics Legislated by Cosmology?", in *Quantum Gravity: An Oxford Symposium*, C. Isham, R. Penrose, and D. Sciama (eds), (Oxford: Clarendon Press, 1975), 556f.

[7] John Wheeler, "Beyond the End of Time", in C. Misner, K. Thorne, and J. Wheeler, *Gravitation* (San Francisco: W.H. Freeman, 1970), 1214.

[8] George Gamow, "Modern Cosmology", in *The New Astronomy*, ed. by the Scientific American editorial board (New York: Simon and Schuster, 1955), 23.

[9] I.L. Rozental, *Big Bang Big Bounce: How Particles and Fields Drive Cosmic Evolution* (Berlin: Springer Verlag, 1988).

[10] M.A. Markov, "Some Remarks on the Problem of the Very Early Universe", in *The Very Early Universe*, G. Gibbons, S. Hawking et al. (eds), (Cambridge: Cambridge University Press, 1983).

[11] Beda Thum, "Theologie und Metaphysik," *in Kairos: Zeitschrift für Religionswissenschaft und Theologie*, vol 26, nos. 1 and 2 (1984): 108f. Beda Thum believes that the idea of an oscillating universe can be dismissed altogether on scientific grounds. He writes: "Die Physik weist aber auch die Idee einer ewigen Sukession kosmischer Zyklen zurück ... . Schon die erste Annahme einer Umkehrung der kosmischen Expansion ist fraglich, weil es ungiwiss ist, ob die mittlere Massendichte im Weltraum gross genug ist sie zu bewirken. ... Aber auch das Entropieprinzip legt sich quer. ... Die Entropie des Weltalls hat auch zu tun mit dem quantitativen Verhältnis zwischen Stranlungsenergie (Photonen) und Kernbausteinen (Protonen und Neutronen). Es entsricht im gegenwärtigen Kosmos ungefähr der Proportionen von 108:1. ... Für das beim Urknall entstehende heisse Plasma hingegen ist eine Proportion von 1:1 anzunehmen. Auch daraus ist zu ersehen, dass sich der kosmische Prozess zu keinem Zyklus rundet".

[12] Ian Barbour, *Religion in an Age of Science* (San Francisco: Harper and Row, 1990), 12.

[13] An expedition of British scientists led by Eddington and Frank Dyson to observe the solar eclipse of 29 May 1919 confirmed that light itself is subject to gravitational attraction, as Einstein's theory predicted.

[14] Arthur Eddington, "The Arrow of Time, Entropy and the Expansion of the Universe", in *The Concepts of Space and Time*, Milic Capek (ed.), (Dordrecht: D. Reidel, 1976), 466.

[15] Sir Arthur Eddington, *The Nature of the Physical World* (Cambridge: Cambridge University Press, 1935).

[16] Cf. for example the comments of R.H. Charles, *A Critical and Exegetical Commentary on the Revelation of St. John* (Edinburgh: T. and T. Clark, 1920), and Henry Barclay Sweete, *Commentary on Revelation* (Grand Rapids: Kregel Reprints, 1977), on Revelation 21:23.

[17] Rudolf Bultmann, *Geschichte und Eschatolgie* (Tuebingen: J.C.B. Mohr, 1964), 180f.

[18] John Barrow and Frank Tipler, *The Anthropic Cosmological Principle* (Oxford: Clarendon Press, 1986), 248f.

[19] A famous quote by Eddington illustrates the power of the suggestion that a theory violates the second law when Eddington suggests that if your theory disagrees with some great thinker, well pity on them, if it seems to disagree with observable data, then perhaps the experiments were wrong, "but if your theory is found to be against the second law of thermodynamics I can give you no hope; there is nothing for it but to collapse in deepest humiliation". Eddington, *The Nature of the Physical World* (London: Dent, 1935), 81.

[20] Steven Weinberg, *The First Three Minutes*, 154.

[21] Cf. Stanley Jaki, "The History of Science and the Idea of an Oscillating Universe", in *Cosmology, History, and Theology*, Wolfgang Yourgrau and Allen Beck (eds), (New York: Plenum Press, 1977), 238; and Tipler, *The Physics of Immortality*, 74ff.

[22] Origen, *De Principiis*, in *The Ante-Nicene Fathers*, vol. 4, A. Roberts and J. Donaldson (eds), (Grand Rapids: Eerdmans, 1979), 341f. (III.V.3).

[23] Ibid., 272f. (II.III.4,5).

[24] Ibid., 240 (preface, 4).

[25] Ibid., 261 (I.VI.2).

[26] Cf. Ibid., 341f. (III.V.3).

[27] Cf. Barrow and Tipler, *Anthropic Cosmological Principle*, 576ff.

[28] Patton and Wheeler, "Is Physics Legislated by Cosmology?", 557.

[29] Cf. John Wheeler, "Genesis and Observership", in *Foundational Problems in the Special Sciences*, R. Butts and K. Hintikka (eds), (Dordrecht: Reidel, 1977).

[30] Ibid.

[31] Cf. *Summa Theologica*, I.46.2 together with I.44.2 and 45.1.

[32] *Summa Theologica*, 1.44.2, 45.1.

[33] For two different approaches to this question see Denis Edwards, "Christ and E.T." in *The Pacific Journal of Theology and Science*, vol 1:1 (Oct 2000), and M. Worthing, "God and the Search for Extraterrestrial Intelligence: A Thought Experiment for Christian Theology", in *Intelligence in the Universe: Science and Theology in Dialogue*, H. Regan (ed.), (Grand Rapids: Eerdmans, 2001).

[34] Cf., for instance, the citations by Medhi Golshani in his chapter in this volume, "Creation in the Islamic Outlook and in Modern Cosmology" of Imam Muhammad al-Baqir "God indeed created thousands and thousands of worlds and thousands and thousands of humankind. You are in the last of these worlds and are the last of those human beings". And also the philosopher Fakhr al-Din al Razi that God is "capable of creating thousands and thousands of worlds".

Part III

Life, Consciousness, and Genetics

Chapter 12

The Contributions and Limitations of Christian Perspectives to Understanding the Religious Implications of the Genetics Revolution

Audrey R. Chapman[1]

Every month, sometimes every week, announcements appear of new breakthroughs in understanding genetics and controlling life processes. The capacity to rearrange the very building blocks of life has made it possible to genetically alter plants, animals, and potentially even human beings. Scientists have managed to clone and produce genetically identical copies of several species of animals, with the prospect of human applications. In June 2000, the Human Genome Project, a $3 billion international effort, completed a working draft of the human genetic code.[2] After a decade of trials, scientists are beginning to have success with human genetic therapies that insert corrective genes to compensate for malfunctioning genes.[3] Some scientists now anticipate developing genetic interventions that could enhance the mental and physical characteristics of patients beyond the normal range. Other prospective therapies being discussed may be able to effect genetic modifications that will be inherited by future descendants.[4]

The genetic revolution offers both a challenge and an opportunity to religious communities and thinkers. To respond adequately will require addressing a central question, "What is God enabling and requiring us to be and to do"[5] with our newfound abilities to intervene within and reshape nature? The ability to alter nature, and possibly human nature as well, raises fundamental questions about the appropriate role and limits of human intervention into the creation. Findings from genetic research about the genetic influences on behavior have implications for understanding what it means to be human, and the nature of human freedom and responsibility. Decisions about genetic applications entail judgments about human moral agency and responsibility to God, to other people, to future generations, and to the created order.

The genetic revolution raises three types of theological and ethical issues. First, what is the theological meaning of our genetic knowledge and our ability to reorder and reshape the genetic composition of living organisms, including plants and animals and potentially human beings as well? Second, under what circumstances is it appropriate to undertake human genetic intervention and alterations, and how should we go about making those decisions? And third, are the findings from genetic science consistent with traditional theistic views of human nature (or what Christians refer to as theological anthropology), and if not, what are the implications? As wave after wave of new discoveries have come, these fundamental questions have become more pressing, as well as ever more complex to address.

It is, however, quite difficult to apply theological reflections developed in pre-scientific cultures to the interpretation and analysis of genetic developments. Sacred texts rarely, if ever, directly address the types of issues raised by genetic advances. Such issues as the fabrication and alteration of microscopic embryos outside the womb from extracted gametes introduce unique quandaries unimagined in canonical texts. In testimony on the appropriateness of undertaking human cloning, Aziz Sachedina, a Muslim bioethicist at the University of Virginia, pointed out to the (U.S.) National Bioethics Advisory Commission that the Qur'ān and the Islamic tradition lack even a universally accepted definition for an embryo. Nor does the Qur'ān or other sacred texts anticipate modern biological data about genetics.[6]

Another problem is that many core theological concepts, particularly in the Christian tradition, function like metaphors or symbols. By this I mean that religious affirmations, such as the assertion that humans are created in the image of God, tend to evoke a range of meanings rather than to have a fixed and carefully defined content. Historically this characteristic has been an asset because it has enabled religious traditions to adjust and adapt to varying situations without entirely losing their original meaning.[7] However, this also makes these symbols or concepts difficult to serve as standards or criteria by which to evaluate scientific developments and formulate action guides.

One example is the concept of stewardship, which Christianity shares with Islam and Judaism. This tradition characterizes the vocation of humanity as a servant or vice-regent given the responsibility for management of something belonging to another, in this case the Creator, to manage in trust, consistent with the intentions of the owner. The classical notion of stewardship predates the scientific understanding of evolution and assumes a static, finished, and hierarchically organized universe in which every creature and life form has its own place. In such a universe, stewardship implies respecting the natural order and not seeking to change it. Twentieth century science contradicts these assumptions though, showing that nature is dynamic and ever evolving. This suggests that it is appropriate for humanity to make at least some changes in the order of things. But on what basis should we draw a line between what is appropriate for a steward as an exercise of God-given intelligence and creativity and what constitutes a transgression in a dynamic and ever changing creation? Although several Christian theologians have sought to address this very complex issue, none has done so in a fully satisfactory manner.[8]

That theology and ethics are based on sweeping, first order principles, such as love of neighbor, and abstract concepts, as for example human dignity, further complicates the interface with science. Religious thinkers have the capacity to expound abstractly on such topics as human dignity, but they lack methodologies to evaluate the long-term implications of particular technologies within specific societal contexts for human dignity. Thus the ability of religious communities to address cutting-edge scientific and technological issues raised by genetics requires the development of new ways to apply theological concepts and ethical norms to complex scientific innovations. Or to put the matter another way, theological concepts must be *operationalized*, that is translated into more concrete precepts with clear empirical criteria.

To date, faith-based reflections on and interpretations of genetics have been written primarily from a Christian perspective. My surveys of the literature written in English and involvement in meetings and projects related to genetics have identified only a few Muslim authors and participants.[9] Quite possibly there is additional literature in Arabic, French, or German. There are also relatively few Jewish, Hindu, or Buddhist reflections on genetics. This reflects a variety of factors. This may reflect the fact that not all faith traditions have developed methodologies and approaches for addressing contemporary bioethical and genetics issues.[10] The absence of a centralized ecclesiastical structure or the existence of an official body to speak for a community is often an impediment. It is also understandable that thinkers situated in regions distant from genetic research and testing centers would be less concerned about these issues.

Significance of Genetic Knowledge

What are the implications of having knowledge about the genetic basis of life? Scientists have compared the decoding of the human genome with the discovery of a biological Holy Grail and a biological Rosetta Stone.[11] James Watson, whose discovery of the helical structure of DNA laid the groundwork for the biotechnology revolution, celebrated the Human Genome Project as nothing less that the attempt "to find out what being human is".[12] At the press conference announcing the completion of the mapping of the human genome and the sequencing of the base pairs constituting the genes, Francis Collins, the director of the (U.S.) National Human Genome Research Institute and the primary funder and coordinator of the Human Genome Project reflected, "It is humbling for me and awe-inspiring to realize that we have caught the first glimpse of our own instruction book previously known only to God".[13]

Christian thinkers early realized the importance of genetic developments, anticipating more than 20 years ago that discoveries in human genetics would revolutionize our fundamental understanding of the world and the role of humanity. A 1984 (U.S.) National Council of Churches' publication, for example, compared the potential influence of genetic developments to the impact of the scientific revolutions based on the works of Copernicus, Darwin, and Einstein. It compared the "bioethical pilgrimage" brought about by the discoveries of genetic science to the journeys of Abraham, Moses, and other leading persons of faith.[14] A number of reflections on genetics also acknowledge that historic Christian teachings about human nature and the meaning and purpose of human life are challenged by these technologies.[15]

The developing capacity to decipher and alter nature has led some religious communities and several theologians to recast the human vocation from that of a steward merely managing the creation to a more active role. Sources variously utilize the terminology of humanity as God's "co-creator",[16] "created co-creators",[17] partner, or co-laborer.[18] These formulations all share a belief that humans now play an active role in shaping the creation. Even theologians refraining from using this terminology concur that "Creation by divine power is not static but dynamic and ongoing. As creatures uniquely made in God's image and purpose, humans participate in the creative process through the continuing quest for knowledge, which now includes unraveling and learning to control the intricate powers compressed in genes of DNA molecules".[19]

Nevertheless, most Christian religious thinkers would take issue with the hyperbole in the characterizations of genetic knowledge by prominent scientists cited above because these statements imply too intimate a connection between the human genetic constitution on the one side and human identity and behavior on the other. Christian theologians and ethicists generally take a strong position against what Ted Peters terms the "gene myth", the belief that genes determine everything about us.[20] One of the most important roles of the religious community in North America has been to serve as a voice against a creeping genetic essentialism. Christian understandings strongly oppose claims that we are our genes.

Religious commentaries have been sensitive both to the potential beneficial and the detrimental applications of genetic knowledge. The Anglican Archbishop of York, John Habgood, who was originally trained as a biologist, addressed the perils of trying to know too much at a 1992 conference. He reminded his audience that "Knowledge is more than an abstract pattern in the mind or in the computer. ... It is an understanding of what to do with such patterns, how to use them".[21]

Christian Attitudes toward Genetic Science Applications

"Playing God" has come to be used as a shorthand for concerns that it is inappropriate for humans to change the way other living organisms or human beings are constituted. The term conveys the view that engaging in genetic engineering amounts to usurping the creative prerogative of God. Ironically, this claim has usually come from secular critics rather than members of the religious community. Christian and Jewish thinkers writing on genetics generally have a favorable attitude toward genetic engineering, affirming that genetic engineering at least in principle does not go beyond the limits of a reasonable dominion over nature. Openness to genetic engineering, particularly among the moral theologians well versed in science, often derives from the realization that nature itself is constantly engaging in a process akin to human genetic engineering, albeit with significant differences. Others believe that our growing genetic knowledge and capabilities reflect God's activity and purposes. According to one theologian, "the purpose of genetic engineering is to expand our ability to participate in God's work of redemption and creation and thereby to glorify God".[22] Another theologian, who understands the *imago Dei* – the image of God embedded in the human race – in terms of creativity, argues that technological intervention into the cell line of a life form, when oriented toward a beneficent end, can be understood as a legitimate exercise of human creativity.[23] Yet others claim that the biblical mandate to humanity to understand and to make something of the creation justifies the technological manipulation of life to serve human welfare.[24]

Like many secular sources, religious commentators celebrate the potential of genetics to provide significant new modalities for the treatment of congenital defects and healing human diseases. Noting that Jesus fed the hungry and healed the sick, many of the sources welcome the new opportunities to help those in need. This theme of the contribution of genetic science plays a major role in shaping attitudes toward genetic research and therapies within the religious community. Virtually no ethicist working within a religious context contests the principle that new genetic knowledge should be used to improve human health and to relieve suffering. This attitude accounts for support for using experimental somatic gene therapies on patients who cannot be treated with more conventional remedies, provided the genetic interventions are found to be safe and effective.

While generally favorable to genetic science, faith-based sources typically reject a position of unconditional acceptance of scientific achievement that is not tempered by humane and ethical considerations. Religious thinkers and communities have taken an important role in attempting to hold genetic research and applications to an ethical standard of evaluation. A 1986 policy statement on genetics of the National Council of Churches of Christ in the U.S.A., for example, states: "We cannot agree with those who assert that scientific inquiry and research should acknowledge no limits. All that can be known need not be known if in advance it clearly appears that the process for gaining such knowledge violates the sanctity of human life".[25]

Many religious thinkers therefore evince what might be characterized as a presumption of caution. By this I mean that they place greater priority on anticipating and preventing potential problems than on favoring technologies and applications because they may bring future benefits. One author aptly characterizes this posture as "critical engagement". He explains that Christians generally support genetic science but are required to evaluate any particular genetic discovery or application according to criteria informed by faith and Christian sources.[26]

Given the presumption of caution, it is essential to ascertain whether a specific intervention (or omission, exception, policy, or law) is likely to promote or undermine human welfare. Recognizing that many of the issues at hand are complex and human motives may be ambiguous, how should determinations about appropriate genetic research and applications be made? Or to put the matter another way, how do we engage in *ijtihad* on genetics? To do so at the least requires the development of a methodology or set of criteria for evaluating whether genetic science is truly in the service of beneficence, the risks involved, and the faith implications of going forward. Unfortunately, to date few religious sources have conducted such a systematic analysis of the potential benefits and drawbacks of potential genetic applications. Most of the faith-based literature is more intent on interpreting the meaning of genetic discoveries than on offering guidance on this critical issue. To put it another way, these resources sensitize readers to the issues that genetic research and applications raise but often fail to offer guidelines on how to resolve these dilemmas. The value of these works is usually more in the questions they raise than in the answers they provide.

This is not to imply that the issues raised or questions posed are not relevant and insightful. A policy statement adopted by the United Methodist Church, for example, identifies four very important questions to ask about genetic research and technologies: (1) Is the research appropriate in terms of benefitting the quality of life for humans, animals, and the environment immediately and over many generations? (2) Will the technology be available at affordable cost? (3) Is the technology the most effective way of meeting the need? (4) Will all members of society have access to the technology?[27]

The Cloning Controversy

Christian thinkers have generally approached each genetic development anew. Positions taken on particular issues are often varied and sometimes can be surprising. This can be seen in the range of views on human cloning and inheritable genetic modifications.

Like secular ethicists, religious communities and moral theologians have offered a wide range of perspectives on the implications of human cloning. With some simplification, these positions may be divided into three categories. A small number of churches, official bodies, and individual theologians have opposed cloning on fundamental theological grounds. The Roman Catholic Church's claim that human cloning is unnatural and therefore contrary to the divine plan[28] represents an example of this view. The Catholic position particularly reflects beliefs not widely shared by other Christian thinkers. Roman Catholicism holds that natural law is both fixed and discernable to the human intellect; few other Christian denominations have the traditionalist bias inherent in the Catholic natural law orientation. On the question of the status of the embryo, the Catholics consider the embryo to have full human status from the moment of conception, whereas other Christian ethicists generally believe that the human embryo gradually gains full human standing as it develops.

Another group of religious commentaries, the largest in number, also opposed cloning but not on theological grounds. Their concerns related more to the lack of safety of the technology for human applications and the likely deleterious impacts of cloning on the family and human dignity. There was considerable apprehension in the religious community that a cloned child would be treated as less than a fully equal and unique person. A related issue was that in a society inclined toward a simplistic notion of "genetic determinism" a child produced by cloning might have an overwhelming burden of expectations that would be incompatible with the freedom necessary for each person to develop an individual identity.[29] A few of these sources emphasized that it is beneficial for children to have two adults' genetic resources recombined to form a unique genotype that is tied to both parents. Some groups also supported a ban on the therapeutic, medical, and research procedures that generate waste embryos.[30] Others, while believing that cloning does not raise fundamental theological issues, considered it to be unwise because it might accelerate the tendency to commodify reproduction, that is to subject it to marketplace logic.[31] Nevertheless, none of these reflections believed that cloning would deprive a child of a full relationship with God or deprive the cloned human being of full legal status and protections.

The third category consists of ethicists who had a qualified acceptance of cloning. Some members of this group did have misgivings but identified limited instances where the application would be acceptable. In several instances ethicists assumed that some form of human cloning was inevitable and believed it would be more realistic to attempt careful regulation rather than a total ban. Others emphasized that the application of the cloning, not the technology, is the most significant moral issue. The one Muslim ethicist who testified before the U.S. National Bioethics Advisory Committee in its hearings on cloning, Aziz Sachedina, fit into this third category. His position was based primarily on the absence of a clear prohibition in Islam and the Islamic support for science.[32]

While cloning represents an example of the religious community scrambling to respond to an unexpected scientific development, a report based on the work of a multidisciplinary working group – sponsored by the American Association for the Advancement of Science (AAAS) on inheritable genetic modifications[33] – offers an example of religious thinkers attempting to anticipate and possibly to shape future scientific applications. Limitations of current medical therapies to treat diseases with a genetic component have led to efforts to develop techniques for treating diseases at the molecular level by altering a person's cells. To date, most of the research and clinical resources related to gene therapy have focused on developing techniques for targeting nonreproductive body cells. Somatic cell genetic therapies currently being attempted seek to restore cell function in an individual with defective genes, but these corrections cannot be inherited. Inheritable genetic modification (IGM), sometimes referred to as germ line therapy, refers to any biomedical intervention that can be expected to modify the genome that a person can transfer to his or her offspring.

Recent advances in animal research are raising the possibility that we will eventually have the technical capacity to modify genes that are transmitted to future generations. Some scientists and ethicists argue in favor of developing such interventions. In theory, modifying the genes that are transmitted to future generations would have several advantages over somatic cell gene therapy. It would then be possible to prevent the inheritance of some types of genetic diseases in families rather than attempting repeated somatic cell therapy in affected individuals generation after generation. There are also situations where it is not feasible to correct irreversible genetic damage after it occurs in the early stages of development.

However, there are significant technical, ethical, and religious issues involved. Because these interventions would be transmitted to the progeny of the person treated, there would need to be compelling scientific evidence that these procedures are safe and effective. Efforts to modify the genes that are transmitted to future generations have the potential to bring about a social revolution, for they offer us the power to mold our children in a variety of novel ways. These techniques could give us extraordinary control over biological properties and personality traits that we currently consider essential to our humanness.

Do we have the technologies, wisdom, ethical commitment, and public policies necessary to go forward with inheritable genetic modification? The participants in the AAAS study concluded that inheritable genetic modification cannot presently be carried out safely and responsibly on humans. According to their assessment, current methods employed for somatic gene transfer are inappropriate for human germ line therapy because they involve addition of DNA to cells rather than correcting or replacing a mutated gene with a normal one. To assure that the procedures used do not cause unacceptable short-term or long-term consequences either for the treated individual or succeeding generations of offspring will therefore require the development of reliable gene correction or replacement technologies.[34]

Guided by the theologians – from mainline Protestant, Catholic, and Jewish traditions – and ethicists on the AAAS working group, the group concluded that inheritable genetic modification did not raise fundamental theological issues. The theologians and ethicists in the group raised many concerns, but these were not uniquely religious or theological in nature. It was determined that such alterations would even be permissible in the Roman Catholic tradition, which treats the embryo as a human person from conception, as long as the technology met certain conditions: the procedure was clearly therapeutic; did not directly or indirectly destroy or injure the human intellect or will, or otherwise impair their respective functions; and did not involve in *vitro fertilization*, experimentation on embryos, or their destruction in the course of developing the therapy.[35]

While religious thinkers on the working group did not believe that such interventions are, in principle, theologically impermissible, they identified a series of fundamental ethical concerns. The implications for equity and justice were considered to be particularly problematic. The introduction of this technology in a society and global community with differential access to health care could pose significant justice issues and could introduce new, or magnify existing, inequalities. It would mean that those persons who can already provide the best "environments" for their children would also be able to purchase the best "natures". Many religious traditions have a commitment to social and economic justice stemming from the belief that the benefits of creation, including those that come in part from human effort, are to be widely shared. Most, but not all of the ethicists and theologians, therefore drew the conclusion that these factors, singularly and jointly, indicate that we are not currently at a point where we should allow the development and use of inheritable genetic modifications.

There was also concern that inheritable genetic modification might change attitudes toward the human person and the nature of human reproduction. Like many secular ethicists, religious thinkers are worried that too great a readiness to attempt to control the genetic inheritance of our offspring will undermine the value and meaning of the parent-child relationship. Simply put, the intrusion of technology, even if well intended, could reduce the child to an artifact, a product of technological design, at least in the mind of the child or of his or her parents. Such alterations could also exacerbate prejudice against persons with disabilities.

Greater knowledge of genetics is also making it possible to contemplate genetic interventions not only to treat or eliminate diseases but also to "enhance" normal human characteristics beyond what is necessary to sustain or restore good health. Examples would be efforts to improve height or intelligence or to intervene to change certain characteristics, such as the color of one's hair. Such interventions could be attempted through either somatic modification or inheritable genetic modification, but the working group concluded that the latter was more likely. Inheritable genetic modification for enhancement purposes designed to produce improvements in human form or function was considered to be particularly problematic. Efforts to improve the inherited genome of persons could widen the gap between "haves" and "have nots" to an unprecedented extent. Enhancement applications might foster attempts to have "perfect" children by "correcting" their genomes. The dilemma is that IGM techniques developed for therapeutic purposes are likely to be suitable for enhancement applications as well. Thus, going forward with IGM to treat disease or disability will make it difficult to avoid use of such interventions for enhancement purposes even when this use is considered to be ethically unacceptable.

Genetics and Human Nature

Religious thinkers realized quite early that findings from genetic science would challenge traditional understandings about the role and nature of humanity. Anticipating developments in genetic science, in 1969 James Gustafson called for the reconceptualization of the traditional non-evolutionary, fixed, unchanging, and essentially dualistic concepts of human nature. He advocated formulating a theological anthropology adequate to conserve inherited biblical and philosophical insights while still responsive to the new scientific knowledge.[36] It is only very recently, however, that theologians have begun this very complex and difficult task. This chapter can only briefly note some of the issues and topics that religious thinkers are beginning to address.

The traditional monotheistic perspective assumes that human beings are at the pinnacle of a fixed order, and are set apart and fundamentally different from the rest of nature by divine design. These beliefs have long infused Western religious concepts of human nature. Genetic science, however, reveals human kinship with all other forms of life. It shows, for example, that we share 98 to 99 percent of our DNA with our two closest primate relatives, bonobos and chimpanzees. Our shared genetic code provides a scientific underpinning for the theological and ecological theme of the interrelatedness of all creation rather than the distinctiveness of humans.

What does genetic science show about the nature of the link between the human genome and human identity? That each person, with the exception of monozygotic (identical) twins has a unique genome is true, but personality and behavior cannot be reduced to genetics. Human development features a continuous and ongoing interaction between the organism and the environment throughout life. The complex and dynamic relationship between genotype and environment influences the manner in which each makes its relative contributions to individual variability.

Moreover, a full concept of human personhood involves more than a self who is the product of interactions between biology and the environment. Human beings are also cultural beings whose language and symbolic capacities enable them to interpret and shape their contexts and choose their course of action. Perhaps most importantly, the human person has an inherent capacity for ethical behavior and spiritual development. Thus genetic science illuminates some facets of human development and behavior, but it has not eliminated the mystery of the human spirit and the apparently unique human capacity for self-transcendence.

Free Will vs. Genetic Determinism

Of the topics considered in the religious literature, one of the most important is the assessment of the extent to which evidence from genetic science recast the age-old theological and philosophical discussions of freedom and determinism and the implications for moral responsibility. While theologians and ethicists acknowledge scientific evidence for genetic influences on human behavior, they generally argue strenuously against biological or genetic determinism. Like many behavioral geneticists, religious interpreters speak in terms of genetic probabilities and dispositions, and not genetic determinism.

The pathways from genes to human behaviors are far more complex than a crude genetic determinism implies. Understanding genetic influences as predispositions or limiting factors still leaves a broad potential sphere of human freedom and moral accountability. An individual's genome sets boundaries on various traits and potential, but it does not determine how someone will organize his or her life within those parameters. Genetic science therefore leaves a broad sphere of choice and personal responsibility intact.

Ted Peters' book, *Playing God? Genetic Determinism and Human Freedom*, contains the most careful analysis as well as the most insightful criticism of the notion that persons are determined by their genes. This book argues forcefully that science does not support the view that humans are the sum total of their DNA and nothing more. He also provides an eloquent defense of the existence of human creativity, moral responsibility, and freedom. Peters concludes that because freedom is exercised at the level of the person in the form of deliberation, decision, and responsible action, determinism at the genetic level, even if proven, does not obviate having free moral will.[37]

Perhaps the most notable challenge for theologians is drawing the implications of genetic science for understanding the human essence, portrayed in classical theology as the soul or spirit. Genetic research, like work in the neurosciences, makes it difficult to maintain a dualistic conception of a self that is divided into a body and soul. The findings from genetic science therefore make problematic religious doctrines which describe the soul as completely distinct from the body and consisting of a fundamentally different kind of being. To take genetic science seriously requires an integrated and embodied view of the human person. This has prompted some theologians and ethicists to reformulate a notion of the human essence that is neither reductionistic nor dualistic.

One promising line of interpretation is the development of a "nonreductive physicalist" account of the person by a multi-disciplinary group of scholars in a collection of articles entitled *Whatever Happened to the Soul? Scientific and Theological Portraits of Human Nature.*[38] Many of the articles in the volume reconceptualize the soul of humans as a physiologically embodied property of human nature and not an entity with a distinctive existence, awareness, and agency. Several of the authors propose an understanding of the soul as a dimension of human experiences that arises out of personal relatedness. According to one of these essays, written by a psychologist, experiences of relatedness to others, to the self, and most particularly to God endow a person with the attributes that traditionally have been attributed to the soul.[39]

A nonreductive physicalist approach is consistent with the work of several theologians defining the human soul as a set of capabilities that is defined by genes, but not entirely determined by them. Ronald Cole-Turner, for example, suggests thinking of the soul or self as the coherence within the complexity of the human organism, a coherence that is genetically conditioned but also transcends that conditioning.[40] In like manner, Karen Lebacqz offers a view of the soul as a symbol of the covenant between God and each person.[41] For Anne Clifford the soul is synonymous with the center of human individuation.[42]

Implications for Islamic Analyses of Genetic Developments

We are still at the very beginnings of attempting to understand what God is enabling and requiring us to do as we proceed with our newfound abilities to intervene and reshape nature. The most important task ahead will be to develop a scientifically-based prescriptive ethics infused with religious insight and values. I believe that now is the time for religious thinkers representing a broad diversity of communities, including those from an Islamic background, to come together in a science and religion dialogue to explore fundamental questions of human life and destiny as challenged and illuminated by the genetics revolution. I very much hope that Muslim ethicists and theologians will be part of this process. I believe that future efforts by Islamic scholars can benefit from examining both the contributions and limitations of the body of work contributed by the Christian community. I would therefore like to draw some broad recommendations.

My first and most important recommendation is the importance of using a method that promotes a two-way dialogue between science and religion, dialogue through which theology and ethics can be informed and even altered by scientific concepts, information, and theories.[43] This process can also sensitize and expand the horizons of scientists to understand the ethical and theological implications of their research and to respond accordingly. It is possible to have such a dialogue take place on an individual and/or a group level. The most successful Christian ethics on genetics has derived from an understanding of relevant science. In a few cases, genetic scientists have written explicitly within a religious framework, alone or paired with a religious thinker. Numbers of successful dialogue projects have taken place where a sponsor has convened a multidisciplinary working group. This kind of mutual learning and transformation has occurred in several of the projects conducted by the Program of Dialogue on Science, Ethics, and Religion at the American Association for the Advancement of Science.

But a word of caution is in order. All cross-disciplinary research, analysis, and efforts to dialogue must cope with differences in methodological approaches, priorities, and vocabularies in the distinct fields. The science-religion divide is particularly difficult to traverse. The science-religion dialogue can in some ways be compared with simultaneous translation of two languages and frameworks on a changing conceptual field. Thus, the science and religion dialogue is a very complex and time-consuming enterprise. It takes time and patience, and it requires a considerable amount of learning and conceptual translation across disciplinary boundaries.

As an example of the potential fruitfulness of science and religion dialogues on genetics, the American Association for the Advancement of Science recently sponsored the work of a multi-disciplinary group of scholars on ethical and theological issues related to inheritable human genetic modifications. This working group included scientists and religious ethicists from a wide variety of backgrounds (Protestant denominations, Catholic, and Jewish, but unfortunately no Muslims) and some members with no explicit religious affiliation. Although most of the religious ethicists initially sought to draw primarily on their own heritage, the issues were so unprecedented that they quickly realized they were in uncharted territory. The process of moral reasoning in this group benefitted from ongoing exposure to scientific development from some of the very persons central to these efforts. There was also continuous re-analysis and refinement of the ethical implications over the two and one half years of the project. In these discussions, the insights and sensitivities of each ethicist stimulated and contributed to the thinking of others. Moreover, many of the scientists became immersed in the process of ethical discernment, sometimes within a religious frame of reference. The final product built on, but went well beyond, the initial frame of reference and expertise of the individual participants, and it likely will have greater standing because it is the outcome of such an inclusive process.[44]

My second recommendation is to shape a prescriptive rather than a descriptive ethics. Much of the ethical literature written by religious thinkers to date focuses more on identifying the meaning of genetic discoveries or describing the issues they raise rather than on providing moral guidance on specific issues. When norms relevant for determining ethical implications are offered, they tend to be presented at such a level of abstraction that they are difficult to apply as action guides.

My third set of recommendations is the need to develop the intellectual building blocks of ethical and theological analysis prior to evaluating the implications of particular genetic discoveries and technologies. Traditional theological precepts or themes, like stewardship (or humanity as God's vice-regent), human dignity, and human identity, as well as newer concepts like humanity as God's "created co-creator", can play important roles in structuring evaluations of the theological and ethical implications of particular scientific and technological innovations. But many of these religious concepts are too abstract and too shaped by philosophical analysis to apply to science and technology. Thus it is necessary to rethink these concepts in ways that would make them more appropriate for evaluating science and technology. One way to do so is to try to *operationalize* broad principles or norms. This entails dis-aggregating the concepts and assessing what each of these components implies for genetic applications. Part of this task is to formulate middle axioms that can apply the principles and norms to specific issues and cases. Middle axioms have been described as "more concrete than a universal ethical principle and less specific than a program that includes legislation and political strategy. They are the next steps our generation must take in fulfilling the purposes of God".[45]

My fourth and final recommendation is to consider the genetic revolution synoptically rather than evaluating research findings and technologies in the piecemeal fashion so characteristic of the Christian response. According to Ian Wilmot, the scientists whose technological innovations produced Dolly, the cloned lamb, we have entered the age of "biological control".[46] Genetic testing, somatic genetic therapies, the completion of the Human Genome Project, cloning, and human stem cell research all offer increased powers to control basic biological processes in human beings. Taken together, these developments have a stunning cumulative impact on our understanding of ourselves and our potential to shape the human future. There are both advantages and disadvantages of the delayed theological and ethical analysis of genetics in the Muslim community. One of the benefits is a greater capacity to view the whole rather than the parts and to do so in a more thoughtful and reflective manner than has sometimes been the case in the Christian community.

Notes

1   Parts of this paper draw on this author's book *Unprecedented Choices: Religious Ethics at the Frontiers of Genetic Science* (Minneapolis: Fortress Press, 1999).

2   The Human Genome Project claims to have cloned 97 percent of the genome, and sequenced 85 percent of it to draft standard.

3   In 2000, articles appeared in scientific journals reporting creditable successes with gene therapies improving the health of patients suffering from hemophilia B and human severe combined immunodeficiency (SCID) disease.

4   For an assessment of this possibility see Mark S. Frankel and Audrey R. Chapman, *Human Inheritable Genetic Modifications: Assessing Scientific, Ethical, Religious, and Policy Implications* (Washington, DC: American Association for the Advancement of Science, 2000).

5   James M. Gustafson, *Ethics from a Theocentric Perspective*, vol. 2, *Ethics and Theology* (Chicago: University of Chicago Press, 1984), 1.

6   Dr. Aziz Sachedina, "Testimony to the National Bioethics Advisory Commission", 14 March 1997, (Washington, DC: Eberline Reporting Service), 56-64.

7   On this point see Jan Christian Heller, "Religiously Based Objections to Cloning", in James M. Humber and Robert F. Almeder (eds), *Human Cloning* (Totowa, N.J.: Humana Press, 1998), 161.

8   Bruce B. Reichenbach and V. Elving Anderson attempt to deal with this issue, not entirely satisfactorily, in their book *On Behalf of God: A Christian Ethic for Biology* (Grand Rapid, Mich.: Wm. B. Eerdmans, 1995).

9   Hassan M. Hathout, M.D., Ph.D., a physician and a Qur'ānic scholar, was involved in some of the early meetings in the U.S. dealing with genetics and religion. The American Muslim Council was among the 180 religious signatories to a 1995 statement opposing the patenting of life. Aziz Sachedina, Ph.D., a bioethicist at the University of Virginia, conveyed a Muslim perspective on cloning in hearings held by the (U.S.) National Bioethics Advisory Committee and also participated in a science-religion dialogue on cloning sponsored by the American Association for the Advancement of Science. Gamal I. Serour, whom I believe is Egyptian, has dealt with issues related to somatic cell gene therapy in his article "Islamic Developments in Bioethics", in B. Andrew Lustig, *Theological Developments in Bioethics: 1992-1994* (Dordrecht, Boston, and London: Kluwer Academic Publishers, 1997). He is also co-editor with A. Omran of *Proceedings of the First International Conference on Bioethics in Human Reproduction Research in the Muslim World* (Cairo: International Islamic Center for Population Studies and Research, 1991).

10   The American Muslim Council has declined invitations from the AAAS Program of Dialogue to participate in science and religion dialogues related to genetics several times on these grounds.

[11] Quoted in Ted Peters, *Playing God: Genetic Determinism and Human Freedom* (New York and London: Routledge, 1997), 6.

[12] Quoted in Ronald Cole-Turner, *The New Genesis: Theology and the Genetic Revolution* (Louisville: Westminister/John Knox Press, 1993), 20.

[13] Colin Macilwain, "World leaders heap praise on human genome landmark", *Nature*, 405 (29 June 2000): 984.

[14] Panel of Bioethical Concerns, National Council of Churches of Christ in the U.S.A., *Genetic Engineering: Social and Ethical Consequences*, Frank M. Harrion (ed.), (New York: Pilgrim Press, 1984), 20.

[15] See for example World Council of Churches, Church and Society Unit, *Biotechnology: Its Challenge to the Churches and the World* (Geneva: WCC, 1982).

[16] The Division of Mission in Canada, "A Brief to the Royal Commission on New Reproductive Technologies on Behalf of the United Church of Canada", approved by the executive of the Division of Mission (17 January 1991), 14.

[17] The terminology of "created co-creator" was first suggested by Philip Hefner and most fully developed in his book *The Human Factor: Evolution, Culture, and Religion* (Minneapolis: Fortress Press, 1993).

[18] See for example, The Presbyterian Church (U.S.A.), 195th General Assembly (1983), "The Covenant of Life and the Caring Community", *Social Policy Compilation* (Louisville: Advisory Committee on Social Witness Policy, 1992).

[19] National Council of Churches of Christ in the U.S.A., "Genetic Science for Human Benefit" (New York: Office of Research and Evaluation, adopted by the Governing Board, 22 May 1986), 14-15.

[20] This concern is a central theme in Peters, *Playing God?*.

[21] The statement of the Archbishop of York, "The Perils of Trying to Know Too Much", is quoted in J. Robert Nelson, *On the New Frontiers of Genetics and Religion* (Grand Rapids, MI: Wm. B. Eerdmans, 1994), 48.

[22] Cole-Turner, *New Genesis*, 51.

[23] See, for example, Peters' discussion in *Playing God?*, 15, 123, and 144.

[24] This position is taken by a working group convened by the Church of Scotland's Society, Religion, and Technology Project. See Donald Bruce and Ann Bruce (eds), *Engineering Genesis: The Ethics of Genetic Engineering in Non-Human Species* (London: Earthscan Publications, 1998), 93-95.

[25] National Council of Churches of Christ in the U.S.A., "Genetic Science for Human Benefit", 15.

[26] Willer, "Introduction", in Willer, ed., *Genetic Testing and Screening*, 8.

[27] "Genetic Science Task Force of the United Method Church", United Methodist Church Genetic Science Task Force Report to the 1992 General Conference, (General Board of Church and Society of the United Methodist Church, Washington D.C., 1992), 4-5.

[28] For the position of the U.S. Catholic Conference see the testimony of the Rev. Dr. Albert Moraczewski to the National Bioethics Advisory Committee on 13 March 1997 (Washington, D.C.: Eberline Reporting Service), 185-192.

[29] See for example, the United Church of Christ's "Resolution on the Cloning of Mammalian Species to the 21st General Synod", (Columbus, Ohio, 3-8 July 1997).

[30] General Board of Church and Society of the United Methodist Church, "Statement from the United Methodist Genetic Science Task Force", 9 May 1997.

[31] Ted Peters, "Cloning Shock: A Theological Reaction", *CTNS Bulletin* 17 (Spring 1997): 1-9.

[32] Sachedina, "Testimony to the NBAC", 14 March 1997.

[33] The outcome of these deliberations, including the group's findings and deliberations are in Mark S. Frankel and Audrey R. Chapman, *Human Inheritable Genetic Modifications: Assessing Scientific, Ethical, Theological and Policy Issues* (Washington, D.C.: American Association for the Advancement of Science, 2000).

[34] Ibid., 15-27.

[35] Ibid., 27-30. The analysis of the Catholic position is based on a paper contributed by Father Albert Morazczewski, "The Catholic Church's Moral Tradition and Germ Line Genetic Intervention", which will be published in Audrey R. Chapman and Mark S. Frankel (eds), *Human Genetic Modifications Across Generations: Assessing Scientific, Ethical, Religious, and Policy Issues* (forthcoming).

[36] James M. Gustafson, "Genetic Engineering and the Normative View of the Human", in Preston N. Williams, *Ethical Issues in Biology and Medicine: Proceedings of a Symposium on the Identity and Dignity of Man* (Cambridge, Mass.: Schenkam, 1973), 46-58.

[37] Peters, *Playing God?*, 160.

[38] Warren S. Brown, Nancey Murphy, and H. Newton Malony (eds), *Whatever Happened to the Soul? Scientific and Theological Portraits of Human Nature* (Minneapolis: Fortress Press, 1998).

[39] Warren S. Brown, "Cognitive Contributions to the Soul", in Brown, Murphy, and Malony (eds), *Whatever Happened to the Soul?*, 99-102.

[40] Ronald Cole-Turner, *The New Genesis*, 88.

[41] Karen Lebacqz, "Alien Dignity: The Legacy of Helmut Thielicke for Bioethics", in Allen Verhey (ed.), *Religion and Medical Ethics: Looking Back, Looking Forward* (Grand Rapids: William B. Eerdmans, 1996), 44-49.

[42] Anne Clifford, C.S.J., "Biological Evolution and the Human Soul", in Ted Peters (ed.), *Science and Religion: The New Consonance* (Boulder, Colorado: Westview Press, 1998), 172.

[43] This perspective is very much like the view of James Gustafson in *Intersections: Science, Theology, and Ethics* (Cleveland: Pilgrim Press, 1996), 4.

[44] See Frankel and Chapman, *Human Inheritable Genetic Modifications*.

[45] John C. Bennett, *Christian Ethics and Social Policy* (New York: Charles Scribner's Sons, 1946), 76-77.

[46] He is so quoted in, Ronald Cole-Turner, "The Era of Biological Control", *Beyond Cloning: Religion and the Remaking of Humanity* (Harrisburg, Pennsylvania: Trinity Press International, 2001), 1.

Chapter 13

Interface of Science and Jurisprudence: Dissonant Gazes at the Body in Modern Muslim Ethics

Ebrahim Moosa

In the classical and post-classical periods the discipline of Islamic jurisprudence was relatively in tune with the scientific discourses of the day. Jurists (*fuqahāʾ*) who were not averse to the "foreign sciences" (*ʿilm al-awāʾil*) ably demonstrated in their legal judgments that they were familiar with scientific disciplines of the day such as astronomy, anatomy, alchemy, physics, mathematics, and geometry. The practitioners, namely the jurists, of the sciences of jurisprudence (*uṣūl al-fiqh*), and the science of positive law (*fiqh*), accepted the working assumptions adopted in the field of science as a reality and there were rarely any major misfits between the two. On the occasion when there was tension it was often resolved in a creative and amicable manner. Most jurists of the classical period, for instance, insisted that in determining the lunar calendar, sighting the crescent with the naked eye was preferable in keeping with the report of the Prophet. A minority of jurists however declared astronomical calculations to be sufficient and a more accurate determination of the calendar.[1] Thus, the position of the Shāfiʿi school of law, while advocating the view in favor of naked eye sighting, also allows those who know astronomy to follow the certainty of their observations achieved by empirical means. Hence, people who hold such knowledge can actually proceed with the rituals associated with the lunar calendar that was determined by scientific calculations. While it is not my purpose to exhaust the examples of the interface between science and jurisprudence in the classical period and later, from the single example provided one can infer that there was some semblance of epistemic coherence between jurisprudence and science.

In the modern period this epistemic coherence between Muslim jurisprudence and science is no longer evident. Several factors can be attributed for this breakdown. Among them is the fact that since the 18th century, Western scientific advances raced ahead, especially in the 20th century, while science education in traditional Muslim institutions was still focused on Euclidean geometry and pre-modern science. In the 20th century science was gradually removed from the syllabi of those institutions where Muslim jurists were trained. So it is not surprising to see an Indian Muslim author of a traditional bent comment, in 1907, that the claim made by science that all life originated from ether and motion was a claim contrary to religion. Although the writer Muḥibb ul-Ḥaqq ʿAzīmābādī was no doubt combating a version of evolution, he was not in principle hostile to science.[2] He actually believed that true science would be in harmony with religion. "Science seeks causes and religion seeks truths", he commented.[3] In addition to the peculiar perception of scientific processes, ʿAzīmābādī and others also viewed science in the same light that medieval Muslims viewed Greek philosophy, called *falsafa qadīma*. Just as Muslims developed an analogous dialectical theology (*ʿilm al-kalām*) to that of Hellenism, there is an expectation that modern Muslims have to develop something analogous to modern science. In other words the defenders of Islam in the early 20th century had the unenviable task of refuting modern science based on empirical positivism with abstract logic and pre-modern philosophy.

Long before the modern period already, the epistemological estrangement between science and the religious sciences, especially law and theology, took place in Muslim societies. The exploration of the causes for this will have to be pursued elsewhere. Suffice it to say that the inherited sciences of religion in Islam and the modern natural sciences share very little in common in epistemological terms and hence the possibility of dialogue is limited. When Islamic law is forced into confronting issues of a scientific nature the conversation is marked by the radical differences in assumptions, forms of reasoning, and perceptions made by each "language": the language of science and the language of religious law. This chapter looks at the way contemporary Islamic law looks at the human body in the context of modern bio-technology.

The earliest debates in Muslim jurisprudence relating to the human body in the modern period emerged in the context of autopsies or post-mortem investigations. At first many Muslim scholars and jurists objected to such invasive surgery of the corpse. Disfiguring a corpse was seen as violating the dignity of the dead and thus objectionable in religious terms. However, as the social benefits of autopsies became more evident and necessary to modern life, where autopsy results can for instance assist in apprehending a criminal and determine the cause of death, the initial resistance to such medical practices gave way to permission. Today, there will be very few Muslim jurists who would oppose autopsies on legal grounds. On this one issue, over a matter of time modern Muslim jurisprudence and medical science began to find a common epistemic vocabulary.

With the possibility of more advanced forms of medical technology becoming more readily available such as organ transplantation surgery, Muslim jurists are faced with the prospect of having to deal with issues of greater scientific, ethical, and legal complexity and sophistication. With the advent of transplant surgery and brain-stem death, the earlier controversy about invasive surgery to a corpse in the case of autopsies pale in significance. These issues now involve complex ethical questions about the donation and reception of organs to living persons, but with it also comes the prospect of new definitions of death. In short, scenarios that may once have been in the realm of science fiction are increasingly becoming part of our existential reality. In addition, organ donation procedures have also developed in complexity. In the past, organs such as corneas were taken from cadavers. Now with advanced technology, organs are harvested from human bodies that visibly appear to have some form of life, albeit by means of life-support apparatuses, but are medically considered to be brain dead. These changed scientific perceptions completely undermine the inherited perceptions, understandings, and definitions of "life" and "death" to which Islamic jurisprudence and ethics had been accustomed.

In order to explore some aspects of contemporary Muslim thinking on bioethics and the body, I will analyze a few legal opinions issued by contemporary Muslim jurists on organ transplantation and brain death. By doing a close reading of these opinions, I hope to present the different kinds of legal and religious logic that these statements reflect. The opinions are no doubt diverse and sometimes diametrically opposed to each other. This chapter does not claim to exhaust the analysis of legal arguments employed by the jurists. The discussions of legal arguments are minimal where possible in order to demonstrate the interface of science and law and the nature of the conversation that takes place. Some of the issues that are explored include questions such as:

> What do these rulings on bio-medical issues tell us about the kind of scientific gaze from which modern Muslim jurists approach these very complex issues? What informs the gaze of the jurists?
>
> Do the presumptions of pre-modern Islamic law inform that gaze? If that is true, then how do jurists in the modern period mediate that pre-modern gaze in their thinking and rulings?
>
> Do these legal narratives reflect existing narratives about the body in Muslim thought?
>
> How do these statements of normativity reflect different representations of the Muslim "self"?
>
> What kind of preliminary conclusions can we draw about how the body is imagined in modern Islamic discourse?

In the late 1960s and late 1970s two opinions were issued on the topic of organ transplantation in two different parts of the Muslim world. These opinions were issued by what some would call "mainstream" Muslim authorities. For the purposes of this chapter I will use the term "traditional" Muslim thinkers as it is more appropriate. The first *fatwā* to be analyzed in this paper was issued by jurists in Pakistan, most of whom were affiliated with the Deoband school.[4] In the Pakistani context, the *fatwā* on organ transplantation was preceded by a juridical consultation by the Research Council on Contemporary Issues headed by Muftī Muḥammad Shafīʿ and Mawlānā Yūsuf Binnawrī. A *fatwā* is a non-binding legal opinion issued by a *muftī* (jurisconsult) in reply to a question. The *fatwā* was endorsed by six senior members of the Research Council in 1969 while the main signatory was Muftī Muḥammad Shafīʿ, a reputable and highly regarded scholar-jurist in Deobandi circles in the Indo-Pak subcontinent.[5]

The second opinion on organ transplantation was in the form of a *fatwā*, issued by the Dār al-Iftāʾ, in Egypt. The Dār al-Iftāʾ is an autonomous body that falls under the Ministry of Religious Endowments (*Awqāf*) and Religious Affairs in Egypt. The *muftī*, has regularly been a scholar whose credentials were acceptable to the al-Azhar University, one of the oldest Islamic universities in the world. The Egyptian *fatwā*, was issued by Shaykh Jād al-Ḥaqq ʿAlī Jād al-Ḥaqq, in his capacity as muftī of Egypt in 1979.[6] He later became the rector of the famous al-Azhar University.

The discussion on brain death was undertaken by the Academy of Islamic Jurisprudence (AIJ). The AIJ is a specialist committee of the Organization of Islamic Conference, a pan-Islamic body. In 1986 the jurists serving on the AIJ held a special consultation on brain death. What is of interest is how the various positions held by the jurists were justified. Their arguments disclose the manner in which issues such as the body and death are imagined within modern Muslim jurisprudence. In this sense it adds to our exploration of the manner in which religion and science have an encounter of some sort.

Pakistan Opinion

The Pakistani jurists declared organ transplantation to be prohibited
(*harām*) in terms of Islamic law. This ruling has not been repealed by
any subsequent decision in the Pakistan context. Two subsequent
consultations of experts and religious scholars in India, in 1989, and
another in Pakistan in 1995, have raised questions about the status of
the earlier *fatwā*. The 1995 consultation in Pakistan could not get the
ulema to agree on a ruling that permitted organ transplantation,
although some individual scholars thought it was permissible.
Interestingly, the 1989 Islamic Fiqh Academy of India issued a ruling
that under extreme circumstances and life-threatening conditions a
Muslim may receive an organ, and only live-donor donation of organs,
such as kidneys, are permitted – since a person can survive on a single
kidney.[7]

To return to the Pakistan *fatwā*, the argument rested on the
reasoning that organ transplantation transgressed the absolute
inviolability of human dignity (*karām wa hurma*). Further, the scholars
applied the legal maxim that repelling harm (*darar*) took precedence
over the acquisition of any potential benefit.[8] In arriving at their
decision, the Pakistani jurists took cognizance of several arguments
within Islamic law. Their key arguments hinged around several issues:

1. Considerations of legal philosophy and principles.
2. The prohibition on consuming expressly prohibited substances as
   a remedy and their use under extreme circumstances of need.
3. The irreducible inalienability and dignity of the human body from
   being expendable.

The Pakistani ruling also integrated issues of law with
considerations of moral philosophy and metaphysics. At the outset the
ruling assumes that organ transplantation is highly problematic in so
far as it violates the dignity of the human being. However, it does
briefly consider transplantation as a remedy. Hence the next step is to

test the validity and permissibility of the remedy in terms of the criteria of Islamic law (*fiqh*). The ruling then creates two categories of needs or necessity: (1) Primary necessity (*ḍarūrī*); and (2) a secondary necessity (*ḥājī*).

A primary necessity is one where a person is confronted with a life-threatening danger where such danger is declared with certainty by qualified medical experts. In such serious contexts there is a well-known legal maxim stating that "necessity lifts prohibition" (*al-ḍarūra tubiḥu 'l-maḥdhūrāt*). A secondary necessity is a non-emergency condition (*ghayr idhṭirārī*). For the treatment of a secondary necessity, the remedy should not violate an explicit prohibition found in the Qur'ān such as wine, carrion, pork, and blood. If the remedy for a secondary necessity violated a source and authority lesser than the Qur'ān, the ruling deemed such violation tolerable. Neither does the ruling see any curative value in prohibited substances following a prophetic report that states, "Allah has not provided a remedy in those things that are prohibited to you".[9] Prohibited substances can only be used as medication if it passes a three-point test: (1) that the remedy only be applicable to cases where there is a life-threatening danger; (2) the danger to life must be known with certainty and be an "actual" danger and not a potential or suspected threat; (3) a medical practitioner should conclusively establish the curative value of the use of the prohibited substance.

After taking into account the social reality, the need for treatment as well as the legal arguments developed within Islamic jurisprudence, the ruling concludes that organ transplantation is not permissible (*nā jā'iz*). The reason it supports this decision is that, while it admits that there are beneficial aspects to organ transplantation, there are also elements of unforeseen harm (*ḍarar*) to the religious, individual, and social dimensions of human existence.[10] In ignoring the harmful aspects of transplantation humanity can be exposed to unforeseen perils, the ruling argued.[11] The imperative to repel harm prior to the acquisition of benefits is scrupulously adhered to in this ruling.[12] According to the Pakistani jurists, human bodies are a "trust" (*amāna*) from God and as such human beings do not have the unfettered discretion to the use of their bodies. Not even consent to donate one's organs is permissible. The ruling emphasizes that transplantation would indiscriminately open up the ethical floodgates that could lead to the slippery slope of large-scale abuse and the sale of human organs. A specific fear was that the rich would exploit the poor in order to purchase their organs. On the grounds of the violation of human dignity and the imperative to avoid harm, the impurity of severed organs, and the prohibition of consuming human flesh, the ruling by way of *argumentum a fortiori* (*bi daraja awlā*) deemed organ transplantation prohibited. The ruling in fact proposed that alternative medical practices such as prosthesis, artificial substitutes described as "plastic surgery", and reconstructive prosthetic devices be explored as remedies to transplantation.[13]

Egyptian Opinion

The centerpiece of the Egyptian *fatwā* is that the issue of organ transplantation does not have any precedent in law and thus is a matter open to juristic discretion (*ijtihād*) *ab initio*. Any decision would have to take into consideration policy concerns about what course of action best considered the "dominant public interest" (*ri'āya maṣāliḥ al-rājiḥa*) or common good.[14] The approach of this *fatwā* is that in the absence of any prohibition the doctrine of "original permissibility" (*ibāḥa aṣliyya*) applied to transplantation. Drawing on opinions from the Ḥanafī, Shāfi'ī, and Māliki schools, the *fatwā* argues that organs severed from a body are not defiled and advances the view that a believer's body cannot be permanently defiled whether living or dead.[15] Faced with a life-threatening danger it was even permissible to eat human flesh.

By means of interpretation the *fatwā* managed to resolve some of the issues that concerned the authors of the Pakistani ruling. One such issue was a report (*ḥadīth*) of the Prophet stating that breaking the bones of the dead was like breaking [the bones] of the living.[16] The meaning of the report, the *fatwā* explained, was to stress the dignity attached to a corpse and that this report could not have prophesied against organ transplantation. The report in question, the *fatwā* explained, stemmed from the Prophet's reproach to a gravedigger who tried to force a corpse into a narrow grave by breaking the bones. Disapproval of such undignified behavior toward the dead was the context for such a report. The Pakistan ruling cited the same report in support of its argument against transplantation, without providing an interpretative framework for the report.

The *fatwā* also explored several analogous precedents that may in some sense resemble elements of organ transplantation. The ruling cited the permissibility of a procedure akin to cesarean-section to remove a full-term viable fetus from the womb of a mother who died in labor. It also argued that past jurists allowed a valuable to be retrieved from the belly of a dead person by way of invasive surgery. Given the permissibility of invasive surgery to dead bodies and the purity of severed organs, the *fatwā* established grounds of comparison with organ transplantation. From these remote precedents the author of the Egyptian *fatwā* extrapolates a very useful principle that cogently supports the philosophy behind transplantation: Securing the dignity of the living and their life/lives is preferable to securing the dignity of the dead.[17] Enumerating the various analogues to procedures remotely resembling elements of transplantation the *fatwā* argued that by way of *argumentum a fortiori* there was an even greater reason to approve the permissibility of organ transplantation. The relevant part of the *fatwā* read:

> It is permissible to cut the abdomen of a person and remove an organ or part of it, in order to transplant it to another living body, given the physician's view based on dominant probability that the recipient (donee) will benefit from the donated organ. [This follows] the jurists' consideration of the preponderant public interest, that 'necessity lifts prohibition' and that a 'greater harm can be offset by a lesser harm' and these are authoritative

[principles] derived from the noble Qur'ān and the sublime Sunna (tradition of the Prophet).[18]

From the evidence provided it appears that the *fatwā* only sanctioned cadaver donations or live kidney donations. The Egyptian *fatwā* did not address the crucial issue of brain-stem death. Besides cadaver and donor organs used in transplantation, the bulk of the organs harvested for transplantation purposes nowadays involve brain-stem death. In fact, the *fatwā* is explicit that no organ can be removed unless death is determined and specifies the application of the conventional cardiopulmonary test for death: fixed gaze of the eyes; limpness of the feet; bending of the nose; sunken temples; and the turgidity of the skin. If there is breathing, heart, and pulse function then these should be accepted as signs of life.

Academy of Islamic Jurisprudence (AIJ)of the OIC

Two diametrically opposed positions were extensively debated by the AIJ, after which it adopted brain death as an acceptable definition of death in terms of Islamic criteria. The details of the legal arguments have been discussed in detail elsewhere.[19] Muḥammad Na'īm Yāsīn, a Jordanian jurist, made a submission to the Academy's consultation advocating that brain death is permissible in Islam. Other scholars with approximately similar arguments supported him. His argument was that since there were no textual ordinances (*nuṣūṣ*, singular *naṣṣ*) offering explicit guidance on this issue, it was a matter that fell in the domain of juristic discretion (*ijtihād*). In the case of the inception of life, there were textual sources that clearly stated such beginnings. However, in the case of death there was no definitive directive from revealed text. Jurists thus employed customary criteria to determine the instant of death. Yāsīn is unequivocal in his stating that the issue of brain death is to be primarily determined by medical specialists. Scholars of religion and jurists should work in collaboration with medical specialists in order to provide ethical guidelines for such complex practices.

Yāsīn's view is that human life ends in the reverse process with which it begins. If life begins with the entry of the soul then it ends with the exit of the soul. While we cannot be certain about the operations of the soul, reasonableness and dominant probability provide us with a working certainty on these matters. Muslim scholars had written extensively on issues of the soul. From this we know that in some of its functions the soul is dependent on the body as long as the body is capable of supporting the activities of the soul. Once the body fails to serve as a locus for the soul it departs. Yāsīn argues further to show that especially in criminology, Muslim jurists made certain assumptions about the instant of death in order to determine the cause of death. These juristic-cum-scientific assumptions were effective in instances where several assailants in a serial fashion perpetrate the crime of murder. In scrutinizing the forensic evidence, Muslim jurists had to make certain determinations about which assailant caused the death and which one only aggravated the injury. Yāsīn's point is to show that already in pre-modern Muslim jurisprudence there were juridico-scientific techniques to determine the cause of unnatural forms of death as to when the "instant of death" was, in order to apportion culpability in criminal cases. In all these rulings the jurists were satisfied in making their findings on the grounds of dominant probability (*ẓann*) and not on certainty (*yaqīn*). With these discussions Yāsīn makes two points that will be helpful in his argument favoring brain-death. There is precedent in Muslim jurisprudence that considers death to occur in various stages and that in such cases certainty was not a criteria, rather the probability of evidence was sufficient. The soul's absence or presence is related to brain function, the seat of human personality. So he is convinced that with the end of brain function, the soul is no longer present and hence death has effectively set in. Signs of pulse, heart beat, and kidney functions sustained by life-support systems are no indicators that the human being is alive. Ashqar, another jurist supporting Yāsīn's position states that Islamic law treats a severely injured person on the verge of death, as symbolically dead. Such a person on the verge of death is not included among the legitimate heirs in the event that his father, mother, or child predeceases him or her since the law does not consider him or her among the living heirs in such a near-death condition.

Tawfīq al-Wā'ī makes a detailed submission opposing brain death. Wā'ī argues from a range of sources, mainly from the Qur'ān, to demonstrate that when the revealed sources speak of death, they primarily speak of the death of the body. Thus to argue that death is tantamount to the death of the brain would go against his reading of the sources. While he is fully aware of the interdependence of the body and soul, he is critical of the view that reduces the definition of life and death to the presence and absence of the soul. Citing the jurist-theologian Fakhr al-Dīn al-Rāzī (d. 606/1209), Wā'ī states that the human body is a composite of several organs and not a single organ. He argues that in the Qur'ānic account the prophet Abraham dismembers animals and then returns them to life, to argue that even radical dismemberment or deterioration of a body is not described as death in the revealed sources. In another account the Qur'ān describes the legendary Seven Sleepers of Ephesus (People of the Cave, *Aṣḥāb al-Kahf*) to have a death-like sleep, but they were never declared dead. Furthermore, he argues that Muslim jurists never made the mind (*'aql*) and sense perception (*iḥsās*) to be the sole criteria for evidence of life in a body. Both features are not fully evident in infants and yet we do not declare infants dead, he argues. The status quo definition of death by cardiopulmonary indicators provides certainty in the determination of death and thus Wā'ī argues that the current conventions of determining death should continue to apply. In the end, the AIJ resolved to accept brain death as an acceptable criterion for death.

Interface Between Jurisprudence and Science

It is fascinating to see how pre-modern notions of law, body, and science are employed in a conversation with phenomena of a radically different and utterly modern provenance, such as organ transplantation and brain death, in the discourses of contemporary Muslim jurists. Most notable is that hardly any of the jurists take on board the language of modern human biology and science from which transplant surgery is derived. The primary reference point is the body of law available in the juristic tradition. Only in the AIJ consultation did medical professionals make submissions to the committee to explain what actually took place in terms of brain death. However, there was little evidence in the deliberations of the AIJ that indicated that they took serious notice of the modern scientific bio-medical technology presented to them. It appears that once the jurists grasped what the practice of transplantation surgery or brain-death involved, they translated the concepts into the framework of legal reasoning with which they were most familiar. There is no attempt to align or create coherence between the two different epistemologies, namely that of science and that of Islamic jurisprudence.

Jurists on both sides of the opinion, for and against these modern bio-medical innovations, translate these modern concepts and practices into the language of Islamic law. Thus there is also an endless translation taking place within the juridical process. The Pakistani and Egyptians all try to translate the modern practice of transplant surgery into the nearest available and analogous legal ruling for which precedent exists within Islamic law. Surely such a method does indeed allow for the continuity of an intellectual tradition, even if at the expense of bowdlerizing the tradition. In the process the logic of the law is expanded and made sufficiently elastic in order to seemingly solve even the most complex and challenging bio-ethical issues. In extending the law and classifying acts as either permissible or prohibited, the jurists clearly succeed in bestowing a certain legitimacy or illegitimacy to practices such as brain death and organ transplantation. With it comes a semblance of authority and authenticity that they lend to the practices. In fact for many Muslim jurists this ability of Islamic law to solve is a sign of it being "divinely enriched" and comprehensive in its principles.[20] The Egyptian lawyer Audah argues that a divinely inspired law has some of the following features:

> That the principles of legislation as well as the text of [the] provisions must be of such elasticity and universality that they would embrace all the requirements of human society regardless of the lapse of time, societal evolution, and the multiplicity and diversification of human needs.
>
> That these principles and texts must be so perfect and comprehensive that they would not fall short in matching the standard of the society at any point in time. In truth, the above logical requirements are inherent in Islamic jurisprudence, and its principles and provisions are universal and elastic to the extreme, and are absolutely far-reaching and perfect.[21]

Audah's viewpoint is not an aberration or idiosyncratic opinion. It is pervasive among large sectors of the contemporary Muslim legal community, namely that the perfection of Islamic jurisprudence lies in the elasticity and perfection of its principles. Audah makes the description of a complex and diverse juridical into an *a priori* statement. Little distinction is made between the rhetoric of ideals and the intellectual rigor that was invested over centuries to create and sustain this juridical tradition.

From the issues discussed above we observed how contemporary Muslim jurists mediated their authority via the texts of the legal tradition and in the process either legitimated or de-legitimated social practices. It goes without saying that the existential conditions of the jurists are undoubtedly also part of the mediation process and thus it is not as simple as saying that they become the vestibules for transmitting pre-modern law into modernity. The very condition of modernity itself modernizes the law in one form or another, be it a thoroughgoing modernization or minimal modernization. And, perhaps it is through this process and almost indirectly that the tradition of Islamic jurisprudence finds some coherence with the modern *episteme*, albeit in an unsystematic and non-programmatic manner. One cannot ignore the fact that traditional Muslim jurists live in modern contexts, experience it, and are required to pass a value judgement on the technologies of modernity such as bio-technology and advanced forms of medical surgery. While modernity undoubtedly infuses itself into traditional sites, there is overwhelming evidence that the language and social imagery of the pre-modern legal discourse is alive and well in the modern era. But whether this language performs the same function it played in pre-modern societies or it is transformed by the new context, is moot and needs to be explored elsewhere.

The question that arises is whether the jurists and the medical practitioners, as well as patients, share a common set of meanings as to what is meant by "death", "life", "harm", "body", "human dignity", and "healing". My provisional response would be that there is dissonance between the perspectives of the jurists on the one hand, and the practitioners and patients on the other hand; but there is also some overlap otherwise there would be utter mis-communication. These perspectives are generated by different and divergent forms of educational training, cultivation of worldviews, and the respective scientific and moral gazes with which these diverse linguistic communities view realities. Thus, each constituency would also have a different language that represents a slightly different worldview, even if they belonged to the same faith community. One would also often find that different languages co-exist within the same person. A Muslim patient or physician may fully comprehend the scientific aspects of brain death or organ transplantation but may feel ambivalent in engaging in such practices due to their religious convictions. Patients in need of a kidney or cornea have refused transplantation on the basis that their religion prohibited such practices. Others, in turn, would have no such compunctions or would be convinced by an alternative religious argument that sanctions such practices.

Returning to the language of the law in the context of modern medicine and the rulings discussed above, one could ask the question whether there is any meaningful dialogue taking place between the language of Islamic law and the practices and philosophy of modern science. From the summarized descriptions of the legal arguments above, one cannot ignore the instrumentalist nature of the discussion in this juridical-scientific encounter. Those jurists who favor organ transplantation (Egyptian *fatwā*) and those members of the AIJ who approved of brain death, start with the premise that juristic discretion (*ijtihād*) is required in this matter because of an absence of legal precedent. Even they, nevertheless, feel compelled to find some kind of rationale to bolster their argument by finding analogous precedents in pre-modern practices of Islamic law. So we have surgical delivery of a viable fetus, the purity of severed organs, and the consideration of public benefits that secure the permissibility of organ transplantation in Egypt. There is no detailed discussion of the ethics of trans-plantation, who decides how organs are donated and transplanted, the sale of organs, the consent of the patient, the ethics of costly transplantation, and high-tech medicine in poor countries lacking in basic health-care facilities. To be fair the Pakistani jurists did raise some of these issues such as the sale of organs.

In permitting brain death, the AIJ jurists ruled that since there was no binding precedent in such matters it was an open question. What remained was to make an argument as to the relation between body and soul and to identify the locus of the soul. Once it could be argued that the locus of the soul is the brain and that consciousness is an indicator of brain function, brain death can easily be justified. Those jurists who opposed brain death and organ transplantation used the same texts and sources as their fellow jurists but arrived at an opposing and differing position. Their emphasis was on the social imagery of the body as inviolable in its dignity. This was bolstered by subsidiary legal arguments about the impurity of severed organs in the case of organ transplantation. In the case of brain death, the opposition was grounded in a demand for a more holistic account of death and opposed the reductionist view that identified death solely with brain function and the absence of consciousness.

The oddity of these analogical formulae will not be lost to more perceptive observers of Islamic law. There is a world of a difference between the surgical recovery of a valuable from the belly of a deceased, or the delivery of a fetus from the womb of a dead mother, and the prospect of donating organs or limbs and having these transplanted onto another human body. The resemblance if any, is tenuous. It is possible that the analogues are meant to serve as persuasive value, rather than adding to any serious formulation of the law. Neither is the legitimating argument of public benefit a persuasive one when there is hardly any exploration as to what contribution organ transplantation makes to society.

The instrumentalist approach does not take into cognizance contemporary debates about a whole range of issues that impact on some of these scientific developments. If Islamic law is to be viewed as a tradition-in-the-making, contrary to Audah's *a priori* perception of law, then there ought to be some point in which the traditional juristic theories begin to update themselves in order to come to terms with some of the assumptions of the contemporary world; otherwise, Islamic law will remain a bastion of resistance to social change and modernity while its rulings will find very little reception among its followers. Updating the tradition of Islamic law does not necessarily mean the slavish adoption of a specific pattern and model of modernity. We now know that there are multiple modernities and alternative modernities to the hegemonic western model. The very general principles of Islamic law based on the analogical model have their own limitations, arguments that were already well rehearsed in the medieval legal debates. For this reason, Muslim legal theorists devised additional theories in order to deal with new contingencies, not imagined by the founding fathers of the law. Changing conditions accelerated the use of doctrines such as public interest (*maṣlaḥa*) and legal preference (*istiḥsān*) with increasing frequency in later generations. Istiḥsān is the legal technique where dead-end analogy is overlooked and a more workable and practical analogue is employed to end the logjam in legal logic contrary to the established rules. However, a discussion of how exactly Muslim legal theory updates itself and enters into a conversation with the modern episteme would take us way beyond the scope of this discussion. What this section attempts to highlight is the non-conversation that takes place between scientific discourses and religious discourses in Muslim ethics and legal practices.

Bodily Cosmology

The divergent approaches that the legal arguments (*fiqh*) yield, forces one to look at broader narratives about the body that may subtly and sub-consciously lay beneath the various juristic gazes of the body. Given that the juristic tradition is intimately tied to the established and diverse Muslim intellectual tradition, it may well be worth exploring what kind of approaches history had bequeathed to posterity on the question of the body. The relationship between the corporeal body and the incorporeal soul or spirit, is one debate that had preoccupied Muslim thinkers from the earliest times. A brief look at the views of the philosopher Ibn Sīnā (d.1037) and Abū Ḥāmid al-Ghazālī (d. 1111) may help us to see if our contemporary perceptions of the body resonate with some of the ideas of an earlier period.

Ibn Sīnā has argued that the soul comes into existence whenever it deems a body fit to be used. "The body which thus comes into being is the kingdom and instrument of the soul", he says.[22] But the body is not the formal or final cause of the soul.[23] Rather, the body and the temperaments are accidental or accessory causes to the soul. Thus, as an effect of an accessory cause (the soul) can and does survive the accessory causes.[24] The body is not informed with the "form" of the soul, nor is the soul imprinted into the composite parts of the body. After evaluating several arguments, Ibn Sīnā concludes that "all the forms of attachment between the body and the soul have proved to be false and it only remains that the soul in its being, has no relationship with the body but is related with other principles which are not subject to change or corruption.[25] From this it follows that the soul is incorruptible and does not die with the body.

The soul, according to Ibn Sīnā, is individuated by the fact of its creation. Even when disembodied it retains its consciousness and the individuality of its history.[26] However, Ibn Sīnā's naturalism has been the subject of critique. Especially his hylomorphism, in allocating all definiteness and definition to the formal aspect of reality as well as the corresponding assignment of mere passivity and inertness of all matter, makes him play right into the hands of Ghazālī. For Ghazālī damaged Ibn Sīnā's argument of naturalism by showing that all movement or action requires a will in order to initiate such action. Ghazālī brings home the point that even the elements of temperament (hot, cold, wet, dry) are inert and not self-sufficient as causes and require something else to activate them into life. In order to explain the miracle of life the philosophers employ the term "formal principles" while the theologians call these angels, and relate these to a realm of spirit and ultimately to God.

While Ibn Sīnā and Ghazālī would both agree that the soul is what makes possible the activities of life, growth, reproduction, sensitivity, and motility of animals, as well as the consciousness and rationality of human beings, there remains a difference between the two with respect to matter. The human body is constitutive of matter. It is here that the qualitative difference takes place between the two viewpoints. For Ibn Sīnā the body is part of a naturalism and enjoys the motions of natural causality. Ghazālī, while not denying causality, actually assimilates natural causality to the work of some spiritual principle of divine causation. This divine spark, or this mere theistic "touch" that Ghazālī brings to matter, in some way generates a continuity of some of the spiritual substance of the soul and the body (matter), but the two are not identical. While there is a difference between the soul and body in Ghazālī's view, there is an ontological continuity too, a continuity that the philosophers fail to acknowledge.

Ghazālī is a useful source and informs us how jurists and religious thinkers in the past may have imagined the body-soul relationship. He raises this issue almost parenthetically in the *Deliverance* (*Munqidh*) when discussing those philosophers whom he describes as naturalists. They are empiricists who have a deep interest in botany and anatomy, with a special interest in animal anatomy.[27] Ghazālī is well disposed toward them in so far as their research discloses to them and others the wonders of God's creation and His unique wisdom as Creator and the perfection of his creation. However, he has some reservations about their overemphasis on the powers that animals possess. The philosophers, he says, believe that the equilibrium of the *mizāj*, meaning temperament or organism, has a decisive influence on the powers and capacity of animals. They take this point to such extremes in believing that the faculty of thinking is also dependent on animal powers. In his own words Ghazālī says:

> Yet these philosophers, immersed in their investigations of nature, take the view that the equilibrium of the *mizāj* (temperament/ constitution/ organism) has a profound effect on the existence (*qiwām*) of the powers of a being. Thus they thought that the human rational faculty is dependent on its constitution (*mizāj*). So that as the *mizāj* (constitution) is corrupted, intellect is also corrupted and ceases to exist. Thus when something ceases to exist then it is unthinkable in their opinion that the non-existent should return to existence.[28]

Although Ghazālī's explicit purpose is to refute the conclusions of this special breed of naturalist philosophers (not Ibn Sīnā in this matter) for rejecting the immortality of the soul, this statement also discloses something about the relationship of the body and the soul. The point that Ghazālī makes is that one should not view the continued existence of the soul, exclusively in terms of its relationship to matter, namely the body. He wishes to refute the crass materialism of the naturalists who argue that the soul dies with the death of the body. Although we do make a practical distinction between rationality and body, we must acknowledge that human consciousness or human rationality is just as much a sign of human existence, as a living body indicates life. Ghazālī describes the body as the mount, on which the soul rides and strives to gain proximity to God.[29] Without the means, i.e. the body, the soul cannot attain its destination. Thus the means (body) is extremely critical to the realization of the ends, namely the perfection of the soul. Even if a distinction is allowed between body and soul, then for Ghazālī in the words of Watt, "the body is just as much the man as the soul".[30] Watt explains this to be the monistic or Semitic view of body-soul continuity. Muslim philosophers on the other hand, like Ibn Sīnā held the dualistic or Greek view according to which humans also consist of the soul and the body; the crucial difference being that to the dualists the body is only the soul's temporary garment. Ibn Sīnā and others believed that the body was dispensable and only valorized the soul. Thus, it was relatively easy for them to conclude that the afterlife will not necessarily be a bodily resurrection.[31] The philosophers, especially Ibn Sīnā, argued that the souls in the afterlife would imagine the pleasures and the torments of that realm through the instrumentation of some kind of celestial body.[32]

Contrary to this view, Ghazālī and some Muslim theologians wished to retain the integrity of both body and spirit, instead of making one dependent on the other; thus both the soul and the body are valorized. In the hands of Ghazālī the valorization of the body even becomes a symbol in doctrinal matters. Thus Ghazālī insists that resurrection will be bodily, in other words corporeal. Prior to him, Ash'arī catechism had made belief in bodily resurrection an important plank of its doctrinal formulation. Ghazālī championed the same argument against the Muslim philosophers. What we should not lose sight of is how the social imagery of the body surreptitiously makes its way into the doctrinal formulations involving the body.

Reading the Legal Opinions

Now that we have some sense of the way in which Muslim thinkers analyzed the body, it may highlight the futility of the situation in trying to configure why jurists, employing the same texts and arguments, arrive at different conclusions. There may surely be interpretative differences in jurisprudence itself that may account for such variations in the law, but one can probe further by asking what causes such interpretative differences. It is eminently possible that the monistic and dualist narratives of the body-soul relationship may still be prevalent in the discursive practices of Muslim thinkers and societies. One can easily see a naturalist hand at work in the account of the pro brain death writers in the AIJ opinion, who valorized the consciousness and the place of the soul in their analysis. In the Egyptian *fatwā* the body is considered dispensable especially if it serves a higher purpose of benefitting fellow human beings. Very little attention is given to the sacred status of the body. In the Pakistan ruling the jurists were extremely reverential towards the body, treating it as sacrosanct, as the soul itself. In fact the Pakistan jurists were not at all unmindful of the relationship between body and spirit and considered the body as much as being human with or without the soul.

To continue with my attempt to provide some explanatory matrix for these different versions of Islamic law, we have to return to the function of law in Muslim society. Most definitions of the subject of positive law (*fiqh*) would describe law as that body of knowledge that informs us of the shari'a values. In other words, it is about the application of the values derived from both revealed sources, such as the Qur'ān and the prophetic tradition, as well as from the socially constructed sources such as consensus and analogy, on which there is general agreement. (There are also a number of controversial sources or instruments of deriving rules from the sources.) In short, positive law provides the rules for good social order and moral conduct. With the assistance of Ghazālī we discover that already in the 11th and 12th centuries, sensitive thinkers like him recognized that law performed poorly if it was only meant to perform as the external regulator of human conduct.

In his own discontent with the jurists of his society, Ghazālī in addition to excoriating the legal practitioners of his day, also made us aware that law has to play an additional function. Failing to fulfill this purpose renders law into a mere performance without realizing its desired effects. In his *Criterion for Action* Ghazālī postulates another meaning for fiqh, which literally means "discernment". He proposes a novel purpose (or not often mentioned one) for the discursive sciences such as fiqh. The purpose of fiqh is to find a reliable manner by way of intellectual exertion (*ijtihād*) in order to discern the state of the spirit.[33] Law does not only have positivistic concerns, but is also ultimately concerned with the state of the soul. It is here that Ghazālī provides us with another meaning of faqih, namely the "discerner". He urges the reader to consider becoming a "discerner of the spirit" (*faqīh al-nafs*) and understand the condition of the soul. To become an expert in understanding the inner realities of the soul and its well being is just as important as understanding the positive law. Discerning the needs of the soul requires practice and application until one develops a habit of understanding the phenomena of the spirit or the law in such a manner that it becomes spontaneous and a part of one's identity.[34]

In my reconstruction of Ghazālī's insights one could venture to say that he is urging us to understand the ritual function of the law. The word "ritual" is not meant in the common sense usage in which people dismiss practices as rituals because they are habitual and uncontemplated activities. Nor do I use the term in the functionalist sense in which rituals create societal unity and balance in order to retain the status quo. From Ghazālī's insights, I derive the sense that he believes that the practice of positive law, the ritual of law for that matter, produces a sense of the self, and a sense of self-identity. Ritual action through the law is not an expression *of* the sacred nor is it a response *to* the sacred. Rather, the ritual of law conveys a sacrality on a thing or a person. For Ghazālī fiqh *per se* performs its ritual function once it is conceived as fiqh al-nafs, an inner discernment, where the ritual action consists of a series of transactions concerning the self and other, true and false, justice and injustice. In other words, rituals truly performed begin to make a difference between various ethical and aesthetic registers of the practitioner. With the rise of legal positivism, certain interpretations of modern Islamic law too had adopted the positivist framework that undermined the Ghazālīan sense of ritual. Johansen has carefully shown that modern 20th century Arab jurists have adapted the legal reasoning of fiqh into a positivist model along the lines of codification and modern national legal systems. In the process, says Johansen, the

> liturgical acts, the ethical content of those norms which cannot be applied by courts but which address the conscience of the individual believers, their *forum internum*, in short the religious dimension of the fiqh, has hardly been considered an object of legal reconstruction and would need a completely different approach.[35]

Johansen's concerns echoes my reconstruction of Ghazālī's notion of "discernment of the self" as the ritual or liturgical function of the law. In fact one could actually argue that Ghazālī develops techniques for asceticizing ritual law. His *Iḥyā'* is possibly the most eloquent testimony of such a herculean effort. In the context of the rulings on organ transplantation and brain death examined above, one could argue that the law performs different ritual functions in each context, within the community of jurists and their respective lay communities. The law for that matter reflects and represents different kinds of Muslim "self" (selves) in their peculiar and unique contexts. In other words, the law is also an index of the Muslim self. The variations and differences in the law – legal practices are not so much occasioned by a difference in the interpretation of texts, although that cannot be ruled out – is more discretely produced by the differentiation that law as ritual asserts *through* the subjects of the law.

Conclusion

In the foregoing I have attempted to show that contemporary Muslim legal practices in the realm of bioethics employ premodern *epistemes* to address issues emanating from a totally different epistemological perspective. I am skeptical whether there is a dialogue between scientific practices and the juridical legitimation or prohibition of such practices as evidenced in the examples of organ transplantation and brain death. I argue that instrumentalist reasoning does the trick in providing a semblance of engagement. However I have tried to show that the different positions towards the body adopted by contemporary jurists may in greater or lesser measure resonate with broader narratives of bodily cosmologies prevalent in different periods of Islamic history. I tried to identify two such approaches, those of the dualists and the monists.

In trying to explain why there are different and variant positions in the law, I employed a Ghazālīan insight to make the case that law also has a ritual and liturgical/religious function. The ritual function of law is to differentiate and individuate different subjects. The effect of differentiation also affects those who authorize the law, since they are also simultaneously the subjects of the law. Notwithstanding my attempt to explain the function of the law, I still believe that there is merit in considering the possible scenarios in which Muslim legal theory can be updated and reconstructed so that Muslim legal thought can meaningfully engage with relevant contemporary issues.

Notes

[1] See Ebrahim Moosa, "Shaykh Aḥmad Shākir and the adoption of a scientifically-based lunar calendar", *Islamic Law and Society*, 5:1, (1998): 57-89.
[2] Sayyid Muḥibb ul-Ḥaqq 'Azīmābādī, "Ahle Sāyins and Sāyins", in *Da'wat al-Ḥaqq* (Patna: Maṭba'a Sayyidi, 1907)14-18, 27-31.

[3]　Ibid., 31.

[4]　Deoband is a seminary founded in India in the second half of the 19th century, near Saharanpur in Uttar Pradesh. It has since developed into a major school of thought on the Indian sub-continent as well as internationally. Colleges and seminaries affiliated to this school mark the landscape of the subcontinent and other regions of the world. See Barbara D. Metcalf, *Islamic Revival in British India: Deoband, 1860-1900* (Princeton: Princeton University Press, 1982).

[5]　Muḥammad Shafīʿ, *Tanshīṭ al-Adhhān fī al-Tarqīʿ bi Aʿḍāʾ al-Insān [Exercising the Mind in Matters [related] to the Joining of Human Organs: In Other Words, Combining Organs]* hereafter referred to as Tanshīṭ (Karachi: Dar al-Ishaat, 1972, 2nd edition).

[6]　Jād al-Ḥaqq ʿAlī Jād al-Ḥaqq, *al-Fatāwā al-Islāmiyya min Dār al-Iftāʾ al-Miṣriyya,* hereafter referred to as *Fatāwā,* fatwā no. 1323 titled: "Transferring Organs from one Person to Another" (Cairo: al-Majlis al-Aʿlā li al-Shuʾūn al-Islāmiyya, 1403/1983), 10:3702-3715.

[7]　*Aham Fiqhī Faysle* (New Delhi: Islamic Fiqh Academy, 1999), 13.

[8]　Al-Imām Zayn Ibn Nujaym, *al-Ashbāh wa al-Naẓāʾir* (Karachi: H.M. Saʿid Company, n.d), 45.

[9]　*Tanshīṭ,* 22.

[10]　*Tanshīṭ,* 30.

[11]　Ibid.

[12]　Further arguments reinforce the ruling of prohibition. According to the Ḥanafī school of law organs severed from a body are viewed as defiled (*najāsa*). This is the position of only a section of the Ḥanafī school but the ruling does not inform us about the status of this view. Furthermore, the ruling argues that past Muslim jurists of the Ḥanafī school also prohibited one from eating ones own flesh in life-threatening circumstances while conceding that other law schools deemed such acts permissible, see *Tanshīṭ,* 14 and 20.

[13]　Another related issue discussed at some length in the ruling was the question of blood transfusion. This discussion is relevant in so far that it gives us an idea of the underlying scientific gaze of traditional Muslim scholars. The authors of the Pakistan ruling were aware of the anomaly of permitting blood transfusion. One will recall that they followed the Ḥanafī view that severed organs were defiled and accordingly blood too would be prohibited. The consumption of blood is explicitly prohibited in the Qurʾān (Q 2:173). Yet blood transfusion is permitted to remedy cases of an "emergency" or "primary" (*ḍarūrī*) type need or necessity. Clearly if there was any analogue for organ transplantation, then blood transfusion could be viewed as a precedent. The legal argument for blood transfusion was constructed on pragmatic grounds. Blood, the jurists argued, was easily transferred and did not involve elaborate surgery nor did it violate human dignity. The analogy for blood transfusion was the use of female breast milk. Past jurists permitted the use of human breast milk for medicinal purposes. Blood transfusion is thus permissible

because it was a choice between the lesser of two competing harms and that necessity had lifted the statutory prohibition on the use of blood. One of the unstated reasons the Pakistani jurists found it easier to permit blood transfusion was that blood was a regenerative tissue, whereas certain organs may not be regenerative. In the context of blood transfusion they also raised a very interesting issue of a psycho-legal and moral nature. The violation of shari'a rules had both material and spiritual consequences. There are thus concerns over that the spiritual condition of the donor can be transmitted to the recipient via organs and blood. Non-Muslims, as well as Muslims who are deemed sinful (*fāsiq*) and profligate (*fājir*) could transmit their negative spiritual conditions to the recipient, see *Tanshīṭ*, 28. The blood of such persons carry "spiritually impure effects (*atharāt-e khabītha*)" and will have an effect on the moral character of the donee. This view is consistent with established positions within Islamic ethics that a sinful wet-nurse, for instance, could transmit her negative moral and spiritual character to the suckling whom she is breast feeding.

14 *Fatāwā*, 10:3705.
15 *Fatāwā*, 10:3708.
16 *Fatāwā*, 10:3707.
17 *Fatāwā*, 10:3705.
18 *Fatāwā*, 10:3712-13.
19 See Ebrahim Moosa, "Languages of Change in Islamic Law: Redefining Death in Modernity", *Islamic Studies*, 38:2 (Autumn 1999); it deals with the opinion of the Academy in great detail.
20 Abdul Qader Audah, *Islam Between Ignorant Followers and Incapable Scholars* (n.p.: International Islamic Federation of Student Organisations, n.d), 85.
21 Ibid., 27.
22 Ibn Sīnā, *Avicennas Psychology: An English Translation of Kitāb al-Najāt*, Book II, Chapter IV, trans. & commentary by Fazlur Rahman (London: Oxford University Press, 1952), 57.
23 Ibn Sīnā, *Najat*, 59.
24 Ibn Sīnā, *Najat*, 59 and Fazlur Rahman, *Commentary*, 107.
25 Ibn Sīnā, *Najat*, 61.
26 Len Goodman, *Avicenna* (London: Routledge, 1993), 128.
27 Ghazālī, "*al-Munqidh min al-Ḍalāl*" in *Majmū'ā Rasā'il al-Imām al-Ghazālī*, Ahmad Shams al-Din (ed.), (Beirut: Dar al-Kutub al-'Ilmiyyah, 1409/1988), 35.
28 Ghazālī, "*Munqidh*", 36.
29 Ghazali, *Ihyā' 'Ulūm al-Dīn, Adab al-Muta'allim wa'l-'Ilm*, 5 vols (Cairo: Mu'assa al-Halabi, 1387/1968), 1:78.
30 W.M. Watt, *Muslim Intellectual* (Edinburgh: Edinburgh University Press, 1963), 61.
31 Ghazālī, *Incoherence of the Philosophers (Tahafut al-Falasifa)*, trans Michael Marmura (Provo, Utah: Brigham Young University Press, 1997), 225.

[32] Arthur J. Arberry, *Avicenna on Theology* (London: Jouhn Murray, 1951), 74.

[33] Ghazālī, *Mīzān al-ʿAmal*, Sulayman Dunya (ed.), (Cairo: Dar al-Maʿarif, n.d), 224.

[34] Ghazālī, *Mīzān*, 253.

[35] Baber Johansen, *Contingency in a Sacred Law* (Leiden: E.J. Brill, 1999), 59.

Chapter 14
Neuroscience and Human Nature:
A Christian Perspective
Nancey Murphy

Pick up any reference work from the Christian scholarly world and read what it has to say about the nature of the human person, the body, soul, resurrection, immortality, and it is likely to tell you more about the assumptions of the era in which it was written than it does about original or authentic Christian teaching. There seems to be no topic in theology or biblical studies into which we humans are more likely to project ourselves. Not surprising. For this reason I shall not presume to write about *the* Christian view of human nature, and even less to presume that I could write anything about *the* Islamic view.

My plan, then, is to piece together a brief account of how these issues have developed throughout Christian history. I shall end this historical account with current arguments against dualism (or trichotomism) and in favor of a position I shall call nonreductive physicalism. Then I shall ask whether such an account should be considered to fall within the range of acceptable positions in the Christian tradition. There are both theological and philosophical issues to consider. I shall touch briefly on some of the theological issues at the end of my paper, but will concentrate on philosophical issues, attempting to further arguments for the possibility of genuinely *non-reductive* physicalism – that is, to show that neurobiological determinism does not threaten our self-image as free and rational creatures.

History

I have failed to discover any comprehensive history of the issue with which I am concerned here – the metaphysical make-up of the human person. One aspect that needs to be included is the history of *oversimplifications* of earlier history – to which I hope I am not now contributing! Nonetheless, here is my amateur historian's account.[1]

Apparently there were a variety of theories of human nature, with correlative expectations regarding death, available to the writers of the new Testament. It is widely agreed among current Christian and Jewish scholars that early Hebraic accounts of the person were holistic and physicalist, and had no well-developed account of life after death. By Jesus' day, however, there was a lively debate as to whether or not the dead would rise at the end of time. The Hellenization of the region had begun several centuries earlier and some Jews had adopted a dualistic view of body and soul, along with a conception of the soul's survival of death. Early Gentile Christians probably held an even wider variety of views. The important fact to note is that there is no explicit teaching on the metaphysical composition of the person; however, the New Testament writers did clearly emphasize the resurrection of the body (as opposed to immortality of the soul) as a guarantee of life after death. Writing to the church at Corinth Paul's apology for the resurrection of the body met resistance from some who found it too good to be true and from others who could not understand why they should *want* to be encumbered again by a body once they had escaped it at death.

As Christianity spread throughout the Mediterranean world and its theology was developed in conversation with a variety of philosophical and religious systems, a modified Neoplatonic account of the person came to predominate in scholarly circles. The *eternal* Platonic soul became (merely) immortal and there was added the expectation that it would be reunited with a body at the end of time. Augustine's account was the most influential until the later Middle Ages.

A major turning point in Christian history, of course, was a result of borrowing from Muslim scholarship in the later Middle Ages. I shall return shortly to Thomas Aquinas' account of the soul, with its dependence on Aristotle and on further developments by Muslim scholars. Thomas' position, based on Aristotle's conception of the soul as the form of the body, may be described as a modified rather than radical dualism.

Two factors at the dawn of modernity challenged the Aristotelian account of human nature. One was the Protestant Reformation's tendency to associate Aristotle with Catholicism and to return to the more Platonic elements in Augustine's thought. The other was the demise of Aristotelian metaphysics as a whole as a result of the rise of modern science – the substitution of atomism for hylomorphism. In response, René Descartes provided modern Europeans with a dualism of mind and body even more radical than Plato's – mental substance is defined *over against* material substance, and the body is purely mechanical.

The interesting twists in this story are the result of critical church history and historical-critical biblical scholarship, beginning especially in the 19th century. At that time many scholars called into question the authenticity of miracle accounts in the Bible, and especially the chief miracle, the resurrection of Jesus. This led to an emphasis in theological circles on an immortal soul as the only basis for Christian hope for life after death. Immanuel Kant's transcendental argument for the immortality of the soul played a complementary role.

At the same time, though, critical scholarship made it possible to ask whether current doctrine (including doctrines regarding the soul) were in fact original Christian (and Hebraic) teaching or whether they were the result of later doctrinal development, read back into the biblical texts. It became common during the 20th century to make a sharp distinction between original Hebraic conceptions and later Greek accretions such as body-soul dualism, and to favor the former as authentic Christian teaching. In addition, both theologians and biblical scholars in the past generation have rediscovered the centrality of the resurrection of the body in primitive Christian proclamation.

Science has affected these debates at three major points. First, as already mentioned, the atomist revolution in physics represented the replacement of Aristotelian hylomorphism, so not only did it become impossible to understand soul as the form of the body, but the very conception of matter involved in speaking of the body changed radically. Second, evolutionary biology pushed many in the direction of physicalist accounts of human nature: if animals have no souls (as moderns, beginning with Descartes, assumed) then humans must not have them either. But others argued that the concept of soul is all the more important in order to account for human distinctiveness. The thesis of this chapter is that the most significant scientific development having a bearing on this long history of debates is now occurring in the cognitive-neurosciences.

Neuroscience and the Soul

In this section, then, I shall argue that all of the human capacities once attributed to the soul can now be understood as brain functions – more precisely, as functions of the brain in the body and in complex social relations. In order to provide evidence for this claim, however, we need an account of what those soul capacities are. I usually use Thomas' account for this purpose because, to my knowledge, it is the most elaborate and perceptive analysis in the Christian tradition. It is a particularly apt choice for this volume because so much of Thomas' work was based on Muslim scholarship.

Thomas had an elaborate account of the hierarchically ordered faculties of the soul, which derived ultimately from Aristotle's distinction among the capacities of the vegetative, sensitive (or animal), and rational souls. The lowest powers of the human soul, shared with both plants and animals, are the vegetative faculties of nutrition, growth, and reproduction. Next higher are the sensitive faculties, shared with animals, and including the exterior senses of sight, hearing, smell, taste, and touch, and four "interior senses" (to which I shall return shortly). This sensitive level of the soul also provides for the power of locomotion and for lower aspects of appetite – the ability to be attracted to sensible objects. This appetitive faculty is further subdivided between a simple tendency toward or away from what is sensed as good or evil, and a more complex inclination to meet bodily needs or threats with appropriate responses: attack, avoidance, or acquiescence. Together these appetitive faculties (all still at the sensitive level) provide for 11 kinds of emotion: love, desire, delight, hate, aversion, sorrow, fear, daring, hope, despair, and anger.

The rational faculties are distinctively human: passive and active intellect and will. The will is a higher appetitive faculty whose object is the good. Since God is ultimate goodness, this faculty is ultimately directed toward God. The two faculties of the intellect enable abstraction, grasping or comprehending the abstracted universals, judging, and remembering. Morality is a function of attraction to the good combined with rational judgment as to what the good truly consists in.[2]

The concept of the soul, in general, has been invoked to explain the existence of capacities such as these since they did not appear to be explainable in physical terms. Now, however, all of them can profitably be studied as biological functions generally or, more particularly, as functions of the brain and nervous system. The soul (*anima*) was, first of all, the life principle, that which *anima*ted the body. Since the end of the vitalist controversy early in the 20th century, though, life has been seen as a function of the organization of the body, not as the result of an additional, nonmaterial substance. The soul was also taken to account for the fact that members of a species always reproduce their own kinds, with some properties being "essential" (such as four-leggedness in horses) and others being "accidental" (such as color). The discovery of DNA, of course, now explains all of this.

The three functions of the vegetative soul – nutrition, growth, and reproduction – are all understood now in purely biological terms. The brain is clearly involved in all the faculties of the sensitive soul: neuroscientists have located the motor cortex, auditory and visual cortices, olfactory lobes, and so forth. It was once thought that all emotions were mediated by the same neural machinery, the "limbic system", but more recent research suggests that there are different systems for different emotions.[3]

The functions of the rational soul are less well understood in neurobiological terms than sensations. However, all involve language and a great deal is known about the brain's role in language use. Broca's area and Wernicke's area have long been recognized as language centers; different regions of the brain have been shown to be involved in recall of different sorts of words – nouns, proper names, verbs.[4] Furthermore, syntax and semantics are processed by different brain systems.[5]

I come back now to Thomas' four "interior senses" attributed to the sensitive soul. There are precursors of Thomas' views to be found in Aristotle, but largely Thomas borrowed here from Ibn Sīnā. The *sensus communis* (common sense) is the faculty that distinguishes and collates the data from the exterior senses – for example, associating the sweetness of honey, its color, texture, and scent in order to allow for recognition of the one substance. The *vis aestimativa* (the estimative power or instinctive judgment) allows for apprehensions that go beyond sensory perception, for example, apprehending the fact that something is useful or friendly or unfriendly. The *vis memorativa* (sense memory) stores the judgments made by instinct regarding the intentions of agents.

Ibn Sīnā recognized two further internal senses: the representational power that preserves the sensations of the common sense even after sensible things disappear, and the imagination that selects and combines some of the objects of the representational power with each other and to separate the rest.[6] Thomas did not believe that animals other than humans have the latter ability and so for him *phantasia* (imagination) is actually Ibn Sīnā's representational power.[7]

In contemporary neuroscience an explanation for what the medievals called the common sense is now referred to as the binding problem, and it is considered one of the most difficult problems in current research, second only, perhaps, to the problem of consciousness itself.

An important question in neuroscience has been the controversy over how the brain comes to recognize patterns. Do brains come equipped with individual neurons designed for recognizing patterns – that is, a "grandmother neuron" devoted to recognition of this one particular elderly woman, and other cells for each pattern that the brain is able to distinguish? It is now believed that recognition tasks depend on activation of large nets or assemblies of neurons rather than on the firing of individual neurons. The concept of a "cell assembly" was introduced by Donald Hebb, and its formation is described as follows: "Any frequently repeated, particular stimulation will lead to the slow development of a 'cell-assembly', a diffuse structure comprising cells ... capable of acting briefly as a closed system. ...".[8] This issue is clearly relevant to an understanding of Thomas' imagination and Ibn Sīnā's representational power.

It appears that the concept of the estimative power was first developed by Ibn Sīnā. This is a particularly interesting faculty from the point of view of neuroscientific investigations, and it needs to be considered along with the sensitive memory. What Joseph LeDoux writes about "emotional appraisal" is relevant to distinguishing the estimative power from the common sense:

> When a certain region of the brain is damaged [the temporal lobe], animals or humans lose the capacity to appraise the emotional significance of certain stimuli without any loss in the capacity to perceive the stimuli as objects. The perceptual representation of an object and the evaluation of the significance of an object are separately processed in the brain. [In fact] the emotional meaning of a stimulus can begin to be appraised before the perceptual

systems have fully processed the stimulus. It is, indeed, possible for your brain to know that something is good or bad before it knows exactly what it is.[9]

The distinction between Ibn Sīnā's representational power and the sensitive memory appears in LeDoux's summary as follows:

> The brain mechanisms through which memories of the emotional significance of stimuli are registered, stored, and retrieved are different from the mechanisms through which cognitive memories of the same stimuli are processed. Damage to the former mechanisms prevents a stimulus with a learned emotional meaning from eliciting emotional reactions in us, whereas damage to the latter mechanism interferes with our ability to remember where we saw the stimulus, why we were there, and who we were there with.[10]

Thomas emphasized that the estimative power is capable of recognizing intentions. Leslie Brothers has contributed to an understanding of the neural basis for such recognition in both humans and animals. Humans and other social animals come equipped with neural systems that predispose them to pick out faces. The amygdala has been shown to be necessary for interpreting facial expressions, direction of gaze, and tone of voice. Brothers has shown that neurons in the same region are responsive to the sight of hands and leg motions typical of walking. Thus, while there are no individual grandmother neurons predisposed to fire in the presence of a particular individual, there are neurons whose function is to respond to visual stimuli that indicate the intentions of other agents.[11]

The foregoing is a sketchy sample of the ways neuroscientists are studying the neural bases of the capacities once attributed to the soul. Of course no amount of empirical evidence can ever disprove the philosophical doctrine of the soul; it can only show that we no longer have need of such a concept.

Defining Nonreductive Physicalism

There are two routes by which to arrive at a physicalist account of human beings. One is to begin with dualism, say, of a Cartesian sort, and then subtract the mind or soul. John Searle has argued persuasively against this move.[12] The other route begins with science. We recognize a certain "layered" feature of reality: subatomic particles at the lowest level combine in increasingly complex structures to give us the features of the world known to chemists, and these in turn combine into incredibly complex organizations to give us biological organisms.

The version of physicalism I espouse denies the complete reducibility of the biological level to that of chemistry and physics. I argue that just as life appears as a result of complex organization, so too sentience and consciousness appear as non-reducible products of biological organization.[13] To conceive of how it is possible to get "mind" out of matter one needs to appreciate not only the development from inorganic to organic, but also from mere homeostasis, through goal-directedness, information processing, goal evaluation, consciousness, and sociality to self-consciousness.

There are a variety of benefits in approaching physicalism scientifically rather than through a reaction against Cartesianism. As Searle has pointed out, it frees one from the (apparent) necessity of attempting to deny or define away obvious facts of experience – such as the fact that we are conscious. Another benefit is this. Arguments against the reducibility of the mental to the physical can draw upon parallel arguments against reductionism in other scientific domains.

The concept of *supervenience* is now used extensively in philosophy of mind. The claim is that, in contrast to earlier mind-brain *identity* theses, it allows for a purely physicalist account of the human person without entailing the explanatory or causal reduction of the mental. In other words, it leaves room for the causal efficacy of the mental.

Development of the concept of supervenience in philosophy began with R.M. Hare's use in ethics; Donald Davidson first employed it in philosophy of mind. Hare used 'supervenience' as a technical term to describe the relation of evaluative judgments (including ethical judgments) to descriptive judgments. Hare says:

> ... let us take that characteristic of 'good' which has been called its supervenience. Suppose that we say 'St. Francis was a good man'. It is logically impossible to say this and to maintain at the same time that there might have been another man placed in precisely the same circumstances as St. Francis, and who behaved in them in exactly the same way, but who differed from St. Francis in this respect only, that he was not a good man.[14]

In 1970 Davidson used the concept to describe the relation between mental and physical characteristics. He describes the relation as follows:

> mental characteristics are in some sense dependent, or supervenient, on physical characteristics. Such supervenience might be taken to mean that there cannot be two events alike in all physical respects but differing in some mental respect, or that an object cannot alter in some mental respect without altering in some physical respect. Dependence or supervenience of this kind does not entail reducibility through law or definition. ...[15]

While I have argued that typical definitions of "supervenience" do not allow for the irreducibility of the mental, it is nonetheless a helpful concept for describing the relation of the mental to the physical.[16]

The Problem of Free Will

The central philosophical problem a physicalist has to answer is this: if mental events supervene upon (or are constituted by or realized by) brain events, and if we assume causal closure at the neurobiological level, how can it *not* be the case that all mental events are merely the product of blind neural causes? If this question cannot be answered then it appears that human freedom is in jeopardy and, even worse, that we are completely deceived about the nature and significance of all intellectual processes – they must be governed by physical causes rather than being governed by reason. In this section of my chapter I shall attempt to shed fresh light on these two issues: the problem of free will, and the problem of mental causation – that is, how can mental events *qua* mental make a difference in the world?

The title of this section is somewhat inappropriate in that there is no such thing as *the* problem of free will.[17] Thus, I need to delimit my topic: I shall not consider the problems raised by theological concepts of predestination, divine omnipotence, or divine foreknowledge. Nor shall I tackle what currently goes under the heading of "the problem of free will" in philosophical circles. Many versions of "the problem" amount to ingenious attempts to do the impossible – to argue for freedom, given the assumptions that the universe is deterministic and that free will requires the absence of determinism.[18]

There are, however, two interesting kinds of threats to human freedom: various versions of environmental determinism and biological determinism, both genetic and neurobiological. It may be argued that neurobiological determinism is the most basic issue. On the one hand, it is widely agreed that there is not enough genetic information in the genome to determine the details of neural wiring in the brain – environment and random growth account for much of it.[19] On the other hand, the kinds of environmental factors we are interested in (such as social pressures) cannot determine our choices without having some impact on our nervous systems. Thus, the threat of neurobiological determinism seems the most important to address.

My approach here will not be to attempt to argue that we do or do not have free will, but rather to assume that we do and attempt to show how agency and free choice emerge out of a neural substrate that may be assumed to be (largely) deterministic. This is an approach to philosophical reasoning recommended by Robert Nozick, who urges philosophers to pursue a particular sort of philosophical explanation in which we bring ourselves to see how something we want to believe could be possible.[20] One not only wants but *needs* to begin with the assumption of free will; to argue the contrary would be hopelessly self-stultifying in that it would amount to giving *reasons* for a philosophical position that *denies* the role of reason in human mental processes.

So the question I shall address is this: how is it possible for agency and free choice to emerge out of a deterministic neural substrate – how do deterministic processes get organized into a system that possesses a degree of freedom?

Freedom as Obeying the Dictates of Reason

Immanuel Kant argued that having free will is a matter of being capable of being moved by reason rather than by natural causes. If this is an adequate account of free will, then the problems of free will and of mental causation turn out to be one and the same. While I shall argue later that freedom involves more than this, we shall have come a long way toward the goal of this section if we can see how reason gets its grip on neural processes. There is a considerable and interesting body of literature on the problem of mental causation.

The Problem of Mental Causation

Jaegwon Kim's statement of the problem of mental causation is probably the best known. He argues that mental properties will turn out to be reducible to physical properties unless one countenances some sort of downward causation. But such downward efficacy of the mental would suggest an ontological status for the mental that verges on dualism.[21] The problem can be evoked using a simple diagram (figure 14.1).

$$\overset{\text{?}}{M_1 \rightarrow M_2}$$

$$\$ \qquad \$$$

$$P_1 \rightarrow P_2$$

Figure 14.1   Diagram of the Problem of Mental Causation

Here M_1 and M_2 represent mental states or properties; P_1 and P_2 represent physical states or properties. The arrow from P_1 to P_2 represents a causal relation, and the dollar sign represents the supervenience relation.[22] The diagram, then, represents the assumed causal closure at the physical level – that is, every physical event (in this case, the neurobiological event P_2) has a sufficient physical cause. It also represents the thesis that mental events supervene on brain events.

The dilemma for the nonreductive physicalist comes down to this: Mental properties can be taken to have causal efficacy insofar as they supervene on physical properties and those subvenient physical properties are causally efficacious. But if the physical properties are causally efficacious, what causal work is left for the mental properties? We seem to be left with a new version of epiphenomenalism.

Some philosophers are happy with epiphenomenalism, but, as I have noted above, we should *not* be happy with this result: in short, it seems to rule out any *reasoned* connection between mental states and to replace them with causal connections. So here I intend to sketch out the basics of an argument for the compatibility of reasoned connections at the mental level with causal connections at the neurobiological level. To do so I shall turn, eventually, to the concept of downward causation.

First, let me make it clear that I am reframing Kim's question. Kim speaks in terms of mental and physical *properties* of events: if the physical property is causally sufficient, what is left for the mental property to do? I want to argue that this way of describing the problem misses the crucial issue. The crucial issue is whether the sequence from

M_1 to M_2 is a *reasoned* sequence or merely a *causal* sequence. So, for example, you read "5 times 7". You think "35". Did that happen because it is *true* that $5 \times 7 = 35$ or because a causal process in your brain made you think it?

Given that we presuppose the truth of $5 \times 7 = 35$, that is, that it is *rational* to think "35" when one reads "5 times 7", we can again reframe the question: how can we reconcile an account in terms of reasons with a physicalist account of the mental without giving up on the causal closure of the physical? Colin McGinn asks: "How, for example, does *modus ponens* get its grip on the causal transitions between mental states?"[23] To sum up the problem of mental causation I would rephrase his question as follows: "How does *modus ponens* get its grip on the causal transitions between *brain* states?"

Resources from Philosophy and Neuroscience

A hint about how I shall proceed: Notice that a calculator obeys the laws of physics *and* the laws of arithmetic. This is because it has been built in such a way that its causal processes model arithmetic transformations. Following Fred Dretske, we can say that the calculator has been *structured* in such a way that any token instance of a series of *triggering* causes – pressing the "5" key, the "times" key, the "7" and the "equals" – causes the machine to display a "35".[24]

So for many purposes it is an oversimplification to represent a causal sequence simply as a series of events: $E_1 \rightarrow E_2 \rightarrow E_3$. Instead we need to think of *two* series of events: those leading up to the triggering of the effect as well as those leading up to the condition under which T is able to cause E. Figure 14.2, adapted from Dretske's diagram, is intended to represent these intersecting strings of triggering and structuring causes:

$$... \, T \rightarrow T \rightarrow E$$
$$\uparrow$$
$$... \, S \rightarrow S \rightarrow (C\text{---}C)$$

Figure 14.2   Triggering and Structuring Causes

Here the *T*s represent a series of triggering causes and the *S*s represent a series of structuring causes leading to the ongoing condition *C* such that *T* is able to cause the effect *E*.

So the present question can be rephrased as follows: are there significant enough analogies between the human brain and a calculator such that we can plausibly assume that the "wetware" has been structured in such a way that its causal processes model or instantiate rational sequences? The disanalogy, of course, is that the calculator has been intentionally designed by a rational agent. Can we provide a plausible account, based on what we now know of neurobiology, as to how such rational structuring might occur without having to presuppose rational agency? I believe that the answer is yes. But here my account necessarily becomes somewhat speculative due to the tentativeness and incompleteness of neuroscientific explanations.

The physicalist assumption is that a mental event, such as thinking of the number 5 or thinking of Grandma, supervenes on a neural event. As mentioned above, it is most plausible to think of such an event as the activation of a cell-assembly. It is in the *training* of such assemblies that we begin to see downward causation. It is better described as downward causation from the environment to the brain rather than mental causation, but insofar as intentionality or reference is an essential ingredient in rationality we have here the beginnings of an account of the rational *structuring* of the brain. Before pursuing this line of thought, however, we need to explore the concept of downward causation.

Excursus: Defining Downward Causation

There has been a developing literature on downward or top-down causation over the past 40 years. Roger Sperry, who has done more than anyone to promote the concept of top-down causation in the field of psychology, sometimes speaks of the properties of the higher-level entity or system *overpowering* the causal forces of the component entities.[25] However, elsewhere in his writings Sperry refers to Donald Campbell's account of downward causation. Here there is no talk of overpowering lower-level causal processes, but instead a thoroughly non-mysterious account of a larger system of causal factors having a selective effect on lower-level entities and their causal effects.

Campbell's example is the role of natural selection in producing the remarkably efficient jaw structures of worker termites and ants. He points out that the hinge surfaces and the muscle attachments agree with Archimedes' laws of levers, that is, with macromechanics.

> This is a kind of conformity to physics, but a different kind than is involved in the molecular, atomic, strong, and weak coupling processes underlying the formation of the particular proteins of the muscle and shell of which the system is constructed. The laws of levers are one part of the complex selective system operating at the level of whole organisms. Selection at that level has optimised viability, and has thus optimised the form of parts of organisms, for the worker termite and ant and for their solitary ancestors. We need the laws of levers, *and organism-level selection* ... to explain the particular distribution of proteins found in the jaw and *hence* the DNA templates guiding their production.[26]

Downward causation, then, is a matter of the laws of the higher-level selective system determining in part the distribution of lower-level events and substances. "Description of an intermediate-level phenomenon", he says, "is not completed by describing its possibility and implementation in lower-level terms. Its presence, prevalence, or distribution (all needed for a complete explanation of biological phenomena) will often require reference to laws at a higher level of organization as well".[27]

Campbell uses the term "downward causation" reluctantly. If it is causation, he says, "it is the back-handed variety of natural selection and cybernetics, causation by a selective system which edits the products of direct physical causation".[28]

We can represent the bottom-up aspect of the causation as in Figure 14.3:

$$
\begin{array}{c}
\text{jaw structure} \\
\$ \\
\text{DNA} \rightarrow \text{protein formation}
\end{array}
$$

Figure 14.3   The Bottom-Up Aspect of Causation

That is, the information encoded in the DNA contributes to the production of certain proteins upon which the structure of the termite jaw supervenes. This is micro-physical or bottom-up causation.

However, to represent the top-down aspect of causation, we need a more complex diagram, as in Figure 14.4, representing feedback from the environment, *E*. Here the dashed lines represent the top-down aspects, solid lines represent bottom-up causation.[29]

Downward Causation of Neural Structure

Let us return to the question of how the brain becomes *structured* in such a way that its causal processes realize rational processes. Many theories of brain function rely on "neural Darwinism".[30] That is, the answer to the question of how neural nets or cell assemblies form is by a process of random growth of dendrites and synaptic connections, followed by selective reinforcement of connections that turn out to be useful.

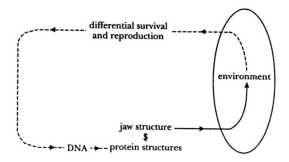

Figure 14.4   Top-Down Aspects of Causation

"grandmother" assembly and the "cookies" assembly) remain strong, while unused connections, (say, between "grandmother" and "frogs") weaken or die off. In this way, neural connections that model relations of various sorts in the world come to be selected.

A central claim of my chapter, then, is that downward causation, in the sense of environmental selection of neural connections and tuning of synaptic weights, provides a plausible account of how the brain becomes structured to perform rational operations. The larger system – which is the brain in the body interacting with its environment – selects which causal *pathways* will be activated.

So far we have an example of a weak form of rationality – presumably it *is* more rational to think of cookies than of frogs in association with thoughts of one's grandmother. Here the connections among things in the world come to be modeled by connections among cell assemblies in the brain. When this happens, free association is replaced by "rational" trains of thought.

We can build from this to consider more interesting forms of reasoning. If interaction with the physical world structures the brain in its image, so does interaction with the social world, with its structures and conventions. Consider the social environment of the primary school classroom and the set of conventions we call arithmetic. How do the brains of children come to be structured so that neurobiological causal processes realize rational operations? Let us speculate about rote learning of multiplication tables. We can imagine that upon hearing the teacher say "5 X 7", neural assemblies are activated and, at first, activation spreads widely and randomly – activating a variety of other assemblies: for example, those subserving thoughts of, "57", "Times Square", "30", "35", "75". But feedback from the environment selectively reinforces one connection, while lack of reinforcement weakens all the others. We can picture this process by means of a diagram formally identical to the one I used to represent Campbell's account of downward causation (See figure 14.5).

Let me emphasize that the foregoing is not intended to be a realistic cognitive-science account of the actual learning of arithmetic. In addition, it begs all of the questions pertaining to the foundations of mathematics. It is simply intended to show that downward causation in the form of environmental selection among neural connections provides a plausible explanation of how rational connections could become instantiated in or realized by causal pathways in the brain.

So if my rephrasing of the problem of mental causation is satisfactory, then we have here the basis for solving the problem. That is, I claimed that the issue is not the causal powers of the mental properties of events (as Kim says) but rather it is to explain how an account of a sequence of mental events ordered in terms of *reasons* can be reconciled with an account of those same events connected by neurobiological causes.

Note that while we have made sense in neurobiological terms of an agent being moved by reason, we have shown that Kant was wrong to contrast this with being moved by natural causes. The important conclusion of this subsection is that certain brain processes are simultaneously free (in Kant's sense) and causally determined.

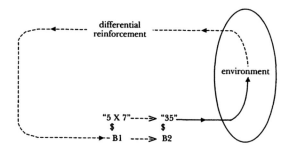

Figure 14.5   Lack of Reinforcement

Freedom to Choose

Kant's conception of freedom as the ability to act in accordance with reason is an unusually narrow analysis of the meaning of free will. In this subsection and the following I intend to build from the foregoing work on top-down mental causation to a broader conception of freedom. We shall have to ask in the end if the result is in fact an adequate account of free will.

One obvious problem with Kant's understanding is that so few of the decisions we make can be determined solely by reason; life would be much easier if it were possible, when facing a decision, to know in advance *the* optimal solution. As an extreme case, consider the medieval philosophical fiction of Buridan's ass, starving to death between two equidistant and equivalent piles of hay. This thought experiment was designed to raise the problem of reasoned choice in the absence of sufficient reason to choose. Nicholas Rescher states that there is almost no discussion in current literature of the logical issues involved in resolving this problem.[31]

Current neuroscience, though, may have solved the problem. Neuroethologists have shown that organisms as primitive as fruit flies and even bacteria exhibit "initiating activity". For instance, the bacterium Eschericia coli has a motor that produces "random" change in the direction it swims. It is able to move to more suitable environments by means of a *delay* in the next change of direction if the milieu im-proves.[32] Fruit flies exhibit similar periodic "random" changes in direction, and it has been possible to control their environments sufficiently to show that these movements are internally generated rather than responsive to external stimuli.[33] These self-initiated "random"[34] changes in behavior provide an optimal solution to the problem of survival in an environment too complex to be met entirely with instinctive behaviors.[35] The organism's behavior thus explores all possibilities in its possibility space (*Verhaltensfreiraum* in Heisenberg's text) and feedback selects the responses that further the organism's goals. Warren Brown (in personal communication) concludes that all organisms with more than the most rudimentary nervous systems have a "chooser" – a program to produce a multiplicity of behavioral plans that may or may not be used. This being the case, Buridan's ass will not starve; nature has designed it to choose one pile of hay or the other despite the lack of any adequate *reason* to do so. Figure 14.6 represents a system capable of initiating actions in pursuit of a goal.

O is an organizing system that produces responses, and C is a comparator, whose role is to compare information coming from the field of operation (I_f) with information about the goal state (I_g).[36] This diagram is designed to represent any mechanism that pursues a particular goal actively by correcting, automatically, conditions that lead away from the goal and helping trends towards the goal. It can as well represent a thermostat as an organism. I am supposing here only a very primitive organizing system, which merely initiates "random" activity. I could have used this diagram as well to represent the feedback from the environment that shapes the student's learning of multiplication tables. So this is again formally identical to Campbell's top-down causation from the environment.

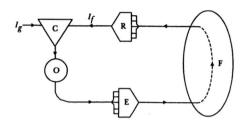

Figure 14.6   Initiating Actions in Pursuit of a Goal

Notice that another capacity with which nature has endowed even simple organisms is the capacity to change or choose among salient goals. If this were not the case, animal behavior would not be flexible enough to shift from, say, pursuing a drink of water to escape from a predator. The following figure (14.7) represents a goal-directed system with the capacity to reset its own goals.

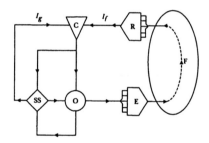

Figure 14.7   A Goal-Directed, Goal-Setting System

In this figure *SS* represents a supervisory system that has the power to change the target settings (I_g) so as to settle for a new target because of some unacceptable mismatch being signaled to it from the comparator.[37]

In one of Heisenberg's articles he speaks of "Free Will in the Fly".[38] He notes that the spontaneous initiating activity he discusses is *not* an adequate model for human free will. Yet the capacity for such activity is an important prerequisite for the evolution of genuine free will.

Free Will as Self-Determination

The foregoing subsection suggests that although we do not attribute free will to animals there is much to learn about our own capabilities by examining simpler forms of life. What we have seen so far is that organisms are goal-directed systems and that when there is no predetermined behavior appropriate to the situation they act spontaneously and "randomly", allowing feedback from the environment to shape their behavior and to alter the goals they pursue.

What conditions need to be added to this spontaneous but goal-directed activity in order for it to qualify as free will? A central contention of this paper is that "free" action is best understood as self-determined or self-caused action. Free will is always a matter of degree –no agent ever acts entirely independently of pre-existing biological drives or environmental influence (and no one should *want* to be free in this sense, since biology and society have been shaped to foster our survival). The question, then, is how self-determination gradually *emerges* within the dynamic interplay between biologically driven activity and reactions to the environment. I hypothesize that the following cognitive capacities, found almost exclusively in humans, are the necessary prerequisites:

1. Symbolic language.
2. Self-awareness and self-transcendence.

3. The ability to imagine behavioral scenarios involving one's own future action.
4. The ability to predict the consequences of such actions.[39]

Language and Self-Transcendence. Terrence Deacon argues that language is essential for detaching behavior from immediate, biologically salient stimuli in order to enable the pursuit of higher-order goals. He describes an instructive series of experiments with chimpanzees. A chimp is given the opportunity to choose between two unequal piles of candy; it always chooses the bigger one. Then the situation is made more complicated: the chimp chooses, but the experimenter gives the chosen pile to a second chimp and the first ends up with the smaller one. Children over the age of two catch on quickly and choose the smaller pile. But chimps have a very hard time catching on; they watch in agitated dismay, over and over, as the larger pile of candy is given away.

Deacon says that the task poses a difficulty for the chimps because the presence of such a salient reward undermines their ability to stand back from the situation and subjugate their desire to the pragmatic context, which requires them to do the opposite of what they would normally do to achieve the same end.

Now the experiment is further complicated. The chimps are taught to associate numbers with the piles of candy. When given the chance to select numbers rather than the piles themselves, they quickly learn to choose the number associated with the smaller pile. Deacon argues that the symbolic representation helps reduce the power of the stimulus to drive behavior. Thus, he argues that increasing ability to create symbols progressively frees responses from stimulus-driven immediacy. So language is one piece of the solution to the free-will problem. It helps to account for our ability to detach our behavior from biological drives.[40]

The experiments with the chimps illustrate a second piece to the free-will puzzle. What the chimps in the first phase of the experiment are unable to do is to make their own behavior, their own cognitive strategy, the object of their attention. This ability to represent to oneself aspects of one's own cognitive processes so as to be able to evaluate them is what I shall call self-transcendence. Dennett follows D.R. Hofstadter in pointing out that the truly explosive advance in the escape from crude biological determinism comes when the capacity for pattern recognition is turned in upon itself. The creature who is not only sensitive to patterns in its environment but also to patterns in its own reactions to patterns in its environment has taken a major step.[41] Dennett's term for this ability is to "go meta" – one represents one's representations, reacts to one's reactions. "The power to iterate one's powers in this way, to apply whatever tricks one has to one's existing tricks, is a well-recognized breakthrough in many domains: a cascade of processes leading from stupid to sophisticated activity."[42]

MacKay has a diagram that represents such a system (figure 14.8). Here the supervisory system of figure 14.7 is divided into two components: a meta-comparator and a meta-organizing system. The *MC* receives information from the environment by means of a feed-forward system. The *MC* is capable of recognizing not only a mismatch between I_f and I_g but also a mismatch between its own activities and its goals. *MC* sends information to *MO*, which in turn directs *O* to adopt a different strategy.

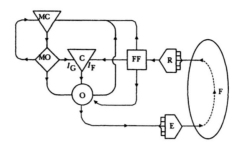

Figure 14.8　A Meta-Comparator and a Meta-Organizing System

Behavioral Scenarios and their Consequences. The combination of sophisticated language and the capacity for self-transcendence contribute to another dimension of human self-determination, the ability to run mental scenarios involving one's possible future behavior and predict their likely consequences. This frees one from the need to implement the behavior in order to receive environmental feedback. Warren Brown writes:

> Consideration of potential future behavioral scenarios allows for these scenarios to be evaluated with respect to the desirability of the imagined outcomes. The evaluation would be of the kind 'good to enact' or 'bad to enact'. Having been evaluated, the behavioral scenario creates a memory trace that affects the future probabilities of expressed behavior. ...[43]

Can we put these four factors together now to formulate an account of a free and morally responsible decision?

We come into the world as goal-directed and spontaneously active systems. Conflict between goals that cannot be pursued simultaneously often brings those goals to conscious awareness. Conflicting goals can become prioritized by running scenarios and imagining long-term consequences of various constellations. Language gives us the capacity, in addition, to describe our actual goals in abstract terms and to imagine ourselves pursuing different goals. Thus, the achievement of higher-order abstract goals, such as acting fairly or pleasing God, may become a criterion for ordering lower-level goals.

I suggest that a hierarchical ordering of goals of this sort is a prerequisite for responsibility. When actions are determined in light of such a hierarchy I claim that the person is acting freely.

Notice that I have described the processes leading up to the action without invoking any agency – no *homunculus* within the person's mind making choices. To do so would set up a regress problem: were any of *those* choices free? Rather, I have described a process that could be deterministic all the way through. More likely it is a mixture of deterministic outcomes and of selection among "randomly" generated alternatives. For example, when faced with a decision there may have been a process of free association resulting in a "random" selection among all of the possible options that might have come to mind. The highest-level goal might be a product of innate temperament and the various concepts of morality available in the person's milieu.[44] For this reason I think that the question of free will should not be taken to hinge on the issue of determinism versus indeterminism.[45] There will always be a host of prior causal events leading up to an act. The important question, as I suggested above, is whether or not the act can be said to be (largely) determined by the person him- or herself, considered as a goal-directed and self-modifying system. I insert the qualification "largely" because a human action that is entirely independent of biological and social causal influences is highly improbable, and if such acts do occur, they are far from the kinds of actions – such as moral choices – that we care about in arguing for free will.

Overview

In this section I have not set out to argue *that* humans have free will, but rather have assumed it to be the case as a condition for the meaningfulness of any scholarly work, this essay included. I have attempted instead to fill in a part of the *explanation* of why it is *not* (always) the case that the laws of neurobiology simply determine human thought and behavior. My explanation involved the key concept of downward causation, and this is in two ways: downward causation from the environment creating patterns of causal pathways that instantiate or realize rational connections; and downward causation from higher-order evaluative or supervisory systems within the agent's cognitive system that reshapes the agent's goals and strategies for achieving them. This downward mental causation also results in the reshaping of the agent's neural pathways.

An adequate treatment of this issue, of course, would require much more space than I have here. What I hope to have accomplished, though, is to show that a physicalist account of the human person is not irreconcilable with our traditional views of ourselves as free and responsible moral agents, and at the same time to suggest that the familiar old battles fought over free will on *philosophical* terrain might better be resolved by taking the issue to be a problem for cognitive-neuroscientists to solve.

Theological Issues

Because the Christian tradition has assumed a dualistic account of the person throughout most of its history there are a number of theological issues that must be reviewed if one adopts a nonreductive physicalist account. The most obvious issue is what happens after death. I have already mentioned that 20th century theologians and biblical scholars have recognized the centrality of the doctrine of the resurrection of the body, and this is entirely consistent with a physicalist account: we *are* our bodies; our survival of death must depend on God's recreation or transformation of our bodies. This emphasis calls for correlative shifts in Christian understanding of eschatology (doctrine of last things). I believe Wolfhart Pannenberg is correct to argue that our eschatological vision must be for a transformation of the entire cosmos comparable to the transformation of Jesus' body in the resurrection.[46]

Deeper and more immediate consequences have to do with the very concept of salvation. Dualism allowed Christians to adopt a Neoplatonic conception of individual escape from nature, society, human history. A physicalist account, with its recognition of the fact that we are essentially constituted by our relations to nature and to other humans (as well as to God) lends itself to a recaptured vision of salvation as bringing the Kingdom of God to its fullness.

Conclusion

The topic of human nature is one of the most fruitful points of contact between science and theology. I have considered only a narrow focus of the dialogue: what Christian theology and neuroscience each have to say about the metaphysical constitution of the human being. I claim that Christian scholars and contemporary scientists can agree on a physicalist account of the person. Nonetheless, there are important philosophical problems still to be solved for physicalists who aim for a *nonreductive* account of human thought and behavior. I hope to have advanced our understanding of how purely physical beings can be both reasonable and free. There is, of course, much more to be done here.

Much more needs to be said, as well, about theological accommodations of a physicalist anthropology since the Christian tradition has assumed a dualist account through most of its history. I believe that this topic will prove to be a fruitful one for Muslim-Christian dialogue since our traditions share so much in other ways, and concepts of human nature have such wide ramifications throughout one's theological system. I hope what I have written here will be sufficient to stimulate lively discussions of these issues.

Notes

[1] For a slightly more comprehensive account, see my Introduction in R.J. Russell, N.Murphy, T.C. Meyering, and M.A. Arbib (eds), *Neuroscience and the Person: Scientific Perspectives on Divine Action* (Vatican City State and Berkeley: Vatican Observatory and Center for Theology and the Natural Sciences, 2000), i-xxxv; and Warren S. Brown, Nancey Murphy, and H. Newton Malony (eds), *Whatever Happened to the Soul? Scientific and Theological Portraits of Human Nature* (Minneapolis: Fortress Press, 1998), esp. my chap. 1 and Joel Green's chap. 7.

[2] Thomas Aquinas, *Summa Theologica*, Ia, 75-83.

[3] Joseph LeDoux, *The Emotional Brain: The Mysterious Underpinnings of Emotional Life* (New York: Simon and Schuster, 1998). Leslie Brothers, in fact, argues that the general concept of emotion does not hold up as a useful category in neuroscience. See her *Friday's Footprint: How Society Shapes the Human Mind* (New York: Oxford University Press, 1997), chap. 8.

[4] See especially Terrence W. Deacon, *The Symbolic Species: The Co-evolution of Language and the Brain* (New York: Norton, 1997).

[5] See Peter Hagoort, "The Uniquely Human Capacity for Language Communication", in R.J. Russell, et al., *Neuroscience and the Person*, 45-56.

[6] Shams C. Inati, "Soul in Islamic Philosophy", in Edward Craig (ed.), *Routledge Encyclopedia of Philosophy*, vol. 9 (London and New York: Routledge, 1998), p. 41.

[7] Thomas Aquinas, *Summa Theologica*, Ia, 78, 4.

[8] Quoted by Alwyn Scott, *Stairway to the Mind: The Controversial New Science of Consciousness* (New York: Springer Verlag, 1995), 81.

[9] LeDoux, *The Emotional Brain*, 69.

[10] Ibid.

[11] See Brothers, *Friday's Footprint;* for a summary see "A Neuroscientific Perspective on Human Sociality", in Russell et al., *Neuroscience and the Person*, 67-74.

[12] John R. Searle, *The Rediscovery of the Mind* (Cambridge, MA: MIT Press, 1992).

[13] This is a view long espoused by Arthur R. Peacocke and Ian G. Barbour. For their most recent formulations, see Peacocke, "The Sound of Sheer Silence: How Does God Communicate with Humanity?"; and Barbour, "Neuroscience, Artificial Intelligence, and Human Nature: Theological and Philosophical Reflections", both in Russell et al (eds), *Neuroscience and the Person*; and other chapters therein.

[14] R.M. Hare, *The Language of Morals* (New York: Oxford University Press, 1966), 145. Originally published in 1952.

[15] Donald Davidson, *Essays on Actions and Events* (Oxford: Clarendon Press, 1980), 214. Reprinted from *Experience and Theory*, Lawrence Foster and J.W. Swanson (eds), (Amherst and Boston: University of Massachusetts Press and Duckworth, 1970).

[16] See Nancey Murphy, "Supervenience and the Downward Efficacy of the Mental: A Nonreductive Physicalist Account of Human Action", in Russell et al., *Neuroscience and the Person*, 147-64.

[17] "Free *will*" is also a poor term. Looking for inner acts of will in addition to one's actions themselves and inquiring whether the willing was free needlessly complicates an already complex problem. Nonetheless, I shall employ this conventional term.

[18] For an excellent critique of many of these puzzles, see Daniel C. Dennett, *Elbow Room: The Varieties of Free Will Worth Wanting* (Cambridge, MA: MIT Press, 1983). Much of what follows is indebted to Dennett.

[19] See, for example, Hugo Lagercrantz, "The Child's Brain – On Neurogenetic Determinism and Free Will", in N.H. Gregersen, W.B. Drees, and U. Görman (eds), *The Human Person in Science and Theology* (Edinburgh: T & T Clark, 2000), 65-72.

[20] Described and adopted by Dennett, *Elbow Room*, 49.

[21] See Jaegwon Kim, "The Myth of Nonreductive Materialism", in *The Mind-Body Problem*, Richard Warren and Tadeusz Szubka (eds), (Oxford: Basil Blackwell, 1994), 242-60.

[22] This use of the dollar sign may be my own most significant contribution to this discussion so far, a fitting symbol to represent the supervenience relation for three reasons: it looks like an 'S' for 'supervenience'; it also resembles one of the symbols for 'approximately equal to', turned on its side and squashed together; and, finally, it has the advantage of using a key on the keyboard that philosophers have little use for otherwise.

[23] Colin McGinn, "Consciousness and Content", in Ned Block, Owen Flanagan, and Güven Güzeldere (eds), *The Nature of Consciousness: Philosophical Debates* (Cambridge: Cambridge University Press, 1997), 255-307, 305.

[24] Fred Dretske, "Mental Events as Structuring Causes of Behavior", in John Heil and Alfred Mele (eds), *Mental Causation* (Oxford: Clarendon Press, 1995), 121-136; 122-3.

[25] Roger W. Sperry, *Science and Moral Priority: Merging Mind, Brain, and Human Values* (New York: Columbia University Press, 1983), 117.

[26] Donald T. Campbell, "'Downward Causation' in Hierarchically Organised Biological Systems", in F.J. Ayala and T. Dobzhansky (eds), *Studies in the Philosophy of Biology: Reduction and Related Problems* (Berkeley and Los Angeles: University of California Press, 1974), 179-186; 181.

[27] Ibid., 180.

[28] Ibid., 180-81.

[29] The most helpful recent account of downward causation is that provided by Robert Van Gulick. See, "Who's in Charge Here? And Who's Doing All the Work?" in Heil and Mele (eds), *Mental Causation*, 233-256.

[30] See, for instance, Gerald M. Edelman, *Bright Air, Brilliant Fire: On the Matter of the Mind* (New York: Harper Collins, 1992).

[31] Nicholas Rescher, "Jean Buridan", in Paul Edwards (ed.), *The Encyclopedia of Philosophy*, vol 1 (New York and London: Macmillan, 1967), 428. Rescher notes that Buridan's opponents were inspired by a similar problem conceived by Al Ghazālī involving equally desirable dates (from date palms, not singles' clubs).

[32] I suspect that *inhibition* of otherwise spontaneous action is an important aspect of the exercise of free will in the case of humans but I cannot pursue this here.

[33] Martin Heisenberg, "Initiating Activity and the Ability To Act Arbitrarily in Animals", by Beatuix Schieffer of "Initiale Aktivitä und willkürverhalten bei Tieven", *Naturwissenschaften*, 70(1983): 70-78.

[34] I enclose "random" in quotation marks because it is not clear whether this is an appropriate term for this sort of event. "Random" is usually defined as uncaused. These movements are *not* uncaused – the nervous system produces them. However, they *appear* to be random in that they lack any discernible pattern and are not responsive to changes in the environment. Heisenberg attributes the neural basis of these behaviors to spontaneous activity in brain cells: nerve cells that without apparent causes give off rhythmic or non-rhythmic potentials have been found in all types of brains. Are these events truly random (in the sense attributed to certain quantum events) or are there "hidden variables"?

[35] Dennett, *Elbow Room*, 66-73.

[36] The diagram is from Donald MacKay, *Behind the Eye* (Oxford: Blackwell, 1991), 42-43.

[37] MacKay, Behind the Eye, 50-51.

[38] Martin Heisenberg, "Voluntariness (Willkurfahigkeit) and the General Organization of Behavior", in R.J. Greenspan and C.P. Kyriacou (eds), *Flexibility and Constraint in Behavioral Systems* (New York: John Wiley and Sons, 1994).

[39] Here I am closely following Warren S. Brown, "A Neurocognitive Perspective on Free Will", Center for Theology and the Natural Sciences Bulletin, 19:1 (Winter 1999): 22-29.

[40] Deacon, *The Symbolic Species*, 413-15.

[41] Dennett, *Elbow Room*, 29; referring to D.R. Hofstadter, "Can Creativity Be Mechanized?", *Scientific American*, 247 (September 1982): 18-34.

[42] Ibid.

[43] Brown, "A Neurocognitive Perspective on Free Will", 27.

[44] It is important here to remember that further iterations of self-transcendence are always possible. As soon as I become suspicious that my moral principles are merely conventional I have made them subject to evaluation and may change them as a result.

[45] Another related issue in the philosophical literature turns on the argument that free will entails that the agent could have done otherwise, or might do otherwise in exactly the same circumstances. Dennett has argued persuasively against this analysis of free will on the grounds that identical circumstances never present

themselves and thus there is no way to know of any given action whether it was free or not. It is a criterion that can never be applied in practice, and it is exactly for practical reasons that we need to know what free will amounts to.

46 See, for instance, Wolfhart Pannenberg, *Jesus–God and Man* (Philadelphia: Westminster, 1968).

Index